STUDIES IN RUSSIA AND EAST EUROPE
formerly Studies in Russian and East European History

Chairman of the Editorial Board: M. A. Branch, Director, School of Slavonic and East European Studies.

This series includes books on general, political, historical, economic, social and cultural themes relating to Russia and East Europe written or edited by members of the School of Slavonic and East European Studies in the University of London, or by authors working in association with the School. Titles already published are listed below. Further titles are in preparation.

Phyllis Auty and Richard Clogg (*editors*)
BRITISH POLICY TOWARDS WARTIME RESISTANCE IN YUGOSLAVIA AND GREECE

Elisabeth Barker
BRITISH POLICY IN SOUTH-EAST EUROPE IN THE SECOND WORLD WAR

Roger Bartlett
LAND COMMUNE AND PEASANT COMMUNITY IN RUSSIA: COMMUNAL FORMS IN IMPERIAL AND EARLY SOVIET SOCIETY

Richard Clogg (*editor*)
THE MOVEMENT FOR GREEK INDEPENDENCE, 1770–1821: A COLLECTION OF DOCUMENTS

Olga Crisp
STUDIES IN THE RUSSIAN ECONOMY BEFORE 1914

John C. K. Daly
RUSSIAN SEAPOWER AND 'THE EASTERN QUESTION', 1827–41

Dennis Deletant and Harry Hanak (*editors*)
HISTORIANS AS NATION-BUILDERS: CENTRAL AND SOUTH-EAST EUROPE

Richard Freeborn and Jane Grayson
IDEOLOGY IN RUSSIAN LITERATURE

Julian Graffy and Geoffrey Hosking (*editors*)
CULTURE AND THE MEDIA IN THE USSR TODAY

Jane Grayson and Faith Wigzell (*editors*)
NIKOLAY GOGOL: TEXT AND CONTEXT

Harry Hanak (*editor*)
T. G. MASARYK (1850–1937)
Volume 3: Statesman and Cultural Force

Geoffrey D. Hosking and George F. Cushing (*editors*)
PERSPECTIVES ON LITERATURE AND SOCIETY IN EASTERN AND WESTERN EUROPE

D. G. Kirby (*editor*)
FINLAND AND RUSSIA, 1808–1920: DOCUMENTS

Michael Kirkwood (*editor*)
LANGUAGE PLANNING IN THE SOVIET UNION

Martin McCauley
THE RUSSIAN REVOLUTION AND THE SOVIET STATE, 1917–1921: DOCU-MENTS (*editor*)

KHRUSHCHEV AND THE DEVELOPMENT OF SOVIET AGRICULTURE

COMMUNIST POWER IN EUROPE: 1944–1949 (*editor*)

MARXISM–LENINISM IN THE GERMAN DEMOCRATIC REPUBLIC: THE SOCIALIST UNITY PARTY (SED)

THE GERMAN DEMOCRATIC REPUBLIC SINCE 1945

KHRUSHCHEV AND KHRUSHCHEVISM (*editor*)

THE SOVIET UNION UNDER GORBACHEV (*editor*)

Martin McCauley and Stephen Carter (*editors*)
LEADERSHIP AND SUCCESSION IN THE SOVIET UNION, EASTERN EUROPE AND CHINA

Martin McCauley and Peter Waldron
THE EMERGENCE OF THE MODERN RUSSIAN STATE, 1856–61

László Péter and Robert B. Pynsent (*editors*)
INTELLECTUALS AND THE FUTURE IN THE HABSBURG MONARCHY, 1890–1914

Robert B. Pynsent (*editor*)
T. G. MASARYK (1850–1937)
Volume 2: Thinker and Critic

Evan Mawdsley
THE RUSSIAN REVOLUTION AND THE BALTIC FLEET

J. J. Tomiak (*editor*)
WESTERN PERSPECTIVES ON SOVIET EDUCATION IN THE 1980s

Stephen White and Alex Pravda (*editors*)
IDEOLOGY AND SOVIET POLITICS

Stanley B. Winters (*editor*)
T. G. MASARYK (1850–1937)
Volume 1: Thinker and Politician

Alan Wood and R. A. French (*editors*)
THE DEVELOPMENT OF SIBERIA: PEOPLE AND RESOURCES

T. G. Masaryk (1850–1937)

Volume 1
Thinker and Politician

Edited by
Stanley B. Winters

Professor of History
New Jersey Institute of Technology

MACMILLAN

in association with the
School of Slavonic and East European Studies
University of London

First published 1990

Published by
THE MACMILLAN PRESS LTD
Houndmills, Basingstoke, Hampshire RG21 2XS
and London
Companies and representatives
throughout the world

Printed in Hong Kong

British Library Cataloguing in Publication Data
T.G. Masaryk (1850–1937).   (Studies in
Russia and East Europe).
Vol. 1 : Thinker and politician
1. Czechoslovakia. Masaryk, T.G. (Tomáš
Garrigue), 1850–1937
I. Winters, Stanley B., *1924–*
II. University of London, *School of
Slavonic and East European Studies*
III. Series
943.7′03′0924
ISBN 0–333–46245–9

Series Standing Order

If you would like to receive future titles in this series as they
are published, you can make use of our standing order
facility. To place a standing order please contact your
bookseller or, in case of difficulty, write to us at the address
below with your name and address and the name of the
series. Please state with which title you wish to begin your
standing order. (If you live outside the UK we may not have
the rights for your area, in which case we will forward your
order to the publisher concerned.)

Standing Order Service, Macmillan Distribution Ltd,
Houndmills, Basingstoke, Hampshire, RG21 2XS, England.

To Zdenka

Contents

Preface

The ideas and achievements of Thomas Garrigue Masaryk, the thinker and teacher, politician and social critic, a founder and the first president of the Czechoslovak Republic, comprise the essence of this book. Scholars from Europe and North America, concentrating on the decades before 1914, discuss Masaryk's relationship to such cultural and political movements as the emancipation of women, liberalism, 'Realism', Decadence, South Slav nationalism, and above all the nationality question as it affected the Czechs: the meaning of their historical experience and their possible destiny as an increasingly numerous, urbanising, and self-conscious minority within the multinational Habsburg Empire, dominated by Germans and Magyars. The editor hopes that the essays here will deepen our understanding of Masaryk's contribution to his nation and to Central European civilisation before World War I, and help us better to appraise his role in history.

The book is the outcome of cooperation between the authors of the essays, the faculty at the School of Slavonic and East European Studies of the University of London, and the editor. The essays were initially commissioned by the editor, who subsequently was invited to merge his efforts with those of the organisers of the T. G. Masaryk (1850–1937) Conference sponsored by the School in December 1986. The Conference simultaneously commemorated Masaryk's death half a century ago and the seventieth anniversary of his speech inaugurating the School in October 1915, following his appointment as lecturer in Slavonic literature and sociology.

The editor appreciates the collegial labours of the authors of the essays, and he gratefully acknowledges help from those who read and evaluated them: Frederick M. Barnard, Ivo Banac, Milan Fryščák, Bruce M. Garver, Erazim V. Kohák, Hans Lemberg, Robert Luft, Robert B. Pynsent, Barbara Reinfeld, Trevor V. Thomas, and Ruben Weltsch. Vital books and photocopies were obtained through the good offices of George J. Svoboda and Steve Maricic. Zdenka Winters helped immensely with proof-reading and constant encouragement. The American Council of Learned Societies facilitated the editor's participation at the London Masaryk Conference with a travel grant.

The School of Slavonic and East European Studies is extremely grateful for funds donated by the British Academy, the British Council, the Ford Foundation and Mr Robert Maxwell towards the holding of the T. G. Masaryk Conference. Most of the essays in the three volumes of Conference proceedings, of which this is the first, were delivered as papers at Conference sessions.

Stanley B. Winters
Newark, New Jersey

Notes on Contributors

Frederick M. Barnard. Professor of Political Theory, University of Western Ontario (London, Canada). Author, three books on Herder and a fourth on Rousseau (forthcoming); contributor to several books and scholarly journals.

Bruce Garver. Professor of History, University of Nebraska at Omaha. Author, *The Young Czech Party, 1874–1901, and the Emergence of a Multi-Party System* (1978); 'Women in the First Czechoslovak Republic', 'Czech-American Freethinkers in the Great Plains', and others.

Irena Gantar Godina. Lecturer at the Faculty of Arts, University of Ljubljana. Author, *Masaryk in masarykovstvo na Slovenskem od 1895–1914* (1987), and articles on Slovene history.

Hillel J. Kieval. Associate Professor of History and International Studies, Chairman – Jewish Studies Program, University of Washington (Seattle). Author, *The Making of Czech Jewry: National Conflict and Czech Jewry in Bohemia, 1870–1918* (1988); co-author, *The Precious Legacy: Judaic Treasures from the Czechoslovak State Collections*; various articles.

Karel Kučera. Historian, Department of the History of State and Law, Faculty of Law, Charles University (Prague). Co-editor, *Stručné dějiny University Karlovy* (1964); author, 'Jaroslav Werstadt', and others.

Hans Lemberg. Professor of East European History, University of Marburg. Co-editor, *Bohemia*. Author, *Die nationale Gedankenwelt der Dekabristen* (1963), and numerous articles, mainly on the Bohemian Lands, in books and scholarly journals.

Thomas D. Marzik. Associate Professor of History, Saint Joseph's University (Philadelphia). Editor for books on Slovakia, *East Central Europe*. Co-editor, *Immigrants and Religion in Urban America* (1977). Has published an article on 'Masaryk's National Background'.

Marie L. Neudorfl. Ottawa. Freelance historian, who has also written an article on 'The Young Czech Party and Modernization of Czech Schools in the 1890s'.

Robert B. Pynsent. Reader in Czech and Slovak Literature at the University of London, has written books and articles on applied linguistics, European and Czech and Slovak literature. Co-author of the Standard Czech-English Dictionary (1986). Most recently he has edited László Péter, *Intellectuals and the Future in the Habsburg Monarchy* (Macmillan, 1988).

Roger Scruton. Professor of Aesthetics, Birkbeck College, London. Editor, *Salisbury Review*. Author, *Art and Imagination* (2nd ed., 1979), *The Aesthetics of Architecture* (1979), *The Meaning of Conservatism* (2nd ed., 1984), *Sexual Desire* (1986), *A Land Held Hostage* (1987), and others.

Eva Schmidt-Hartmann. Historian, Collegium Carolinum (Munich). Editor, *Bohemia*. Author, *Thomas G. Masaryk's Realism. Origins of a Czech Political Concept* (1984), and several articles.

Arnold Suppan. Reader in the History of East Central Europe, University of Vienna. Co-author, *Innere Front. Militarassistenz, Wiederstand und Umsturz in der Donaumonarchie 1918* (1974); author, *Die Kroaten 1848–1918* (1980), *Die österreichischen Volksgruppen* (1983), and similar writings in books and journals.

Stanley B. Winters. Professor of History, New Jersey Institute of Technology (Newark). Managing Editor, *East Central Europe*. Co-author, *Intellectual and Social Developments in the Habsburg Empire* (1975). Author, *From Riot to Recovery: Newark after Ten Years* (1979) and articles on Central Europe, Czechoslovakia, and urban history.

The Writings of T. G. Masaryk

LIST OF CZECH WORKS QUOTED BY THE AUTHORS OF ESSAYS IN VOLUME I

With an English translation and the date of first publication

AMERICKÉ PŘEDNÁŠKY (American Lectures), 1929.
ČESKÁ OTÁZKA. SNAHY A TUŽBY NARODNÍHO OBROZENÍ (The Czech Question. The Strivings and Aspirations of the National Revival), 1895.
'ČEŠTÍ VOLIČOVÉ!' (Czech Voters), 1908.
DNEŠNÍ POLITICKÁ SITUACE DLE NÁZORU PROF. T. G. MASARYKA (The Current Political Situation According to Prof. T. G. Masaryk), 1911.
IDEÁLY HUMANITNÍ (Humanist Ideals), 1901.
JAK PRACOVAT? PŘEDNÁŠKY Z ROKU 1898 (What is Work? Lectures from 1898), 1898–99.
JAN HUS. NAŠE OBROZENÍ A NAŠE REFORMACE (Jan Hus. The Czech Revival and the Czech Reformation), 1896.
KAREL HAVLÍČEK. SNAHY A TUŽBY POLITICKÉHO PROBUZENÍ (Karel Havlíček. The Strivings and Aspirations of Political Awakening), 1896.
'LIST REDAKTORA ATHENEA' (A Letter of the Editor of *Athenaeum*), 1886.
MISTR JAN HUS A ČESKÁ REFORMACE (Master John Huss and the Czech Reformation), 1910.
MNOHOŽENSTVÍ A JEDNOŽENSTVÍ (Polygamy and Monogamy), 1899.
MODERNÍ ČLOVĚK A NÁBOŽENSTVÍ (Modern Man and Religion), 1897–98.
'MODERNÍ NÁZOR NA ŽENU' (A Modern Opinion on Woman), 1904.
MRAVNÍ NÁZORY (Moral Opinions), 1925.
NÁRODNOSTNÍ FILOSOFIE DOBY NOVĚJŠÍ (The Philosophy of Nationality in Recent Times), 1905.

PRÁVO PŘIROZENÉ A HISTORICKÉ (Natural and Historical Rights), 1900.

'PŘEDNÁŠKY PRO DĚLNÍKY' (Lectures for Working Men), 1893.

PŘEHLED NEJNOVĚJŠÍ FILOSOFIE NÁBOŽENSTVÍ (A Survey of the Most Recent Philosophy of Religion), 1905.

PŘECHOD ZE STŘEDNÍ ŠKOLY NA ŠKOLU VYSOKOU (The Transition from Secondary School to University), 1913.

RAKOUSKÁ ZAHRANIČNÍ POLITIKA A DIPLOMACIE (Austrian Foreign Policy and Diplomacy), 1911.

RÁMCOVÝ PROGRAM ČESKÉ STRANY LIDOVÉ (REALISTICKÉ) (Outline Programme of the Czech People's [Realist] Party), 1900.

'ŘÍŠSKÁ RADA' (The Reichsrat), 1891.

RUSKO A EVROPA (Russia and Europe), 1919–21.

SEBEVRAŽDA HROMADNÝM JEVEM SPOLEČENSKÝM MODERNÍ OSVĚTY (Suicide as a Mass Phenomenon of Modern Culture), 1904.

SLOVANSKÉ STUDIE I. SLAVJANOFILSTVÍ IVANA VASIL. KIREJEVSKÉHO (Slavonic Studies No. I. The Slavophilism of Ivan Vasil. Kiryevsky), 1889.

'SOCIALIZEM IN UMETNOST' (in Slovene: Socialism and Art), 1903–04.

'SCHVÁLENÍ ROZPOČTU S POLOŽKOU PRO ŠKOLU V CELJI – SBLÍŽENÍ JIHOSLOVANŮ A KONSERVATIVCŮ' (Authorisation of the Budget with an Item for the School in Celje – The Rapprochement of the South Slavs and the Conservatives), 1898.

SLOVANSKÉ PROBLÉMY (Slav Problems), 1928.

STUDENT AND POLITIKA (The Student and Politics), 1909.

STUDIE O F. M. DOSTOJEVSKÉM (S RUKOPISNÝMNI POZNÁMKAMI) (A Study of F. M. Dostoyevsky – with manuscript notes), 1932.

SVĚTOVÁ REVOLUCE. ZA VÁLKY A VE VÁLCE 1914–1918 (The World Revolution. During and in the 1914–1918 War), 1925.

'SVOBODOMYSLNÍ ČECHOVÉ V AMERICE' (Freethinking Czechs in America), 1902–03.

'V ČEM JE VÝZNAM KARLA HAVLÍČKA' (Where the Significance of Karel Havlíček Lies), 1906.

'VŠEOBECNÉ PRÁVO HLASOVACÍ A ČESKÁ DEMOKRACIE' (Universal Suffrage and Czech Democracy), 1906.

'VÝŇATKY Z 3. ČÁSTI DÍLA *RUSKO A EVROPA*' (Excerpts from Part 3 of *Russia and Europe*), 1938.

ZÁKLADOVÉ KONKRETNÉ LOGIKY. TŘÍDĚNÍ A SOUSTA-VA VĚD (The Fundamentals of Concrete Logic. The Classification and Organisation of Science), 1885.

ZA SVOBODU SVĚDOMÍ A UČENÍ (written with F. Drtina) (Towards Freedom of Conscience and of Teaching), 1908.

'ŽENA U JEŽÍŠE A PAVLA' (Woman according to Jesus and Paul), 1910.

'ŽENSKÁ OTÁZKA V AMERICE A V ČECHÁCH' (The Women's Question in America and Bohemia), 1894.

'ŽIVOT CÍRKEVNÍ A NÁBOŽENSKÝ ROKU 1904' (Church Life and Religious Life in 1904), 1905.

'ZOLŮV NATURALISMUS' (Zola's Naturalism), 1895.

ZRCADLO KATECHETŮM (A Mirror for Catechists), 1906.

Introduction
Stanley B. Winters

'Biography', wrote Carlyle, 'is the only true history', and he could have added, the most difficult. In Masaryk's case, the historian or philosopher dealing with the grand middle phase of his life up to 1914, as in this volume, faces two specific challenges. He or she must see Masaryk squarely in the setting of his native Central Europe, particularly Prague and Vienna, with their mix of traditional and modernising cultures, and not through the lens of his presidency of the first Czechoslovak Republic and its collapse after his death, or of later campaigns to malign or glorify him. He also must tackle an abundance of Masarykiana, written mainly in Czech and German – Masaryk was an indefatigable correspondent, his handwriting is sometimes undecipherable and his expressions enigmatic – and sufficient in quantity to daunt the most intrepid scholar. Should the scholar surmount these obstacles, he or she is obliged to say something new about this much studied subject. Indeed, the authors of the following essays have tried to be original, in their approaches and conclusions, and to avoid the twin pitfalls of uncritical hagiography and dogmatic partisanship that have ensnared many others who preceded them.

Dead now for fifty years, Masaryk is less well remembered than his contemporaries such as Woodrow Wilson, Lloyd George, and Lenin; yet measured on the scale of his small nation, arguably his deeds are comparable in significance. The favourable reputation that he enjoys perhaps stems more from his seventeen-year tenure as President of Czechoslovakia than from his activities under the Austrian Empire as a politician and social thinker, which are better known to historians than to the general public. Hans Lemberg, in his essay here, suggests that had World War I not broken out so soon after Masaryk published his major study, *Russland und Europa*, he might have completed its third and final volume and be best recalled as an interpreter of Russian thought and culture. It was Masaryk's pre-war career, coupled with his odyssey while in self-imposed exile during the war, that laid the foundation for his subsequent enduring reputation. His fame was fixed and embellished during his presidency, when he became the subject of a flood of books and articles, medals and postage stamps, that did not cease until the Germans occupied Bohemia and Moravia in March 1939. By then his own writings had been reprinted many times, every statement culled from obscure journals and pamphlets, his thoughts and sayings anthologised as part of the Czech nation's cultural treasury. No wonder that Czechoslovakia's post-1918 generations grew up in an atmosphere of profound respect for 'tatíček Masaryk' (affectionately, Daddy Masaryk), the patriarch who embodied qualities of wisdom, personal concern, and strict self-discipline.

More than any other new state in inter-war Central Europe, Czechoslovakia perpetuated many of the administrative practices of the defunct Austrian Empire.[1] Like the Empire, she was a state of many nationalities, the most multinational in Europe west of the Soviet Union, except for Yugoslavia. By a twist of circumstances, Masaryk became the modern successor to the ancient Habsburg rulers in that portion of the old Empire. Indeed, he held office as long as many monarchs. He wore the traditional mantle of the Czech scholar-statesman, like František Palacký and F. L. Rieger from the nineteenth century. In keeping with the republican tide, he attained his presidency by the vote of an elected parliament. From these elements was fashioned his imposing and durable public image of philosopher-king that posterity must reckon with.

This public image is exemplified in a widely sold book of striking photographs of Masaryk the President in various settings.[2] We see him meeting foreign dignitaries, cuddling infants, relaxing with his family, attending official functions, touring villages, and buried in deep, solitary thought. His immense dignity is occasionally leavened by traces of a smile or a twinkle in his eyes. He wears a dark peaked cap, dresses simply, dons knee-length leather boots ('so I won't have to lace them up'), and mounts a horse. Masaryk on horseback became a national icon. He came across as larger than life yet intensely human, at one with the people while incarnating noble virtues befitting his great age. In his republic, when youth still respected seniority, when the old transmitted custom and experience to the young, such propaganda must have struck home.

The hazard of viewing Masaryk through the lens of later events is evident when we note the ravages of World War II in Czechoslovakia and the political upheavals after the war. Under Nazi wartime restrictions in Bohemia and Moravia only innocuous or sycophantic works were published. Records were removed or destroyed. Tens of thousands of Czechoslovak citizens, including political and cultural figures who knew Masaryk, fled the country or perished in concentration camps. His name was eclipsed. When it surfaced again after 1945 the atmosphere was different; a new political and moral climate prevailed. Some of his writings, and the popular books about him by Karel Čapek and Jan Herben, were reprinted. Histories again mentioned his contributions to the nation.[3] But after the Communist assumption of power in February 1948, a line was drawn between his early and late careers. For example, a popular magazine of the socialist regime, marking the centenary of his birth, hailed him as 'the champion of all who suffered from injustice' under the Habsburgs but accused him of 'taking no positive measures against the aggressive bid for power by Czechoslovak big capital' under the republic.[4] By the early 1950s an official campaign to deflate his reputation was in full swing, sometimes utilising works with the trappings of scholarship.[5] Monuments to his memory were dismantled. The major Marxist history of Czechoslovakia from those years contrasted his 'progressive' bourgeois-liberal role under Austria with his 'reactionary' pro-imperialist stance during World War I and as president.[6] From a fighter for national liberation, he was turned into an enemy of the people. Yet within the ranks of Czech and Slovak historians, changes were brewing that gradually led from the 1960s onward to a more balanced and factual account of his place in the country's past.[7]

Considering Masaryk's eventful life and favourable image, one is startled to learn that no recent full-scale biographies about him exist. The last one in German was that of 1930 by Ernst Rychnovsky, an editor of the *Prager Tagblatt* who served as a link for Masaryk with the German-Jewish community in Czechoslovakia.[8] The best biography in Czech was a reprint in 1947 of Jan Herben's classic, which had appeared in its essentials twenty years earlier.[9] Herben drew deeply upon his insider's knowledge and personal experience, having served since the early 1880s as Masaryk's votary and, in effect, his press attaché. In English, W. Preston Warren sympathetically blended biography with an analysis of Masaryk's philosophical ideas in a study published early in World War II.[10] Paul Selver, a London-born Czechophile and translator, produced a readable biography that emphasised Masaryk's career up to 1918 and paralleled Herben's in depicting Masaryk as the martyred victim of reactionary enemies.[11] Nothing comparable in scope appeared in English until Zbyněk Zeman's 'dual biography', which knit Masaryk's personal life and political activities with that of his son Jan.[12] Regrettably, none of these useful works fully meets the criteria of comprehensiveness and critical scholarship.

There are, to be sure, many specialised studies on specific aspects of Masaryk's career, and quite a few are cited by the authors of the essays here. The most ambitious of these is the four-volume un-finished biography by historian Zdeněk Nejedlý, who covered Masaryk's development in wondrous detail from youth to the mid-1880s.[13] Using many unpublished sources, Nejedlý worked in a positivist vein that left interpretation up to the reader. Jaroslav Opat, a present-day Prague historian, in a monograph that resembles Nejedlý's in its microscopic focus and biographical intent, carries the story forward until Masaryk's political debut in the early 1890s.[14] The most fluid and sensitive, if selective, portrayal of Masaryk in recent Czech writing is in Otto Urban's panoramic synthesis of Czech intellectual and social history from 1848 to 1918.[15] A compact but conventional article-length survey of Masaryk's life, with special attention to his wartime diplomacy and presidency, has appeared in Rumania.[16] Masaryk's flawed participation as editor during the 1880s of the greatest Czech encyclopaedia is the subject of an article by this writer.[17] A new, impressively documented book by Roland J. Hoffmann, a German scholar, throws new light on Masaryk's concept of the contentious Czech Question at the turn of the century.[18] With these and other recent special studies, and those from the Masaryk Conference in London, the scholarly basis for a new, reliable biography is coming into being.

Many authors begin from a stance favourable towards Masaryk rather than one of – at least conscious – neutrality. This may be due partly to their admiration for the man but also to a desire to refute attacks on him over the years from Right and Left. Some see him at the vortex of a struggle between good and evil. Under Habsburg Austria, the context of the essays here, evil is represented by the imperial bureaucracy, the Roman Catholic hierarchy, German-Austrian national chauvinists, conservative aristocrats and great landowners, scheming diplomats and bloodthirsty generals, opportu-nistic Czech bourgeois politicians, and other alleged defenders of outworn, absolutist institutions – a mighty host indeed! The bias of such authors sometimes mirrors that of Masaryk's own small group of Realist followers, who stigmatised his critics as foes of enlightenment and progress. The critics, in turn, denounced the Realists as sectarian true believers willing to bend reality to fit their ideological needs. In her essay, Eva Schmidt-Hartmann argues that Masaryk's Realism was derived from a preconceived mind-set and not from the historical record he claimed to analyse. The passionate intensity of those old debates was, nonetheless, a sign of intellectual vitality at a time when Czech national consciousness was maturing. Pursuing this theme, Karel Kučera's essay traces the running dispute between Masaryk and Josef Pekař, a leading historian in the first third of this century, over their variant conceptions of the nation's Hussite and Reformation pasts. The protagonists in those quarrels are long gone, but the issues they raised abide with us in one form or another.

Bibliographies of Masarykiana offer some idea of the enormous number of publications available to the curious. The voluminous but not quite definitive list from 1935 by Boris Jakovenko cited 340 items by Masaryk plus over 700 about him written by others.[19] A year later, the Prague City Library prepared an inventory of its holdings in biography that listed 318 books and brochures on Masaryk's life (contrasted with 290 on Jan Hus and 119 on Napoleon I).[20] A recent bibliography that covers the years 1935 to 1979 noted another 1100 items, mostly in Czech.[21] Even allowing for duplications in these lists, they enumerate well over 2000 published works. Not included are dozens of articles by Masaryk in newspapers and periodicals, although some thereafter were reprinted as pamphlets or chapters in his books. Many of these, and similar pieces, are listed in the print-out of the vast Masaryk-Beneš Collection at Berkeley.[22]

Unpublished sources remain the last frontier of Masaryk studies. The key trove is the Masaryk Personal Archive (Masarykův osobní archív, 1875–1914) in Prague. Assembled between the wars, after 1948 it was virtually closed to foreign (and to most Czech) scholars. After being opened briefly in the 1960s it was again closed. A few historians who worked there were able to make copies of material. Now, reportedly, the archive is in disarray. No inventory of its holdings was prepared; items have been lost or removed. Another important repository is the Archive of the Chancellery of the President of the Republic, also restricted in access. Valuable portions of Masaryk's correspondence are located at other Czechoslovak archives under the auspices of the Literary Archives of the National Museum and of the Literary Archive of the Memorial of National Letters, many of which are accessible upon request through official channels. Holdings in Yugoslavia, Austria, Germany, England, and the United States, and even Japan,[23] may yield new finds. It is unlikely that such foreign sources will bring major revisions in the appraisal of Masaryk, but they could fill gaps in knowledge.

The essays in this book resist simple classification. Some deal with

Masaryk's ideas, some with his deeds, others with both. For convenience they have been arranged under two headings, and within each
roughly by chronology. The group entitled 'Masaryk as Philosopher
and Teacher' is opened by two essays that explore his intellectual
roots in the eighteenth-century Enlightenment. The first, by
Frederick M. Barnard, analyses Masaryk's debt to Johann Gottfried
Herder. Barnard sees Masaryk as following Herder in breaking with
the Enlightenment by denying that maximising rationality maximises
freedom. Action requires will in addition to knowledge; will involves
choice, choice clothes our actions in morality. The exercise of
conscious, moral choices led Masaryk to religion and the concept of
humanita. He saw in religion a vital component of human self-
expression, because religious norms rest on acceptance of a transcen-
dent authority, as also on the realisation of finitude and hence of the
inherent limits of human agency.

Barnard writes, '*Humanita* or *Humanität* consists thereby precisely
in this conscious *coming to terms* with both the scope and limits of
self-direction and self-determination.' For Masaryk, belief in God
offers man protection against a false humanism, a danger he sub-
sumed under the concept of titanism; that is, the human attempt to
overextend oneself, to ignore and thus reach beyond mortal limits.
Such striving is properly curbed by religion, in its vital role as a
measure of the possibilities of human attainments. In the form of
Christianity, religion is to project godliness onto one's neighbour,
thus bringing about the interpenetration of the universal and the
particular. This idea of human mutuality, according to Barnard,
connects closely to that of Herder on nationality. Nationality needs
humanity 'in order to acquire moral status as a political claim', just as
humanity needs nationality in order to acquire concrete meaning.
Barnard sees Masaryk as following Herder in accepting this reconciliation of nationality and humanity in 'a concrete universal, the
nation'. Since this belief may have given Masaryk the strength to
persist in his public career, its importance should be apparent.

The essay by Roger Scruton examines Masaryk's attitude toward
philosophers Franz Brentano, Edmund Husserl, and above all Immanuel Kant. Masaryk was initially hostile towards Kant's 'moral
aristocratism' and exclusively philosophical morality, yet he relied on
him for the ultimate justification of his views. Masaryk saw no conflict
between truth and morality. As Scruton writes, '"To live in truth" is
to acknowledge the absolute right to live in reason', so long as
rational beings retain 'the moral space' within which reason is

embodied. From this arises Masaryk's rejection of collectivism set forth in his book, *Otázka sociální*. While the individual occupies a sovereign sphere in society that permits *práce drobná* or the everyday small-scale work that will improve his or her condition, Masaryk equally rejects an extreme individualism that pits each against all in their pursuit of ego gratification.

Masaryk's major failing as a philosopher, in Scruton's view, was his retreat from metaphysics, instead substituting religion. He steered a middle course between Kant's attack on national sovereignty and those who worshipped the nation-state. His book *Česká otázka* stimulated valuable discussion on the existence of a unifying Czech national consciousness, but its historical grounding was weak and its separatist politics rested on the paradoxical humanitarian morality of the Enlightenment. His philosophical deficiencies prevented him from resolving the tension between the universal demands of morality and the specific loyalties of national politics. Instead, 'by a consummate intellectual manoeuvre – which was more rhetoric than philosophy', he fused and confused the liberation of the Czech lands from outside domination with the inner enlightenment of the nation. Scruton concludes that this papered over the real difficulties in nation-building such as those between the Czechs and the Slovaks until hostile outside interventions obliterated 'the happy compromise' of Masaryk's republic.

Robert B. Pynsent's essay on Masaryk's view of the turn-of-the-century literary and aesthetic movement of Decadence illustrates how Masaryk could use literary criticism to advance his moralistic principles. The Decadence manifested morbidity, pessimism, extreme individualism, aberrant sexuality; it separated art and artist from morals. Masaryk rejected pessimism; he opposed all excess but had to reconcile his moderation with his distaste for unoriginality and philistinism. The *maladie du siècle* lay in its negativeness, its Romantic passivity, its expectation that new barbarians would arise to conquer a sick Europe – ideas antithetical to his 'humanitism'. His criticism rested on a concept of a Europe in crisis, but he pushed the beginnings of the process far back into the Hussite era of Czech history. This simplification, according to Pynsent, was 'utterly forgivable ignorance', because of the state of knowledge at the time he wrote.

Pynsent links Masaryk's obsession with the sexual factor to his rejection of absolute freedom: individual liberty brings no happiness to people unprepared for it. It can lead instead to moral laxness, despair, depravity, suicide. Masaryk loathed Paris. He saw it as a cesspool generating impurity, adultery, the decay that was ruining Czech society and modern literature. Nor had he patience for art for art's sake or science for science's sake. Always seeking the middle road, Masaryk rejected asceticism, but the Decadents go to another extreme with their eroticism, their worship of life for life's sake. Equally, Roman Catholic emphasis on the celibacy of the clergy unduly magnifies sexuality, whereas the problem is basically moral: the unhealthy 'sexification of life' that contaminates France and other Catholic countries, in fact all of society. Here Masaryk is the moralising pedagogue par excellence.

Pynsent chides Masaryk for seeing Decadence merely as 'a sick literary trend', for failing to analyse its origins as a literary current or to penetrate its surface. At the same time he notes that, in perceiving the Czech Decadents as symptoms of a 'literary famine' arising from the artists' sense of transience, insecurity, and dependency in the Czech and Austrian *Fin-de-siècle*, Masaryk provided a lasting interpretation of those cultures.

Never one to avoid quarrels, Masaryk often provoked them and perhaps enjoyed their give and take. One of his most bitter and long-lasting was with Josef Pekař over the meaning of Czech history. As presented in the essay by Karel Kučera, the quarrel concerned the question of the importance of an interpretation of the nation's history to a people striving for autonomy, if not yet for full independence, in an era of imperialism and world war. Pekař was the student and colleague of Jaroslav Goll, the most influential of Czech academic historians. Pekař was more combative than Goll, more sensitive to the challenge posed by Masaryk and his Realists to academic orthodoxy both as a way of life and as an accommodation to Habsburg Austria. The dispute passed quickly from one over facts to one of ideology. The Realists sought a new national programme, the historians wanted adjustments to existing conditions. The Realists saw active involvement in public affairs as a means of translating ideas into action, a step that Masaryk's academic colleagues at the Czech university were unprepared to take.

Masaryk's underlying principles were set forth mainly in his books *Česká otázka*, *Naše nynější krise*, *Jan Hus* and *Karel Havlíček*, from the mid-1890s. In them he expounded a philosophy of Czech history based on the continuity of the religious ideas of the Czech Reformation. His interpretations, according to Kučera, were too rigid to stand up to contrary historical evidence. Masaryk's followers took up the cudgels on his behalf, and Pekař responded by stressing the importance of 'the national *motif*' in Hussitism. Soon the Realist organs *Čas* and *Naše doba* were aligned against *Český časopis historický*, the leading historical journal edited by Goll and Pekař. Kučera believes the conflict of views to have been irreconcilable because each side came from different directions, and Masaryk's tactic of going outside of academe to influence public opinion was unacceptable to many scholars.

During World War I, Goll openly supported the Austrian war effort, while Pekař, although lacking faith in Masaryk's actions abroad, was less of an Austrophile than his post-war critics were to claim. The war's outcome, writes Kučera, 'raised Masaryk to unheard-of heights . . . *Finis coronat opus.*' Meanwhile, he had begun to modify his earlier views by giving more weight to national and political factors in the National Revival, although retaining his fundamentally religious conception. Pekař, refusing to bend, turned to a close study of the Baroque and Enlightenment intervals between the defeat at the White Mountain and the Revival, in an effort to counter Masaryk's theory that the real kernel of Czech history lay in the Hussite era. Ultimately, both he and Masaryk were united in their acceptance of a non-oppressive, non-integrative nationalism, although Pekař went beyond discreet bounds towards conciliating the Germans. The long dispute between the two men therefore was not just an academic matter but involved each man's conception of the nation's past as a guide to its future.

One means by which Masaryk's influence was carried to the far corners of the Austrian Empire was the several generations of Slav students who came to Prague for higher education. In the case of the Slovenes, they were motivated by the lack of a university in Slovenia, a desire to learn how to resist Germanising pressures in their homeland, and an interest in preserving their national language and traditions. Irena Gantar Godina's essay discusses the ingredients in Masaryk's teachings that specifically attracted Slovene youth. On the theoretical side, they included his advocacy of the rights of small nations, a moderate approach to Slav reciprocity and tsarist Russia, and support of demands for national autonomy. In practice, he supported universal suffrage, deinstitutionalised religion, and all-class cooperation within each nation for cultural progress. By 1899–1900 the first steps were taken in Ljubljana to propagate Masaryk's emphasis on *práce drobná*. The author sees the Masarykians serving as intermediaries between the Social Democrats and the liberal-

bourgeois parties. Numerically, they were far too few to found their
own party; they went beyond Masaryk in seeking a Slovene type of
socialism that would appeal, not to the industrial workers, but to
rural people and to small-scale entrepreneurs. They helped to spread
progressive ideas among the youth and encouraged schooling and
social involvement as means to national advance.

Summing up, Godina feels that Masaryk's own interest in the
Slovenes up to 1914 was limited, but that he stimulated intellectuals
by his teaching, principles, and actions. He offered 'an intermediate
ideology between liberalism and socialism.' Masarykism in Slovenia,
as transmitted through several student generations, was a transitional
outlook that raised national consciousness at a time when various
political approaches were being tested.

The final essay in the group is by Eva Schmidt-Hartmann. She
seeks to demonstrate, using the Czech Question as her reference
point, that Masaryk's Realism was actually not realistic as she
conceives the term. Intrigued by the seeming lack of relevancy of
Realism to Czech society and by the controversies it provoked, she
cites its imprecision and impracticality as paradoxical qualities that
undermined its validity. Masaryk's critical method – the so-called
Realist approach – was highly selective and subjective. It utilised
insufficient data and fostered an emotional rather than a rational
response among his audience. Schmidt-Hartmann particularly indicts
Masaryk's use, or rather misuse, of history, which approached the
past in the light of 'subjectively defined' present needs. He politicised
the study of history by ignoring evidence that did not fit 'the political
reality'. In shifting the Czech Question from one of statehood to one
of nationhood, he reduced its historical context to the history of the
Czechs in isolation from other peoples such as the Germans, also
long-time residents in the Bohemian crownlands. This gave
Masaryk's views a prophetic quality when they were seemingly
fulfilled in the peace treaties that ended World War I; but their
one-sidedness fanned the nationality conflicts under the republic and
retarded the growth of sensitivity within the predominant Czech
group to the needs of the minority nationalities, according to
Schmidt-Hartmann.

Schmidt-Hartmann believes that Masaryk engaged in ideological
reductionism by positing 'the idea of humanity' as the guiding thread
in Czech history, and holding that history is worth studying only when
that thread is present in certain eras, such as the Hussite and later
Reformation, and the National Revival. She sees a radical change in

Masaryk's career path from 'unpolitical politics' before 1914 to revolutionary action thereafter. This change, Schmidt-Hartmann writes, cannot be explained by any new insights he gained on the Czech Question but rather his decision to seek change in the political order through political activity. Schmidt-Hartmann suggests that her critique of Realism indicates a need for further analysis of Masaryk's political philosophy.

With the second group of essays, our attention shifts to a sphere dominated by Masaryk's involvement in Czech and Austrian politics, social criticism, and Slav matters. The setting is the public meeting hall, the columns of party newspapers, the Reichsrat in Vienna and the Bohemian Diet in Prague. The opening essay by Stanley B. Winters surveys twenty-five years in the sometimes cordial, often abrasive relationship between Masaryk and Karel Kramář. Kramář entered politics as Masaryk's junior partner in the late 1880s, when both teamed with Josef Kaizl as Realists to join the Young Czech Party just before its great electoral triumph over the fading Old Czech Party. Winters discusses Masaryk's uneasy position in the party, his reasons for breaking with it, and the effects of his subsequent open feud with the party on his relations with Kramář. Despite Kramář's respect for Masaryk, he saw politics quite differently; hence, he worked within the party and within the parliamentary system for reforms that would bring the Czechs increased governmental autonomy and full civil equality within the Austrian Empire. Masaryk was clearly less patient and less resilient than Kramář regarding the Czech brand of liberal politics; he was unwilling to subordinate his freedom of action to party discipline. After resigning his elective positions in parliament and the Diet in 1893, Masaryk held no public office from 1894 until 1907, but he founded his own party in 1900 and wrote constantly about politics, thus keeping abreast of developments and his name in the public view.

Winters sees Kramář as asserting his independence of Masaryk by staying with the Young Czechs, and Masaryk as holding it against him that he did, just as Masaryk never forgave the party for not acceding to his demands for reforms in its organisation. By 1914, relations between the two men bordered on hostility, a mood which worsened seriously in that fateful year because of the notorious Šviha affair, in which they both were involved. Winters sees Masaryk as less successful in practical politics than Kramář over the time-span surveyed, but grants that Masaryk nonetheless did succeed in gathering about him a band of loyal followers while fighting his unpopular causes against alleged official wrongs and ubiquitous prejudices. Both men aspired to be acknowledged as *the* national spokesman. Although neither succeeded, Kramář came closer to filling that position, at least until the Young Czech setback in the 1907 parliamentary elections. Ideologically, both represented variants of Czech democratic liberalism in a period of transition and uncertainty in the nation's attitude towards itself and its future.

Thomas D. Marzik's essay examines Masaryk's relations with Karel Kálal, and Masaryk's influence via Kálal on Czech efforts at promoting Czech-Slovak cooperation and reciprocity.[24] Masaryk has a reputation for pioneering in bringing the Czechs and Slovaks together; perhaps for this reason a popular reference work erroneously calls him 'an ardent Slovak',[25] something he never claimed to be. Masaryk learned of Kálal in the late 1890s, when the latter's writings and organisational work made him 'one of the most effective advocates of Czech-Slovak reciprocity in Czech public life.' Since his activities paralleled those of the Realists and he had friendly relations with members of the Masaryk-inspired 'Hlas' movement, Kálal acceded to Masaryk's request that he write two pieces on the Slovaks: one would reveal Magyar oppression of the Slovak people, the other would criticise the conservative Slovak leadership. The first piece, published as a brochure, became one of the first intimations to reach beyond Central Europe about the extent of Magyar oppression in Slovakia. The second, appearing as a series of articles in *Naše doba*, sharply assailed the Slovak leaders in Turčiansky Svätý Martin for authoritarian methods, uncritical Russophilism, and other failings that disarmed the Slovak intelligentsia and frustrated Czech-Slovak reciprocity. In a Masarykian vein, the articles chastised the Slovak Roman Catholic clergy and even the intelligentsia for leaving the masses without sound moral guidance. Kálal's prescription for altering these conditions was drawn along Masarykian lines: self-purification through an end to alcoholism, prostitution, and commercial corruption; a strong campaign to upgrade education, and local economic self-help.

Masaryk was condemned for instigating the articles, and Kálal, who had written them anonymously, was exposed as the real author, to his intense mortification. His work thereafter among the Slovaks was undoubtedly crippled; but the affair was a not untypical one for Masaryk, who soon moved on to other concerns. Masaryk's long-term direct influence on the Slovaks was through the Hlasists, but his association with Kálal helped bring the Slovak plight to wide attention. His interest in the Slovaks overall 'was not as constant and intense' as that of some other Czechs, or as successful; but through Kálal, a representative of his Realism, he did exert influence upon the Czech Slovakophile movement before World War I.

Few of Masaryk's actions were as productive for him in the long term as his interventions in two South Slav treason trials of 1909, the subject of Arnold Suppan's essay. Masaryk not only demonstrated thereby his critical grasp of Austrian foreign policy, but he also helped expose its duplicity and irresponsibility. He strengthened his reputation among South Slav activists and, through the reporting of foreign journalists, made a favourable impression on liberal circles in Western Europe, Masaryk's previous interventions in controversial trials – such as the Hilsner ritual murder case and the Wahrmund affair – showed him to be, as Suppan puts it, 'an implacable enemy of despotism, bondage, and ideological terror.' Apparently he saw anti-human factors operating in the Zagreb and Friedjung trials, when he criticised prosecutorial methods and the factual substance of the charges. His legal research may not have been the most thorough, but it sufficed, and worth noting is Suppan's comment on Masaryk's perceptive conclusion: that the Zagreb treason trial was an anachronism from an era of aristocratic absolutism in foreign policy, whereby a few persons could make vital decisions without the understanding or consent of the broad masses affected. Masaryk's use of his Deputy's mandate in parliament to discuss the trials reveals the valuable public exposure and freedom of action his elective position afforded him. More significantly, he drew from the trials negative conclusions about Austria's viability under its untrustworthy and incompetent leaders.

Without the help of a political party and a parliamentary seat, Masaryk's place in history – notwithstanding his theoretical works – might have merited just a footnote or passing mention. Politics toughened him emotionally; it schooled him in the realities of power. Bruce Garver's essay, 'Masaryk and Czech Politics, 1906–1914', discusses how Masaryk's party was structured, his influence on its programmes, and his use of the party to advance his ideas. External and internal factors impelled him and his colleagues to enlarge and reorganise the Czech People's (Realist) Party, founded in 1900, as the Czech Progressive Party in 1906. The keystone to reorganisation was creation of a permanent party secretariat to handle finances and party administration, which under Masaryk earlier had been unsystematic. Thus, while Masaryk remained the predominant force, his associates, particularly František Drtina and Alois Hajn, provided the help needed to free him to concentrate on writing, public speaking, and political negotiations. Neither Masaryk nor other party founders expected it to become a mass party; its members were drawn largely from the professional intelligentsia. They hoped to influence other parties while keeping control of their own, and to secure for Masaryk forums beyond his classroom and the press. Garver attributes the continuity of the party programmes of 1900, 1906–08, and 1912 to Masaryk's role in composing and editing them.

The 1912 programme of the Czech Progressive Party revealed Masaryk's 'slightly changing views of Czech history and politics', according to Garver, in that it discussed such specific issues as the emancipation of women, the expansion of public education, the democratisation of local government, and, most important in Garver's opinion, 'the need for the Czech nation . . . to achieve the greatest degree of its political independence.' Garver explains Masaryk's 'relative unpopularity among Czech voters' as partly due to his objective approach to issues and his attacks on injustice from all sides, Czech and non-Czech. He sees Masaryk maturing politically by 1912 and as having come to recognise that the Empire was unlikely to accept his programme for its reform. As one of the few Czechs with political contacts abroad, including his influence among Czech immigrants in the United States, Masaryk was well prepared, Garver concludes, to conduct a resistance movement in other countries when he left Austria in December, 1914.

Whereas other Czech males supported Masaryk on issues involving religion, foreign policy, the nation's history, and the rights of labour, hardly any did on the woman question, as Marie L. Neudorfl relates in her essay. His approach to the question was largely pragmatic: once he became convinced of women's equal capacity for growth with men, he sought practical implementation. Specifically, he advocated increased cooperation and openness between the sexes in family and public life. His ideas on democracy here dovetailed with those on women as equal partners in marriage and politics. While criticising unwarranted male privileges, he equally deplored, as Robert Pynsent also notes, the then fashionable views that made personal happiness dependent upon sexual gratification. Yet male-female equality never meant the identity of genders but rather their complementarity.

Masaryk's views on marriage were of long standing: marital love was not mere romance but mutual dedication based on a pure life free from drink, recourse to prostitution, and other infidelities. He fought what he felt were immature attitudes among Czech young people on sexuality, premarital relations, free love, and divorce, some of which he blamed on the teachings of August Bebel, the German socialist. In turn, he excessively praised prominent nineteenth-century Czech writers like Božena Němcová for seeing women as equals. These thoughts on literature may have been too narrow and self-righteous, Neudorfl writes, but they were derived from Masaryk's perception of literature's signal role in many people's search for self-knowledge.

Masaryk actively participated in the Czech temperance movement, which he helped to found in Moravia. He wanted the educated class – the clergy, teachers, other professionals – to set good examples in temperance and thus alleviate women's lot. Neudorfl credits Masaryk with seeing the women's question as part of a broad social and moral problem. Realising that major changes in legislation and social practices were unlikely under old Austria, he stressed the need for personal initiatives and greater frankness between the sexes on an individual level. His stands were forthright for that time but his actual impact, Neudorfl believes, is difficult to estimate. Clearly, he was one of the few Czech males to have been consistently involved in the battle for the emancipation of the sexes.

Hans Lemberg's essay on 'Masaryk and the Russian Question' traces the composition and publication of Masaryk's most ambitious scholarly work, one that more than any other built his critical reputation in Western Europe and the United States. This was *Russland und Europa* (1913), published later in English as *The Spirit of Russia*. Lemberg concentrates on the book's influence in Germany and Masaryk's position on Russia in the light of German and Czech attitudes towards that country. The role of Masaryk's publisher, Eugen Diederichs, was crucial to Masaryk's success, for Diederichs had noted the growing interest by Germans in Russian affairs and the relative dearth of reliable works on Russia in German. Masaryk's book filled a definite need. By using the same method he had employed in his *Česká otázka*, Masaryk drew on the history of ideas by using selected events and themes from Russian history to provide an interpretation of contemporary Russia. His book, according to Lemberg, served as the major overview of Russian thought in any Western language through the 1940s, and it became a key force is shaping German ideas about Russia.

In view of the mainly positive, but hardly uncritical, reception accorded *Russland und Europa*, Lemberg asks why Masaryk never finished his contemplated third volume, especially considering the resources he commanded as president of Czechoslovakia after 1918.

He feels that the march of events since 1905–06, when Masaryk was preparing it, had rendered the Russian Question as it had then existed obsolete. (Russia's survival was no longer in doubt by the 1920s; and Masaryk's experiences there in 1917–18 had given him many insights and enabled him to make a realistic appraisal of the significance of the Bolshevik Revolution for Czech policy toward Russia.) Karel Kramář, Masaryk's former associate in Realism and under the republic his rival for power, possibly emulating Masaryk with a book on Russia, strove to maintain a pro-Slavonic thrust to Czech policy by writing his *Ruská krise* (1921); but his ideas were consigned to a minor role in shaping Czechoslovak foreign policy, which remained securely in the hands of Masaryk and his devoted follower, Edvard Beneš. Official foreign policy prudently avoided Kramář's rightist hostility towards Soviet Russia and moved carefully towards eventual diplomatic recognition. Masaryk's studies on, and experiences in, Russia thereby played an important role in determining policy in the new Czechoslovakia.

The final essay in the second group is entitled 'Masaryk and Czech Jewry: The Ambiguities of Friendship'. One of the givens in Masaryk's reputation is his amity for the Czechoslovak Jews. This applies not only to those under the Republic but also extends back to those of Bohemia and Moravia under Austrian rule. The author, Hillel J. Kieval, is well aware of this positive image but sees paradoxes in it. One is that Masaryk at times was 'highly ambiguous' and 'overtly negative' towards Jews, and that he seems never to have overcome his 'fundamental ideological discomfort' at the prospect of full Jewish assimilation into the Czech national community. The Czech-Jewish movement for assimilation arose in the 1870s and at first allied itself with the rising liberal Young Czech party. By the late 1890s, due to growing anti-Semitism and equivocations on the part of the Young Czechs, these 'Czech national Jews' looked elsewhere for political allies, settling on Masaryk's Realists. They saw in Masaryk and his party strong opponents of anti-Semitism and supporters of Jewish strivings for social and political integration.

These Czech-oriented Jews welcomed Masaryk's positions on natural rights, evolutionary change, anti-clericalism, and positivism. The major Realist impact was due to their rejection of any form of anti-Semitism. Articles in *Naše doba* on this theme, and Masaryk's denunciation of the blood libel in the Hilsner affair, inspired Jewish hopes for integration into the Czech national movement. Unfortunately, the Jews underestimated the depth of Masaryk's commitment to the Czech national movement and his disapproval of cultural assimilation. In 1909 he called assimilation 'impossible and in fact laughable'. Asked to explain, he hedged by saying, 'Of course the Jews can become culturally Czech, but there still remains a difference: that of separate origins, or race . . .'. He was not being inconsistent here, as Kieval notes, for he had voiced similar opinions in 1883, and regarding the Hilsner affair, he admitted to having been led to it, not out of Philo-Semitic reasons, but 'to defend Christians from superstition'. In *Otázka sociální* he had criticised Jews for lacking 'the self-criticism of the prophets' and for being 'self-satisfied'. Other Realists, including Jan Herben, made similar statements.

Not surprisingly, therefore, Masaryk praised Zionism as opening the way for a moral regeneration of Jewry, just as he himself was urging a moral regeneration of the Czechs. Masaryk's sympathy with Jewish nationalism, according to Kieval, was consistent with his belief that rarely, if at all, could Jews become true Czechs; yet despite his favourable view of Zionism, increasing numbers of Czech Jews (in contrast to German-oriented Jews) opted for integration into Czech society.

Although the essays in this volume are thematically heterogeneous and leave many gaps in Masaryk's career and ideas, some of these will be filled by essays in the two volumes that follow. Having come this far, we may now assess Masaryk's achievements in this phase of his activity. By 1914 he had not succeeded in creating the unity that he desired among the Czech people. The debate that he had initiated over the Czech Question was unresolved. The nation's political parties were more divided and jealous of each other than ever. The public's attitude towards Austria was sceptical, occasionally defiant and rebellious, but unrevolutionary. Signs of Masaryk's own final disaffection with the Empire were not yet definitive, either, no matter how mistrustful he might have been.

Masaryk's following was tiny, but it occasionally stimulated other parties into action on important issues. He had numerous critics and enemies, but this did not dissuade him. A lifelong dissenter, he went his own way, possessed of an inner mission. Since coming to Prague in 1882 he had been controversial, an acknowledged fearless critic of outworn traditions and aristocratic privileges, a sturdy advocate of liberal rights and democratic forms of participation. His influence elsewhere in the Empire, such as it was, became tangible mainly in his second and third terms as a parliamentary deputy, when he focused on Empire-wide issues. His ideas on reforming the Empire and on the crisis in European civilisation impressed several generations of Czech and South Slav students, many of whom later entered public life.

In foreign affairs Masaryk was one of a handful of gadflies who criticised Austria's adherence to her alliance with Germany and her risky Balkan policy. His exposés irked and may have embarrassed Habsburg officials, but did not change their ways; if anything, they became more stubborn and unyielding. Many of the issues he raised were deep-seated problems, particularly in Central Europe: women's emancipation, the democratisation of local and regional government, anti-Semitism, or such timeless needs as broader public education, the rights of small nations, and the long view of the development of humanity. He called for self-criticism and moral cleansing among his fellow Czechs as preconditions for progress. Tough, often impatient, or even impetuous, unduly self-righteous and uncompromising, Masaryk was also fearless in trying to stem the tide of common opinion on religious intolerance and sexual licence. His occasional brusqueness was directed not so much against specific individuals – although he suffered neither fools nor demagogues – as against organised prejudice and generalised insensitivity to his message. Unfortunately, while embracing all of humanity with his fears and hopes, he seems not to have embraced many of his fellow human beings as feeling individuals with justifiable opinions and personalities of their own.

Could Masaryk's future European and world eminence have been predicted from the course of his pre-1914 career? Not from the evidence in the time-span covered here. In those thirty-odd years he had his 'moments of greatness'[26] but lacked the sustained and decisive impact on large-scale events or on the history of thought that 'greatness' implies. In 1914 he seemed at a dead end, weary, even strident. The war's outbreak re-energised his whole being. It opened the way for his escape from the Habsburg Austrian miasma that was befuddling and entrapping many of his compatriots. He left his homeland for Western Europe as an exile, but not as an emigrant. His crucial 'moment of greatness' came with the war, which he used to glorious advantage. Yet the opening of that chapter at the same time brings to an end the purview of this volume.

NOTES

1 Helmut Slapnicka, 'Der neue Staat und die bürokratische Kontinuität.
   Die Entwicklung der Verwaltung, 1918–1938', in Karl Bosl (ed.), *Die
   demokratisch-parlamentarische Struktur der ersten Tschechoslowakis-
   chen Republik* (Munich: Oldenbourg, 1975) pp. 121–7.
2 *Masaryk ve fotografii. Slovem uvádí Karel Čapek*, 9th ed. [1932]
   (Prague: Čin-Orbis, 1947), p. 2. See also the anecdote humanising
   Masaryk as related in Jiří Voskovec, 'TGM and Culture in the First
   Republic', in Milič Čapek and Karel Hrubý (eds), *T. G. Masaryk in
   Perspective: Comments and Criticism* (New York: SVU Press, 1981)
   esp. pp. 261–2.
3 Otakar Odložilik, *Nástin československých dějin*, 4th ed. (Prague:
   E. Beaufort – Národní správa, 1946) pp. 132–5. František Roubík,
   Přehled českých dějin (Prague: Orbis, 1947) p. 210.
4 'T. G. Masaryk, 1850–1950', *Czechoslovak Life*, 4, no. 3 (March,
   1950) p. 7.
5 František Nečásek et al. (eds), *Dokumenty o protilidové a protinárodní
   politice T. G. Masaryka* (Prague: Orbis, 1952). František Nečásek and
   Jan Pachta (eds), *Dokumenty o protisovětských piklech československé
   reakce. Z archivního materiálu o kontrarevoluční činnosti Masaryka a
   Beneše v letech 1917–1924* (Prague: SNPL, 1954). Jurij Křížek, *T. G.
   Masaryk a naše dělnická třída; Masarykův boj proti revolučnímu
   dělnickému hnutí před světovou imperialistickou válkou* (Prague: Naše
   vojsko, 1955). Richard Hunt, 'The Denigration of Masaryk', *Yale
   Review*, 18, no. 3 (March, 1954) pp. 419–26. Karel Hulička, 'The
   Communist Anti-Masaryk Propaganda in Czechoslovakia', *American
   Slavic and East European Review*, 16 (1957) pp. 160–74.
6 Josef Macek et al. (eds), *Přehled československých dějin*, 3 vols
   (Prague: ČSAV, 1958–60); here, vols II and III.
7 Stanley Z. Pech, 'Ferment in Czechoslovak Marxist Historiography',
   Canadian Slavonic Papers, 10, no. 4 (1968) pp. 502–22.
8 Ernst Rychnovsky, *Masaryk* (Prague: Staatliche Verlagsanstalt, 1930).
9 Jan Herben, *T. G. Masaryk*, 3 vols. (Prague: Spolek výtvarných
   ůmělců Mánes, 1926–27); *idem*, *T. G. Masaryk. Život a dílo presidenta
   osvoboditele*, 4th ed. (Prague: Sfinx-Janda, 1938); 5th ed., 1947. The
   study by Milan Machovec, *Tomáš G. Masaryk* (Prague: Melantrich,
   1968), is not a biography; it contains references to Masaryk's life,
   excerpts from his writings, and a religion-centred view of the applica-
   bility of Masaryk's ideas to mankind's present condition.
10 W. Preston Warren, *Masaryk's Democracy. A Philosophy of Scientific
   and Moral Culture* (London: George Allen & Unwin, 1941).
11 Paul Selver, *Masaryk: A Biography*, with a Foreward by Jan Masaryk
   (London: Michael Joseph, 1940).
12 Zbyněk Zeman, *The Masaryks. The Making of Czechoslovakia* (New
   York: Barnes and Noble Books, 1976).
13 Zdeněk Nejedlý, *T. G. Masaryk*, 4 vols. (Prague: Melantrich, 1930–
   37).
14 Jaroslav Opat, *Filozof a politik. Tomáš Garrigue Masaryk, 1882–1893*

(Köln: Index, 1987). Cf. Jurij Křížek, *T. G. Masaryk a česká politika. Politické vystoupení českých 'realistů' v letech 1887–1893* (Prague: SNPL, 1959). This is a detailed and informative monograph based on contemporary sources that emphasises the ideological and social-class motives of Masaryk and his associates over the moral, national, and pedagogical.

15 Otto Urban, *Česká společnost 1848–1918* (Prague: Svoboda, 1982).

16 Eliza Campus, 'Thomas G. Masaryk 1850–1937', in *Diplomaţi iluştri* (Bucharest: Politică, 1983) IV, pp. 244–300.

17 Stanley B. Winters, 'Jan Otto, T. G. Masaryk, and the Czech National Encyclopedia', *Jahrbücher für Geschichte Osteuropas*, 31, no. 4 (1983) pp. 516–42.

18 Roland J. Hoffmann, *T. G. Masaryk und die tschechische Frage* (Munich: Oldenbourg, 1988).

19 Boris Jakovenko, 'La bibliografie de T. G. Masaryk', *Bibliothèque Internationale de Philosophie, Publication périodique*, vol. I, no. 9–10 (Sept.–Oct. 1935) pp. 331–422; reprinted with index, Prague, 1935.

20 Zdeněk Gintl (ed.), *Postavy a osobnosti. Seznam životopisů a osobních monografií* (Prague: Melantrich) 1936.

21 'Masarykova bibliografie', in Milan Machovec, Petr Pithart, and Josef Dubský (eds), *T. G. Masaryk a naše současnost* (Prague: Typescript, 1980) pp. 697–757. I wish to thank Eva Schmidt-Hartmann for lending me a copy of this publication.

22 'Masaryk-Beneš Collection' (Berkeley: Univ. of California, 1985). Over 1400 items are listed. Also valuable is the index to Masaryk's pieces in *Naše doba* before World War I; see *Bibliografie Masarykových prací v předválečné Naší době*, František and Marie Laichter (comp.) (Prague: Laichter nakladatelství, 1936).

23 George J. Kovtun (with the assistance of Szugao Kawamura), 'Masaryk in Japan', *Kosmas*, 4, no. 2 (1985) pp. 83–99.

24 The term 'reciprocity' (in Czech *vzájemnost*) as applied generally to inter-Slav relations means mutual cultural (or other) relations; exchanges between peoples on the basis of equality and autonomy on all sides.

25 *Chambers Biographical Dictionary*, rev. ed. (Cambridge University Press, 1984) p. 900.

26 For this phrase and the idea behind it, I am indebted to Erazim V. Kohák of Boston University. This in no way implies that Professor Kohák agrees with my interpretation.

Part 1
Masaryk as Philosopher and Teacher

1 Humanism and Titanism: Masaryk and Herder

Frederick M. Barnard

It is, I believe, no exaggeration to say that the similarity between the ideas of Thomas G. Masaryk and those of Johann Gottfried Herder (1744–1803) is at times so striking as to be truly breathtaking.[1] Perhaps the most characteristic affinity lies in a persistent desire on the part of both men to bring together concepts that are usually held to be in tension, 'dialectically' opposed, if not altogether contradictory. In this paper, I wish to focus on one such tension, the tension between autonomy and heteronomy, which, in their thinking, largely parallels the tension between human beings' understanding of themselves as self-directing agents and possessors of freedom, on the one hand, and as other-directed servants, instruments or victims, within an order not of their own making, on the other. It is the central thesis of both Masaryk and Herder that it is modernity's separation and opposition of these modes of self-understanding which bring them into internal conflict, thereby creating the prevailing malaise of modern man.

Comparative discussions present snares that are not easily eluded. I do not wish to suggest that Masaryk was a mere carbon copy of Herder, nor do I wish to imply that Herder was the sole influence on Masaryk's humanist philosophy, or that the influence, for the most part, was a direct influence. Although Masaryk more than once acknowledged his intellectual debt to Herder, many of the ideas that he shared with him, he derived from his reading of earlier Herderians, such as Josef Dobrovský, Josef Jungmann, Jan Kollár, Pavel Josef Šafařík, František Palacký, Karel Havlíček, and Augustin Smetana. As to the Herderian heritage itself, Masaryk expressed the view that it was essentially a retransmission of the heritage of the Czech Reformation, of Jan Hus and Jan Amos Komenský (Comenius), a view doubtlessly open to question.[2] What, however, is beyond challenge is that Herder's pro-Slavic sentiments, voiced particularly in his chapter on the Slavs in the *Ideas Toward a Philosophy of History of Mankind*, originally attracted Masaryk to Herder, as it had attracted his Czech and Slovak predecessors.

Beyond challenge, too, is the fact that, among the major German thinkers, Masaryk rated Herder above Goethe and Kant, and did so chiefly because he found Goethe wanting in ethical conviction and Kant too aprioristically rationalistic.[3] In one important respect, however, the resemblance between Masaryk and Herder breaks down: Masaryk actually accomplished what Herder could only dream of. Instead of a life of active public service that was to put a Solon or Lycurgus to shame, Herder found himself confined to the inkpot, as he himself lamented (in his *Travel Diary*),[4] and although he carried out some educational reforms during his office as church superintendent in Weimar, his record as a doer is a pale reflection of Masaryk's record.

In *Modern Man and Religion*, Masaryk speaks at some length of Herder and points to four themes that had drawn him to Herder's thought: (1) Herder's doctrine of *Humanität*, in that it identifies the concept with tangible human goals in their manifold diversity, and not with any single and unchanging ideal, and, no less significantly, in that it relates the concept, rather than opposes it, to religion; (2) his theory of causation and continuity in history and its attempt to combine the idea of humanity's self-determination with the idea of a providential order; (3) his vision of the future of the Slavs as the bearers of a cultural and ethical mission; and (4) his belief in the compatibility of particularism and universalism in the interpretation of nationality.[5]

Although I shall focus on the first theme, I shall, in varying degrees, touch also on the other themes, since these frequently are but extrapolations, if not entailments, of Masaryk's conception of *humanita*.

For both Masaryk and Herder, humanism has at once ethical and ontological connotations, in that what human beings might be is seen through the prism of what they are, with all the limitations of being human. And, in contrast to common understandings of humanism, Masaryk's conception shares with Herder's the necessity of a religious grounding. Religion, for both of them, is an essential source of the authentic self-understanding of a human being. In elaborating upon 'religion', Masaryk, it is true, is much clearer in describing the *function* of religion, or in telling us what religion is not, than he is in telling us what it is. Religion is to provide the norms or standards that enable human beings to understand and come to terms with the limits of what existentially they *can* do and ethically they *ought* to strive for. It is to guard against what Masaryk calls titanism, the assumption of tasks for which one is unable or unwilling to take personal responsibility, or the indulgence in schemes which have their source in wishful thinking, delusions of grandeur, or an utter loss of measure and realisability. Titanism, for Masaryk, is the very opposite of authentic humanism, and, interestingly, he holds it to be most acutely present in the relation between the sexes. Titanism, he says, *feeds* on the male's imagined superiority over the female, treating her not as a subject of intrinsic worth like himself, but as an object of his desires.[6] Masaryk, like Herder before him, sees in man's treatment of woman the touchstone of civilisation and the most telling clue for distinguishing humanism from titanism.

The fact that he became best known in the world as a statesman and the founder of Czechoslovakia may suggest that politics assumed central importance in Masaryk's thinking. This, however, is not quite so, although Masaryk himself retrospectively claimed that all he ever wrote was politically motivated.[7] *Humanita*, admittedly, became increasingly associated with the virtues of democracy, but Masaryk did not so much as even mention democracy throughout the greater part of his philosophical and sociological writings, as Milan Machovec correctly observes in his monograph on Masaryk.[8] It would seem closer to the truth, therefore, to regard Masaryk's vision of democracy as the culmination rather than the source of his theory of 'humanism' in terms of individual self-direction and social mutuality. But if not inherently political, this theory is unmitakably human-centred. What human beings are, what they ought to be, and what they can be, by themselves and in acting with others: these are the questions which occupied Masaryk throughout his life. It is to the credit of a number of Marxist commentators, from Zdeněk Nejedlý to Machovec and Lubomír Nový, that they firmly located the fulcrum of Masaryk's thought in the study of humanity. They recognised, too, that this study had an ethical as much as an anthropological foundation, in the sense in which Masaryk always strove to blend fact and value, the ontologically given and the transcendentally aspired. Ethics, for Masaryk, was chiefly *practical* ethics, the doctrine of right-*doing*, but it nonetheless presupposed standards of right-*choosing*, principles of the will, as much as the determination of will. What these commentators, however, failed to recognise, or failed to recognise adequately, is the degree to which religion formed an *integral* component in Masaryk's ethics as well as in his phenomenology of humanity. As a result, they generally looked upon the religious dimension in Masaryk's conception of *humanita* as a mere prop of his ethical theory. In this they were, I believe, fundamentally mistaken. While humans were certainly at the centre of things in Masaryk's theory of right-doing, for him human choice was not unbounded. Human beings may have the capacity for autonomous, and hence for moral, action, but they have to start from somewhere; they cannot wholly choose the ground upon which they stand or find themselves. Humanity is not alone in the world, and no one, as Herder never ceased to remind us, made themselves by their own efforts alone.[9] Purposes are not entirely the product of individual choice; they confront us for the most part as alternative *givens*. Masaryk's human-centred conception of *humanita*, therefore, was a qualified form of human-centredness. And what qualified it was religion. Religion, in its Masarykian understanding, conferred on humanism a meaning that was as pre-modern and non-secular as it was modern and typically secular. This mingling of two distinct traditions characterises not merely Masaryk's ethics and philosophical anthropology, but also, to a significant extent, his philosophy of history.

In Masaryk's ethical humanism, religion structures the manner in which human beings grasp their existence in the world of Nature and in the world of others, or more precisely, their *relation* to nature and to others. Masaryk views religion as the prime category of cognition and perception, as the basic way of responding to the world around, as well as being the anchorage of our individual security and mental sanity.[10] In and through religion we first encounter 'God, men, the world, and our own selves.'[11] By means of religion, human beings acquire a certain sense of measure and proportion, an understanding, or, at any rate, intimation, of the distance between what they are and what they might be, between the imperfect and the perfect, between the attainable and the unattainable. Religion thus generates an awareness of limits, a consciousness of the boundedness of human existence and human agency. And it is in recognising these limits, rather than in ignoring them, that Masaryk, very much like Herder, sees the possibility of human freedom and human autonomy. To ignore the limits which religion brings home to us is not to promote humanism; it is to invite titanism.[12]

Masaryk, as one commentator put it, always fought 'on two fronts',[13] against irrationalism and mythic religion, on the one hand, and dogmatic rationalism and Positivism, on the other. Although Masaryk conceded, and indeed stressed, that reason and scholarly method are indispensable to the striving for truth, he nonetheless held them to be insufficient for the discovery of meaning. Humanity's belief in itself as a free and self-directing agent demands, above all, an act of faith that goes beyond reason, a conceptual leap that defies the methods of natural science. Indeed science, by eschewing questions of intrinsic meaning – the 'why' as distinct from the 'how' of existence – is capable of undermining human beings' understanding of themselves as autonomous agents by treating them as the mere products of natural processes, or as something wholly reducible to the causality of antecedent conditions. To expect, therefore, from the natural or mechanical sciences what neither is capable of delivering is to court profound disenchantment. Worse still, since people cannot accept a world in which they see no meaning, they turn to unreason and myth. Disillusion and despair drive them into magic; they fall victim to pseudo-science, the 'religion' of modernity.[14] And yet Masaryk could never accept Kant's dualism of science (scholarship) and morality. Kant was as aware of the threat of science to human beings' understanding of themselves as autonomous and moral beings as was Masaryk, but he saw no way out of the dualism. Masaryk, on the other hand, somehow wished to believe that inherently there was no conflict between true religion and true science – that, although each may discover different aspects of truth, they both contribute to the discovery of one and the same truth.[15] Together, he seemed to hold, they *can* disclose true causes and true meaning. It is only the belief that science can achieve by itself what religion must supply to it, which leads to pseudo-religion, which blurs rather than illuminates meaning and which creates the illusion of limitless possibilities and endless infinity.[16]

It is not altogether clear in what sense science and religion reveal the same truth, nor what, precisely, Masaryk meant by 'truth', but generally it seems that he thought of truth as factual or empirically verifiable truth, that is, as scientific truth.[17] All the same, Masaryk never tires of warning against reductionism, against a causality of human agency, in which all we say and do is ascribed to antecedent psychosomatic conditions, uncontrollable instincts, social and economic pressures, or impersonal commitments, which enable individuals to take cover behind such reifications as parties, classes, the masses and so on, or behind blind obedience to authority in the execution of their duties.[18] We cannot rely on 'instinct' and 'causes' and 'duties' if we wish to view ourselves as responsible beings, capable and willing to account for what we do. To make instinct the sovereign of human action is to invite moral chaos.[19] And to speak of mechanical causes as though they were effective motives of moral action is to mistake ethics for engineering. 'Why', says Masaryk, 'are Marx and Engels against capitalist exploitation? Merely because the capitalist system is economically unsound? Or because it is wrong, because it offends the feelings of humanity?'[20] If what people do inexorably results from causes over which they have no control, then individual self-direction and, with it, individual responsibility are meaningless notions. In order to act in the proper sense of acting, a person has to know what he or she is doing, for what reasons and upon what principles. To find things right and wrong, not technically but morally, we must have a knowledge of right and wrong, a moral consciousness, which enables us to judge and evaluate choice. Masaryk does not belittle the role of feelings in action or in moral choice, since, like Hume and Herder, he cannot view reason as the sole moral causality. At the same time, he does not equate feeling with blind impulse to an extent that would deprive what we do of a basis upon which it could be judged, or render the consciousness of choosing wholly irrational.[21] We must have some knowledge at the time and in retrospect why we did what we did. Otherwise we are unable to accept personal responsibility and are most liable to overreach ourselves and ignore the limits inherent in the human condition, limits that, indeed, according to Masaryk's religious conception of humanism, *define* one's humanity, and distinguish humanism from titanism. But how are we to know the limits of our capacity to act, how are we to recognise the boundaries of accountable autonomy? What, indeed, does it mean to act upon accountable principles of one's own? If humanity alone is not the measure of things, who or what is?

It is in attempting to come to grips with these questions that Masaryk reveals his *qualified* belief in human-centred humanism. And it is precisely in formulating this qualified humanism, a humanism tempered by religion, that Masaryk also discloses his remarkable affinity to Herder's philosophy of *Humanität*.

Herder, like Masaryk, endorsed the principle of individual self-direction and personal accountability, and, again like Masaryk, expressed serious misgivings about its exclusively secular and rationalist underpinnings. This is not because he was the inveterate antagonist of the Enlightenment that he is at times taken for, but because he specifically questioned the cosmopolitan and excessively rationalist understandings of the inherited concept of *Humanität*. We are not rational automata, nor are we constitutively capable of global brotherhood, for no human love is as extensive as that.[22] Herder also objected to the belief, widespread in his age, that enlightenment was a smooth and cumulative progress. Instead he urged that every advance has its price; all actuality is purchased at the cost of excluded possibilities. Modern people travel in ships, but primitive people know how to *build* their boats. Not everyone who makes use of inventions has the skill and the knowledge of the inventor.[23] Every advance, moreover, knits a new pattern of thinking and acting; new techniques create new needs, and these in turn generate new problems, new hazards, as well as new opportunities. Few inventors know or *can* know, let alone determine, to what use their inventions might eventually be put. Outcomes are frequently other than intentions, and mankind can be no greater ass than when it tries to play God.[24] Here, too, Herder and Masaryk speak with one voice.

Humanität, then, is not simply indiscriminate love, the cumulative happiness of mankind, nor the progress of technology. Nor is it solely a matter of augmenting knowledge or skills, for in themselves neither of these gives structure nor lends meaning to human actions. There is another 'causality' at work. Humanity, Herder concedes, is part of Nature and subject to her laws; at the same time it inhabits the realm of culture, the realm of art, religion, justice, love, and so on, in which it is subject as well as object, agent as well as instrument, and in which realms, choice rather than necessity prevails. It is by virtue of being an inhabitant of both realms that human beings can be said to have a 'will of their own', that they are not only subject to law, but also 'a law to themselves'.[25] Humanity, in short, possesses freedom in that it is not only determined but also determining. Yet, whatever freedom human beings have is neither unconditional nor absolute. Freedom, like love, is not unbounded. Freedom, like human love, to be effective and meaningful, requires 'scale', a space that is bounded by our inherent humanity. In humankind, consciousness of freedom and the capacity for self-direction give rise to the optimistic belief in continuous self-perfection, but may also create illusions. What worries Herder most, therefore, is not sanguine optimism *per se*. Rather it is what he perceives to be a lack of measure, a tragically defective grasp of what it is to be human. The very fact that human beings are creatures of language, which shapes and moulds the basic categories in the mind, compels them to think of themselves as being determined as well as determining, and as sharing a space with others. It is therefore the first germ of attaining consciousness of our *Humanität* (as also of our freedom) to recognise the limits within which we can choose, within which we *are* agents.[26] Language and religion go together for Herder; indeed religion would be inconceivable, in his view, without the existence of language. Language enables us to form concepts, to reason and to think, to have and share ideas, feelings, attitudes, hopes and fears. Without language consciousness would not be what it is. And, *with* consciousness, religion is born. While language constitutes, as it were, the soil in which religion can grow, religion itself is the fruit on which our consciousness of limits feeds – to use Herder's own images. Freedom, according to Herder, assumes meaning only if and when we attain consciousness of the limits within which we can impose our own will and choose our own ends. 'The strongest and most free among men perceive this most deeply and yet they strive on'.[27] Although Herder does not go so far as to *equate* freedom with the recognition of objective necessity, he does insist that the idea of limitless freedom is incompatible with the idea of being human. Human beings may be a law unto themselves, but they are not monads; and though they may choose for themselves, the choice is not unbounded. To make self-direction or autonomy contingent, therefore, on the complete absence of limits, influences, interferences, and restraints, is to lose sight of what it is to be human.[28]

Just as the existence of choice makes human freedom possible, so also, for Herder as for Masaryk, freedom provides the ground for the operation of practical rationality. At the same time Herder is not prepared to support the 'faculty' conception of reason as an independent entity. Reason, he argues, is neither a super-faculty that reigns sovereign nor an innate and self-sustaining 'automaton' (Herder's term).[29] Echoing Locke, Herder persistently affirms that reason is acquired, that it is formed by experience, and thus is neither spontaneous nor *a priori*. Being itself the fruit of experience, reason cannot instruct us before we have the experience; being itself formed, it cannot causally form us. Yet no one, nor mankind as a whole, can live long enough to acquire experience enough to gain perfect rationality. To rest optimal autonomy, therefore, on absolute or perfect rationality, is to misconceive both the nature of human reason and the nature of human autonomy. The matter goes deeper, though. Even if absolute rationality or perfect knowledge were attainable, it would not enhance our capacity to make choices, or, for that matter, the morality of our actions.[30] Masaryk, despite his Positivist moods, substantially shares Herder's conception of reason and freedom. The perfectly rational person who, by definition, knows what to do, cannot but act the way he or she does. Choice will not be a burden, but neither will praise or blame be ascribable. Moral action will be like solving a mathematical problem to which there is only one correct solution. But is such action *moral* action? Is it not that we act morally only when we have no perfect knowledge and therefore have to weigh diverse and often competing alternatives? Besides, Masaryk agrees with Herder that knowing is one thing and doing quite another. Knowledge, Masaryk points out, is not enough for action, for knowing without willing does not engender doing.[31] It is choice that confers morality on our actions, and not sophistication, and we recognise this most acutely when we are confronted with more than one possible solution to a problem. We then realise that to act morally *means* choosing, and that to choose may cause pain precisely because we are faced with options that clash, not simply because some options are good and some evil, but because several *may* be good.[32] It is above all this insight which forms the bedrock of Herder's as well as Masaryk's pluralism, and of their plea in support of freedom of thought and expression in their utmost diversity. That Masaryk here probably followed John Stuart Mill rather than Herder is of little moment, for Mill made no secret of his debt to Herder.[33]

On Masaryk and Herder's theory of reason and freedom, then, the relation between rationality and autonomy is a good deal less direct and more tenuous than a number of 'humanists' of their time (and ours) have held, or than Kant, especially in his pre-critical days, would have us believe. Herder was among the first of modern thinkers to insist that maximising rationality (however defined) does not *mean* maximising freedom. This insistence, together with the recognition of the multiplicity and possible incompatibility of values, ends, or principles, marks a decisive break with the mainstream of thought in his own time. By the second half of the nineteenth century, however, Herder's thinking had become so much part of the intellectual fabric of European thought that Masaryk may well have been unaware of its Herderian origins. Possibly, too, Masaryk may have owed his belief in the limits of reason to an earlier source, to Hume's philosophy of human nature, a likelihood made all the greater by Masaryk's known interest in Hume. Reason, Masaryk agreed, may tell us *what* we are at and (possibly) also *why*; but it does not inform us *that* we ought to do what, rightfully, we should do, nor

does it *make* us do it.[34] By saying therefore that someone acts
rationally, we could be merely describing how, in what manner, a
person says, believes, or explains things; we do not necessarily imply
that it was the right thing to say, believe, or bring about. The idea of
Humanität, as that of *humanita*, in so far as it is a moral idea, cannot
accordingly rest on reason as the sole foundation of morality. Since
both Masaryk and Herder failed to see how reason itself could
generate principles of moral causality, they understandably shared a
reluctance to accept Kant's claims in support of morality as the
exclusive work of practical rationality.

In this connection, Herder's comments on Kant's postulates of
practical reason are of interest. They add force to Masaryk's basic
and virtually axiomatic tenet that *humanita* in action, as the exercise
of conscious and moral choice, cannot dispense with certain principles which in essence are religious principles. Kant's postulates,
Herder declares (in the *Metakritik*), contain a definite contradiction.
'If it is unconditionally necessary', he says, 'that you always obey the
moral law because *reason* commands it, and because it is your maxim
to obey a moral precept thus commanded, then surely it [reason]
should suffice.'[35] Introducing God, as Kant does, only confuses the
issue. 'Clearly, you abrogate the law of reason as soon as you enlist
the aid of an extraneous and unknown Being (*Wesen*) that you had to
invent (*erdichten*) in order to confer upon that law practical validity.
And, in so doing, you admit that it is *in*sufficient, that it is null and
void.'[36] The very fact that Kant has to enlist religion to press reason
into service as a moral causality proves to Herder two interrelated
things: that practical reason by itself is not intrinsically sufficient to
ground moral action and, secondly, that only religion structurally
serves to make a moral precept tangibly intelligible and practically
effective. To appeal to rationality, therefore, as though it were some
kind of moral filter, simply will not do. Acting upon reasons, while it
helps to define human agency, does little to define substantive
morality, just as acting upon one's own reasons defines self-direction
and not the difference between acting rightly and acting wrongly.

Humanita or *Humanität*, then, though it may involve the merging of
self-choosing and right-acting, does not *entail* that merging. What is
clear enough from both Masaryk and Herder's understanding of
humanism, is the existence of a tension inherent in the human

condition. Herder, perhaps somewhat more successfully than Masaryk, leaves no doubt that it is one thing to regard self-directed and reasoned choice as a formal requirement of acting morally, but an entirely different thing substantively to identify this formal requirement with morality *tout court*. Rational grounds, in short, are not of necessity morally binding unless rationality definitionally *implies* morality. But then this implication is not *established* by argument, it *presupposes* it. Rationality, on Herder's (or Masaryk's) showing, cannot by itself ground moral conduct in the absence of a generally accepted framework of distinct moral sanctions. And such a framework, for both men, is virtually inconceivable without religion.

But, if some such supportive framework is required to make autonomy 'work' in the service of ethical humanism, does this not undermine the very principle of individual autonomy? No doubt it was this worry which prevented Kant from admitting religion as a *constitutive* basis of moral conduct. And it can hardly be gainsaid that, if people act within a matrix of custom and tradition, and are wholly guided by its norms, in a passive and entirely unreflective manner, they cease to act morally because they do not autonomously choose the principles or maxims of their conduct. One cannot have it both ways: one cannot uphold individual autonomy and personal accountability as the touchstones of *humanita* or *Humanität* and, at the same time, claim authority for religiously entrenched standards of conduct. For does not veneration of religious traditions, let alone blind obedience to them, stifle the scope of individual self-choosing? Is not freedom from the constraints of any such external authority, as Kant insisted, the only legitimate condition under which human autonomy and moral responsibility can find expression?

These objections are not easily put to rest. There can be little doubt about the risk of a tension between the simultaneous affirmation of a secular belief in human self-determination and a religious belief in a divinely ordained world. Clearly, if religious traditions, of whatever source or form, are to assume primacy, if they are to *ground* the conception of ethical humanism, then an authority other than the self-legislating individual *does* come into play. Such an authority *is* an external authority, and its acceptance *does* create a problem for individual autonomy, as Kant correctly saw. Religious standards of conduct are things to be discovered, not created; they are not born within an individual, but are something into which the individual is born, and are therefore, in this sense, external to him or her. Similarly, to mean anything at all, traditions have to be authoritative or they are nothing. A tradition that ceases to command respect and compliance ceases to be a tradition. Is, then, the acceptance of religious standards tantamount to a denial of autonomy?

Intriguingly, both Masaryk and Herder see in religion the only intelligible way by means of which the scope *and* the limits of human self-determination can find expression, and in which the principle of individual freedom and individual responsibility can have a viable source. Without such a tradition, men and women are adrift, forced upon themselves, and yet not able to cope with their autonomy. In despair they create, and turn to, Titans, to secular supermen, who displace the God or gods of their foreparents. Yet, in thus vicariously bolstering their faltering faith in themselves, they help destroy the moorings of their lives as ordinary men and women. By desperately attempting to rise above themselves, they turn themselves into less than themselves, if not to utter nothingness, and, with it, to abject nihilism. The gods they thought had failed make way to idols who use them and destroy them.[37]

All the same, neither Masaryk nor Herder advocates blind acceptance of religious norms or of tradition *per se*, nor does either maintain that conduct governed by religious precepts is self-evidently moral conduct, or that self-choosing within a framework of accepted traditions ensures right-acting. But Masaryk and Herder do seem to think that religious standards of mutuality could guard against wholly subjective forms of behaviour, that they could act as reminders of the existence of a realm of other beings and a world that is not entirely the work of their own creation, and could thus conceivably reduce the risk of solipsism and titanism, and of total disregard of the effect one's actions have on others. Religious standards, in short, are to provide perimeters of choice which cannot and should not lightly be dismissed. And while such perimeters undoubtedly constitute constraints, the recognition of such constraints does not imply for Masaryk or Herder the denial of human autonomy. Rather, the recognition of constraints implies that humanity has to come to terms with an inescapable fact of human existence, that is, the limits of human agency. To a very real extent, it seems, *humanita* or *Humanität* consists therefore precisely in this conscious *coming to terms* with the limits of both self-direction and self-determination. If this necessarily makes autonomy less than total, it evidently is a price that Masaryk and Herder are not unwilling to pay. Total freedom in the choice of norms or principles of action, if it were at all possible, could, they might grant, enhance the chances of new discoveries in science and technology, yet they might less readily concede that it would at the same time augment the chances of greater justice and social mutuality in social relations. The untrammelled search for truth does not *entail*, for Masaryk or Herder, a certain gain in knowledge of how to act, by oneself or in concert with others. Enlightenment by itself may not, for either of them, usher in the good society, just as self-choosing by itself may not usher in right-acting.

What Masaryk, after Herder, wished to convey to modernity is that modern humanism is beset with difficulties as puzzling and potentially tragic as those which beset cosmologies or *Weltanschauungen* that view humanity other than at the centre of things. Whether or not they succeeded in salvaging what they saw of value in a pre-modern and pre-secular age, they unmistakably sounded a warning in pointing to the dangers of ignoring norms which reminded human beings of their finitude. They revealed considerable sagacity and insight in averring that, outside a religious tradition of one form or another, there is no known way of reconciling self-understanding as a self-determing being with the realisation of dependence, imperfection, bounded- ness, and instrumentality. In the absence of religion, however defined, Masaryk and Herder simply could not envision any tangible conceptualisation of *humanita* or *Humanität* as a condition in which human beings view themselves as *at once* instruments and agents, created and creating, determined and determining. Both men were anxious to advance some sort of interpenetration between subjectiv- ity and objectivity, between the self as an autonomous being and the self as a heteronomous being, in a world which human beings help to create, but which they do not create by themselves alone. They may be the authors of their own history, but they do not make it out of whole cloth, as Marx conceded. To transcend or transform the present to create something new, human beings cannot dispense with inherited categories of thinking; they cannot do without 'borrowed language', from whatever tradition it may originate.[38]

Masaryk saw in humanity's belief in God a safeguard against a false or non-authentic form of humanism, to which he applied the concept of 'titanism'. Humanity's attempt to overreach itself was, according to Masaryk, bound to flounder. In the absence of religion, Masaryk feared, *hubris*, an overweening pride in one's own unaided capaci- ties, may easily prompt a human being to turn him- or herself into God, and thus confuse the imperfect with the perfect, the true with the false, and the secular with the divine. Like Herder, who feared that by supermoralising themselves people are apt to ex-moralise themselves,[39] Masaryk could not accept humanism as a substitute for religion, for a belief in God. Although he did not categorically deny that *humanita* might be obtainable without religion, he believed that without it *humanita* would run the risk of utopian expectations whose non-fulfilment would in turn create a danger of dehumanisation and decay.[40]

Masaryk, however, like Herder before him, strove to deny any dualism or antithesis between the religious and the secular. To bring secular values to religious concerns, and religious values to secular concerns, appears to have been their joint resolve. 'What a wonderful idea it is to apply religion for the benefit of man and society', Herder wrote.[41] Religion was to constitute an active component in human affairs by being suffused with secular mutuality in people's conduct. The better it succeeded in achieving this fusion in social and political life, the more conducive it became to the furtherance of authentic humanism. Indeed, Herder went so far as to suggest some form of interactive causality: just as *Humanität* was to be suffused with religion, so religion was to be suffused with *Humanität*. 'The purer a religion was', Herder declared, 'the more genuinely it strove to promote the good of humanity. This, in truth, is the very touchstone of all religions.'[42]

To reconcile belief in human autonomy with belief in a divine order, and thus bring about the joint causality of humanity and God (the sort of thing Masaryk called synergism) was the shared aim of Masaryk and Herder in their philosophies of humanity and their philosophies of history. But both were careful not to identify 'religion' with Church dogma or the belief-system of a particular orthodoxy or creed. Church and religion are not one; religion unites, but dogmas divide; dogmas breed fanaticism and intolerance.[43] In essence, therefore, religion is not a matter of organisation, but the innermost concern of each individual, and is, as such, inalienable; each person is his or her own priest.[44] This was for Masaryk and Herder the supreme message of the Reformation, the heritage of Jan Hus and Martin Luther. Religion means *conscientiousness* in all human duties, the coming into play of conscience as well as 'duty'.

Christianity, in its purest form, is the expression of this conscientiousness in action, in practical conduct; it is the source and the manifestation of people's attitude to their fellow human beings. For Christ, in Masaryk's understanding, morality is always social morality, but, to be fully human, social morality has to project God onto one's neighbour. This is Christ's principal message, and we can learn it best from Him directly rather than from the Church that speaks in His name.[45] This projecting of God onto others is not a 'natural' inclination, but an effort of the mind and the will, which, when regularly practised, becomes a disposition, a frame of mind or general outlook, to which Herder applies the term *Gesinnung*. And for him, as for Masaryk, it is such a *Gesinnung*, and not a set of theological principles, doctrines, or dogmas, that exemplifies what is the essence of Christianity, what is supreme in the teachings of Christ. In Christ they therefore see above all a teacher of *Humanität*, although, at the same time, neither feels that it matters greatly whether or not the label 'Christian' is applied to this humanist-religious *Gesinnung*.[46] A *Gesinnung*, thus conceived, is at once universal and particular: universal, in that its conceptual impulse is the most general and all-encompassing that human beings are capable of experiencing; particular, in that its concrete realisation demands a context of action in which its meaning is capable of tangible translation into the here and now. The projection of God onto our neighbour therefore implies the generation of a *concrete* universal, of a mode of feeling and thinking which involves the constant interpenetration of the universal and the particular. By this means, the manifold experience of particulars receives its structure, its *Gestalt* or configuration *as* experience. Although universals (which are what they are *of themselves*) cannot be assimilated to particulars (or *vice versa*), there is need for their interpenetration if universals are to regulate or structure human conduct. This kind of interpenetration characterises, in one form or another, the thought of both Masaryk and Herder and, in so doing, sheds significant light on their 'humanist' brand of nationalism. 'Humanity' *needs* nationality to acquire substantive and intelligible meaning, just as nationality *needs* 'humanity' to acquire moral status as a political claim. In practical terms, this means the acceptance of diverse and multiple interpretations of Masaryk's form of *humanita*, in spite of certain unchanging root-meanings. Masaryk, like Herder before him, recognises that this pluralism can give rise to conflicts and tensions. Masaryk therefore pleads for tolerance, and it would not be wrong to say that tolerance is a built-in requirement for the political application of his concept.[47]

Neither Masaryk nor Herder had any illusions about the prospect of translating *humanita* or *Humanität* into palpable human action, since each recognised that such a translation demanded the existence of conditions which do not come about easily. Tolerance, the acceptance of diversity, the enlisting of choice, the shouldering of personal responsibility: none of these requirements can be taken for granted.[48] All the same, each, in his own way, succeeded in transforming the concept from an abstract idea (in the Platonic sense) into an operative idea, converting it from an essentially philosophical ideal into a dynamic principle of action. Such a transformation or conversion has its dangers. No idea can, in the process of its practical implementation, wholly escape the risk of distortion or, indeed, corruption. As 'levers of action', humanist claims or goals may easily become mere slogans, rhetorical weapons in the political struggle for supremacy. And yet, though real enough, these dangers do not detract from the intrinsic value of Masaryk and Herder's groping for an authentic form of ethical humanism. This groping launched on the world a number of exceedingly intriguing, complex ideas. If I were to summarise these ideas, I would cite, first, the distinction between ethics and religion, and, at the same time, their interpenetration in and through action; secondly, the affirmation of individual self-direction, as a condition of personal accountability, and, simultaneously, the recognition of limits in the scale and scope of human aspirations and moral strivings; thirdly, and related, the need to connect ethics with a phenomenology of humanity, not, to be sure, of humanity as an absolute, but nonetheless as a datum which, however circumscribed by cultural and historical conditions, cannot ultimately be omitted in the reckoning of human expectations of the realisable; fourthly, the notion that humanism, though it refers to ultimate ends or values, equally refers to the means necessary for their attainment, since, if means cannot be justified in themselves, the end which they serve can add little to the moral quality of an action. The manner in which ends are attained forms an integral part of what is to be achieved; means are never only means.[49]

Finally, the idea that change is meaningless, and as empty as the concept of development, if it is cherished for its own sake, outside a context of values, or totally divorced from the flow of history, from whatever links the present with the past. If everything is subject to change, Masaryk observes, if human values are *wholly* relative to the time and place of which they are the mere 'results' or 'products', rather than their intrinsic generating agents, then we have no benchmarks to guide us, no way of coming to any appraisal of where or whence we are going. 'First come things, then development.'[50] We need to see change *qua* development as embedded in a continuum, and view this continuum *sub specie aeternitatis*, as if there were eternal, unchanging standards by means of which we *could* assess the direction and desirability of change. We have, in short, to see change as part of tradition.[51]

Humanita, then, while not an incontestable concept (since it allows for different expressions and interpretations within diverse historical and cultural contexts) embodies universal, immutable values. To preserve these values, and to achieve some balance in the tension between belief and action, between self-destruction and self-limitation, between means and ends, between continuity and change, is, for Masaryk, a matter not chiefly of correct theoretical formulation (though it is this too) but rather a matter of practical understanding, of perceiving the diverse interpenetrations in such and such a situation, in order to discover for oneself what can and ought to be done here and now, and done in a genuinely 'human' way. And every generation (Masaryk echoes Herder) has to recognise this anew, in the light of its self-understanding and of its understanding of contextual interpenetrations.[52] This kind of knowledge is not the cumulative knowledge of science and technology. Understanding what it is to be human is a form of groping and grasping which, in its search for answers, is invariably converted into new questions, and which, in confronting problems, implies the recognition of possibly never wholly or permanently resolving them. Essentially, therefore, knowledge of what to do, in the form of practical as distinct from technical judgement, demands, in Masaryk's view, not the possession, primarily, of formal knowledge, but the possession of personal knowledge, of knowledge gained through the exercise of moral choice, by means of which universals assume meaning within the particular of the here and now. The growth of Czech national consciousness is, thus, not a parochial phenomenon, not the product of an exclusive national past, nor the specialised form of a general pan-Slav movement, nor even the particularised expression of universal nationalism. For Masaryk it is, first and foremost, the coming together of the particular and the universal: the particular national characteristics of a people and the universal characteristics of an ethical and religious tradition.[53] It follows that the particular is never *mere* particularity for Masaryk; the particular always goes hand in hand with the universal; nationality and humanity are one: the nation is but the expression of a concrete universal. In this reconciliation of opposites – or what are generally perceived as opposites – Masaryk is a true follower of Herder, the humanist of nationalism. This merging of the particular and the universal is what provided the chief source of Masaryk's humanism and, conceivably, the chief source also of his personal strength as an actor in the public space.

NOTES

1   Alexander Gillies, in 'Herder and Masaryk: Some Points of Contact', *Modern Language Review*, XL (1945) pp. 120–6, writes: 'No more instructive or illuminating approach to Herder can be found than in the writings of Thomas G. Masaryk, the philosopher-President' (p. 120). The theme of the two men, Gillies observes, was fundamentally the same, the diagnosis and cure of modern ills. And their cure, for Masaryk and for Herder, according to Gillies, was the same: the doctrine of *Humanität*.

2   Thomas Garrigue Masaryk, *The Making of a State* (New York: Stokes, 1927) p. 421. It is only fair to add that Masaryk was himself extremely critical of the Slav Messianic theory and preferred to speak of a 'synthesis' of cultures (p. 424).

3   Masaryk, *Modern Man and Religion* (Freeport, NY: Books for Libraries Press, 1938 [Reprint 1970]), pp. 274–5, concerning Goethe; and, concerning Kant, he wrote : 'Why should I trust in *a priori* knowledge?' (p. 89): and distanced himself from 'Kant with his aprioristic subjectivism' (p. 90). See also pp. 200–2.

4   Johann Gottfried Herder, *Werke*, ed. Bernhard Suphan (Berlin: Weidmann, 1877–1913) vol. IV, p. 346. (For an English translation, see F. M. Barnard, *Herder on Social and Political Culture* (Cambridge University Press, 1969) p. 64. Hereafter this translation is cited in brackets.)

5   Masaryk, *Modern Man and Religion* (subsequently cited as *Religion*), pp. 121–4.

6   The theme of titanism forms the third part of *Religion*, pp. 215–315 and is further developed in the third volume of Masaryk's *Spirit of Russia* (New York: Barnes and Noble, 1967) especially ch. 15. Goethe's depiction of woman, in Masaryk's view, derives from and in turn supports titanism, apart from corresponding with the ideals of the 'contemporary German bourgeoisie', the ideal of the German *Hausfrau* (p. 261). 'Goethe', says Masaryk, 'cannot conceive of an independent woman [*sic*], or of the love and marriage of two beings loving [*sic*], but also thinking and working together. . . . The titanic superman can only tolerate woman as subman [*sic*], because of whom he feels himself most vividly a superman'. (pp. 260–61.)

7   Karel Čapek, *Hovory s T. G. Masarykem* (Prague: Borový and Čin, 1936) p. 282. (Subsequently cited as *Hovory*.)

8   Milan Machovec, *Tomáš G. Masaryk* (Prague: Melantrich, 1968) p. 12.

9   Herder, *Werke*, vol. XIII, pp. 343–8. This point is discussed further in my *Herder's Social and Political Thought* (Oxford: Clarendon Press, 1967) and in a forthcoming study, *Self-Direction and Political Legitimacy: Rousseau and Herder*. See also my 'Self-Direction', *Political Theory*, 11 (1983) 343–68.

10   Masaryk, *Moderní člověk a náboženství* (Prague: Laichter, 1934) p. 245, cited in Otakar A. Funda, *Thomas Garrigue Masaryk: Sein philosophisches, religiöses und politisches Denken* (Berne: Lang, 1978) p. 124; see also *Religion*, pp. 207–8: 'You are carrying on a fight – but master of it all you are not, and without a master you can see for yourself that it cannot go on; you are fighting, but precisely through this fight of yours you recognise that master; you are a general defending, or perhaps only a private, nothing more. You are not God. Who, then, is that master?'

11   Čapek, *Hovory*, 243; see also Masaryk, *Der Selbstmord als sociale Massenerscheinung der modernen Civilisation* (Vienna: Konegen, 1881) pp. 143–5. (Hereafter cited as *Selbstmord*.)

12   This is the central theme of Masaryk's doctrine of titanism. See especially *Religion*, Part Three, Chap. 3, and Masaryk, *Die philosophischen und sociologischen Grundlagen des Marxismus* (Vienna: Manzscher Verlag, 1899; reprinted Osnabrück: Otto Zeller, 1964) pp. 456–63. (Subsequently cited as *Grundlagen*.)

13   René Wellek, 'Masaryk's Philosophy', *Essays on Czech Literature* (The Hague: Mouton, 1963) p. 66.

14   Masaryk, *Religion*, p. 55; see also *Selbstmord*, pp. 115–17, 170–2, and *Grundlagen*, pp. 460–81, 498.

15   Masaryk, *Religion*, pp. 55–61.

16   Ibid., pp. 62–75; 204–9.

17   For a most perceptive (and contrasting) interpretation of Masaryk's conception of truth, see Erazim Kohák, 'To Live in Truth: Reflections on the Moral Sense of Masaryk's Humanism', in Milič Čapek and Karel Hrubý (eds), *T. G. Masaryk in Perspective: Comments and Criticism* (New York: SVU Press, 1981) pp. 37–61.

18   Masaryk, *Ideály humanitní* [Prague, 1901] 9th ed. (Prague: Melantrich, 1968) p. 17; Čapek, *Hovory*, pp. 227–9; see also *Grundlagen*, pp. 498–500.

19   Masaryk, *Grundlagen*, p. 499.

20   Ibid., p. 486; see also pp. 149–50, 176–8, 227–30; and Masaryk, *Česká otázka* [Prague, 1895] 6th ed. (Prague: Čin, 1948) pp. 342–3.

21   Masaryk, *Religion*, pp. 209–11.

22   Herder, *Werke*, vol. V, pp. 513–54 (pp. 189–211).

23   Herder, *Werke*, vol. XIII, p. 371 (p. 315). *Yet Another Philosophy of History* (1774) is a scathing attack on glib progressivism.

24   Herder, *Werke*, vol. XIII, pp. 372–3 (pp. 316–17); vol. V, p. 557 (p. 214).

25   Herder, *Werke*, vol. XV, p. 133; vol. XVII, p. 143; vol. XVIII, p. 339.

26   Herder, *Werke*, vol. V, pp. 134–47 (pp. 170–7). This is a major thesis in Herder's original (and influential) essay *On the Origin of Language* (1770).

27   Herder, *Werke*, vol. VIII, pp. 201–2.

28   Herder, *Werke*, vol. V, pp. 134–7 (pp. 170–2).
29   Herder, *Werke*, vol. V, pp. 29–47 (pp. 130–41); vol. XIII, p. 143 (p. 264).
30   Herder, *Werke*, vol. V, pp. 554–86 (pp. 211–23).
31   Masaryk, *Religion*, pp. 208–9.
32   For a sophisticated contemporary version of this argument, to which I am greatly indebted, see Isaiah Berlin, 'From Hope and Fear Set Free', in Henry Hardy (ed.), *Concepts and Categories* (London: Hogarth Press, 1978) pp. 173–98, esp. pp. 195–7.
33   For an expression of Mill's indebtedness to Herder, see his *On Bentham and Coleridge*, F. R. Leavis (ed.) (London, 1950).
34   Masaryk, *Religion*, pp. 69–75, 205–10.
35   Herder, *Werke*, vol. XXII, p. 288.
36   Ibid.
37   Masaryk, *Religion*, pp. 206–12, 253–5; see also *Grundlagen*, pp. 152–8, 458–63; *Selbstmord*, pp. 198–9, 220–2; and *Spirit of Russia*, vol III, pp. 215–25.
38   Karl Marx, 'The eighteenth Brumaire of Louis Bonaparte', *Selected Works* (London: Lawrence and Wishart, 1968) p. 96.
39   Masaryk, *Grundlagen*, pp. 456–63; see also Čapek, *Hovory*, p. 278, and *Religion*, pp. 295–7. On Herder, see *Werke*, vol. XXII, p. 276.
40   Masaryk, *Grundlagen*, pp. 152–8, 458–63; *Selbstmord*, pp. 198–9, 220–2; and Čapek, *Hovory*, pp. 264–5, 272.
41   Herder, *Werke*, vol. VI, p. 63.
42   Herder, *Werke*, vol. XVII, pp. 121–2.
43   Herder, *Werke*, vol. XIV, pp. 541–2; vol. XV, pp. 130–1; vol. XVII, p. 273; vol. XX, p. 145; vol. XXII, p. 10.
44   For an interesting account of Masaryk's own religious beliefs, see Friedrich Thieberger, 'Masaryk's Credo and the Jewish Religion', in Ernst Rychnowsky (ed.), *T. G. Masaryk and the Jews*, trans. Benjamin Epstein (New York: Pollak, 1944) pp. 48–73. Funda offers a critical account of Masaryk's religious thinking from the perspective of contemporary Christian theology in *Thomas Garrigue Masaryk*, pp. 121–44.
45   Masaryk, *V boji o náboženství* [Prague: Jan Laichter, 1904] 2nd ed. (1927) p. 27.
46   Herder, *Werke*, vol. XX, pp. 159, 264–5; vol. XIV, p. 320.
47   Masaryk, *Česká otázka* [Prague: 'Čas', 1895] 4th ed. (1935) pp. 337–52, 373–8; Masaryk stresses patience as the quintessential requirement in politics, and sees in it the means for gradual development in place of 'utopian revolutionism'. See also Čapek, *Hovory*, p. 307.
48   Masaryk, *Ideály humanitní*, pp. 13–14, 55–60, 104–5; see also Čapek, *Hovory*, pp. 112, 228–9, 244–6, and Masaryk, *The Making of a State*, pp. 336–40.
49   Antonie van den Beld gives a fascinating account of this problem in 'Masaryk's Morality of Humanity and the Problem of Political Violence', in *T. G. Masaryk in Perspective*, pp. 191–201. See also his *The Political and Social Philosophy of Thomas G. Masaryk* (The Hague: Mouton, 1975). Roman Szporluk, *The Political Thought of Thomas G.*

Masaryk (New York: Columbia University Press, 1981) is an excellent companion volume to van den Beld's study, and a pleasingly urbane approach to Masaryk's political thought, embedded in a frame of reference that is a good deal more comprehensive than one usually finds in comparable monographs. See also Otakar Odložilík, 'Enter Masaryk: A Prelude to his Political career', *Journal of Central European Affairs*, 10 (1950) pp. 21–36; Josef Kalvoda, 'Masaryk in America in 1918', *Jahrbücher für Geschichte Osteuropas*, 27 (1979) pp. 85–8; and Stanley B. Winters, 'Kramář, Kaizl, and the Hegemony of the Young Czech Party, 1891–1901', in Peter Brock and H. Gordon Skilling (eds), *The Czech Renascence of the Nineteenth Century* (University of Toronto Press, 1970) pp. 282–314. All of these offer penetrating analyses of Masaryk's political activity during the period prior to his presidency.

50   Masaryk, *Grundlagen*, p. 76; see also pp. 547, 555; and *The Making of a State*, pp. 444–9, 454–9, 465–75. On the use of violence as a permissible means, see van den Beld, 'Masaryk's Morality of Humanity and the Problem of Political Violence', especially pp. 196–9.

51   Masaryk, *Ideály humanitní*, pp. 55–62; see also Čapek, *Hovory*, pp. 295–9.

52   Masaryk, *Ideály humanitní*, pp. 13–14; Herder, *Werke*, vol. XIII, p. 196, and vol. XVII, p. 138.

53   Draga B. Shillinglaw (ed.), *The Lectures of Professor T. G. Masaryk at the University of Chicago, Summer 1902* (Cranbury, NJ: Associated University Presses and Bucknell University Press, 1978) provides a clear presentation of this thesis. Although the lectures in bookform appear somewhat shapeless and loosely connected, they are rich in explanatory illustrations and often challenging. Moreover, they offer a rare opportunity of capturing the flavour of Masaryk's mode of lecturing, and of demonstrating his capacity for combining scholarly complexity with appealing simplicity, detachedness with personal commitment, and utter seriousness of purpose with urbane humour. There is a vast secondary literature in Czech on Masaryk's national-religious-democratic thesis (of which Funda's study provides an admirable survey), best-known of which are the works of Josef Hromádka, Josef Pekař, and Emanuel Rádl. Václav Lesák, in a recent article, discusses some of Masaryk's critics, in particular Milan Machovec, Václav Černý, and Jan Patočka, but I must admit I have difficulty in understanding his main argument as well as his frequent references to Heidegger. Lesák's article, 'Filozofický význam Masarykova pojetí náboženství a jeho výkladu smyslu československých dějin', in *T. G. Masaryk a naše současnost* (Prague: Typescript, 1980) pp. 328–45, has a tendency to obscure the issue by using 'democratic religion' and 'religious democracy' as though they were interchangeable terms – a rather irritating feature of this highly polemical but not very enlightening piece. One of the most lucid and, at the same time, critical expositions in English is still R. R. Betts, 'Masaryk's Philosophy of History', *The Slavonic Review*, 26 (1947) pp. 30–44.

2 Masaryk, Kant and the Czech Experience

Roger Scruton

Masaryk's ideas are more notable for their influence than for their intellectual power. It is a mistake to attribute to him a philosophical profundity which, had he really possessed it, would assuredly have impeded the brilliant career which made him the envy of philosophers. Masaryk was an intellectual in the Czech mould: wide-ranging, self-consciously European, seeking for ideas which could be clearly and simply expressed, and which would have an impact on the world of men and women. He looked on the university not as a scholarly retreat but as a podium, and his philosophical writings were couched in the same discursive language, and the same didactic tone of voice, as his speeches to the Austrian parliament.[1] If Masaryk was accepted, in his presidency, as teacher of the Czech and Slovak nations, this was partly because he had not the habit of pursuing ideas beyond the daylight realm of public discussion and political controversy. His writings appealed directly to the ideas and feelings of the *obyčejný člověk*, who was partly the product of Masarykian democracy, and partly the cause of its downfall.

Anyone who searches in Masaryk's writings, therefore, either for a metaphysics or for an ethics comparable to those which had influenced his philosophical mentors, searches in vain. Masaryk frequently expressed his distaste for metaphysics, and sought to found his moral and political doctrine in humanitarian ideals rather than extended philosophical argument. Even when he overreached the human world in the direction of the transcendental, the result was a religion so stripped of its liturgical discipline, so emancipated from the bonds and trappings of the sacred and the holy, as to be more like a moral posture than a system of theological doctrine, Nevertheless, Masaryk had much to say about philosophers and philosophies. Not only did he write the first truly systematic critique of Marxism.[2] He also expressed a vision of human beings and society that is undeniably philosophical, and which deserves the kind of careful exposition which he himself never afforded it.

In Čapek's *Hovory*, Masaryk, with the confidence of a man who has fulfilled his mission, summarises his outlook in a single word: 'concretism'. The reader might imagine that Masaryk is referring back to the arguments of the *Versuch einer concreten Logik*, which was published at the outset of his academic career.[3] However, this latter work is not really a defence of 'concrete' thinking, in the sense in which Masaryk was later to oppose concrete thinking to the systems of German philosophy. It is an exercise – profoundly influenced by Comte – in intellectual taxonomy. Concrete logic, Masaryk argues, has the task of uniting the rules governing the various sciences in a single system.[4] He compares this logic favourably with the 'abstract' logic of the philosophers,[5] but gives so unsatisfactory an account of it, and shows himself so little aware of the importance of the true science of logic that was (at the very moment when he was writing) being teased into reality by Gottlob Frege, that we can hardly consider his work to constitute either a genuine assault on the pretensions of German philosophy, or a real contribution to a philosophy of Masaryk's own.

Nevertheless, the emphasis on the 'concrete individual' was to remain dominant in all Masaryk's philosophical writings, and to form the refrain of his political rhetoric. In the *Versuch*, Masaryk associated the idea of individuality with the priority which he accorded to the Cartesian *cogito*. It was Masaryk's belief that the Cartesian argument provided the definitive refutation of philosophical materialism, and the premise of all genuine knowledge. The *cogito* must be taken as 'the starting point of our scientific thinking',[6] since it alone can be established with the complete, foundational certainty that is necessary for knowledge: *'Bewußtsein ist ein Phänomen sui generis, und ist uns – Descartes: cogito ergo sum – in sich selbst gesichert'*.[7] The sentence is typical of Masaryk's style, in its conversational looseness, and its codified reference to arguments that are never properly stated. Nevertheless, it expresses an idea which was, for Masaryk, as important as any other in the history of thought.

Like his teacher Franz Brentano (1838–1917), Masaryk combines the Cartesian theory of consciousness with a repudiation of 'subjectivism' and 'idealism': and in particular of the German idealism which, arising out of Kant's *Critique of Pure Reason*, had found such overwhelming expression in the philosophy of Hegel. Although consciousness is self-guaranteeing, and although this guarantee is offered to each of us *subjectively*, this does not authorise the idealist's division of the world into subject and object (a division which, once admitted, can never be overcome). I too am an object, both for myself and for another,[8] and the fact of consciousness is a fact about a real and objective world.

At the same time, we must not become so objectivist as to deny the existence of the conscious self, or to represent the world as containing nothing but 'material' processes, upon the stream of which the individual rides helplessly like a cork on the tide. In what is perhaps his most important contribution to critical thinking – *Otázka sociální* – Masaryk tried to show that the 'ultra-objectivism' of Marx is as destructive of true science as is the pure subjectivism of the idealists. Indeed, Masaryk argued, in their attempts to read the whole social world as nothing but a material process, Marx and Engels had been driven to describe the world as though it were really mental. Dialectical materialism understands nature through laws that have their true application only in the world of concepts.[9] Marxism, like every form of extreme objectivism, is really an illusionism: its attempt to displace consciousness from the centre of our knowledge leads, by an inevitable paradox, to a description of the material world as itself a kind of conscious process.[10]

Masaryk's hostility to idealist philosophy is partly explained by his horror of collectivism – whether in its Hegelian or its Marxian form.[11] A student of Marxism is brought face to face with the destructive results that follow, when pseudo-profundities take hold of half-educated minds. In his study of suicide, Masaryk had identified this 'half-education' (*Halbbildung*) as a major cause of modern humanity's disorientation.[12] And the diagnosis was only confirmed by his subsequent analysis of Marxism – a philosophy which entered the world already fitted to the emotional needs of the autodidact, and already armed with an impenetrable shield against criticism. Observing the effect of Marxism, first on the German critical tradition, and then on that Russian soul whose peculiar mixture of primitive mysticism and moral audacity he was to analyse in *The Spirit of Russia*,[13] Masaryk could not fail to recognise Marxism as a most dangerous intellectual contagion. If one wishes to find the roots of Masaryk's opposition to German idealism, they are to be sought partly here, in his justified apprehension of what ensues when collectivist theories are poured into half-educated minds.

Masaryk's hostility to Kant (1724–1804), the founding father of German Idealism, dates however from the earliest days of his university career, long before his interest in Marxism. It is a hostility which goes to the root of Masaryk's intellectual personality. Kant was condemned for his 'moral aristocratism' – for his defence of a morality whose form and whose terms were exclusively philosophical, the property of elaborately self-conscious beings. Even so, however, in the last analysis, Masaryk's moral, political, and religious ideas are profoundly Kantian, and dependent on Kant's arguments for their ultimate justification. Masaryk recognised that Kant was the intellectual superior of his immediate successors – and in particular of the left-oriented Hegelians such as Feuerbach, who had had such an influence on Marx. And even in *Otázka sociální* he writes approvingly of Kant's moral philosophy, and of the attempt to confront and to refute the premises of Humean scepticism. Unlike his successors, Masaryk argues, Kant saw the whole meaning of the world as concentrated in morality.[14] Nevertheless, Masaryk never admitted that, without the arguments of the *Critique of Pure Reason* and *Perpetual Peace*, his own moral outlook would be little more than a bundle of humanitarian platitudes.

This deep intellectual need for Kantian philosophy will be more clearly understood if we return for a moment to the thinker who was to become, directly or indirectly, one of the greatest influences on modern Czech philosophy – Franz Brentano. Masaryk's particular understanding of the Cartesian *cogito* was derived from Brentano. The *cogito* attributes self-evidence neither to a mathematical proof nor to a law of logic, nor to any other kind of 'eternal truth', but to a concrete, empirical, and contingent fact – the fact of consciousness. It therefore provides the key whereby philosophy can move out of the realm of necessities, into the world of concretely existing things. Starting from this premise, we can hardly avoid the conclusion that consciousness and its intentionality are the basic objects of knowledge, and that nothing about the world can be more certain to us than the truths that are presented in our own mental life. Such was the starting point of Brentano's *Psychology from an Empirical Standpoint*, and of the later philosophy of Brentano's other famous pupil, the Moravian Edmund Husserl (1859–1938).

Brentano and the phenomenologists took as their primary study the 'intentional' character of mental processes – the fact that our states of mind represent the world, and endow it with 'sense' or 'meaning' (*Sinn*, *smysl*). Through the writings and seminars of Husserl's pupil Jan Patočka (1907–1977), this idea was later to play an important role in the evolution of Czech thought. And in Husserl's treatment of it we find important connections with the themes of Masaryk's philosophy. Like Masaryk, Husserl believed that the 'sense' of the world is to be found in its moral aspect; in a letter of

1935 he even describes Masaryk, the friend of his youth and his 'first teacher', as the one who had awakened in him 'the ethical conception of the world and of life'.[15] Husserl's philosophy culminated in a study of the European 'crisis' which recalls, in its anxieties if not in its style, the central concerns of Masaryk's social philosophy – in particular, the disorientation and fragmentation of humanity, under the impact of a knowledge that delivers no account of its place in the world.

Despite the similarities and the mutual influence, Masaryk had little in common with Husserl. Phenomenology was too contemplative and too 'subjectivist' an exercise for Masaryk, who saw the meaning of life not as something to be received, like the Eucharist, through private experience, but as something to be won and tested through deeds. Husserl looked for forms of knowledge and understanding which would return the human subject to a central place in the scheme of things. Only then, in a final victory over the false objectivism of science, would the sense of the world be restored to us. For Masaryk, this pursuit of a 'knowledge in subjectivity' was too obscure and too theoretical an enterprise, and too remote from that real engagement with the moral life which was, for him, the only cure for humanity's anxiety. The conscious subject was certainly, for Masaryk as for Husserl, the centre and foundation of the human world. But to believe in a 'subjective essence' – a 'first-person substantiality' – is to mistake the true significance of the 'I', which resides not in reflection but in activity.

How then should we interpret Masaryk's frequent emphasis on truth in human conduct, and his adoption of the Hussite motto that 'truth will prevail'? There cannot be a conflict, Masaryk argued, between truth and morality;[16] indeed, ethics asks us to serve the truth diligently and wholly.[17] This 'living in truth' (as recent Czech writers have described it)[18] demands much of us. But, Masaryk implies, it is the only course of action that is compatible with our conscious nature. If that is so, however, it is surely because of the reasons made clear to us by Kant – namely, that a self-conscious being is a rational being, and as such is compelled to respect reason in his actions, and in the actions of others. 'To live in truth' is to demand and to acknowledge the absolute right to live by reason. It is to obey a law which is binding on all, to bow before reason in all its forms, and to leave around every rational creature the moral space which its reason needs for its embodiment. It is to live without special pleading and to treat each rational being as an end in itself. In short, it is to obey the categorical imperative of Kant.

If we look for the true justification of Masaryk's hostility to collectivist thinking, therefore, and of his defence of liberal egalitarian values, it must be found not in Brentano, but in the great and resounding argument given by Kant. From this argument many things (a wary philosopher would say, too many things) follow. Not only is the sanctity of the individual provided with a philosophical guarantee – a guarantee more real, and more imbued with meaning, than any that Brentano and Husserl were able to derive from the Cartesian *cogito*. The place of the individual in society, and the legitimate sphere of his or her activity, are determined unambiguously for every rational being. Those vast collective schemes for the remaking of the human condition are instantly condemned: to instigate them we must do what we are categorically forbidden to do by Kant (and categorically enjoined to do by Lenin) – we must treat the individual person not as an end, but as a means to his or her own replacement, a 'stage on the way' to a future and more perfect being. In place of the grand totalitarian schemes we have only small-scale work – *práce drobná* – which permits us to strive for the improvement of our situation, while remaining obedient to the moral law. Each individual is endowed with an equal store of rights, and a sphere in which he or she alone is sovereign. Others may intrude into this sphere only by invitation, or else to their disgrace. The body politic becomes legitimate when it is established, not by a collective or a general will, but by the individual wills of individual people, to each of whom it leaves that sacred sphere of right without which obedience is unfree. At the heart of every legitimate order, therefore, is the precious core of self-reflecting, self-validating existence, the sacred hearth at which the self is warmed by its own self-emanation: the sphere of *svébytnost*.

Of course, Masaryk would not have presented those ideas as I – borrowing from Kant – have presented them. His defence of Palacký's *práce drobná* was conditioned by his belief that, in the liberal conditions of the Habsburg Empire, the Czech question, however deeply it enquired into the depths of political order, could be gradually and peacefully resolved. Nevertheless, we should leave aside – in searching for the philosophical foundations of Masaryk's political thinking – the historical context of its utterance. To look for a philosophy is to search for what justifies, and not for what explains. Suffice it to say, then, that the main contours of Masaryk's worldview follow so naturally from Kant's theory of the individual that we ought to experience some surprise at Masaryk's hostility to Kantian philosophy. Despite his rejection of the extreme form of individualism

espoused by Max Stirner[19] – the form of individualism which sets
everyone at variance with their fellows, in the pursuit of a power and
a gratification that is uniquely theirs – Masaryk believed in the rights
and freedoms of the individual. And it is a lamentable fact that, in
looking for a basis for his individualism, he turned not to Kant but to
that most slippery of all foundations – the Cartesian *cogito*, with its
attendant idea of consciousness as an 'immaterial' process. The
existence of the soul was, for Masaryk, the indisputable truth upon
which rested the entire structure of religion and morality, and which,
properly understood, would provide the sole and sufficient justification for an egalitarian and democratic politics:

> The existence of the soul is the true foundation of democracy – the
> everlasting cannot be indifferent to the everlasting, and immortal is
> equal to immortal. It is from this that love of one's neighbour
> acquires its peculiar – one might say metaphysical – significance.[20]

That was the furthest that the ageing Masaryk was prepared to go by
way of a metaphysical commitment – and of course it was no further
than those instinctive apprehensions of the world which had informed
his first prayers as a child. How does the fact of consciousness
establish the immortality of the soul? And why should one soul be
equal to another, simply because they are each immortal? Those are
questions which Masaryk does not ask.

Generally speaking, a belief in the immortality of the soul has
made the acceptance of human inequality easier, rather than harder.
It is one result of religious decline, and of humanity's loss of hope for
an eternal salvation, that human equality (equality *here and now*) has
become the unquestioned basis of moral sentiment, and the principal
object of political aspiration. We can see, therefore, what a slippery
basis Masaryk has chosen for his democratic individualism, and how
much safer his outlook would have been had he entrusted it to the
arguments of Kant. For whether or not the *Critique of Practical
Reason* justifies democracy, it at least establishes that all rational
beings are, as moral subjects, equal citizens of a 'kingdom of ends'.
Their equality before the moral law justifies their equality before the
human law. This, in my view, is the only political equality that
philosophers should value, and the only concession that they should
make to the egalitarian fashions of our time.

The moral egalitarianism of Kant may not justify democracy. What
it *does* justify, however, is a theory of human rights, and the political
practice which follows from it. The categorical imperative provides

the 'natural law' of the medieval jurists with a secular grounding – and it is to this natural law that Masaryk looked in explaining what he meant by the *ideály humanitní*.[21] Since every rational being is to be treated as an end in himself or herself, it follows that no one can be rightly enslaved, killed, injured, or violated. Moreover, each rational being must be addressed as such: he or she must be given reasons for doing what we wish him or her to do, and cannot be coerced in defiance of his or her conscience. The individual therefore has inviolable rights, and above all the right to 'live in truth', in obedience to a moral law which is valid only so long as it is freely obeyed, and consciously adopted.

The Kantian path to the defence of human rights has had an influence, direct and indirect, over Czech thinking – over Jungmann, Palacký, and Havlíček, and more recently over Emanuel Rádl and Ladislav Klíma. So far as I know, however, it has not been properly set out by a Czech philosopher in our century, even though there is nothing more vivid in the Czech experience than the sense of what someone loses when they lose their rights – when men and women can no longer live in truth except at an unacceptable cost to themselves and their families. Masaryk's own reconstruction of the moral law barely advances beyond a Wordsworthian 'intimation of immortality'. Such has been the influence on Central European thought of Brentano's attempt to identify the constants of morality through axiology and the study of moral consciousness,[22] that the source and ground of morality has been repeatedly referred to something 'inner' – to a subjective awareness which is also the focus of an infinite 'care'. Thus when Husserl, in his influential work *Die Krisis der europäischen Wissenschaften und die transzendentale Phänomenologie*,[23] addressed himself to the problem of modern disorientation, he saw it as a problem of consciousness. Mankind, Husserl argued, has renounced the immediate forms of knowledge, in which meaning and certainty are contained, and has embarked on an uprooted science, whose pretence at objectivity is little better than a denial of the thinking subject. Science threatens to undermine the *Lebenswelt*, which is the first object of our apprehension. It threatens, therefore, to rid the world of meaning. Husserl made much use, in this work and elsewhere, of the idea of a 'transcendental self'. But he seems to have had little knowledge of Kant's earlier exposition of the idea, and no recognition of the powerful arguments for the conclusion that the transcendental self has reality only in the practical reasoning which subjects it to a moral law.

Husserl's pupil, Jan Patočka, takes these ideas further – though with a consciousness now of the opposition between Kant and phenomenological thinking. Patočka (whose obscurity transcends even that of Husserl) seems expressly to contrast the morality of the categorical imperative with that which derives from the phenomenologist's search for the 'sense' of the world. The 'morality of sense' provides the necessary corrective to the Kantian 'morality of goals'.[24] For Patočka, the disorder of the modern experience comes not only from the false subjectivism of the empiricists and the triumph of the scientific view of humanity, but also (and here Patočka consciously adopts one of Masaryk's most important ideas) from the over-excited addiction to action, and from the attempt to justify all that we are in terms of a purpose. This attempt, beginning from the self-limiting moral law of Kant, ends at last in the explosive nihilism of the Russian revolutionary – a nihilism which Masaryk, in his study of Dostoyevsky, had encountered in its most alluring and spiritualised form. Only a renewed acquaintance with the sense of life, as this is created and bestowed in the act of self-conscious awareness, can fill the terrible emptiness that ensues when the morality of goals is divorced from its religious teleology. This self-conscious awareness is the true subject-matter, not only of the philosophy, but also of the politics, which were bequeathed to European civilisation by the Greeks. And if, as Husserl and Masaryk supposed, our civilisation has now entered a state of crisis, then this was, according to Patočka, because it has removed the 'care of the soul' from the centre of its social, political, and intellectual interests.[25]

I do not pretend to understand Patočka's work – nor even his language, which is far removed from the homely, everyday Czech of Masaryk. Nevertheless, it is interesting to note that Patočka, partly on account of his gesture in becoming the first spokesman of Charter 77, is now widely received in Czechoslovakia as the true exponent of the philosophy of 'human rights'. In his obscure pages, modern Czech intellectuals search for, and sometimes even appear to find, the metaphysical basis for that 'life in truth' which is their source of spiritual comfort. By what roundabout means, and by what dark and muddy paths, has it been necessary for the Czech mind to recapture the clear high ground of Enlightenment!

Patočka thought of himself, indeed, as a servant of the Enlightenment. He criticised Masaryk, not only for the 'indignant' rejection of Kantian philosophy, but also for the Cartesian theory of the soul which was Masaryk's final metaphysical resting place. (For Patočka, as for Heidegger, human beings are mortal, and can redeem themselves only through the acceptance of their mortality.) Nevertheless, Patočka showed as little understanding of Kant's achievement as did Masaryk; and, like Masaryk, he failed to recognise the relevance of Kant, not only to his own search for a secular morality, but also to that peculiar application of moral reasoning which one might call the philosophical 'Czech question'.

Patočka put his finger on the principal weakness of Masaryk as a philosopher, which was

> his lack of courage for independent philosophical thinking, his positivistically-inspired distaste for metaphysics ... his refusal to regard philosophy as an independent activity of the spirit, detached from positive science.[26]

Although Masaryk needed metaphysics, Patočka adds, he put in the place of it a mere instinctive conjecture, which had come to him through religious experience.[27] I have tried to lend some substance to Patočka's criticism (a criticism made also, and in similar terms, by Josef Pekař and Arnošt Procházka). And it is precisely Masaryk's retreat from metaphysics, I believe, which explains his greatest intellectual weakness, which is his failure to reconcile the universalist morality of humanism with the particularist politics of national emancipation.

Kant mounted an attack on national sovereignty in the name of international law. Only when sovereigns would be bound together in a league of nations, and willingly subject to a common law, could there be that peace which is the aim and justification of government.[28] Sovereignty is perfected, therefore, only by limiting itself. To the extent that nations, crowns, and loyalties subordinate mankind to local custom; to the extent that neighbour remains joined to neighbour by bonds of piety; to that extent are human beings, even in a state of truce, fundamentally at variance with one another, and ready always for war. The universalist morality of the Enlightenment seems to require the universalist politics of international law. How then, can such a morality be reconciled with the quest for a national identity which so many Enlightenment and post-Enlightenment writers identified as the major concern of modern politics?

Masaryk, it should be said, was never, in his formative years, an advocate of the nation-state as the ideal political unit. Nor did he wish the Czechoslovakia over whose birth he presided to sever those vital links with the international order of Europe which had been provided by the Habsburg Empire, by the German language, and by the German schools and universities which had been so important in spreading the ideals of enlightenment among the Czech and Slovak peoples. His idea of Czech emancipation was conceived along the lines laid down by Herder – the bringing into consciousness of a shared historical experience and a natural linguistic tie, while retaining the overriding 'civility' which gave preferment to no particular nation, and authority to no particular lineage. Masaryk sought, not for a Bohemian state, but for a Czech and Slovak *národ*, within the legitimate order of an imperial crown. It was only in 1915, with the adoption by the Austrian authorities of a 'Grossdeutschennationalismus', and its attendant hostility to the Slavic peoples, that he took the decisive steps towards the creation of an independent Czechoslovakia. In his speeches to Czech and Slovak soldiers in Russia, he outlined his new conception of the Czecho-Slovak nation, as the natural obstacle in the path of the *Drang nach Osten*, a nation whose formation as an autonomous state was now necessary for the preservation, not only of the non-European nations of the empire, but also of the European order itself.[29]

If the *Česká otázka* had a function, it was precisely to create the 'Czech national consciousness', without which the new state would have no ground for its identity. Even Masaryk, however, could not conceal the fact that there was no common history which could unite the Czechs and the Slovaks as a single nation. All that was available, as a unifying aspiration, was the humanitarian morality of the Enlightenment. And this was, for the reasons given by Kant, a paradoxical source for any truly separatist politics.

The problem exercised Masaryk in many of his writings. His own solution to it owes much to Palacký, who defended what we might call, following Sir Herbert Butterfield, a 'Whig interpretation of Czech history'.[30] According to Palacký, humans are progressive beings, solvers of problems. Human history is a story of emancipation: from superstition, moral darkness, and uncomprehended obedience. History shows a slow breaking down of privilege, a questioning of authority, in favour of a society that is equal and free. For Masaryk, as for Palacký, the critical moments in Czech history were those when the quest for freedom erupted. According to Palacký, the freedom sought by the Czechs was primarily a freedom from the cultural influence of the Germans. Dalimil's *Chronicle* of c. 1314, which had been frequently banned, and which was published in 1849, was cited by Palacký and his followers as proof of a permanent and underlying Czech consciousness, which was the moral reality against which the Germanising authorities had constantly to pit themselves.

Masaryk saw the Czech consciousness in other terms, however – as tending towards a universalist morality – the very same morality which had received its canonisation through the German Enlightenment. The path of Czech nationalism was not so much a positive attempt to establish a tribal state, as a *via negativa* – a throwing off of the yoke of oppression, an emancipation which, while achieved locally, and by the uniting of local forces around local goals, had the universal freedom and natural right of humanity as its justifying cause.[31] True patriotism (*vlastenectví*) was therefore progressive, emancipatory, a form of liberation of the human individual from the bounds of arbitrary power. Hence the emancipation of the Czechs and Slovaks incorporated the goal of all other nationalist movements within the empire. A true patriot must strive for the liberation of *all* subject peoples, and not merely for the liberation of his or her tribe.

Although Palacký was to some extent a Herderian romantic, he respected the international order of the empire, and, until 1867, advocated a federation of autonomous regions within a common jurisdiction. Masaryk's humanitarian ideals turned him in Palacký's direction. It was the experience of World War I which persuaded him that these ideals must now be used against the order which had nourished them, and in favour of the particularist state. Like Palacký, Masaryk distanced himself from pan-Slavism – that yearning for a new international order in opposition to the Enlightenment values of Europe. His study of the Russian spirit made him aware of the distance that separated the Czechs and the Slovaks from the great Slavonic empire of the East. Masaryk was an anglophile, with a profound respect for law and constitution, and a profound distaste for the 'mystical' unity invoked by the Slavophiles. The Czechs and the Slovaks, in his account, were profoundly European in their outlook, and, in their centuries of troubled subjugation, had absorbed and internalised the European idea of law. He therefore distanced himself from the false forms of nationalism: true nationalism, he argued, is an extension of individual freedom, and is built on the free cooperation between individuals. False nationalism is based on the loss of freedom in a collective and unthinking crowd.[32] The contrast here is not exactly pellucid: but presumably Masaryk had in mind something similar to the distinction made by Ferdinand Tönnies, between *Gemeinschaft and Gesellschaft*, and the finer distinction, made by the Austrian economists, between a spontaneous order arising from free choices, and the 'unity about a common purpose', in which individual ambitions are overwhelmed by the collective feeling of the tribe.

It is here that the paradox in Masaryk's philosophical position becomes most vividly apparent. In his study of suicide, he had expressed his conviction that the crisis of the modern conscience was due partly to the breakdown of those shared, unspoken certainties of which religion has always been the guarantee. Masaryk's own religion, however, was, in keeping with his Enlightenment philosophy, an explicitly 'personal' faith: an emancipated Protestantism, in which the individual is alone with God and redeemed through a direct encounter with Him. Christ is held up as a model, since His 'entire life . . . is truth . . . . Nothing external clings to Him and His life, no formalism, no ritualism; all came from within Him.'[33] Already, therefore, in *Suicide*, we sense a deep tension in Masaryk's thinking. The intuitive certainties which he lamented do not come to the ordinary person as they came to Christ. Nor do they come through the kind of radical pietism that motivated Masaryk. They arise from, and find confirmation in, the act of worship, undertaken by those whom history and circumstance have thrown together in a single place. Religion – as experienced by the ordinary believer – is a form of *concrete* attachment to the world: a sense of the holiness of given things. To worship is indeed to transcend the world; but transcendence is achieved only by identifying more closely and more immediately with its local holiness. Despite his 'concretism', Masaryk undervalued pieties, rituals, customs and ceremonies, not understanding that they are the prime instruments of fellowship, and ways in which life obtains a meaning beyond the present moment. Such things are essentially local, and resistant to the universalising attitudes of the Enlightenment moralist. And it is from such things that a nation-state is made.

It seems to me that the tension between the universal demands of morality and the concrete loyalties which form the basis of a national politics can be resolved. Indeed it was resolved by Hegel. But Hegel's argument took, as its starting point, the philosophy of Kant, and pursued to its logical conclusion that tension between the universal and the particular which is already implicit in the categorical imperative. Masaryk's deficiencies as a philosopher closed this majestic path to him. Instead, he invented for the Czechoslovak state a 'national idea' which could never justify the particularist policies that he pretended to derive from it. The ideal of humanity, until qualified by those obligations of piety and allegiance which tie a people to its given circumstance, can never be a sufficient basis for the nation-state. By a consummate intellectual manoeuvre – which was more rhetoric than philosophy – Masaryk represented the emancipation of the Czech lands from 'foreign' domination and the inner enlightenment of the Czech people as *one and the same process*, which was both universalist in its moral foundations and particularist in its social goals. In this way he was able to conceal, not only the real intellectual difficulties of his own moral standpoint, but also the political difficulties which the Czech and Slovak nations were finally to confront, when the happy compromise of the first republic – a compromise made possible by the legacy of Imperial law – was swept away, first by a state which served the particularist God of nationhood, and then by a state which served the universalist God of progress.

NOTES

1 One of the best examples of Masaryk didactic manner is the speech of 4 June 1908 to the Reichsrat, defending the values of a liberal and scientific education against the theologians: T. G. Masaryk, *Freie Wissenschaftliche und Kirchlichgebundene Weltanschauung und Lebensauffassung* (Vienna: Carl Konegen, 1908). See also the selection of Masaryk's speeches and responses in *Slovo má poslanec Masaryk*, ed. Jiří Kovtun (Munich: Arkýř, 1985).

2 T. G. Masaryk, *Otázka sociální*, 2 vols., 3rd ed. (Prague: Čin, 1946).

3 T. G. Masaryk, *Versuch einer concreten Logik, Classification und Organisation der Wissenschaften* (Vienna: Carl Konegen, 1887).

4 Ibid., p. 206.

5 Ibid., p. 216.

6 Ibid., p. 58.

7 Ibid., p. 117.

8 Karel Čapek, *Hovory s T. G. Masarykem* (Prague: Fr. Borový a Čin, 1937) p. 220.

9 *Otázka sociální*, vol. I, p. 71.

10 Ibid., pp. 202–3.

11 T. G. Masaryk, *Světová revoluce* (Prague: Čin and Orbis, 1925), p. 415.

12 T. G. Masaryk, *Suicide and the Meaning of Civilisation*, tr. W. G. Weist and R. G. Batson (University of Chicago Press, 1970).

58   *Masaryk as Philosopher and Teacher*

13   T. G. Masaryk, *The Spirit of Russia*, tr. Eden and Cedar Paul, 2 vols. (London: Allen and Unwin, 1919).
14   *Otázka sociální*, vol. I, p. 29.
15   The letter, to F. Jančík, is reproduced in the Afterword to the Czech edition of Husserl's *Cartesian Meditations*: Edmund Husserl, *Karteziánské meditace*, tr. M. Bayerov (Prague: Svoboda, 1968) pp. 162–66. (This Afterword is by Jan Patočka.)
     Some letters of Masaryk to Husserl, from the Louvain Husserl archive, have been published, in Jan Patočka, *Masaryk* (a selection of papers, lectures and notes) issued in *samizdat* (Prague, 1979) pp. 297–307.
16   Čapek, *Hovory*, p. 194.
17   Ibid., p. 195.
18   Cf. Erazim Kohák, 'To Live in Truth', in Milič Čapek and Karel Hrubý (eds), *T. G. Masaryk in Perspective* (New York: SVU Press, 1981) pp. 37–61.
19   See T. G. Masaryk, *Ideály humanitní* (Prague: Melantrich, 1968) p. 23f.
20   Čapek, *Hovory*, p. 225; see also pp. 300–1. Milan Machovec has noted how rarely Masaryk refers to democracy in his political writings (*T. G. Masaryk* (Prague: Svoboda, 1968) p. 12). We should see this, however, not as a sign that he was unwilling to defend democracy, but rather as a sign of his reluctance to elaborate those aspects of his world view which stood in need of a philosophical justification.
21   *Ideály humanitní*, pp. 10f.
22   See Franz Brentano, *Vom Ursprung sittlicher Erkenntnis* (Leipzig: Duncker & Humblot, 1889).
23   Husserl's work was issued by Martinus Nijhoff at The Hague, 1954.
·24   Jan Patočka, *Dvě studie o Masarykovi* (Toronto: 68 Publishers, 1980) pp. 79–80. The distinction here reflects Weber's distinction between *Zweckrationalität* and *Wertrationalität*.
25   See Patočka's lectures, *Platon a Evropa* (soukromé přednášky z roku 1973) (Prague: Typescript, 1979). Translated by Erica Abrams as *Platon et l'Europe* (Paris: Verdier, 1983).
26   Ibid., p. 65. It should be noted that this later criticism stands in direct conflict with Patočka's earlier regard for Masaryk as an independent thinker; see the articles written between 1936 and 1949: Jan Patočka, *La Crise du sens*, trans. Erica Abrams (Brussels, Ouisa, 1985).
27   Ibid., p. 66.
28   Immanuel Kant, *Perpetual Peace*, Tr. M. Campbell-Smith (New York: Garland Publishers, 1972).
29   See E. Čapek, 'Masarykovy projevy v Rusku', *Nové Čechy*, 4, nos. 2–7 (1920–21) pp. 47–58, 107–12, 162–74, 221–4, 271–6.
30   Franz Palacký, *Die Geschichte von Böhmen*, 5 vols. (Prague, 1836–67). Herbert Butterfield, *The Whig Interpretation of History* (Cambridge University Press, 1931).
31   T. G. Masaryk, *Česká otázka* (Prague: Čin, 1895).
32   See, for example, Čapek, *Hovory*, pp. 201, 207–8, 310–11. Also Antonie van den Beld, *Humanity. The Political and Social Philosophy*

of *Thomas G. Masaryk* (The Hague: Mouton, 1975) pp. 58–9.
33 Masaryk, *Suicide*, p. 154.

An earlier version of this paper was read by Robert Pynsent and Jiří Němec, and I am very grateful for their detailed comments and suggestions.

3 Masaryk and Decadence
Robert B. Pynsent

The critic Arne Novák (1880–1939) called Masaryk 'the judge sentencing the decadent Austro-Hungarian state at the very hour of the twilight of the idols.'[1] That is a hyperbole or at least a misleading aggrandisement. Masaryk was a man of his age. Czech intellectuals of his time were, most of them, judging and condemning Austrian society as a whole and Czech society in particular. Masaryk was not a man of literary taste; he was not an aesthete; he was a moralist and a student of literary phenomenology. That was unusual in Czech literary studies. First and foremost, however, Masaryk was a criticiser. The period was a criticising period in Czech culture and Masaryk possibly contributed more than any other Czech intellectual of the last years of the nineteenth century to the spirit of criticism. In the first chapter of *Naše nynější krise* (1895) he speaks of all the main new camps in art and in political thought as growing out of the critical spirit. The new ideas like those of the Realists, Progressivists, Modernists, Socialists, and even Clericals and Aristocrats were produced from mutual criticism and conflict. In *Otázka sociální* (1898) he rebukes Marx and Engels for being outmoded, for lacking the spirit of true criticism, the spirit of the 1890s. Masaryk himself is as dogmatic as the other Czech turn-of-the-century polemicists, K. M. Čapek-Chod (1860–1927), Arnošt Procházka (1869–1925) and F. X. Šalda (1867–1937), when he writes that Marx and Engels do indeed constantly criticise their opponents, but that 'that criticism always relates to given individual problems; they accept their own philosophical bases without any truly philosophical criticism. Marx and Engels are typical representatives of materialist dogmatism.'[2]

One of the most important sides of this criticising among Czech intellectuals, the Decadents as much as the so-called Realists, was critical patriotism. Masaryk's *Česká otázka* (1895) manifests that critical patriotism in, for example, his warnings about the quietist enemy within or about the Czech martyr complex. Simultaneously, however, this work and *Naše nynější krise*, *Jan Hus* (1896), *Karel Havlíček* (1896), and 'Palackého idea národa českého' (1898), manifest something like neo-Revivalism, especially in their mythopoeic treatment of the historian František Palacký (1798–1876) and journalist-political Karel Havlíček (1821–1859) and in their mythicisation of Protestantism. Masaryk's critical patriotism is not as single-minded as that of his Realist comrade, J. S. Machar's (1864–1942), or his Decadent opponents, Procházka, Viktor Dyk (1877–1931), or J. K. Šlejhar (1864–1914). To be sure, it is not easy to determine how single-minded some of these writers might have been without Masaryk's stimulus. Furthermore, the conventional nationalism of the end of the century clearly irked all thinking writers. Like, say, Procházka, Masaryk was disgusted by the way Czech 'pseudoradical politicians try to impress foreigners and their political opponents with their unbandaged bruises and little scabs, just like beggars at a fair.'[3] Like Šalda or Dyk he inveighs against the Czechs' mercurial enthusiasms: 'One day we are wildly rebellious and the next we try to whitewash that over by being compliant; both manners of behaviour are equally insincere.'[4] That comports with that typically Czech vacillation which lies at the root, he says, of 'the present, not only political, crisis'.[5] And the words he uses to complain about 1890s Czech political life could issue from the pen of any contributor to *Naše doba, Rozhledy, Moderní revue* and so forth: 'How petty Czech life is at present; we are almost completely lost in worthless politicking and agitation, and how feeble all expressions of national life are or of what today passes for work for the nation!'[6] Czech political life is summarised by the somewhat Decadent-sounding word 'mrtvota' (deadness).[7] That stagnancy is so great today, claims Masaryk, because of Czech political immaturity.

Masaryk suggests that the political extremism common among intellectuals of the time, especially the Decadents and the Decadent fringe, results from years of subjugation. He calls it the immaturity of anarchism, which he here defines more specifically than elsewhere as 'a peculiar inability to be self-confident and thus always in charge of ourselves'.[8] That is mythologising, but a form of mythologising which did lend form to the 1890s – even if fallacious form. He might have said the same about the French, but the French political situation was only distantly comparable with the Czech. Czech anarchism also grows from discontent, a discontent Masaryk seeks to exploit practically, politically, where the majority of his contemporaries sought to exploit it aesthetically. Unlike the Decadents, Masaryk saw no place for despair; Czechs should look for the sources of their discontent in themselves, 'not outside themselves like children and young people'.[9] One need not doubt Masaryk's wisdom there, but one might also see something like moral aristocratism – an aristocratism parallel or opposed to Decadent aristocratic amoralism or aestheticism. Masaryk was a man of the age.

In contrast to the Decadents' apparent or affected pursuit of excess, Masaryk firmly proposed moderation in all things, from his *Habilitation* work, *Der Selbstmord als sociale Massenerscheinung der modernen Civilisation* (1881) onwards (see, for example, para. 40, heading 2). Masaryk objects to all extremism but considers the notion of the Golden Middle Path repulsive; in the latter he agrees with most Decadents. He conceives of the striving for that Path as one of those cursed phenomena which arise out of Czech prudentialism: 'People live in extremes for the excitement of it. Czech history is a great, if sad, example of it. Now it is Žižka, now Comenius! And then along come [Calyxtine] Rokycanas praying, 'Lord God, grant us the ability to keep to the middle path!' A terrible prayer; the Czech curse. That repellent so-called Golden Mean.'[10] On the other hand Masaryk can entirely un-Decadently sentimentalise, for example on Prague pubs and cafés, which 'bring together unimportant people in joy and grief, so they can enjoy themselves together and exchange ideas, so they can dance and work.'[11] Simultaneously, like a Decadent, he abhors philistines of the kind he would find in those pubs: 'We have the police for thieves and murderers, but we are powerless against the inactivity and pussyfooting of so-called good people, i.e. inactive, indifferent people.'[12] And, like the Decadents, Masaryk considers art to be beyond the purview or appreciation of the bourgeois. 'The bourgeoisie', he states, 'does not, however, have much sense of art. Their slogan is, "lots of it cheap", which can have nothing to do with true art.'[13]

In general terms, though not at all in particular, Masaryk's view of art, of the value of art, is more or less the same as that of the Decadents – and, indeed, of other nineteenth- and twentieth-century idolators of art. Masaryk gauges 'artistic cognition to be the summit of human endeavour'[14] and, like the Decadents and his own followers (at least temporarily) in the Česká Moderna manifesto (1895), Masaryk denies there can be nationalist art; it is natural that an artist will treat subjects which surround him in everyday life, but that need not render him parochial nor prove him a good patriot. Although he ends his brief aesthetical study on an anti-Modernist note, declaring his mistrust of radical innovation in art, simultaneously he pleads the same understanding of true art as the Czech Decadents were to plead, mainly in the subsequent decade: true literary art just suggests ('naznačí')[15] and leaves it up to the reader to complete the picture.

There he is contrasting true art with Zola; in his study 'Zolův naturalism' (Oct. 1895–Feb. 1896), which is frequently overtly anti-Decadent, he compares the scientist with the artist as any *Moderní revuista* might: 'The scientist explains the world; the artist constantly re-creates it in himself.'[16] Masaryk's attitude to what Positivist critics called plagiarism is also the same as the Decadents'; the Decadents well-nigh programmatically adapted or expanded earlier literary and oral-tradition works. Here again one might catch a glimpse of Masaryk's moral aristocratism:

> One does not lose one's independence through someone else's thought. The independent writer is he who lives through, experiences someone else's thought and produces from it new thoughts. You cannot find in someone else's world what you do not have in yourself. The weakling takes or imitates others' thoughts; the strong man makes them his own. The strong, independent mind can draw conclusions from someone else's thought and so insert it in his own system of thought. The independent man, however knowledgeable and learned, observes Nature and the world through his own eyes; he who lacks independence, sees the world through someone else's glasses.[17]

Masaryk points out that, though Karel Hynek Mácha (1810–1836) may have used odd motifs from Byron's works in his *Máj* (May, 1836), since he had truly lived what he wrote about, there is no question of plagiarism. Similarly Machar's use of a straight quotation from Jan Neruda (1834–1891) in his *Zde by měly kvést růže . . .* (Here roses should grow . . . , 1894) does not diminish the poem's emotional warmth.[18] Masaryk also puts a Decadent's emphasis on the need for decent psychology in literature: 'At the moment it is great writers who are concrete psychologists par excellence'.[19] One might say that was banal, but certainly less banal, and still more important to Decadent thinking, is Masaryk's statement that art is necessarily contrived. In fact nothing could be more obvious than that, but the nineteenth century with its ridiculous belief in progress and the perfectability of man and of man's knowledge tended to see 'contrived' as a pejorative term. 'Every more or less strong artist', Masaryk avers, 'must be a contriver'.[20]

Masaryk's stated anti-historicism also comports with *Moderní revue* ideology. He makes it the cornerstone of what he calls Realism: 'Realism is to confront historicism, excessive historicism. Things, not history, things, not evolution: that is the motto of Realism, as I understand it.'[21] Masaryk very reasonably understands Czech historicism to arise from the Czechs' lack of communal self-awareness: 'We have lost our consciousness of historical continuity more than other nations. Because of that we immerse ourselves into the past more than other nations, seeing ideals for the future in that past of ours.'[22] The Czechs' 'unfortunate historicism and romanticism lie in their highly partial observation of history; they look for gold only in gold.'[23] In *Zur russischen Geschichts- und Religionsphilosophie* (1913; Czech version, *Rusko a Evropa*, 1919–21) he claims that the Romantic movement had led to the glorification of 'Old Russia' and of the medieval in manners, religion and art; he sees that not simply as a perversion of history, but also as a distortion of the present. Historicism is a central aspect of Marxism Masaryk cannot respect. Marx and Engels's historicism, he maintains, derives from their revolutionariness (for Masaryk, revolution is Romantic and wrong), 'from their excessive innovativeness', and he again says his Realism may be set up as a defence against Marxist 'excessive historicism'; and he uses almost the same words in *Otázka sociální* as he had used in *Česká otázka*.[24] As a true Man of the Nineties, Masaryk attacks the nineteenth-century worship of facts: 'mankind's "sacred discontent" is a protest against the so-called logic of facts. Historicism is nothing but a version of this brutal logic. Though, then, Engels and Marx insistently demonstrate that communism existed in the most ancient times, it in no way follows that communism was *eo ipso* good and so must come again.'[25] For Masaryk, socialist historicism also fails because it has to treat the past inhumanely. Like the Decadent critics or essayists, Procházka, Jiří Karásek (1871–1951) and Arthur Breisky (1885–1910), Masaryk saw historicism as lacking in the same thing as most historiography: 'Materialism does not provide the historian with satisfactory psychology. The true explication of historical facts . . . is impossible without psychology.'[26] In his 1887 critique in *Čas* of the Parnassian Vrchlický's (1853–1912) play, *Exulanti* (The Exiles, 1886), Masaryk states the view which was to be repeated by both *Moderní revuisté* and Šalda, that Czech historical novels and, indeed, most historical novels – Masaryk's exception is Tolstoy's *War and Peace* – fail because 'the ideas and emotions of the heroes are generally modern; only the exterior, only the clothes, comport with a given historical period.'[27]

Very much in accordance with his own ideology, Masaryk himself describes the process of history as a 'realisation of our longing and yearning for perfection.'[28] One sees in that the essential difference between Masaryk and the Decadents. Like very few intelligent men, Masaryk was an optimist. (Or at least he wrote as if he were an optimist.) He looked like an optimist in an age when pessimism constituted the starting point of serious thinking, but was also highly fashionable. At least, according to Karel Čapek (1890–1938) in *Hovory s T. G. Masarykem* (1928–36), from his childhood until shortly before his death he had 'always been an optimist'.[29] Also, unlike most serious contemporancous writers, Masaryk rejects a totally negative perception of the modern technological age. In 1895 he writes: 'But I see life in locomotives and stations and factories, etc. I can see "darker" sides in that life, but I can also see many better, fine, attractive sides.'[30]

That apparent optimism did not prevent him from recognising the *maladie du siècle*, which he considers both a spiritual and a moral problem; a reader will often imagine that Masaryk is writing either to prove misguided all those who are century-sick or to cure them as a preacher-physician. He particularly dislikes the modern spirit of 'negation', negativeness. As early as in *Selbstmord* he is speaking of Europeans' souls being plagued in their tenderest years by the modern spirit of negation. Then in his 'Život církevní a náboženský roku 1904' (1905), he writes, 'Negation is the slogan of the era; very few people act in a spiritually positive manner. Mankind is accustoming itself to living in ruins . . .'[31] What he relentlessly labels his humanitist programme is spiritually positive and will work against negativeness, as it will overcome the nineteenth century's 'mysticism of Romantic passivity'.[32] That passivity, usually linked with determinism, was evident in most Decadent writers. Furthermore, the Decadents waited for their *barbares blancs* to come to destroy and renew sick European civilisation. That side of Decadent passivity was even more heinous to Masaryk. It was a surrendering to all that was bad in modern civilisation. He considers suicides the victims of that civilisation and the cultural battles it had entailed. Like Matthew Arnold, Masaryk sees modern humanity today as the subject of self-destructive meditation. He blames the alienation of modern men and women on German philosophy: 'With its subjectivism German idealism can easily lead man to loneliness. Man becomes entangled in his own ego and completely loses himself in his inner self. The man who is lonely and immersed, lost, in himself becomes restless, uneasy, unhappy. The man who believes only in himself begins to have doubts, begins to lose faith of any sort.' He continues that argument by stating that suicide is the 'extreme subjectivism' one

could expect from philosophies like Schopenhauer's. Suicidality, as
well as the growing rate of psychotic behaviour are, for him, the
'other side' of the German idealist 'coin'.[33] Masaryk also links
psychiatry or psychopathology with the *maladie du siècle*: 'The
weakness of psychopathology is that, by one-sidedly studying the
inner self, it leads to mysticism and fruitless brooding. Furthermore,
because of the transience and interfluence of the objects to be
studied, psychology can easily lead to fantastic inexactitude and
indefiniteness.'[34]

Masaryk considers this problem again, with clearer relevance to
Decadent art and literature, in his 'Moderní člověk a náboženství'
(1897–1898). Here, as frequently, he connects the *maladie du siècle*
with Roman Catholicism; alienation is identified with instability.
Masaryk uses Flaubert's term, and calls the sickness, Catholic
melancholy:

> It is a complex state consisting in several elements (sensual
> fantasising, various degrees of insincerity, self-deception and the
> deception of others, analysing one's own state, oscillating between
> the extremes of impurity and purity, periodical repentence, fear of
> ecclesiastical authority, etc.). We may study that state not only in
> Musset, but also in a whole series of French (Catholic) writers:
> Baudelaire, Barbey d'Aurevilly, Guy de Maupassant, Zola, Pré-
> vost, etc.[35]

Modern man, Masaryk says in *Otázka sociální* feels unwell, is ill at
ease and is 'neurotic, split within himself, staggering uncertainly
between the past and the future'. Masaryk then, is recognising,
indeed accepting, as his own, the sense of belonging to an age of
transition. That sense of belonging to something in flux and uncertain
constituted something like an obsession in the Czech Decadents
(though its source was French Romanticism). Masaryk asserts that
socialism emerged from that sense, that 'mood', like suicidality.
Suicidality originated in nineteenth-century pessimism, but socialism
replaced that pessimism with non-pessimistic objectivism: socialism's
'driving emotion is anger, fury – objectivist emotions'.[36]

The implied alignment of suicidality with socialism is typical of the
period; both are forms of destruction for 1890s men and women, but
they are opposites. Suicide may express the supremacy of the ego;
socialism expresses the supremacy of the masses, a national collective. Masaryk imagines the existence of suicides resulting from
taedium vitae, but such suicides are most common among ascetics and

debauchees. Most suicides, however, result from depression, which Masaryk conceives of as a delirium of *amour propre*. Suicide is a sickness of a sick, selfish century. Depression itself results from real or imagined unhappiness. For Masaryk such unhappiness must be pathological, for any healthy *Weltanschauung* places a high value on life and therefore needs to preserve life. Suicide and the *maladie du siècle* are agents working against humanitism. For the Decadent, death is a part of life, indeed may be the orgasmic zenith of life. Probably the majority of Czech Decadent prose works has as its action structure the process of dying. The picture at the end of Zeyer's (1841–1901) novel, *Dům 'U tonoucí hvězdy'* (1897), where a prostitute has committed suicide by coal-gas and eventually the whole house catches fire and its physically or mentally sick inhabitants are consumed, could be seen as a summary of Masaryk's conception of suicide and the *maladie du siècle*.[37]

In Masaryk's and the Decadents' lexicon, suicide is or may be an aristocratic act. Masaryk conceives of titanism as part of the century-sickness, and titanism constitutes a form of aristocratism. He sees Musset's debauchee Rolla (in the 1833 poem of that name) as the typical aristocratic suicide; Rolla is driven to suicide by the experience of his Marie's chaste love. Musset's Octave (*La Confession d'un enfant du siècle*, 1836), equally an aristocratic titan, considers, but does not commit suicide. In *La Confession*, Musset depicts a prostitute as the sickness: 'C'était la maladie du siècle, ou plutôt cette fille l'était elle-même, et ce fut elle qui, sous ses traits pâles et moqueurs, avec cette voix enrouée, vint s'asseoir devant moi au fond du cabaret.'[38] Masaryk combines that metaphorical depiction with Rolla's death, not quite logically, though such a combination comports with Masaryk's interpretation of the century's sickness as intimately connected with excessive real or imaginary copulation. 'Almost all titans have an aristocratic, undemocratic way of thinking. It is certain that Rolla's end is the *maladie du siècle* as we read of it in *La Confession* when [Octave; T.G.M. has no subject; it could be, nonsensically, Rolla] describes his wandering into a nightbar and getting to know a prostitute: 'That was the *maladie du siècle*, actually the girl ['*dívka*', sic!] herself was the sickness'.[39] For Masaryk, titanism often appears to be synonymous with extremism of practically any kind. Thus he speaks of the activities of the small left-wing group in 1848 Prague as 'Whitsun radical titanism'.[40] He sees the century as a history of titanism, a history reflected in the first fighting with God of Goethe's Faust, who then ends as a ruler or politician.

As literature had developed further and further into materialism, so had politics: 'Gottfried Keller, like Marx, consciously built on Feuerbach', and Keller, like Marx, is concerned primarily with the common people.[41] That apparently contradicts Masaryk's rejection of aristocratism; certainly his comprehension of titanism always remains somewhat blurred. At one point he explicitly fuses author with author's subject, when he makes Marx himself into a typical nineteenth-century titan, makes Marx into a hero of his time: 'Musset's Rolla, Goethe's Faust, Byron's Manfred, Mickiewicz's Konrad, Krasiński's Pankrac, Tolstoy's Levin, Dostoyevsky's Ivan; the ideas and longings which these titans express in the name of their era, just as Marx expresses his ideas and longings, may certainly not be reduced down to environment or economic discontent'.[42] To interpret Marx as a hero of his time is acceptable, particularly given the subsequent development of European history, but surely it is the proletariat who would then become Marx's mass titan, not Marx himself. If Masaryk spoke of collective titanism as a Marxian conception, his argument against socialism would be stronger – and the reader would be faced with a damning sentimentalisation which would concur with Decadent writing (mainly Arnošt Procházka) on Marxism and communism. Masaryk complicates his interpretation further by averring that Marx represents the 'capitalist as an exploiter, a modern Faust, lurching to and fro between avarice and epicurism.'[43] In the end Masaryk obfuscates this line of argument further and makes Marx into a Modernist, albeit a better, healthier Modernist than most, because Marx is essentially, says Masaryk, an optimist. (In fact, Modernists do not generally have solutions; perhaps, then, early Freud was not entirely a Modernist, however Decadent a writer he might have been.) Masaryk's argument is barely convincing, but it is important for anyone concerned with his conception of titanism or Decadence:

> Marx's *Das Kapital* is an economic transcription of the Faustian Mephistopheles.
> In its negation Marxism eclectically seizes what is at a given moment fashionable – Naturalism, Positivism, Darwinism, the Decadence, the *Moderne*, Zola and so on – everything in a muddled miscellany. Marxism is fatalistic. It puts all its money on one horse.
> Only dilettantism protects it . . . from extreme consequences.[44]

Masaryk, however close to Decadence he may himself sometimes come, fairly despises the merest whiff of Decadence. Jaroslav Vrchlický's version of the Polish Faust, Twardowski, is a naive titan, something of a 'šosáček' (petty *bourgeois* philistine), and Masaryk shows his ignorance of Decadent, French, pictures of Salome when he writes: 'Max Nordau would say Twardowski was a proper Decadent. Certainly he has wild, coarse desires, as we see from the interest he shows in watching [in Venice] these naked "she-dogs" and lascivious women from whose eyes burn "the anger of tigresses". In keeping with all the rules the tigresses themselves are Decadently sensuous – Herodias thirsted for John's blood because he would not accede to her desires.' Masaryk rightly points out the fact that the temptations of Goethe's Faust are of a different order from the lewd pictures presented to Vrchlický's Twardowski. The result is that Twardowski, in Masaryk's view, in the end loses all claim to titanism. Or, if he had been a titan, he ceases to be a titan once he falls prey to 'ultra-decadent [ultra-Decadent?] temptation'.[45] Vrchlický's hero has nothing to do with Faust as modern man; he is superficial and fails to embrace the global restlessness which now besets the world. Elsewhere Masaryk says, 'Modern man senses a certain tension, discontent, wages war against Fate and history. That war is not, however, directed against definite individuals or classes; its nature is philosophical, metaphysical'.[46] Unlike Vrchlický, both Masaryk and Marx take as their starting point a Europe in a state of decay.

Masaryk's perception of national historical decay, ('úpadek') is based on the early Revival interpretation of Bohemian culture and political history. Writers like Josef Dobrovský (1753–1829) and Josef Jungmann (1773–1847) conceived of Czech culture going into decay with the Battle of the White Mountain (1620) and the Counter-Reformation. Palacký saw that decay coming with the Battle of Mohács (1526). The Revival (particularly Palacký and Havlíček) is a revival from decay. That Masaryk followed the Revivalist propagandistic interpretation of Czech history is clear from the sub-headings in the last chapter of *Česká otázka*. For Masaryk the first Czech decay set in after the Battle of Lipany (1434), and its pace only accelerated with the White Mountain.[47] Elsewhere he spoke of the seventeenth and eighteenth centuries in Bohemia as a 'decadent era'.[48] Masaryk's untenable view is founded on utterly forgivable ignorance, at least until he comes into conflict with the historian, Josef Pekař (1870–1937). Such a view was encouraged by the awareness of decay which had started to spread in the later stages of Romanticism and had become intense all over intellectual Europe by the 1880s and 1890s.

European intellectuals had seen one revolution after another fail to improve the lot of humanity; they had experienced the growth of atheism and agnosticism, the overtaking of Nature by machinery and the subsequent increase in urban squalor, and now they had seen uncivilised Prussia soundly defeat civilised France. The spread of education had led to subjectivity (in Masarykian terms, the uneducated savage, is, obviously enough, objectivist); spiritual education may lead to refinement, but not to betterment. In Masaryk's view, suicidality spreads with education (or: semi-education) and general sexual immorality. (Masaryk is peculiarly possessed by sexuality, perhaps under the influence of Nordau and Bourget.) The nineteenth century had also witnessed an expansion of individual liberty, but the freer the country (Masaryk makes exceptions of the Anglo-Saxon lands), the higher the suicide rate. The social ills of the modern age also derive from the immoral overvaluing of objects of physical satisfaction. Masaryk sees modern European humanity in a crisis of degeneracy. In retrospect he wrote in *Světová revoluce* (1925): 'To demand moral discipline was declared old-fashioned moralising and piety or religious living was condemned as superstition. Scepticism, world-weariness, restlessness, discontent, pessimism, anger, despair, ending in suicidality, militarism, war-mongering – those are the shady sides of modern man, the superman.'[49] To some degree that echoes what he had written in *Naše nynější krise* in 1895, where he conceives of social decay based on incontinence and indiscipline. He writes there that the 'unbalancedness, world-weariness, restlessness and discontent of a major section of young people derive simply from an impure life, from sexual depravity – an impure imagination corrupts life. Impurity is death to true ideals; impurity is the source of the lie upon which modern society rests.'[50]

Masaryk sees everything in terms of crisis at this period. In *Naše nynější krise*, he is speaking of the Old Czech Party (and their rivals, the now dominant Young Czechs) as in decay, the decay of politics, especially of liberalism. That 'derives from a *chauvinism of not working and of ignorance*, the source of the present crisis.'[51] He is careful to say that this crisis of decay in the Old and Young lines does not indicate anything like national decay. On the contrary, he says, the present crisis is a 'stipulation for and, indeed, a part of progress and revival.'[52] Thus Masaryk does consider crisis a positive force, though he does not seem to have gone quite so far as to see decay as necessary for innovation, in Nietzschean or Decadent terms. (He is not quite consistent in his attitude to the nation as a whole, for, towards the end of the book, he writes, 'The Czech student body is indeed sick, but no sicker than all of us, than the whole nation.'[53])

After the moral, national, and political crisis, we have the crisis of religion. Goethe, Musset, Byron, Dostoyevsky and even Kant, he says, have struggled for a 'suprapositivist' religion, but today religion is in a state of crisis, for which religion itself is largely to blame.[54] Masaryk claims that this crisis lies not only in the Christian Church but also in Jewry; 'the religious problem is a problem of the whole of humanity.'[55] He regards modern Marxism to be in a state of 'scholarly and philosophical crisis',[56] indeed he states that 'the crisis in Marxism is not merely a problem for the Social Democratic Party but for philosophy and scholarship altogether.'[57] In Decadent literature, this sense of crisis is reflected in the depictions of individuals going out of their minds or becoming mortally sick.

Very much part of the crisis for Masaryk is what he conceives of as the decay of individualism. Sound, free individualism has tended to be driven out by either collectivism (of the Socialist brand) or subjectivism (solipsism of the Decadent brand). Masaryk defines his own individualist ethic thus: 'The modern ethic considers the individual's and humanity's life *sub specie aeternitatis*; it believes in progress, believes that social solidarity will build ever stronger individuals. Individuals, not egoists.'[58] Masaryk cannot see egoism and altruism as opposites, and he conceives of the relationship of the individual to society as an amalgam of solidarity and antagonism. (Even egoism can be useful to society, to use Masaryk's terms.) He cannot accept that there is an absolute conflict between the individual and society (as most Modernists pleaded). In opposition to Nietzscheans and Decadents, Masaryk demands a moderate individualism, and his thinking here approaches the woolly, or begs too many questions: 'Moderate individualism, truly philosophical and ethical individualism, desires that definite types, characters, personalities be fashioned in society through a common endeavour, on the basis of love'.[59] The individual conscience must not be responsible to any external authority. That is a theme of his *Jan Hus*, where he sensibly sees the Reformation as a reformation of the individual's relationship to society – and to his or her God. Masaryk then sees the National Revival also as a reform of individuals, as a movement working for the liberty of the individual. (The Hussite reformation, he would plead, reacted against ecclesiastical decay, as the Revival reacted against national cultural decay.) That has nothing to do with Romantic individualism, which Masaryk consistently sees as the mother of two social evils, nationalism and revolutionism. He rejects the socialist idea of a collective consciousness on the basis that society must consist of individuals:

> What is called collective consciousness signifies that, by coexistence and constant, ever increasing reciprocity, individuals have created a spiritual state which manifests itself as the so-called intellectual atmosphere, public spirit or *Zeitgeist*, public opinion, intellectual *milieu* and so forth. That social atmosphere is never, indeed society is never, possible without individuals.[60]

Cogently enough, Masaryk has little time for the extreme anarchist individualism of Max Stirner, a philosopher Czech and German Decadents admired. For Masaryk 'Stirnerian egoism [that is, solipsism] becomes straightforward nihilism.'[61] He links Stirner's Individual with Goethe's titanic Faust: 'German idealists made a god of the individual. It is as if Stirner with his *Der Einzige* were writing a commentary to Faust's egoism.'[62] Such extreme individualism has no moral or theoretical justification, according to Masaryk. The ego may not be 'placed on the same level as God' and, anyway, 'no ego is or can be alone', totally independent.[63] Similarly, extreme individualism like Bakunin's eventually 'leads to the negation of individuality, to absolutism.'[64] As Stirner's solipsism constitutes for Masaryk nihilism, so the other leading German philosophical influence on the Czech Decadence, Schopenhauer, with his pessimism, is likewise a nihilist. Schopenhauer's pessimism was also 'born of excessive individualism'. It was and is popular with readers, no doubt because 'Schopenhauer lays so much stress on emotion instead of reason.'[65] Masaryk also notes there that Schopenhauer's pessimism derived from anger rather than despair; that reminds us that he claims that Marx's socialism derived from anger. Both philosophies reflected the industrialisation of Europe and embodied an intellectual optimalist rejection of it. The aspect which divorces Marx and Engels from Schopenhauer, and Nietzsche, is that the former pair have no sympathy: 'Even Zarathustra', Masaryk quips, 'surely had sympathy with his superman.'[66] Masaryk considers that Marx and Engels, as much as Schopenhauer, are at least in part responsible for the despairing state of the soul of modern human beings, as it is depicted in literature; the following constitutes an assessment of the Modernist state of mind:

> Modern man does not despair only because of poverty and need, just as, on the other hand, his anger does not derive only from

poverty. This mood has its source elsewhere. In the head and in the heart. In philosophy. In Marx himself we can pretty easily see where this mood came from; he says it himself: from the time Feuerbach destroyed Heaven there was nothing left for philosophy to do but revolutionise the world. Faust, too, and Cain, Manfred, Rolla, Ivan Karamazov, all these modern titans begin with a battle against the supernal and end with revolutions or their own deaths. Schopenhauer disposed of God in the same way and declared a blind will directed towards nothingness to be the essence of the world. Marx and Engels set up material in the place of God and surrendered themselves to blind chance. Engels 'entirely consistently' sees blind Evil as the motive force of the world; history is driven by the blind passions of avarice and the desire to dominate. In a blind, worthless world there is no time or place for love and joy.[67]

Masaryk links Schopenhauer with Faust through his 'psychological romanticism', but he sees in Nietzsche, particularly in the superman, a fusing of Faust and Schopenhauer. Nietzsche was the most discussed thinker of the Decadent period. Masaryk mocks the superman (but even Arnošt Procházka had little time for the idea): in Nietzsche, Masaryk says, 'the Faustian superman is debased and becomes a blind lout; the philosophical out-and-out Promethean surrenders himself to evolutionary chance of selection. . . . The storming of the Nietzschean superman manifests neither strength nor weakness; the superman has simply become an anti-man of sheer negation.'[68] On the influence of Nietzsche as an 'infallible teacher' of young Czech intellectuals, Masaryk makes the significant observation that in Bohemia, as in Russia, foreign (Western) ideas are eagerly snapped up and then ill-digested; that results in moral anarchy.[69] (Hence central and eastern Europe's tendency towards extremism.) Masaryk utterly rejects the anarchism he considers inherent in Nietzsche's conception of the superman, indeed he rejects *fin-de-siècle* intellectual anarchism altogether. Presumably because he has not seriously read Decadent literature, Masaryk separates the Decadents from writers with an anarchist tendency; he appears to consider the disciples of Nietzsche as having nothing to do with Decadence: 'Anarchist writers often regard themselves as belonging to Socialism, even if this anarchism with its aristocratic superman is the very opposite of Socialism'.[70] He is, however, aware of a by then usual trend for writers of the fleshly school or for Decadents at least to flirt with socialism.[71] In *Česká otázka* he welcomes the two founders of

the main organ of the Czech Decadence, *Moderní revue*, Procházka
and Jiří Karásek, as young criticisers fighting against the old and
stodgy. He soon condemns *Moderní revue*, however, for its aristocratism and its 'ethical nihilism', especially over the trials of Oscar
Wilde.[72]

Masaryk sees Vrchlický as a precursor of the Decadents, which is
one of the things he has against him. He finds in Vrchlický what he
lists as typical Decadent elements: 'a predilection for external,
sensual forms, aristocratism and subjectivism, a love of the exotic'.[73]
When writing about Zola, he makes the comment that Zola and other
Modernists (that is, including the Decadents) use *bourgeois* means to
épater le bourgeois. This is an empty argument, given that most
writers of the time are by origin petty *bourgeois* or *bourgeois* and that
the very point of Modernists was to revolt against the society they had
been brought up in. The following words contain Masaryk's essential
indictment of the *Fin de siècle*:

> That peculiar love of the fantastic in Romantics and in many
> modern schools is nothing but superstition; it is thus that it acquires
> its particular significance in modern endeavour. The fact that Zola
> for all his superstition wants to be a Positivist is, I beg to inform
> you, again particularly characteristic for a whole series of modern
> philosophical revolutionaries and titans: frightened philistines
> whistling and shouting in the dark wood of scepticism, Positivism
> and modern thinking altogether. And it stands to reason that those
> who fear these moderns are also thoroughly philistine . . .[74]

Modernists speak of a sickness of the will and, Masaryk maintains,
'these aristocratic Decadents and Positivist dilettanti are really sick
with intellectualism.'[75] The *Moderne* itself, he says aphoristically, 'is
both a child of Decadence and, simultaneously, an attempt to be rid
of decadence.'[76] Decadence is part of a general fashionable escapism.
Everyone says they are avoiding materialism and looking for something else: 'hence these various trials by *psychologistes*, neo-Realists,
Symbolists and Decadents, magi, neo-Christians, and hence these
various 'conversions' of Verlaine, Maupassant, Bourget, Huysmans,
et al.'[77] Masaryk himself manifests no compassion whatsoever when
he describes the lostness of the *fin-de-siècle* generation:

> The attempts of *Impossibilistes*, Positivists, Naturalists, Dilettanti,
> Symbolists, Decadents, Naturists, etc., are shallow, insincere
> objectivist endeavours. Thus stagger the descendants of Octave
> and Rolla to and fro between superstition and faith, between

tear-jerking and emotion, between public opinion and the truth, between sensuality and love, between Satan and God: the titan has become an old *roué* dandy. And an old dandy, as anyone who knows the latest literature of perversity would admit, is a terrible creature, a terribly sad creature.[78]

Masaryk despises Decadent revolutionism, and is plain sarcastic about it; when writing about Wagner he seems to be reacting against Decadent arrogance by being condescending himself: 'The *bourgeois* Decadent likes to play at being a revolutionary and is filled with joy that he will be able to shake off the whole of this hateful civilisation at one stroke and then he will be tough, a real man . . . .'[79] Decadence is part of that morally unhygienic literature produced by Paris, the Great Mother: 'Impurity is the ruin of Czech society and of modern literature. The Parisian novel, Parisian drama, Parisian literature, Parisian art . . . manifest impure living.'[80] Masaryk, the literary moralist, admires the Marxists for their opposition to decadent literature:

Marxists find the reasons for the Decadence in the capitalist social system. Pessimism, idealism and mysticism are merely different expressions of the same general *taedium vitae* which characterises the decay of the old era with its satedness and enfeeblement. . . . It is understandable that some Decadents use Social Democracy and even revolution as a stimulant: the Decadent lurches between church and brothel and so, in his physical and moral exhaustion, he also sometimes gets lost and wanders to the barricades.[81]

As one would expect from a literary moralist, Masaryk has no time for *l'art pour l'art* or, indeed, say, for 'science for science's sake'.[82] Although he is capable, if condescendingly, of understanding *l'art pour l'ait* in its true meaning. Thus, in 'Moderní člověk a náboženství' he writes, 'The slogan *l'art pour l'art* should not make us pause. If it has any meaning, it is at most that the artist, the true artist, will always pay as much attention as possible to artistic form; but even with that form art is an expression and exudation of life. It stands to reason that no artist works to order or for a *Tendenz* which is alien to him.'[83]

A tendentious artist Masaryk had little time for was Zola, *the* Naturalist. The actual difference between Naturalism and Decadence is slight. And, if one accepts the generalising definition that Decadent writing consists in depicting in as artistically effective and as sensuous a way as possible the decay of nineteenth-century society or mentality, it is altogether difficult to say where any borderline might lie between Naturalism and Decadence. In his early critical writing, Masaryk denies that 'the Naturalist method may be at all identified with art.'[84] In his major article, 'Zolův naturalism', he writes of the novels, justly though unclearly (or clumsily), 'Where we expect realist truth and clarity, we find Decadent symbolism, but even that is without rhyme or reason. Instead of accurate observation we are offered an unsuccessful symbol.'[85] Masaryk mocks Zola's old-fashioned, essentially Romantic, personifications:

> Zola's rife aptitude for personification is connected with his symbolism. The modern Positivist, no less than the ancient poets who believed in Olympus and the gods, likes to indulge in anthropomorphisation. . . . Zola very much enjoys personifying the soil – the soil empathises with man's joy and grief. In *La Terre* the soil is a straightforward fate-goddess and fetish. . . . In *Le Docteur Pascal* we have a zoomorphic image when the author compares Nana with a golden firefly flying up from these miasmal morasses.[86]

Masaryk considers Zola a Romantic or neo-Romantic fantasiser, a superstitious man who likes materialist mysticisations. He is, in fact, 'the very opposite of a modern Positivist, though he lacks the courage to admit it.' That is, Masaryk believes, 'a weakness he shares with many "modern weaklings".' He is also a fatalist.[87] Zola, Masaryk sarcastically maintains, 'anthropomorphised and zoomorphised instincts, created wonderful and imaginary beings, dressed them in prehistoric garb and that was the end of any psychology.'[88] Masaryk does not agree with Max Nordau that Zola was clearly a sexual psychopath, but he, no doubt accurately, suspects that a man who is so keen on male sexual prowess is somewhat inhibited. He labels him the 'pedant and scholast of sensuality'.[89] The one thing he appreciates in Zola is that 'one could not say he was a pessimist'.[90]

Masaryk spends far less time on the Italian Decadent Gabriele D'Annunzio, who was more popular than Zola among the *Moderní revuisté*. In retrospect he writes of D'Annunzio (and Giosue Carducci), thus incidentally commenting also on the political development of such as Procházka and Dyk: 'The blasphemous hymn to Satan is a natural component of what I call Decadence. . . . D'Annunzio's political activity well suits the fulfilment of his Decadent spiritual emptiness.'[91] Satanism, he says elsewhere, is always blasphemous and feeble; in that, 'D'Annunzio could have been a French poet . . . but even in Czech literature titankins go to French school because of an inner urge.'[92]

According to Masaryk, the zenith of Decadence in Russian literature was achieved by Artsybashev in *Sanin*. The way he describes that
Decadence in *Zur russischen Geschichts- und Religionsphilosophie*
reminds one of the ranting Nordau himself:

In literature Decadence expounds on excited and exciting sexuality; the borderline between art and pornography is often blurred. It
has even gone so far that free-love clubs and societies have been
established, even among schoolboys.... This Decadence takes
great pleasure in religious mysticism [*sic*!]. While one part of the
intelligentsia considers hedonism a consequence and, to an extent,
a salvation from revolutionary disillusion, the other part falls
victim to a most decisive pessimism, which often ends in suicide.[93]

According to Masaryk, Russian youth took the epicure Sanin as
gospel. Sanin is also a solipsist. He 'believes only in his own pleasant
or unpleasant sensations (he could not care less about others, for "I
live only for myself")'.[94] Masaryk sees him as a 'Decadent Bazarov';
Bazarov's active nihilism has become 'passive sexual nihilism; the old
motto, *carpe diem*, has been perverted to sexual deviance'.[95]
Masaryk remarks sardonically that modern Russian literature contains a fair number of writers 'who have established for themselves a
trade in sexual excess and perversion.' He names Fedor Sologub,
Kuzmin, Kuprin, Rukavishnikov, Potemkin, and Nina Petrovskaya.
'The most repulsive of them are', he says, 'those Decadent Jesuits
who sanction perversity with their religious hocus-pocus, like, for
example, Merezhkovsky'.[96] Masaryk, still a disciple of Nordau, sees
in Russian Decadent literature a sure sign of social degeneration.
   That sounds melodramatic, whereas there is solid good sense in his
statement that in Richard Wagner one sees a 'genius of a synthesis
between Decadence and Prussianness'.[97] Wagneromania did spread
all over Western Europe during the Decadent period – and it infected
not only Bernard Shaw, but also Beardsley. 'Wagner', Masaryk
rightly says elsewhere, 'is a full-blooded Decadent, and there he
differs from Goethe, who was only an embryonic Decadent. To put it
more clearly: Wagner is a Decadent Romantic. In Wagner Romanticism ripened into Decadence.'[98] One notices here, even more forcefully than before, that Masaryk identifies the whole nineteenth
century with Decadence. Where the Decadents followed Walter
Pater in surmising that all art aspired to music, that music was
supreme, indescribable art, Masaryk was far more rational than

Pater, Nietzsche and the rest. On the subject of Wagner, Masaryk
makes the aesthetically most important statement of his life as a
writer. He accepts Schopenhauer's observation that music embodies
the essentials of the world just as well as the exterior world itself,
when he says that 'music is a melody to the text called the world'. But
Masaryk goes on: 'Music replaces and supersedes language'. He adds
to that melodramatically (his own over-rational interpretation of
Pater?) that 'the fact that music is so influential in modern times
proves that modern man is resisting civilisation'.[99] The point is that,
as Masaryk maintains, music speaks to human beings with the music
of the soil itself. Music is the most primitive of all the arts. (As the
twentieth century progresses, so the cultural snobbery attendant on
concert-going increases. As the twentieth century progresses, so
humanity depletes itself further and further into primitivism.)
Masaryk continues the argument with a closely ironic description of
what Wagner means:

> Historically evil manifests itself as the global agglomeration of that
> which we call civilisation or culture. Particularly the state, as organ
> of civilisation, must be overcome and replaced by pure religion; as
> we have heard, language will be overcome by music. The back of
> civilisation will be broken by Nature. Being reason, civilisation will
> be dispensed with by instinct. That Nature, that natural force is the
> nation [which for Wagner means] only those who, out of sheer
> humanity, draw strength for revolution against the unnatural
> pressure of civilisation; the nation is constituted by all those who
> feel communal wretchedness. . . . Morally, culture manifests itself
> as the depravity of sensual saturation, as sexual unnaturalness.[100]

Quite rationally Masaryk maintains that Wagner killed himself with
his own cure: 'For that reason Decadence has such an important
place in his works; Decadence is more effective than its cure – but the
cure itself is, of course, Decadent.'[101]

In that notion of self-sufficiency, one gains a hint of Decadent
aristocratism, an aspect of Decadence Masaryk claimed entirely to
reject. He imagines that the Decadents' denigration of base human
needs involved the total aesthetic rejection of those needs: 'I can see
nothing base in human needs . . . I do not judge economic materialism from the standpoint of some sort of Decadent aesthetic and
ethical aristocratism. I try to judge it entirely along psychological and
sociological lines.'[102] According to Masaryk, Roman Catholics are
more or less necessarily aristocrats.[103] The figure of the dandy

belongs (conventionally and somewhat inaccurately) to Decadent aristocratism. When he is discussing the Dilettantism of Paul Bourget's *Le Disciple* (1889) and *Cosmopolis* (1892), he fails explicitly to delineate its parallels or identify with dandyism, although he does appear to have noticed some proximity. Masaryk abhors dandyism or any attempt at it. 'The Dilettante', he says, 'has artificially to numb his nerves, so that he can try to stifle his emotion.'[104] Elsewhere he states, somewhat inaccurately, that:

> The French dandy is a peculiar type. He is a philosopher, but his tailor and his magazine have considerable authority with him. His tailor looks after his corporeal clothing, his magazine after his intellectual. He is proud and arrogant and constantly dreams of fame, but he also has in him something of the classic theatrical hero. The French dandy is courageous; he sacrifices his life to elevated ideas, but he cannot endure taunts and can still kill himself because of some silly trifle. He is a blameless knight, but the worm of doubt continues to gnaw away at his inner self. . . . He performs his titanic revolution only in thought and idea, never morally or socially. He is the most violent radical in word and theory, but a conservative and reactionary in deed. He is a fervent revolutionary, but always remains an old-fashioned *bourgeois*.[105]

Nevertheless the dandy contributes to the aristocratic, aestheticist side of Decadence, not to the trend's force as an indictment of modern industrial society.

Concerning that, Masaryk comes close to calling Karl Marx a Decadent; it is impossible to determine whether unwittingly or not. He summarises that 'Marx complains about the degenerating influence of capitalism, that capitalism had gripped the strength of the people at the very root of their life. Now even farm labourers are beginning to become degenerate (*abzuleben*); the putrefaction of humanity is nigh and "in the end uncontrollable depopulation." '[106] Stated thus, it sounds as if Marx really was a Decadent catastrophist. Marx does himself state, for example, that 'the degeneration of the industrial populace is slowed down only by the constant absorption of Nature-bound life elements drawn from the countryside.'[107]

Marx had little time for religion, and Masaryk none for what he saw as Roman Catholic religiosity. For Masaryk, the Decadence was primarily a Roman Catholic phenomenon. Certainly the Decadence was in the 1890s a major literary trend only in avowedly Roman Catholic countries, (German) Austria, Bavaria, Belgium, the Bohe-

mian Lands, France, and Italy. In English literature it was hardly
important, *pace* Swinburne, Pater and Wilde. Masaryk takes that
understanding to an extreme when he aligns the abortive Czech idea
of the revived Cyril and Methodius tradition with the French
Decadence. The idea of that tradition, he maintains, is 'nothing but a
specifically Czech Decadence and Symbolism, which comprises all
the vagueness and pseudo-sentimentality of the French Decadents,
who now kiss the feet of St. Francis.'[108] With gross exaggeration,
Masaryk states that, as a result of the Welsh Evan Roberts's visions,
in England 'Decadents, Symbolists and various other *littérateurs* and
artists of a mystic inclination are deriving strength for their religious
Romanticism . . .'[109] And on the publication of some of Zeyer's
letters in the periodical issued by the Bohemian National Museum,
Masaryk sarcastically glosses that, on the basis of these letters,
'anyone who does not realise it from his literary works, will be able to
see that weakling Decadent's literary fetishism, which some admirers
reckoned to be – religion.'[110]

Roman Catholic influence manifests itself most clearly in Decadent
attitudes to woman and sexual intercourse. (Masaryk appears to be
unaware that there were female Czech Decadent writers.) After all,
he would maintain (his wife was a Unitarian) that Roman Catholics
officially regarded marriage as 'an evil, only a means whereby the
impure human being can be less impure.'[111] No literary critic of today
can have any doubts but that Engels, at least, had the makings of a
Decadent. Masaryk was probably the first to point that out. At least
in his conception of the family, Engels was, indeed, a Decadent.
Masaryk overstates his argument (nowadays there are women who
claim Engels as an early feminist); but still Masaryk does have a
serious point, however overinterested in the sexual aspect of human
life Engels may be:

> The essence of Engels's Decadence lies in the fact that, just like all
> Decadents, he acknowledges the absoluteness of the sexual drive
> and he judges all family relationships and intersexual contacts
> exclusively from that standpoint. That is what the Romantic-
> Decadent view consists in, what has been philosophically formu-
> lated by Schopenhauer. One can only call that the fetishism of
> sexuality, sexual titanism. Precisely that titanism manifests weak-
> ness, Decadence. Sexual titanism is always weakness. True
> strength has no need sexually to scholasticise.
>
> Strength comprises modesty. Engels, however, accepts the current

Decadent view that the sexual drive is absolute. There lies his fundamental, fatal self-deception.[112]

From Masaryk's moralist viewpoint, both sexes need to be liberated. He writes as a vociferous anti-Decadent. As Roger Scruton said in his comments on the first version of this essay, the Decadent is fundamentally striving for the 're-capturing of social order.' Masaryk wrongly implies that Decadent amorality contains no ethical element. Both sexes may well need to be liberated from 'both animality and Decadent depravity', and it may well be true that that can only come about 'once we have rid ourselves of the pseudo-scientific prejudice that the sexual urge constitutes the centre of all life.'[113] The Decadents, in their own way, sought just such a liberation, not because they denied the centrality of sexuality, but because they considered that intellectual maturity must comprise the suppressing of that centrality or, at least, a dislodging of the sexual urge. Masaryk is himself sometimes an absolutist; he fails to interpret. What he says about Goethe's embryonically Decadent Faust and his attitude to woman is, however, accurate: 'The titanic superman can only bear a female subman; after all, only by having a subman can the superman feel truly alive.'[114] He regards Zola's 'sexual Naturalism' as a result of that 'ascetic materialism Roman Catholicism produces.'[115] Often Masaryk fears his readers might suspect him of asceticism. He writes, for example, 'No, I am not preaching asceticism; I do not recommend any violation of Nature and the body. On the contrary. I cannot make a distinction between the body and the soul in the way the Decadence does. I decidedly reject that dualism. I do not consider the flesh less pure than the spirit and, because of that, I reject not only asceticism, but also the catholicking Decadence.'[116] He does actually say shortly after that that there is both a Roman Catholic and a Protestant Decadence – and that Engels adheres to the Protestant variety. That is quite different, he says, from Paris-inspired Decadence, which he describes as 'sexual mysticism constantly vacillating between the Madonna and Venus Vulgivaga, . . . a sophisticated Jesuitism of sensuality which, in its coarsest perversity, declares its allegiance to an ascetic ideal.'[117] In 'Moderní člověk a náboženství', he speaks of that French Roman Catholic sexual mysticism or mysticisation in more detail. He describes it as 'a cult of the instinct, . . . a ceremonial apotheosis of the material and of sensuality clad in a religious or metaphysical or scientific veil.' Proliferating, he says, on the ruins of the Ancien Régime, the adherents of the Decadent approach to life are not seriously interested in love; they are 'content with just the exusions of hair and arm-pits.'[118] Masaryk hisses out his anti-Parisian venom anew in his general assessment of Bourget's *Cosmopolis*: 'The whole story is pure-bloodedly Parisian: adultery with all its props, for example, duels, vile anonymous letters, suicide . . .'[119] When he discusses Baudelaire, he finds himself compelled to moralise about pure love and about the way any form of perversion is bound to destroy such love. He finds perversion in Anacreontic poets, whom he then aligns with the Decadents. He inveighs against the extreme eroticism of the Decadents, their allegedly manic sexuality, in much the same terms as he later dismisses Marxism: 'Of course, there are people who see the whole world *sub specie Veneris*. This venereal anthropomorphism, however, has about as much to do with love as fetishist anthropomorphism has to do with true religion.'[120] His argument against Zola follows similar moralistic lines. He condemns the worship of life, life for life's sake. He perceives Zola as a life idolator: 'For Zola, life is the omnipotent saviour and, simultaneously, his only hero, but Zola conceives the self-manifestations of this hero in accordance with his materialist art, mainly in unacceptable forms: brutality and various forms of perversion, particularly female sexual perversion. Perversion is for Zola life. Because of that his chief psychological apparatus consists in blind instinct and ardent passion.'[121] For Zola 'woman becomes Nana and society a brothel.'[122]

In Masaryk's sociological interpretation, the Roman Catholic insistence on the celibacy of priests and the subsequent veneration of celibacy makes for an abnormal concentration on human sexuality and, thus, on sexual deviance. From childhood, anyone brought up as a Roman Catholic will be guided towards exaggerating the importance of the sexual aspect of living. 'The problem', he says, 'is moral, first and foremost moral. The fact is that revolution against the Ancien Régime – in the end that means Catholicism – descends in France to excessive naturalism and sexification, a sexification of life which is unhealthy and, thus, actually decadent. It is in this decadence that I see the great problem of France, but also of the other Roman Catholic nations, indeed of contemporary society altogether.'[123] (I would point out that here Masaryk appears to use *úpadkový*, 'decadent', 'decaying', as a synonym of *dekadenční*, 'Decadent'.)

Masaryk clearly considers the Decadence as simply a sick literary trend, where writers discuss their own sexual aberrations. He makes no serious attempt to analyse why that literature arose in the form it did, and he shows little or no knowledge of Czech Decadent literature. He appears to be incapable of going far beyond the facts recounted in a given work. On the other hand, Masaryk more or less coincidentally provides the key interpretation of the Czech Decadence, an interpretation which has been used by critics and scholars of Czech literature to this day. The most important work to follow Masaryk's interpretation was Fedor Soldan's (1903–79) *Karel Hlaváček, typ české dekadence* (1930). That interpretation derives from his conception of the Bohemian cultural atmosphere as an atmosphere of famine. The Czech Decadence arose out of famine or hunger rather than out of surfeit. It is possible that Hlaváček himself, in his poetic cycle, *Mstivá kantilena* (Cantilena of revenge, 1898) conceived the idea of his Manon's being sick through hunger rather than *ennui* under the influence of Masaryk. In his review of Vrchlický's *Twardowski*, Masaryk writes, 'I see in the activities of Mr Vrchlický a clear proof of the Czech literary famine and of the fact that the Czechs still very much need foreign ideas.'[124] So too, in *Naše nynější krise*, even more pregnantly, he writes: 'we are all intellectually hungry; our fathers and elder brothers oppress us with their satedness (I do not ask what they are sated with) and nothing remains for us but to draw sustenance from foreign sources.'[125] Later in the same work he writes: 'Young people are positively tormented by literary hunger; they want to know about the problems and trends which are now *the* motive forces; they want to read and learn.'[126]

Masaryk grew out of the late nineteenth-century spirit of criticism, like the Decadents. He was preoccupied with the notions of decay and decadence. He abhorred the Decadents and yet he may have unwittingly supplied the Czech Decadents with the most important interpretation their aims received. The Decadents were young Czech writers who felt culturally and socially starved. On the other hand, one might see them as those Czech writers who were particularly acutely aware of the state of transience in which Austrian or Czech culture found itself at the turn of the century. The Czech Decadents expressed primarily insecurity, a state Masaryk strove against.[127]

NOTES

1   Arne Novák, *Krajané a sousedé. Kniha studií a podobizen*, 2nd ed. (Prague: Aventinum, 1930) p. 95.

2　T. G. Masaryk, *Otázka sociální. Základy marxismu filosofické a sociologické* (Prague: Laichter, 1898). An improved, expanded German version appeared as *Die philosophischen und sociologischen Grundlagen des Marxismus* (Vienna: Carl Konegen, 1899) and a Russian edition in 1900. Masaryk's editor, V. K. Škrach, collated the Czech and German editions for a third edition which appeared in 1936. Here I use a new impression of the third edition, 2 vols. (Prague: Čin, 1946) I, p. 85.

3　T. G. Masaryk, *Česká otázka. Snahy a tužby národního obrození*, 7th ed. (Prague: Melantrich, 1969) p. 225.

4　Ibid., p. 109.

5　T. G. Masaryk, *Naše nynější krise. Pád strany staročeské a počátkové směrů nových*, 2nd ed. (Prague: Bursík a Kohout, 1908) p. 360.

6　T. G. Masaryk, *Jan Hus. Naše obrození a naše reformace*, 4th edn. (Prague: Bursík a Kohout, 1923) pp. 41–2.

7　*Naše nynější krise*, p. 243.

8　T. G. Masaryk, *Karel Havlíček. Snahy a tužby politického probuzení*, 2nd rev. ed. (Prague: Laichter, 1904) p. 115.

9　*Naše nynější krise*, p. 252.

10　*Otázka sociální*, II, p. 305.

11　*Naše nynější krise*, p. 291.

12　T. G. Masaryk, *O ženě*, 2nd edn. (Prague: Čin, 1929) p. 24.

13　*Otázka sociální*, II, p. 245.

14　T. G. Masaryk, *O studiu děl básnických* [1884] 2nd edn. (Prague: Voleský, 1926) p. 19.

15　Ibid., p. 46.

16　*Naše doba*, vol. III, p. 138.

17　Ibid., vol. II, p. 318.

18　Ibid., p. 399.

19　*Základové konkretné logiky* (Prague: Bursík a Kohout, 1885); for this article I have used the somewhat expanded German version, *Versuch einer concreten Logik. Classification und Organisation der Wissenschaften* (Vienna: Carl Konegen, 1887) p. 120.

20　*Naše doba*, vol. I, p. 221.

21　*Česká otázka*, p. 171.

22　*Naše nynější krise*, p. 209.

23　Ibid., p. 213.

24　*Otázka sociální*, I, p. 103.

25　Ibid., I, p. 181.

26　Ibid., p. 175.

27　'J. Vrchlického "Exulanti"', reprinted in *Masarykův sborník. Časopis pro studium života a díla T. G. Masaryka* (Prague: Čin, 1927) II, p. 333.

28　*Otázka sociální*, I, p. 103.

29　Karel Čapek, *Hovory s T. G. Masarykem* (Prague: Borový, 1937) p. 16.

30　*Naše doba*, vol. II, p. 564.

31　Ibid., vol. XII, p. 448.

32　*Karel Havlíček*, p. 262.

33　*Otázka sociální*, I, p. 260.

34 *Versuch einer concreten Logik*, p. 138.
35 *Naše doba*, vol. V, p. 151.
36 *Otázka sociální*, I, p. 260.
37 Even the title is significant. It refers to the coat of arms of Paris, thus also to the *Stella Maris*, the BVM as star of the sea, sinking (the failure of religion), the sinking astral self of the hero, to the sinking sun (the evening of the century, the twilight of the gods, idols), and to the end of the world or some other impending catastrophe (*fin-de-siècle* catastrophism). It depicts just that total nihilism which Masaryk loathed.
38 Alfred de Musset, *La Confession d'un enfant du siècle* [1836] (Paris: Gallimard, 1973) p. 83.
39 *Naše doba*, vol. V, p. 144.
40 *Karel Havlíček*, p. 72.
41 *Otázka sociální*, I, p. 31.
42 Ibid., pp. 236–7.
43 Ibid., p. 381.
44 Ibid., II, p. 261.
45 *Naše doba*, vol. II, pp. 331–2.
46 *Otázka sociální*, I, p. 236.
47 *Česká otázka*, p. 228.
48 T. G. Masaryk, 'Palackého idea národa českého', *Naše doba*, vol. V, pp. 769–95; here, *Palackého idea národa českého*, 2nd edn (Prague: Čin, 1925) p. 432.
49 T. G. Masaryk, *Světová revoluce. Za války a ve válce 1914–1918* (Prague: Čin, 1925) p. 432.
50 *Naše nynější krise*, p. 314.
51 Ibid., pp. 217–18.
52 Ibid., p. 253.
53 Ibid., p. 413.
54 *Otázka sociální*, II, p. 192.
55 *Naše doba*, vol. XII, p. 522.
56 *Otázka sociální*, I, p. 8.
57 Ibid., II, p. 360.
58 Ibid., I, p. 234.
59 T. G. Masaryk, *Ideály humanitní (Několik kapitol)*: [1901]; here, *Ideály humanitní, Problém malého národa, demokratism v politice* (Prague: Melantrich, 1968) p. 33.
60 *Otázka sociální*, I, p. 249.
61 *Ideály humanitní*, p. 27.
62 *Naše doba*, vol. V, p. 490.
63 *Ideály humanitní*, pp. 32–3.
64 T. G. Masaryk, *Zur russischen Geschichts- und Religionsphilosophie. Soziologische Skizzen* [1913]; here, reprinted version (Düsseldorf–Köln: Diederichs, 1965), II, p. 23.
65 *Ideály humanitní*, p. 42.
66 *Otázka sociální*, I, p. 231.
67 Ibid., II, p. 315.
68 *Naše doba*, vol. V, pp. 490–1.
69 *Naše nynější krise*, p. 366.

70 *Otázka sociální*, II, p. 315.
71 Ibid., p. 243.
72 *Naše nynější krise*, p. 364.
73 *Naše doba*, vol. II, p. 665.
74 Ibid., vol. III, p. 134.
75 *Otázka sociální*, II, p. 306.
76 *Naše doba*, vol. V, p. 491.
77 Ibid., vol. III, p. 436.
78 Ibid., vol. V, p. 157.
79 Ibid., p. 596.
80 *Naše nynější krise*, p. 319.
81 *Zur russischen Geschichts- und Religionsphilosophie*, II, p. 340.
82 *Karel Havlíček*, p. 241.
83 *Naše doba*, vol. V, pp. 33–4.
84 *O studiu děl básnických*, p. 17.
85 *Naše doba*, vol. III, p. 13.
86 Ibid., p. 14.
87 Ibid., p. 133.
88 Ibid., pp. 226–7.
89 Ibid., p. 294.
90 Ibid., p. 90.
91 *Světová revoluce*, p. 50.
92 *Naše doba*, vol. V, p. 150. (Cf. his comment on Marx/Marxism.)
93 *Zur russischen Geschichts- und Religionsphilosophie*, I, p. 169.
94 'Saninism', *Naše doba*, vol. XVII, p. 31.
95 Ibid., p. 33.
96 Ibid., p. 37.
97 *Světová revoluce*, p. 414.
98 *Naše doba*, vol. V, p. 591.
99 Ibid., p. 592.
100 Ibid., p. 593.
101 Ibid., p. 594.
102 *Otázka sociální*, I, p. 166.
103 See, for example, ibid., p. 203.
104 *Naše doba*, vol. I, p. 216.
105 Ibid., vol. V, pp. 147–8.
106 *Otáka sociální*, I, p. 375.
107 Karl Marx, *Das Kapital* (Berlin: Dietz, 1962) I, p. 285.
108 *Česká otázka*, p. 219.
109 *Naše doba*, vol. XII, p. 277.
110 Ibid., p. 357.
111 *O ženě*, p. 41.
112 *Otázka sociální*, II, p. 91.
113 Ibid., p. 113.
114 *Naše doba*, vol. V, p. 388.
115 Ibid., vol. III, p. 423.
116 *Otázka sociální*, II, p. 93.
117 Ibid., p. 95.
118 *Naše doba*, vol. V, p. 153.
119 Ibid., vol. I, p. 214.

120 Ibid., vol. II, p. 666.
121 *Naše doba*, vol. III, pp. 290.
122 Ibid., p. 293.
123 *Světová revoluce*, p. 125.
124 *Naše doba*, vol. II, p. 316.
125 *Naše nynější krise*, p. 227.
126 Ibid., p. 299.
127 The most exhaustive study of the Czech Decadents thus far is Robert B. Pynsent, *Julius Zeyer, the Path to Decadence* (The Hague: Mouton, 1973).

4 Masaryk and Pekař: Their Conflict over the Meaning of Czech History and its Metamorphoses
Karel Kučera

As an historian, the factual background of the conflict between T. G. Masaryk and Josef Pekař (1870–1937) is of deeper interest to me than the divergent ideas it mirrors or the dialogue between these two men. Much that was written about their exchange of views years ago is practically unknown today. Things have reached a point where disciples of Jan Patočka describe Pekař's views as religious and Masaryk's, by contrast, as 'national'. This shows that even students of a learned philosophy professor can only rely upon instinct, and on the traditional tendency of Catholic thinkers to rally round Pekař and his works, when they discuss the past.

The above example is cited not for the sake of argument but to suggest the value of comparing the two attitudes towards the meaning of Czech history – those of Masaryk and Pekař. In this essay, however, I attach greater importance to the onset of the controversy. I will also try to trace how the dispute, which began well before World War I, continued after it under the impact of Czechoslovak independence. At that stage, the dialogue became virtually a monologue; for although others espoused Masaryk's cause when he, after becoming president, no longer spoke on it, Pekař continued to elaborate the pre-war arguments he had advanced against Masaryk's conception of the national past. The controversy largely determined the direction of Pekař's work from then on. Everything he wrote after the war, all the scholarly goals towards which his lively mind strove, aimed to prove that the arguments he had put forth against Masaryk were correct.

The controversy around Masaryk's Czech philosophy emerged relatively late, some seventeen years after the author formulated it, as a reaction to Jindřich Vančura's paper celebrating Masaryk's sixtieth birthday and assessing his significance for Czech historiography.[1] The first scholar to devote attention to the reasons for the divergence of scientific and political realism was Zdeněk Nejedlý.[2] In his paper published shortly before World War I, as part of the discussion aroused by Pekař's reply to Vančura, Nejedlý explained some of the causes of this divergence. He suggested that dissension among the teaching staff of the Czech university, breaking up the hitherto united critical attitude of scientific Realism, began when Masaryk and his friends wanted to add to the agreed emphasis on methods in scholarship the philosophical aspect of the subjects of research.[3] This approach assumed that besides the scientific aspects, an educational aspect should be taken into account, and that in this way Realist principles would be brought to bear on the life of the nation. From here it was but a step to active participation in political life, and this was a step which the majority of those who believed in academic Realism were not prepared to follow Masaryk in taking.

Masaryk's membership of the Young Czech Party in the early 1890s was a negative experience. And when he parted ways with Josef Kaizl and Karel Kramář, breaking up the original Realist triumvirate, he acted in his role of social reformer, inspired by ethical and religious principles and in revolt against the superficiality of the liberalism of the Young Czechs.[4] 'We did not part company because of trivial, but because of serious differences in our attitudes towards life . . . You and Kaizl will go your way, I . . . will go mine . . . ,' he wrote in a letter to Kramář.[5] The factors behind Masaryk's decision, and the principal motives guiding his ethical orientation, can be seen clearly in *Česká otázka*, *Naše nynější krise*, *Karel Havlíček* and his work on Hus, which was based on a thorough study of František Palacký, Havlíček, and other writers of the Czech National Revival. This was work that occupied him completely. 'I wanted to start anew from the very beginning; I wanted to find a different political approach, one which would revive and reform, which would act on the minds of our people', he confided much later to Karel Čapek in the *Hovory*.[6] An essential part of his analysis of the 'Czech question', intended at the same time as a view of the Czech future, was Masaryk's philosophy of Czech history, based on the continuity of the religious ideal of the Hussite reformation.

Turning to the question of why dissent appeared so late, why the generally negative attitude of most Czech historians to Masaryk's standpoint took so long to emerge, we cannot be satisfied by the supposition that Jaroslav Goll (1846–1929) and his school felt a natural distaste for the philosophy of history as such. There were

certain controversial points in Masaryk's view of Czech history – the
stress he laid on the religious aspect of the Hussite movement, as
against the nationalist view, or his interpretation of the Battle of the
White Mountain as the rejection of the popular ideal of the Reformation. These ideas might have met with some degree of tolerance,
since they expressed his strong personal views, in which the moral
aspect was predominant, informing his own attitude towards the past
and his desire to select those specific ideas whose moral roots would
provide the strong ethical motivation which his programme required.
Yet Masaryk's interpretation of the Revival, with religious humanism
as the central point, going back to the Reformation, was too definite,
too uncompromising, to withstand the weight of historical evidence
compiled by scholarly research.

The categories of ideas Masaryk was working with, and to which he
referred, were so obviously alien to the methods of the historians of
his day that at first they refused to reply to his pronouncements.
Partly this was due to their solidarity with him in the affair of the
Forged Manuscripts, a solidarity which had not yet collapsed. Most of
Masaryk's writings at the time were regarded by his public as critical
analyses of the contemporary political scene, and it was from political
circles that criticism was expected. Kaizl, who was charged with the
defence of the Young Czech party within which his successful public
career was to run its course, was the first to put forward in his
well-balanced reply fundamental reasons for rejecting Masaryk's
interpretation of the Czech National Revival.[7] Goll, however, remained extremely considerate even in private, when expressing his
doubts about it. 'I have been reading Masaryk's *Havlíček* over here',
Goll wrote to Pekař from a holiday abroad in July 1897. 'It is better
than I thought, but I still do not really understand what he means by
his specifically Czech humanism.'[8] It was not until a year later that
the two historians made their disagreement with Masaryk public,
when the Palacký anniversary left them no choice but to discuss the
fundamental conception of the National Revival. Nevertheless, they
accompanied their criticism with a profound appreciation of
Masaryk's work.[9]

Much valuable information can be acquired from the correspondence of these historians, in particular regarding the relations between
Goll's followers and Masaryk. We learn how Goll and Pekař, over
the next few years, gradually lost their feeling of solidarity with
Masaryk, while their respect for his work also diminished, as his
devoted Realist followers tried to propagate his ideas even more

forcefully. The stronger the pressure from this latter quarter for recognition of Masaryk's view of Czech history, the harsher the critical voices raised in *Čas* attacking the slightest sign of dissension, and the more disillusioned became his historian colleagues. Nonetheless, Goll himself, even under such pressure, never relaxed his position of scholarly reticence. In 1899, the year of the Hilsner affair, he not only condemned in his lectures the demonstrations organised against Masaryk by ultra-nationalistic students,[10] but also was hesitant about publishing in the *Český časopis historický (ČČH)* a review of Masaryk's *Otázka sociální* which took a critical stand.[11] He did not want to seem willing to join in the more violent attacks being launched on his university colleague from other quarters.

Pekař, of a more volatile temperament, and more often the target of Jan Herben's journalistic attacks, gradually allowed his pen a sharper edge. After a lecture in Slaný in 1900, dealing with the Hussite heritage, Pekař was accused in *Čas* of underestimating the religious and ethical aspects of Hussitism. In his replies, printed in *Politik*, he took a decidedly anti-Masaryk stand while writing personally to Goll: 'I am not afraid of them, and will not keep silent even if the Great Prophet himself [i.e. Masaryk] comes onto the battlefield.'[12] It was not until two or three years later that he met the Great Prophet in open polemics, and the cause was a lecture on Hus.[13] The discussion was notable in that Pekař finally formulated quite clearly his view of the importance of the national motif in Hussitism. Politics also came into play, since Pekař decidedly rejected the idea that the German 'Los von Rom' movement was mainly ideological, as Masaryk and his supporters believed, as they were drawn ever more closely to Czech Protestantism. Even then Pekař did not reject Masaryk's conception of Czech history completely; he merely protested in the pages of *ČČH* against Masaryk's conclusions published in *Naše doba*.[14] This discussion could not lead to an understanding, since each side approached it from quite a different aspect: Masaryk was concerned to define the main line of thought behind the Hussite movement (basing his approach on the principle that the idea of nationhood was a modern one, which should not be applied to earlier times); Pekař, on the other hand, stressed the consequences of the Hussite movement for the later history of the nation.

These two confrontations (the first, between Pekař and Herben, drew comments in 1930 by Kamil Krofta,[15] who was seeking the roots of Pekař's evolution) are useful today in helping us to measure the distance Pekař had already put between himself and the other Realists. Characteristically, Pekař believed that Masaryk's followers, not the historians, had changed their opinions. 'We no longer supported *Čas*, because we wanted to remain Realist', he wrote in *Politik* in August 1900, defending himself against Jan Herben's suggestion that 'personal opportunism had caused his ideas to change'.[16] Since this was the year in which Masaryk founded the Czech People's Party, it is obvious that, in the eyes of Goll and his supporters, the fact that Masaryk began trying to influence public opinion was a grave step in the wrong direction; his social commitment, the impatience with which he wanted to put the ideas of the Czech Reformation into action in political life, were unacceptable. Among Czech university teachers of both Masaryk's own and younger generations, the attitude towards political activity tended to be one of disapproval – politics encouraged neglect of the scholar's true vocation; they tolerated it only when a man of nationwide reputation put his knowledge and experience at the disposal of the public in the intricate mysteries of law-giving. To experiment with radically new forms of political activity, and to attempt only too openly to bring about changes in the quality of Czech public life, was bound to be seen as a break with the unwritten conventions of academic life.

Masaryk's repeated forays into public life were incompatible with the unbroken serenity of academe, where quiet genius unrecognised by the world was most highly prized. Even in his writings, Masaryk was careless of academic conventions. Shortly before Masaryk's death, F. X. Šalda quoted in his *Zápisník*[17] the opinion of the foremost scholars of the day criticising Masaryk in the years before World War I. They condemned him pitilessly because his activities did not accord with what most of them believed systematic scholarly research should be like and what its purpose should be. On the other hand, whenever in later years Masaryk recalled these early polemics, he showed unusual open-mindedness in assessing the stand he had taken, and he admitted that he might often have provoked and repelled his antagonists.[18]

The long pent-up tension between those around Goll and the supporters of Masaryk broke out suddenly, propelled into the open by Vančura's articles.[19] In 1910 the Realists celebrated Masaryk's sixtieth birthday on a grand scale; it could be said that this was the culminating point of his pre-war career. The situation was very different from that in the 1890s when, in spite of Masaryk's undeniable influence among the students, the 'progressive' movement was becoming more radical in opposition to his views; by 1910 he had many supporters among the younger generation. Next to the progressives, the Realists were the strongest body of student opinion and led most student societies. Masaryk's activity in parliament, to which he had been recently elected, and particularly his sharp attacks on Austrian foreign policy in the Balkans, had made his name popular among the South Slavs. A number of their leading personalities sent contributions to the birthday volume,[20] as did writers from among other Slavonic nationalities.

Reviewing Masaryk's work, Vančura could not ignore his subject's attitude towards his nation's past. Vančura's first article in the special number of *Česká mysl* devoted to Masaryk, 'The influence of Masaryk on the Czech view of history' (Vliv Masarykův na dějinné nazírání u nás), and an article in the same issue by Josef Hanuš, dealing with Masaryk's part in the affair of the Forged Manuscripts, both received Goll's approval in *ČČH*.[21] He stressed the importance of Masaryk's work in bringing Czech scholarship to wider notice in the world at large. Goll was certainly thinking of the man and not of the general tone of Vančura's article about him; indeed, he specifically mentioned the inspiration Masaryk often gave even to men who did not share his views on all subjects.[22] The leading figure of the historical school found an elegiac line of Vergil *(et olim meminisse juvabit)* to illustrate his reminiscences of Masaryk's part in the so-called Battle of the Manuscripts. Not so his disciples, who were displeased with the grandiloquent tone of Vančura's paper. Those historians who had not attended Masaryk's seminars could not appreciate the advantages of a unified approach to the nation's history as elaborated by a non-historian. Their spokesman was Kamil Krofta, who objected[23] that Vančura had credited Masaryk with much that others had done in the interests of the study of the Czech Reformation. His reply appeared in *Přehled*, the organ of the Realist opposition, which had parted ways with the leadership of the Realist Party. This gave the article, though it was non-political, a certain political impact.

While Vančura's first article might have been expected to arouse some opposition, the second, with the provocative title 'What Masaryk has done for Czech historiography' (Čím se Masaryk zavděčil českému dějepisu) was bound to encounter far more. The translator of the work of the French historian of Bohemia, Ernest Denis, was hardly the only historian to accept Masaryk's philosophy of Czech history, but Vančura's devotion to the cause was enhanced by his Protestant beliefs; this in itself ensured that the stand historians took on the question of the Czech Reformation was the prime focus of his attention. This was for him the only criterion by which to assess the contribution each made to the spiritual growth of the nation. Vančura found the majority of Czech historians wanting in this respect; almost all those who had succeeded Palacký had accepted the Austrian view of Czech history, so that all that had been done to throw light on this crucial period must be credited to Masaryk's efforts. He was also ahead of other historians with his programme of historical studies.[24] Vančura based his conclusions on concrete evidence, but his schematic sketch, almost a panegyric, presented the reader with two contrasting types of scholar: Goll and Masaryk. One was the scholar in his study engaged in 'pure' research, an aristocratic soul. The other was the democratic politician trying to put his scholarship at the service of his people. Vančura seemed to be drawing on sociological observation, but his references to Goll's loyalty to Church and State came close to social demagogy.[25] Young historians were accused of many faults; that most of them had little sense of the urgency of what the nation needed was taken by Vančura as evidence of Goll's strong personality influencing his students.

Hitherto this polemical tone had been reserved for newspaper journalism. Although Vančura admitted the methodological contribution of Goll's school,[26] this was not enough to tone down that school's astonishment that he could put this endeavour to give an objective interpretation of historical events in second place, and so make it less important than the historian's ideological grounds. The reactions of those so impugned were commensurate. It is certainly to the credit of Goll himself that even in this tense situation, he urged his followers to moderation.[27] He had no objection to their defending the honour of the school in their replies, but they should deal with specific accusations and not attack Masaryk personally. Goll, as the official delegate from the Upper Chamber of parliament to the Pest conference on Austro-Hungarian foreign policy, had followed Masaryk's rhetorical battle with Foreign Minister Count Aehrenthal.[28]

Goll was successful with only some of his followers; Pekař was convinced that attack was the best defence. He rightly concluded that, if Masaryk's view of Czech history were forced on the public by Realist circles, and if the degree to which this view was applied were to be the measure of success of all historical research, whatever its subject or ideological aim, then not only had this false assumption to be publicly disproved, but Masaryk's theories themselves must be refuted. After a short rebuttal in *ČČH*[29] in which he rejected Vančura's attacks on Goll and his school, and particularly some of his political insinuations, and in which he recapitulated briefly the reasons why Masaryk did not impress his generation, Pekař published his 'Masaryk's Czech Philosophy' in the next number;[30] this was a detailed critical analysis of the question.

Much of the emphatic tone of Pekař's arguments was due to his need to cope with a broad campaign in the press. Jan Herben had expanded some of Vančura's ideas in a series of *feuilletons*, published as a pamphlet.[31] Comparing what Pekař now wrote about Masaryk with his earlier views, however, we see how much more critical he had become. He now felt that Masaryk's part in the Manuscripts affair had been overvalued and that his personal contribution to proving the forgery had been very slight.[32] In a brilliant polemic he cast doubts on the assumption that the humanism of the Revival had been the natural outcome of the ideas of the Czech Reformation. Tracing the genesis of Masaryk's ideas, he showed him as illogical in his treatment of concepts and phenomena, and neglecting the evidence in his sources. According to Pekař, Masaryk elaborated his philosophy of Czech history by 'starting with himself and then seeking himself in the traditions of the past.'[33] Equally suspect was Masaryk's attempt, as a convinced theist, to trace the hand of Providence in Czech history. His historical construction precluded his critical realism as a scientifically-based theory, Pekař wrote in conclusion; he devoted no little space to a personal polemic against Masaryk's political following.[34]

Pekař's attempt to interpret Masaryk's ideas as reactionary[35] was aimed, ironically, at the latter's innovations in Czech political life, but at the same time was meant to stress the unbridgeable abyss between the thought of actively Christian times and contemporary thought. One of Pekař's recurrent themes was the uniquely medieval character of the Czech Reformation. An historian who thought in terms of Positivist research, he found it absurd to apply religious categories in the rationalism of the modern world. His arguments pointed out the weak spots in Masaryk's heuristics, and convincingly demonstrated that the leaders of the Revival could not have consciously drawn on the traditions of the Czech Reformation. It was precisely this use of historical method, however, that the other side could not accept; it seemed pedantic and trivial to a philosopher of history. This was clear from Masaryk's reply, published in *Naše doba*,[36] where he criticised the lack of philosophical training among Czech historians in an unusually tetchy and scornful manner.

Naturally, the outcome of this polemic was seen among academics (and not only historians) as a great victory for Pekař; but there was another, no less important aspect alongside the historical argument. In the spirit of political Realism, the controversy between Goll and Masaryk and their followers was presented as a conflict of ideologies.[37] The Realist endeavour to find a new, worthy national programme was pitted against the political opportunism of academic historians to whom any reference to radical trends in Czech history was anathema. Goll and his school accepted a general sort of compromise with the contemporary distribution of power within the Austrian Empire, and with the place it allowed for Czech national aspirations.[38] This seemed to put them on one side, while Masaryk and his followers encouraged opposition to that situation on another. In the Realists' journal, the controversy appeared as one between a distaste for politics and surrender to cultural reaction, and the courage to take a stand for scientific progress and freedom of research. 'Masaryk and Goll – the struggle between conscience and opportunism', wrote the chief editor.[39] Jan Herben was certainly a brilliant journalist, but his ingenious comments could hardly have influenced public opinion as they did, were it not for the recent Wahrmund affair and other similar revelations about the cultural policy of the Austrian state.

The next few years were to show that what had perhaps been exaggerated by the Realist Party for their own purposes was confirmed in the course of the war.[40] As the situation developed and Czech society gradually split into different groups of opinion, the leading figures around Goll took a wait-and-see attitude with regard to Austria. This was not true of Goll himself, whose mind was full of historical reminiscences of the Austrian wars of succession ('the times of Maria Theresa are back again') and who thus became an enthusiastic supporter of the Austrian war effort. He came out against the manifesto of May 1917 drawn up by the Czech writers, and he maintained his pro-Austrian stand even at the end, when he dissociated himself from his colleagues in the Upper Chamber, who rejected the Emperor's declaration.[41] The attitude of Pekař was less clear-cut; a strong sense of legal statehood distinguished him from his teacher. This he expressed in a number of newspaper articles, from January 1917 onwards, which were eagerly and enthusiastically read, particularly just before the calling of parliament, a time which can still be described as one of stagnation and opportunism in Czech policy towards the war.[42] These articles reacted to the persecution by the government of attempts to spread the consciousness of national statehood among the Czechs. On the other hand, in them Pekař also stressed the role of the Czech state in building the political power of the Habsburg Empire. This in itself was in line with Austrian policy.

The widely held view today, that Pekař did not agree with the dismemberment of the Austrian Empire, seeing the future of the Czech nation in a federal state, is not indisputably correct. Although much that he wrote would confirm this, it is often forgotten that he based his stand on how he calculated the war would end. Pekař remained convinced for a long time that the Central Powers were the stronger side and could not lose the war.[43] The situation on the fronts after the breakthrough at Gorlice strengthened this view. It would seem, too, that his study of Czech history also affected his view of the present. An historian such as he, thoroughly versed in the story of the Wallenstein rebellion and the vain, desperate efforts of Czech exiles during the Thirty Years War to turn the course of history against the Habsburgs, had no faith in Masaryk's campaign abroad. This was partly due to the opinions he had formed when criticising Masaryk's philosophy, and during the polemics which followed. He retained, rightly or wrongly, the deep-rooted feeling that Masaryk's romanticism was stronger than his ability to judge reality objectively, and this was an opinion he intended to stick to.

Nor should we neglect what Jaroslav Werstadt said about the conservative traditionalism of Pekař, which would not allow him to write off the old social forms and orders, nor to give due weight to the new democratic forces which were struggling for change.[44] Even if he counted on Austria's ability to overcome the difficulties of the war, that did not necessarily mean that he counted on Austria as an unchangeable essential in the Czech future. Even if, like Werstadt, we question the explanation Pekař repeatedly gave later,[45] that he longed for Czech independence but could see no power capable of achieving it, today there is other evidence. In 1917 the Czech National Council, under Antonín Švehla, was considering the future constitution of Austria. Pekař was the only Czech speaker to support Weyr's proposal for personal union between the future Czech state and Austria. All his colleagues were content with the idea of Austria as a federal state.[46] Mindful that it would have been taking a great risk for a professor at the state university to speak out for complete independence, even in the somewhat freer atmosphere that emerged toward the end of the war, we believe that Pekař was decidedly less of an Austrophile than his post-war critics claimed. It makes no difference that the effect of these later accusations was a psychological reaction towards the distortion of facts, and that in his proud isolation Pekař took on the likeness which had been forced on him.

The post-war years form a new chapter in the controversy over the meaning of Czech history. The outcome of the war raised Masaryk to unheard-of heights. It was clear that even without the blessing of academic historians, Masaryk's philosophy of history had proved itself effective enough to form the basis for successful negotiations. *Finis coronat opus.* As opinions on his personality changed, so his ideas were admitted, and the official world of Czech scholarship began stressing the points of contact they found in the man and his work. Perhaps the accommodation was sometimes a conscious one, but certainly it was often only a late avowal.[47]

It must be stressed, however, that like some of his other views, Masaryk's philosophy of Czech history underwent modification as a result of the time he spent abroad and his political activities during the war. Even before the war he had tempered his one-sided emphasis on the religious aspect of the Hussite movement,[48] so that as early as 1915, at the Hus celebrations in Zurich which marked the beginning of his revolutionary work, he emphasised the national political significance of the martyr. In his articles in *New Europe* during the war we find a new attitude towards the Czech National Revival;[49] he went furthest in this changed approach in *Světová revoluce* after the war. He no longer spoke of the humanism of the Slav peoples, and he even gave a much freer interpretation of the democratic traditions of Hussite thought, about which he had had so much to say in his earlier writings, finding in the Czech Reformation only 'the foundations of modern humanism and thus also of democracy.'[50] Here, too, he developed the theme of the connection between the National Revival and the Hussite Reformation, but he placed the influence of the latter on a line with the ideals of the Enlightenment and the French Revolution. In Masaryk's view, it was characteristic for the evolution of Czech thought that opposition to the absolutism of Counter-Reformation Austria had led the Czechs of the Revival to the ideas of Enlightenment and ultimately to those of the French Revolution. They began to accept what was fundamentally part of Hussite thought, thus coming full circle back to the moral bases of the Czech Reformation.

These deviations from his earlier postulates were intended by

Masaryk to provide support for his continued belief that the Czech National Revival was basically religious in character. They were insufficient, however, to satisfy those historians who had been persuaded by the results of his work abroad to recognise the value of his conception for the moral uplifting of the nation. As an example we cite Kamil Krofta, who published his objections in print.[51] All that he would accept was Masaryk's assessment of the Hussite movement, in which he agreed with Palacký that it represented the climax of Czech history. Significantly, this question, on which Masaryk's pre-war critics came to agree with him under the weight of Palacký's authority, was the one which gradually shifted the ground of renewed discussion about the meaning of Czech history. Of all the moot points in Masaryk's philosophy of history, this fundamental point aroused the greatest attention.

The background against which the discussion was revived was very different from that of the pre-war years. Masaryk's opponents then were concerned purely with his philosophy, while his followers were accused of introducing political judgements, and generalising them in the context of intellectual discussion. Now, in the highly politicised atmosphere of the post-war years, intellectual argument became the safety valve of political controversy. Before long, the interpretation of Czech history became only one of many subjects of debate, from the 'liberation legend' to the question of the part played by opposition at home in achieving independence, all of which stirred the waters of public life. In most cases, the argument started from the side of the opposition political parties, and conveyed criticism of the policies of leading figures in the state and government. Although Pekař's motives always differed from those of the majority of critics, arose from his intellectual reservations, and had no consistent political goal, this background cannot be neglected when one recalls the atmosphere of the time and the reactions of a part of public opinion to the views he expressed.

Whatever his ideas about the future of the Czech nation during the war, after it was over Pekař welcomed Czech independence from the unenviable position of a man whose forecast had not been confirmed, whereas his intellectual opponent had succeeded in doing what he had thought impossible. The idea that he had been wrong led him to feverish study of the events of the recent past, especially of the sources concerning the war. His articles were printed in journals and the daily press and published in a volume entitled *Světová válka*.[52] Over half the material dealt with the question of a separate peace, a good indication in itself of the direction of his thoughts. His *Bílá Hora*, another volume of essays, would appear to have a similar aim, although written from a different angle. This was inspired by the anniversary of the Czech Estates' defeat in that battle (1620) but its significance went beyond the usual ceremonial observance.[53] These essays were in fact the signal that he was entering the fray; that is clear from those passages in which he emphasises the good side of Czech Counter-Reformation culture. A hint of this discussion of the interpretation of history is visible in the lecture Pekař gave at the university in Prague on the occasion of the first anniversary of Czechoslovak independence, in October 1919, where, without attribution, he quoted Emanuel Rádl's negative view of patriotism.[54]

For open rejection of Masaryk's Reformation theory of the National Revival, however, we have Pekař's review[55] of the standard work by Josef Hanuš, *Národní Museum a naše obrození*. This book, which showed that the ideas of the older generation which led the Revival were national-Catholic, conservative and only slightly influenced by the Enlightenment, played a considerable part in strengthening the views Pekař held on the question. Since at the same time Hanuš appreciated the role of the aristocracy in forming the subsequent national tradition, Pekař drew support from his arguments for some of his own public declarations. Many aspects of post-war life distressed him because they were linked to the erosion of the old social order, which his conservative civil-law principles could not accept. This inspired his efforts to protect the old institutions, and especially institutional relationships hallowed by centuries-old tradition. These included his warnings against leaving the Church, his safeguarding of the cult of St. John Nepomucene and his attempts to protect the Czech aristocracy from the confiscation of their lands under the terms of the postwar agrarian reform.[56] Some of his reactions were provoked;[57] others came from his own interpretation of events, but the chief source of his irritation remained the propagation in the new Czechoslovak Republic of Reformation traditions in a decisive manner, propagation often linked to, if not directly replaced by, leftist democratic policies and socialist theories. In 1930, reviewing his life's achievements on the occasion of his sixtieth birthday, Pekař wrote to a friend: 'My declarations since the war, for John Nepomucene, against the Czechoslovak Church, against the manipulation of Hus for propaganda purposes, were primarily the result of my anger at the actions of the progressive sect, their insolent casuistry trampling the truth under foot, led by their new evangelists *à la* Herben and Bartoš'.[58]

The attention Pekař paid to the period after the Battle of the White Mountain, and to Baroque culture was initially an attempt to counterbalance the consequences of Masaryk's one-sided theory that the real core of Czech history lay in Hussite times. For Pekař, the Czech idea of nationhood ran throughout the country's history as a continual stream of resistance from which no one period could be cut off, and so much the less could history dispense with the period in which he himself saw the onset of conscious Czech patriotism. The more he met with opposition to his view, however, the greater the emphasis he placed on the unique importance of the period following the White Mountain. The time of 'darkness', the popular term he constantly objected to,[59] became not merely one of the periods, but the principal period, the foundation of Czech life in the modern age. This attitude brought him closer to Catholic circles; the ageing Jaroslav Goll was astonished at their eagerness to enrol Masaryk's rival.[60]

On the other hand, this constant wrangling with the so-called progressive camp lessened his admiration for the work of Palacký, who was always being quoted against him by those who disagreed with the stand he now proclaimed. Pekař made public this change in his attitude towards the work of the great historian in the speech he delivered on the fiftieth anniversary of Palacký's death.[61] He suggested that the work of Palacký, and the programme he had elaborated, could not be the 'motto and the guide' for the future that they had been in the past. 'There can be no doubt', he said, 'that the impact of the ideas of Palacký's *History* which captivated earlier generations because they saw mirrored there their own revolutionary ideas of liberation, will now lose much of its force.'[62] He believed that the importance of Hus, too, would be substantially reduced in the work of future historians. An independent country needs to elaborate a different conception of history, 'to search for a different meaning in the past than that sought a hundred years ago, when men longed to free themselves from material and spiritual subjection.'[63] Pekař declared that the most valuable part of Palacký's legacy to posterity would remain nationalism, the idea of the nation, to which he dedicated his life, and which he understood in the enlightened sense as a means of gaining higher cultural goals through competition.[64]

In this speech, Pekař expressed his objections to Palacký's conception in discreet terms, as indeed the situation demanded, but in articles on Jan Žižka[65] and in the book *O Žižka a jeho doba*[66] which followed, he showed how far he was willing to go in his rejection. The

latter expressed direct criticisms and an eloquent negation of earlier
beliefs in the positive contribution of the Hussite movement to the
intellectual and spiritual evolution of Europe, stressing on the
contrary its medieval, Gothic character and locally limited sphere of
influence. The haste with which Pekař set out to stress the darker side
of the movement can be seen in the construction of the book: the first
chapter, dealing largely with an analysis of the source materials, also
includes a passage setting forth the author's intention to refute
Masaryk's excessive appreciation of Tábor democracy.[67] His exhaustive study of Žižka led Pekař to conclude that Hussite times had done
more to damage than service to the Czech national cause. This
provoked a discussion which focused principally on method. Just as
Rádl had once defended Masaryk's views by criticising the historical
methods of Pekař,[68] so now Jan Slavík claimed that the opinions
Pekař put forward revealed gaps in his historical epistemology.[69]
Basing his criticism on Max Weber's conclusions, Slavík opposed
Pekař's contention that his representation of the Hussite revolution
utilised more reliable knowledge of the sources and more careful
objectivity; Slavík imputed the differences between Palacký and
Pekař on this question to the different criteria each of them applied.[70]

There is no room here for a discussion of Slavík's other objections,
some of which Pekař overcame by the suggestive power of his style. It
is more important that while he was writing the book on Žižka, he
found it imperative to give more concrete form to his conception of
Czech national history.[71] Unlike Masaryk, whose philosophy had
from the outset covered not only the past but also possible developments in the future, Pekař as a historian was in principle sceptical
about the present, and even more so about tracing trends which led
into the future.[72] His empirico-historical standpoint narrowed the
whole question down to a number of factors. The prime factor was
the influence and example of Western Europe, which, together with
the geographical position of Czechoslovakia and the fact that it was
wedged into German territory and subjected to that influence, were
the primary forces directing the course of Czech history.[73] Pekař also
attributed considerable significance to the element of chance (by
which he meant the phenomenon of an individual affecting world
affairs)[74] and to Czech history itself, with its traditions and cultural-
political content. Just as a national society could not be the vehicle
for one single programme, one idea, in the course of history, so he
believed no nation could be credited with one single, well-defined
meaning to its history. The aims and desires of a nation change to the

degree that it passes through changes itself. Pekař was more concerned with the periodisation of these changes; his secondary-school textbook presented Czech history in periods that corresponded to the evolution of styles in art, for it was in art that this friend of the art historian Max Dvořák saw the most characteristic expression of the spirit of the age.[75]

This alternation of epochs brought him to the notion that the law of action and reaction was at work, so that periods of classicist character in which authority, order, discipline, and reason reigned (the Renaissance and Enlightenment) were preceded and followed by periods of a romantic nature (Gothic, Baroque), when freedom, mobility, and desire were predominant. This apparent concurrence with Palacký's idea of the polarisation of opposing forces and ideas was received with some satisfaction by those who took it primarily as proof that Palacký's contribution to the Czech cultural consciousness had not lost all authority in Pekař's eyes.[76] Pekař himself, however, who had only introduced the question of periodisation in general terms,[77] was thinking rather of some parallel with the dialectics of Hegel. This can be inferred from the lecture he gave when he was installed as Rector of the University, 'On the Periodisation of Czech History'.[78] Here, while he did not desert his empirical creed, he showed an understanding of the intuitive approach to the past, sympathetically quoting among other modern thinkers Heidegger and his view of history as existence in time.[79]

While Pekař does not seem to have had a profound interest in the philosophical aspects, and may only have been making a tactical answer to his theorising critics,[80] he showed remarkable powers of adaptation in this field; his gift of formulation certainly played a large part here, but it also shows how the question of the meaning of Czech history kept his mind active. It was typical of the evolution of his line of thought that, while Masaryk gradually tempered the sharp lines of the convictions he formulated before the war, and allowed closer and closer links between the religious and the other aspects of Czech history,[81] Pekař moved in the opposite direction, making ever clearer distinctions between them. This deepening of the differences between the two thinkers, most clearly visible in the negative attitude of Pekař towards the Hussite movement, was the greatest obstacle in the way of reconciling their views on the religious and national aspects of history, a task which Krofta[82] and others of the 'Castle' group took upon themselves.

It is difficult, so many years later, to assess the impact of the rivalry of ideas between Pekař and Masaryk on Czech historians, and indeed on broader intellectual circles in the First Republic, since much that is fundamental to it was overshadowed by the political atmosphere described above. The followers of integral nationalism headed by Arne Novák gave their support to Pekař and his ideas, while his disciples who specialised in Baroque culture, led by Zdeněk Kalista, had studied along the lines Pekař laid down. The events of World War II and its aftermath made it difficult to take the side of Pekař even after his death, and then the captivating force of his charismatic personality began to fade. To give an example: the successor to Pekař in his university department, reviewing his book on Žižka, had elaborated and set out clearly some of the ideas the author had only suggested, but after the war he refused to accept a thesis by a student of Pekař who demonstrated his teacher's view of the Baroque roots of the Czech National Revival on the basis of detailed and specific analyses.[83]

During World War II the Nazis clearly turned Pekař's work to their own use. The rival of Masaryk and critic of Palacký seemed ideal for their purpose, which was to use Czech weapons to wipe out the memory of recent independence – the paradoxical outcome of the author's contrary intentions. It is noteworthy that these were intentions on which both Masaryk and Pekař were fundamentally agreed, however far apart their basic principles, and in spite of their differing assessment of the causes and circumstances of political events. When, for instance, Pekař justified his secession from Palacký's standpoint with reasons of state, the need to refrain from celebration of the revolution in order to strengthen the authority of the new state,[84] he unconsciously came close to the way of thinking of the President who (although he could never have agreed with Pekař on this question), had welcomed the victory of the 'civil' parties in the previous year's elections. Pekař welcomed their victory in the interests of the Republic. Recent years had dampened his earlier hopes of finding an understanding of his attempts to solve the difficult problem of nationalities among the left wing, and in particular among the Czech and German socialist parties. It was precisely here that the second and more fundamental cause for agreement with Pekař is to be found, for just as the ideal state as Pekař saw it would include the German part of the population, so his Czech nationalism lacked any trace of anti-German feeling. That Masaryk shared this view, and opposed nationalist animosity towards the German population in the country, was one of the admirable sides of Masaryk's personality in his opponent's eyes (although he was less inclined to admit, with him, that this animosity was the natural outcome of nationalism). He expressed this admiration in the speech he made at the university's celebrations of Masaryk's eighty-fifth birthday.[85]

As we have seen, Pekař was reluctant to accept revolutionary ideas, or political parties that proclaimed a new democratic social order. This led him to seek allies for his Czech-German entente in the right-wing German camp alone. He was the only Czech to be misled by the proclamations of loyalty with which Konrad Henlein's movement masked its real goal successfully for some time, but it was a graver matter that Pekař did not object to the anti-Semitism proclaimed by this new party, which concealed their intention to use his name and popularity for the purposes of Nazi propaganda.[86] I have mentioned this, not only because for years this war-time episode outweighed the influence of his work, but also because it meant the end of the subject under discussion for a long time to come; what happened after the war threw a different light on that, too.

It was long clear, especially to historians, that the controversy about Czech history, between Pekař and Masaryk, was not a question that could be settled in the scholarly field. Masaryk's conception had the merit of being a cogent programme and also affected public and political life, while that of Pekař, in its scholarly integrity, could only offer the idea of nationhood, which even so outstanding a hidden rival and critic of Masaryk's as F. X. Šalda found historically too variable and inconsistent to acquire broader validity.[87] Each side had its supporters and its opponents; their sympathies were attracted primarily by the strong personalities of two very different individuals.

If the questions raised then are now coming alive again, this is undoubtedly because arguments about the meaning of history have never quite vanished from Czech consciousness. It would not be a bad thing if they became topical once more in their old form of intellectual discussion, in which opponents, however aggressively they debated, never failed to treat the other's views with tact and objectivity.

NOTES

1 Mainly the article 'Čím se Masaryk zavděčil českému dějepisu', in Edvard Beneš, František Drtina and Jan Herben (eds), *T. G. Masarykovi k šedesátým narozeninám* [1910] 2nd ed. (Prague: Čin, 1930) pp. 155ff.

2 Zdeněk Nejedlý, *Spor o smysl českých dějin. Pokus o filosofii českých dějin* (Prague: 'Pokroková revue', 1914).

3 Ibid., p. 9.

4 I have used Werstadt's term here, taken from his description of Masaryk's pre-war activity in *Od 'České otázky' k 'Nové Evropě'* (Prague: Klecanda, 1920) pp. 10ff.

5 In a letter to Kramář of 16 August 1895, Masaryk explained why he parted company with him and Kaizl; he also reacted to Kaizl's attack on his *Naše nynější krise.* The sentence just before my quotation is, 'This is not just the mood of a moment; it has dragged on for years, and now finally we have cleared things up.' Posthumous papers of Kramář, Archives of the National Museum, Prague, ANM 2–3/6364. Cf. also what Kaizl wrote to Kramář on 25 August 1895: Josef Kaizl, *Z mého života*, ed. Zdeněk V. Tobolka, vol. III/1 (Prague: Vilímek, n. d.) pp. 378–9.

6 Karel Čapek, *Hovory s T. G. Masarykem*, 2nd ed. (Prague: Aventinum, 1937) p. 47.

7 Josef Kaizl, *České myšlenky* (Prague: Beaufort, 1896).

8 *Listy úcty a přátelství, Vzájemná korespondence Jaroslava Golla a Josefa Pekaře*, ed. Josef Klik (Prague: Vyšehrad, 1941) p. 79.

9 Jaroslav Goll did so in the extended text of his university lecture on František Palacký, 13 June 1898, printed in *Český časopis historický* [Hereafter *ČČH*], IV (1898) pp. 211–79. He rejected Masaryk's interpretation of the National Revival, quoting Palacký: 'Palacký himself did not see the revival in this light' (p. 223). Elsewhere, discussing Palacký's idea of political life, he quoted Masaryk's *Česká otázka* and added: 'I could not explain at every point in what respect and how far I agreed or disagreed with the book. There are certainly many points of agreement, although even there our interpretations do not always agree' (p. 276). In the same issue of *ČČH*, Pekař discussed Masaryk's conception in a full bibliographical note on the literature commemorating Palacký; specifically he wrote: 'Great credit is due to Professor Masaryk for the way his writings have inspired us to think deeply about our past and our present, and especially about the period of National Revival; everything he writes is of permanent value both for the wealth of his ideas and for his original approach. I do not conceal the fact that I cannot agree with some of the basic ideas he advances (the view of the Revival as the continuation of the Reformation or a return to its ideas, the religious idea as the major guiding force in Czech history, the humanist idea ruling the Czech Revival and anchored in religion), but that is not so important, after all . . .' (ibid., p. 283). On the reaction of both historians, Goll and Pekař, to criticism of their comments in *Čas*, see *Listy úcty a přátelství*, pp. 126–9.

10   Jan Herben, *T. G. Masaryk* (Prague: 'Mánes', 1926) vol. I, pp. 201ff.
11   On 26 December 1899 Goll wrote to Pekař: 'I have been looking again
      into Masaryk's *Otázka sociální*. I do not think we can peremptorily
      dismiss the book in *ČČH*; it would be better not to mention it at all.
      Perhaps not at all. We'll discuss that later and come to some decision.
      It seems ungallant to attack Masaryk just now. I have written a few
      lines of introduction to a paper which may never be written. The
      introduction gives Masaryk a great deal of credit . . .' *Listy úcty a
      přátelství*, p. 219. Goll's paper appeared in *ČČH*, vol. VI (1900) pp.
      142–56.
12   *Listy úcty a přátelství*, p. 233. The articles in *Politik* appeared on 8 July
      and 5 August 1900.
13   Pekař published the lecture on Hus that he gave at the Old Town Hall,
      Prague, in July 1902; it appeared as *Jan Hus, Přednáška* (Prague:
      Bursík a Kohout, 1902).
14   *ČČH*, vol. IX (1903) pp. 233–5, 354–6.
15   Kamil Krofta, *Josef Pekař 1870–1930* (Prague: Historický klub, 1930),
      a lecture given on 21 May 1930; also published as a supplement in
      ČČH, vol. XXXVI (1930) pp. 19ff.
16   In the discussion in *Čas* (25 July) Herben was referring to Pekař's
      earlier attraction to Realism, which he suggested Pekař had recanted
      because the Realists were now out of favour.
17   Commenting on his failure to win election to the Czech Academy,
      Šalda wrote in 1935: 'I could not help thinking of Masaryk these last
      two days. So long as he was just a professor he was not a member of the
      Academy, not even Dean of the Arts Faculty. When he came back to
      this country as President, the Academy could not resist the farce of
      making him an honorary member, perhaps of all Academy classes.
      Once he had power, he also had brains. . . . The Czechs are always the
      same: impressed by gold braid, impressed by gold epaulettes. And they
      start to respect you only when you have power and might take it out on
      them. So long as he was merely a professor, just a writer, without
      power or influence, I heard this sort of thing about him from
      honourable scholars and scientists: 'He's more like a cheap journalist
      than a scholar.' I was not a magician enough for them, my writings
      did'n' have enough learned terms in them, I didn't spend enough time
      cooking and hashing up brews in their secret occult laboratories',
      Šaldův zápisník, vol. VIII (1935–36) pp. 85ff.
18   'When I had to fight I hit out all round and more than once it was
      unnecessary. I have wronged people, it is true, but I got as good as I
      gave. I scorned people, often, because I was conceited; but above all I
      was impatient, I thought people ought to accept what was right
      straightaway, and start carrying it out.' Čapek, *Hovory*, p. 48.
19   Antonín Hajn, *Výbor prací 1889–1909* (Prague: Hajn, 1912) vol. I, pp.
      391–429.
20   *Česká mysl* (1910) Nos. 3–4.
21   *ČČH*, vol. XVI (1910) p. 253.
22   Ibid. Referring to a critical review of Masaryk's *Otázka sociální* in
      ČČH, vol. VI (1900), Goll wrote 'What has been said in our journal
      once can be said again today. That was Masaryk's great contribution –

he opened the windows through which a rush of fresh air from the outside world reached us. Recalling what was said then, that Masaryk set forth every theoretical question as a practical one, we can speak in the same terms today (looking back on his long, active life and especially the years 1880 to 1900): to his own work we must add that of others who were inspired by him. Masaryk often gave ideas to those who did not agree with him in everything and at all times, and even to those who opposed him in specific matters.'

23 Kamil Krofta, 'Vliv Masarykův na české dějepisectví', *Přehled*, vol. VIII (1910) Nos. 39–42.

24 Vančura, 'Čím se Masaryk zavděčil českému dějepisu', pp. 172ff.

25 'Goll, the son of a physician in a count's family and later in the city, enjoyed a carefree youth and peaceful studies at home and abroad; he was able to prepare for a university career at leisure; his appearance and behaviour were those of an aristocrat. He lived all his life in harmonious agreement with the governing circles in scholarship, politics, and the Church. Goll never entered the political arena; he was not even provoked by Mommsen's arrogant challenge, although Goll's words would have had far greater weight than those of [Oswald] Balzer and Pekař. A true academic soul, he took no part in spreading the results of scholarship among the broader strata of the population. He may even have regarded such efforts as a profanation of scholarship.' (Ibid., p. 176.) [The reference is to a provocative letter written by the German historian Theodor Mommsen in support of the Austrian German efforts to block implementation of the language ordinances issued by the premier Count Casimir Badeni in April 1897, and to vigorous rebuttals to Mommsen by Polish legal historian Balzer and by Pekař.] Vančura painted a similar but even sharper picture of Goll in another article with the same title, intended for the volume dedicated to Masaryk on his seventieth birthday, a project that was not realised. Vančura's article appeared in a later collection as 'Čím se Masaryk zavděčil českému dějepisu (Doslov po deseti letech)', *Masarykův sborník*, vol. II, 1926–27 (Prague: Čin, 1927) pp. 219–24.

26 Vančura, 'Čím se Masaryk zavděčil českému dějepisu', *T. G. Masarykovi k šedesátým narozeninám*, 2nd ed. (Prague: Čin, 1930) pp. 179ff.

27 The 1910 Masaryk volume appeared towards the year's end and most of its discussions were at least one year out of date. Goll disagreed, for example, with some of Krofta's conclusions that revived the defence of Goll's school in *Přehled* (Krofta, 'Masaryk, Goll a české dějepisectví', *Přehled*, vol. X (1912) pp. 349ff, 531ff). Goll replied similarly when Pekař objected to the mild tone of Julius Glücklich's articles in *Národní listy*, 'Realistická žaloba na profesora Golla a jeho školu', 28 April and 5 May 1912. Goll wrote: 'It was my wish that Glücklich should stop attacking Masaryk. I did not ask him to write for *Národní listy*, neither did I do anything to stop him. The first article was better; I did not like the second, but we must not react like the Realists and start looking for moral flaws in a puritan spirit. There was much that could have been expressed differently in Krofta's articles, too'; see *Listy úcty a přátelství*, p. 558.

28 Ibid., pp. 536ff. In another article after the war, Vančura attacked Goll

for having voted for Aehrenthal's policy while a member of the joint Austro-Hungarian delegations in 1910; *Masarykův sborník*, vol. II (1926–27) p. 220.

29 *ČČH*, vol. XVIII (1912) pp. 130–6.

30 Ibid., pp. 170–208. An expanded version appeared as *Masarykova česká filosofie* (Prague: Historický klub, 1912).

31 Jan Herben, *Masarykov sekta a Gollova škola* (Prague: Pokrok, 1912).

32 'Masarykova česká filosofie', *CCH*, vol. XVIII (1912) p. 130.

33 Pekař explained Masaryk's approach as follows: 'It is clear that he only looked for aspects that were related or similar or at least appeared similar. We found, for example, that the real Dobrovský, Dobrovský as critical empiricism revealed him, was fundamentally different from the Dobrovský Masaryk discovered. It was Masaryk's basic error that he not only started from his own self but that he also sought those features that resembled himself, in a way that is academically inadmissible, that goes against the scholarly approach, that is to say, that he passed over whatever did not fit in, while he drew over-hasty conclusions from a distant resemblance to his ideas, accepting it as expressing what he thought'; *Masarykova česká filosofie*, p. 30.

34 Particularly in Chapters 7 and 8 ('Humanita v praxi', 'Věda a agitace'), ibid., pp. 37ff.

35 Ibid., p. 32.

36 'Ke sporu o smysl českých dějin', *Naše doba*, vol. XX (1913) pp. 6–19; cf. the concluding comments in this article. Hromádka noticed that the form of the reply had no small impact on the impression created by this discussion. See J. L. Hromádka, *Masaryk* (Prague: YMCA, 1930) pp. 253ff.

37 Herben, *Masarykova sekta a Gollova škola*, p. 115.

38 Jaroslav Werstadt, 'Masaryk jako filosof a tvůrce našich dějin', *Přerod*, vol. I (1923) p. 150.

39 Herben, *Masarykova sekta a Gollova škola*, p. 116.

40 Werstadt, 'Masaryk jako filosof a tvůrce našich dějin', p. 151.

41 *Národ*, vol. II (1918) 24 October 1918, p. 530.

42 Cf. Heidler's review of the book by Pekař, *Z české fronty*, in *ČČH*, vol. XXVI (1920) pp. 249ff.

43 The last scholar to deal in much detail with his standpoint was Milada Paulová, *Tajný výbor: Maffie a spolupráce s Jihoslovany v letech 1916–1918* (Prague: Academia, 1968) pp. 161ff; she made full use of all the available literature. Cf. also Josef Pekař, 'K českému boji státoprávnímu za války', *ČČH*, vol. XXXVI (1930) pp. 520–51. Pekař first clarified his wartime stand in *Národní listy*, 30 November and 14 December 1919. He wrote then, 'I admit that until the year 1918 I did not believe that Germany or Austria would collapse, or at least I thought it very improbable. I believed that either there would be a draw or else, if things looked bad for Vienna and Pest, I feared that Austria might ask for a separate peace, to save herself. I declared that it was not possible that the Hungarians, knowing that everything was at stake, would not, in their so-often proved political intuition, find a way of at least partial salvation; I believed that the same instinct for self-preservation would influence the dynasty'; Josef Pekař, *Světová*

válka. Stati o jejím vzniku i jejích osudech (Prague: Vesmír, 1921) p. 113.

44   Jaroslav Werstadt, 'Příkladná oslava aneb: Kamil Krofta o Josefu Pekařovi', *Sobota*, vol. I (1930) pp. 321–4. Werstadt later published part of this article in his 'Josef Pekař a česká politika za války. Diskuse mezi učitelem a žákem', *Naše revoluce*, vol. XIII (1937) pp. 21–48.

45   In a letter to Werstadt of 1 October 1930 reacting to this article (see n. 44), Pekař wrote: 'Unfortunately I do not have your article to hand, but as far as I remember it included a sentence to the effect that from the beginning of 1917 I was (or worked) against Masaryk's programme for liberation. The words pained me because they were written by someone who could have known my standpoint during the war, or ought to have known it later (since we talked together quite frequently), and as they were formulated the words contained an untruth. I longed wholeheartedly for the campaign abroad to succeed ... the articles I published in the press, striving to awaken the nation to consciousness of its being, and taking the Czech side in every way, could have contributed just as well to independence without Austria as independence within it' (ibid., pp. 29ff). Cf. also the reminiscence of Hubert Ripka about the reaction of Pekař to Woodrow Wilson's declaration that the peoples of Austria had a right to autonomy: 'He was unusually restless, clearly moved. We felt he had something exceptional to say. He looked at his notes again and suddenly thrust them aside almost angrily (he was lecturing on some aspect of Czech medieval history at the time) and began to speak in a hesitant, breaking voice: "Ladies and gentlemen – have you read today's newspapers? Have you?" He looked closely, almost anxiously at us. From our glowing gaze he could tell that we had. "Yes, ladies and gentlemen, this marks a great, decisive, and historic turn in our affairs. Wilson's declaration (his voice broke) – Wilson's magnificent declaration is a declaration of hope for our people, too." He stopped, gulped, and turned aside, but then made no attempt to hide the tears that flowed from his eyes. He paced back and forth in front of us, looking at us happily, and finally got out the words, "Now I believe, at last we can really believe it!" and went out.' See *Lidové noviny*, 24 January 1937.

46   Professor Weyr recalled this in his letter to Masaryk of 18 April 1923. The president was then working on his book *Světová revoluce* and sent part of the manuscript to Weyr with a request for his opinion on when the Czechoslovak state legally began to exist. If we bear in mind the dispute then going on over whether resistance at home or abroad came first, this was a highly political question. With his normative legalistic views, Weyr attempted neither a jurist's justification nor opposition to Masaryk's political thesis. He simply replied that he would not recommend that the constitutional focus (*Ursprungsnorm*), and therefore basically the origin of the Czechoslovak state in recognition by the warring countries, be acknowledged before 28 October, since that would mean that the internal legal order would be dependent on international law and thus would lose its supremacy and normative independence.

Weyr believed the appropriate method to be 'recognition of 28

October 1918, when the first Czechoslovak law was promulgated, as the metanormative moment' of the establishment of what we call 'the Czechoslovak legal system'. On the other hand, he gave full support to Masaryk's view of the decisive nature of the campaign conducted abroad: 'Our revolution here at home was simply an account kept of successes abroad, and this account came into being at a time when no particular political danger threatened', we read in his explanation sent to Masaryk. 'I do not wish to reproach the home leadership with their political caution; it may have saved much blood, but it is necessary to admit the fact openly. To the best of my knowledge, during the war there were (and still were in 1918) a number of pro-Austrian "optimists", and also many sceptics who would have liked independence but did not believe it would ever come.'

About his proposed constitution Weyr said: 'My proposal was called 'maximalist' and some experts declared it unrealisable and its author a crazy visionary. Rejecting my explanation of the proposal they declared that an independent state with no access to the sea was unthinkable; equally unthinkable was an independent currency, and so forth. Historical evolution could lead only to triadism (the Austrian, Hungarian, and Bohemian Lands) – and yet the speakers were men whose patriotism could not in the least be doubted. They simply did not believe that it could happen – the thing that actually did happen. The only colleague who stood by me was not a legal expert: Professor Pekař. I am putting this on record so that it is clear that there were far fewer "revolutionaries" present then than would appear today. We were just waiting to be liberated, but that does not make us revolutionaries.' The author quotes this from a copy given to him by Professor Josef Borovička.

47 As one example, we cite a lecture by Václav Novotný, *Z dějin vědeckého poznávání Husa* (Prague: Společnost musea Husova, 1919) pp. 5–16.

48 There were signs of this in his lecture, *Mistr Jan Hus a česká reformace* (Tábor: Jiskra, 1910), delivered at Kozí Hrádek on 17 July 1910.

49 T. G. Masaryk, *Nová Evropa. Stanovisko slovanské* (Prague: Gustav Dubský, 1920) p. 162.

50 T. G. Masaryk, *Světová revoluce, za války a ve válce 1914–1918* (Prague: Čin and Orbis, 1925) p. 583.

51 Kamil Krofta, *Masaryk a jeho dílo vědecké* (Prague: Česká Akademie věd a umění, 1930) pp. 32ff.

52 Pekař, *Světová válka* (Prague: Vesmír, 1921).

53 Josef Pekař, *Bílá Hora; Její příčiny a následky* (Prague: Vesmír, 1921).

54 *Říjen 1918, Slavnostní přednáška Josefa Pekaře pronesená ve velké aule university Karlovy dne 28. října 1919* (Prague: Levná knihovna Národa, 1920) p. 25. Rádl's negative view of Czech nationalism, put forward first in his pamphlet *Rasové theorie a národ* (Prague, 1918), was frequently aired in the daily press. It is possible, however, that Pekař was not referring to Masaryk himself. Shortly before this, his earlier pamphlet, *Národnostní filosofie doby novější*, had appeared in a second edition ('Mladé proudy, No. 2.').

55 *CCH*, vol. XXVIII (1922) pp. 469–77.

56   *Omyly a nebezpečí pozemkové reformy*, 2nd ed. (Prague, 1923).
57   Cf. the opening of his first article on St. John Nepomucene, 'V den svatojánský', *Národní listy*, 16 May 1920; reprinted in the collection of his writings, *Z duchovních dějin českých* (Prague: J. Klik, 1941).
58   In a letter to Kamil Krofta, 10 June 1930, in which he thanked Krofta for the speech he had made at the celebrations of Pekař's sixtieth birthday, and added some personal comments when he saw a galley proof of the speech before it was printed. It appeared as a supplement to *ČČH* (see note 15 above). The letter is in the archives of the National Museum.
59   'I heartily dislike your reference to "dreadful darkness". This is the style [F. M.] Bartoš and [Jan] Herben use. I am not going to discuss why this is purely a political slogan, but I beg you not to lend your scholarly authority to support an unhistorical assumption' (ibid.).
60   *Listy úcty a přátelství*, p. 681.
61   Published as 'K jubileu Palackého', *ČČH*, vol. XXXII (1926) pp. 237–42.
62   Ibid., p. 240.
63   Ibid.
64   Ibid.
65   The correspondence between Pekař and Krofta provides some details on how the book about Žižka came into being. Pekař asked Krofta on 12 March 1924 to write an article for *ČČH* about Žižka: 'I need an article about Žižka for the next number, in the second half of June. You can understand why – and then, it wouldn't do for the *ČČH* to pass the great anniversary over in silence. Naturally I thought of you. Would it be possible? Six to ten pages would suffice. What and how you say it would depend on your own ideas and wishes. Let me know what you think.' After Krofta had refused, Pekař returned to the subject in a letter of 19 May 1924: 'I have enough material for the next number, but nothing about Žižka. Šusta refused. I could write something myself, but I would be bound to place the question of the theory and practice of the Four Articles in the forefront, as well as the problem of whether Silvius was right about Sigismund's agreement with Žižka in 1424. I would still have to reject all of Bartoš's fantasies – but can we still write freely about matters where the public admits only one interpretation, and that a glorifying one? Do you see how the popular interpreters of Hus, those who uphold his faith, lie like one man, and insolently? Bartoš, Herben, Vančura – next time I shall have to attack what that pathological fanatic wrote about me and about you in his Denis [reference here is to Vančura's edition of Ernest Denis, *La Bohême depuis la Montagne Blanche*, 2 vols (Paris, 1903), translated into Czech and expanded as *Čechy po Bílé Hoře*, 2 vols (Prague, 1903–5), with a fourth, enlarged edition appearing in 1931]; . . . . You cannot be surprised that the Catholic side seems to me much more attractive.' Pekař's article ('Žižka u Eneáše Sylvia') did in fact appear in *ČČH*, vol. XXX (1924) pp. 413–33, and together with other articles that followed in 1925 formed the basis of his study of Žižka.
66   *Žižka a jeho doba*, 4 vols (Prague: Vesmír, 1927–33).
67   Cf. Jan Slavík, *Pekař contra Masaryk. Ke sporu o smysl českých dějin*

(Prague: Čin, 1929) p. 22.

68 Emanuel Rádl, *O smysl našich dějin; Předpoklady k diskusi o této otázce* (Prague: Programu, 1925).

69 Jan Slavík, *Nový názor na husitství (Palacký či Pekař?)* (Prague: Knihovna Národního osvobození, 1928).

70 Ibid., pp. 38ff.

71 *Smysl českých dějin, O nový názor na české dějiny* (Prague, 1929). Appearing as a 'second edition', this was a fuller reprint of a lecture in the series 'O smysl našich dějin' that was published in several instalments in *Národní osvobození* (1928), with the addition of comments by Jan Slavík.

72 Ibid., pp. 5ff.

73 Ibid., pp. 14ff.

74 Ibid., pp. 17ff.

75 Pekař elaborated this approach in his inaugural lecture as Rector of the University, published as 'O periodisaci českých dějin', *ČČH*, vol. XXXVIII (1932) cf. pp. 3ff.

76 Jaroslav Werstadt, *O filosofii českých dějin, Palacký – Masaryk – Pekař* (Prague: Knihovna Národního osvobození, 1937); cf. pp. 25ff.

77 The most recent writer to discuss Pekař's approach was František Kutnar, *Přehledné dějiny českého a slovenského dějepisectvi*, vol. II (Prague: SPN, 1977) pp. 104–10.

78 'O periodisaci českých dějin', pp. 5ff.

79 Students and followers of Pekař have always stated that 'his entire work on history was fundamentally and intuitively informed by philosophy'; see Jan Hertl, 'Prožití dějin. Poznámky k Pekařovu budování dějinnosti', in *O Josefu Pekařovi, Řád* (Prague, 1937) pp. 217–40.

80 See Werstadt, *O filosofii českých dějin*, pp. 14ff.

81 Krofta, *Masaryk a jeho dílo vědecké*, pp. 34ff.

82 This was in a review published in the periodical *Bratislava*, vol. I (1927) pp. 291–7.

83 This was František Kutnar, Archives of Charles University, Faculty of Arts documents.

84 See note 63 above.

85 The speech was published in *Universita Karlova T. G. Masarykovi 1850–1935, Projevy a přednášky* (Prague: Orbis, 1935); see p. 20.

86 See the discussion between the Nazi historian Josef Pfitzner and Jaroslav Werstadt after Pekař's death. Werstadt published his articles between February and November 1937 in *Prager Presse*; under the title 'Pře se "sudetoněmeckým" historikem o české myšlení historické a politické a o jeho představitele', he also issued them in Czech in a collection of his writings, *Odkazy dějin a dějepisců* (Prague: Historický klub, 1948) pp. 187–213. The subject also was treated by Karel Schwarzenberg, 'Politická myšlenka J.P.', in *O Josefu Pekařovi, Řád*, pp. 247–53.

87 *Šaldův zápisník*, vol. IX (1936–37), 'O Josefu Pekařovi, historikovi a politikovi'; see especially p. 129.

5 The Influence of T. G. Masaryk on the Slovenes up to 1914

Irena Gantar Godina

This article attempts to illustrate the main characteristics of the Slovene followers[1] of T. G. Masaryk and their work at the end of the nineteenth and beginning of the twentieth century. In contrast to the state of affairs in Croatian historiography, not much has been written on the Slovene Masarykians, especially since 1945. What has been published is mainly confined to the activity of the Yugoslav Social Democratic Party before World War I.

The parliamentary crisis in the Austrian part of the Habsburg Monarchy began with the fall of Prime Minister Eduard Taaffe (1879–1893), who wanted to extend the franchise, thus provoking the protests of German liberals and Hohenwart's conservatives.[2] The next government (Windischgraetz – from 11 November 1893 to 19 June 1895) fell primarily because it had intervened on behalf of the Slovene junior high school in Celje (Cilli),[3] and this only served to strengthen national antagonisms between Germans and Slovenes. After Casimir Badeni's language decrees[4] in 1897 were issued in Bohemia and Moravia, the obstructionist policies of German extremists paralysed the work of the Reichsrat, and this caused an even deeper parliamentary crisis until Count Clary[5] revoked the decree in 1899. That year the National Whitsun Programme of the German liberals was accepted by a coalition of German nationalist parties in parliament. This amounted to the revocation of the language decrees, which allowed the Poles, Italians, and Czechs to use their languages for internal official purposes. The Slovenes, however, were not included. The German nationalists insisted on having the leading role in Austria and were strongly against any concessions to the Slovenes, since they considered the area populated by Slovenes to be part of the German heartlands. The Germanisation of the Slovenes greatly intensified in this period; consequently, the Slovene national struggle was mainly orientated towards achieving equal rights for the Slovene language in all fields of public life, especially after 1896, when the pressure from Italian irredentism on the Littoral also increased.

In spite of the fact that the Austrian economy was expanding, the Slovenes were experiencing a major economic crisis which was mainly reflected in large-scale emigration, above all to North America. German economic power in the Slovene lands was strong; administration, education, and culture were also mainly in German hands. This facilitated Germanisation, since there was a serious lack of Slovene schools. That is why many private Slovene schools were established, mainly in the most threatened areas.[6] There was only a negligible number of Slovene junior high schools.[7] In such conditions it might have seemed unrealistic to fight for a Slovene university, but the idea was included in the programmes of both Slovene bourgeois parties and of many student societies, such as 'Slovenija' in Vienna, 'Tabor' in Graz, or 'Adrija' in Prague. Meanwhile, each party favoured a different university for Slovene students to study at, the clericals preferring Vienna and Graz, after 1909 also Cracow and Lemberg, and the liberals Prague. By this the students also demonstrated their personal political affiliations.

The two main bourgeois parties, the clericals and the liberals, were not able to create an effective opposition to Germanisation, being unable or – perhaps selfishly – unwilling to overcome the obstacles they faced. The Slovene clerical party (Slovene People's Party) managed to gather the majority of the rural population under its wing and, thanks to the adoption of its labour programme, many workers as well. Although the liberals (National Progressive Party)[8] were intellectually and financially stronger, they were smaller in number and less powerful than the clericals, who had more influence in culture and education. The liberals consisted largely of the intelligentsia, officials, landowners, and teachers. Though they had a national programme, they did not envisage universal manhood suffrage, which isolated them from the mass of the population.

In this period the numerically small Slovene intelligentsia began to increase its interest in political and cultural activity, in order to provide a more effective response to Germanisation than that of the two established parties. This artistic, scientific and political *'fin-de-siècle'* generation included a number of artists who subsequently became famous: the 'Moderna' with the poets, Dragotin Kette and Josip Murn, and above all, the writer Ivan Cankar; distinguished scholars: Dragotin Lončar the historian, and Ivan Prijatelj the literary historian, and also such political workers as Anton Kristan and Albin Prepeluh. These people, in particular, greatly influenced Slovene students by underlining the urgent need to transform Slovene culture and politics, so as to increase national consciousness and resistance to Germanisation. In addition, the preoccupation of the bourgeois parties with their mutual power struggles apparently created sufficient scope for fresh ideas and principles; furthermore, even after the acceptance of the national programme in the Brno Congress in 1899, the Yugoslav Social Democratic Party (Jugoslovanska socialnodemokratska stranka)[9] was too foreign and too radical for the intellectuals; the Social Democratic principle of internationalism led both bourgeois parties to consider them to be 'anti-national'.

This was the background[10] in the Slovene lands when the Czech university was established in 1882 and Masaryk's political and cultural activities began. It is hardly surprising that many Slovene intellectuals saw Prague as the most promising intellectual centre for developing their Slovene and Slavonic consciousness. Numerous students attended Masaryk's lectures and saw valuable ideas in his writings, especially those on the national question, which they later tried to apply to Slovene conditions. They were attracted by Masaryk's idea of national unity, the idea of viable small nations, the demand for national autonomy, the overcoming of historicism by Realism, the priority he gave to natural rights over historical.[11] (Masaryk proceeded from the thesis that the Czech cause did not derive from the historic privileges of the Bohemian *Staatsrecht* but from natural rights.) Masaryk's moderate Slavism, with its realistic approach and its scepticism towards Russia, struck a chord among his Slovene listeners. They also accepted his demands for universal suffrage, for undogmatic and non-institutionalised religion as well as the demand for socialisation of culture, education, and politics, by which he meant the cooperation of all classes in educational, cultural, and political activities. The Slovene students in Prague were attracted by Masaryk's criticism of liberalism and clericalism against which they wanted to fight at home. All these ideas created among Slovene students great enthusiasm and a will to work. As early as 1897,[12] with their first written contribution about Masaryk in Slovene newspapers, they attempted to transplant these ideas onto domestic soil.

Slovene students had already cooperated with Croat and Serb students in Prague within the Serb students' society 'Šumadija' and in the paper *Novo doba*[13] (founded 1898), in which they published their ideas, mostly in the spirit of Masaryk, about the tasks of youth, education, self-education, economic affairs, and so forth.

After finishing their studies, they returned[14] to Ljubljana in 1899 and 1900, where they hoped to propagate immediately these principles of Realism among the Slovenes. At a meeting in Ljubljana in September 1900, they established ideological foundations for their activity, which they did not at first conceive of in party-political terms. The main items of their programme were: a greater degree of national autonomy, the creation of a Slovene university, universal, equal, and secret suffrage, and educational and cultural work among the people, which they intended to realise by means of lectures, popular books, and reviews. Such work they called 'small-scale work', (*drobno delo*).[15] They also agitated against the influence of the two Slovene bourgeois parties. In 1901 they published *What We Want – An Epistle to Slovene Youth*,[16] in which they presented the main ideas accepted a year before. Along with an article 'Our philosophical standpoint towards liberalism, clericalism, and social democracy', they utilised František Drtina's *Ideály výchovy*. With this book, Slovene youth had their own 'manifesto', a call to the young and to intellectuals to concern themselves with politics, education, 'upbringing' and culture in order to achieve general progress.

An analysis of the *Epistle* demonstrates that its authors relied largely or even completely on Masaryk's definitions in various questions. The bases of their writing were two works of Masaryk, *Česká otázka* and *Otázka sociální*. In their discussion of the national question, in contrast to the Croat students (who had a clear idea of how to solve this problem), Slovenes shaped a more general declaration on the nation and the national question, in the spirit of Masaryk: 'Nationality is not an idol to us; we also have other, more far-reaching ideas, and international unity is necessary to achieve them. Internationalism is thus increasingly becoming a more natural factor than nationality, not as a negation but as solidarity and a national tolerance, and as a way to achieve collective cultural interests.'[17] The Slovene Masarykians defined themselves in the same way as Masaryk with respect to Slavism or Slavonic unity/mutuality: 'We look more critically at Slavism and Slavonic unity/mutuality. We are not satisfied with mottoes and popular tradition. Let us not be brothers in our imagination to everybody and in reality to nobody!'[18]

Criticism of liberalism, clericalism, and social democracy or historical materialism is also important in the *Epistle*. Like Masaryk, its authors saw liberalism as a movement which, in its heyday, had accomplished much positive economic, political, and cultural progress; but its positive role ceased at this point. They considered that 'today, liberalism does not have a progressive character, but a reactionary one, because it wants to maintain the existing situation. Liberalism necessarily entails individualism; the individual needed to be liberated but liberalism carried this out too mechanically, and as a result it is now in decline.' They were against liberalism also because it was 'one-sided rationalism, which negates the religious and ethical meaning of life.'[19]

They were even more critical of clericalism; they emphasised that religious indifference, which is a product of liberalism, was a major contributor to the strengthening of clericalism, which is 'our main philosophical enemy. It is the socio-political exploitation of religion for personal aims and concern for the church which suffocates genuine and true religion.'[20] Like Masaryk, they stressed the fundamental difference between religion and clericalism, and they considered religion itself to have great ethical and social significance. They tried to overcome the idea of its dominance by the formation of a new, unitary, universal scientific outlook, and they believed in Masaryk's idea of a new religion and a new ethic derived from the new philosophy: 'We have to return to Christianity and exalted ideas ... Although modern man has ceased to believe in Christian supernaturalism or the supernatural, he is now increasingly running to the positive shelter of Christianity, to loving his neighbour, and thus searching for salvation ... Modern man sees in Christ's morals the meaning of life, which is to abandon books and stories and enter life directly'.[21]

The relation of Slovene Realists to socialism and social democracy was defined in Masaryk's terms: 'Socialism is the opposite of individualism. In contrast to individualism, socialism stresses the whole and sees prosperity only in this. The individual, who is subordinated to the whole, is given as much freedom as accords with (the needs of) the whole. In socialism, the freedom of the individual is limited to the welfare of the whole.' Masaryk stressed that socialism is above all a social question, related not just to one stratum or class but to the whole of society. Slovene Masarykians also defined socialism as a social question: 'Social questions are being solved in the form of socialism.'[22]

Their opinion of the philosophical foundations of Marxism was also based on Masaryk's judgements. Without regard to the validity of the demands of Social Democracy, they considered the philosophical foundations on which socialism was based, that is historical materialism, to be unacceptable since 'this was materialism, so-called historical materialism, which teaches that economic, productive relations are the most important, that they create history, and that philosophical, religious, and other principles are built only on economic foundations. Since economic relations always influence the origin of ideas, they can provide no means of orientation.'[23]

In his work *Otázka sociální*, Masaryk saw the main crisis of Marxism and Social Democracy in the questioning of revolutionary tactics, and the greater acceptance of parliamentary solutions, all of which he considered to be very positive. The Slovene Masarykians also dealt with this question in their *Epistle*; they stated that the Social Democrats 'reject historical materialism . . . (and) revolutionary tactics'; thus a possible agreement to cooperate with the Social Democrats would involve confirming their legitimate demands, but not their philosophical foundations. The Masarykians believed in giving active support to solving concrete problems, because they felt 'a direct moral obligation' to support the Social Democratic programme, including its international outlook.

The principle of internationalism, one of the key elements of Social Democratic ideology, was not disputed either by Masaryk or the Slovene Realists. They linked the principles of nationality and internationality. In particular, they supported the resolution of the Brno Congress of 1899, whereby the Austrian Social-Democratic Party and its national Czech, Slovene, and Italian parties formulated and accepted the national programme. At Brno the Czech and Slovene socialists were unique in protesting against the German definition of the national question, which considered it to be mostly a cultural and linguistic phenomenon. Both Czechs and Slovenes demanded that the national question should be treated as an economic question as well, and called for equality of national rights.[24]

We could ascribe the concluding thought of the *Epistle* to Masaryk: 'This crisis could be expressed in two words: revolution-evolution, instead of violent revolution, radical reforms. To achieve such social change, we must completely transform our current opinions. We need revolution in our hearts and in our minds.'[25]

Although the *Epistle* has the same title as the 1897 programme of the Croat students – 'What We Want' – the Croat students mainly stressed actual conditions and problems in Croatia, and concrete proposals for solving them, while the Slovene *Epistle* can be understood primarily as a theoretical encounter with the then prevailing thought among Slovenes.

The Masarykians did not want to define themselves as a separate party or a movement, but immediately joined the Slovene political and cultural arena. As early as 1902, some of them began to cooperate with *Naši zapiski* (Our Records),[26] although it was the unofficial organ of Social Democrats. But with a compromise in the subtitle – 'A Social review' – the publishers managed to gain the collaboration of the Masarykians.

The influence of Masaryk was mainly visible in *Naši zapiski* in the early years of its publications, when it published his studies and lectures.[27] After the third volume, however, there were no further Masaryk studies, with the exception of tributes on the occasion of his sixtieth birthday in 1910.[28] The contributions of the Masarykians mainly discussed a programme of theoretical and practical activity, that is, how to spread education among the widest strata: the organisation of popular science, lectures in various regions, and the implementation of widespread educational work among ordinary people. In their programme they also included the struggle against the influence of clericalism and liberalism, which they planned to defeat with their own educational programme. In this programme they pointed out the significance of economic and cultural societies, which explains why as early as 1904 they established the educational society 'Akademija', on the Czech model. The society organised cultural, economic and political lectures. Evidence of the society's attraction, at least at the beginning, is the fact that, in 1904, 14 812 participants attended its lectures, an average of over 220 at each lecture.

As a follow-up, the Masarykians tried to formulate a clear political programme with which they could implement these progressive ideas and not just attack the programmes of other parties. In *Naši zapiski*, they demanded a programme which would be 'an original product of people and conditions' and cited Masaryk's view that politics is a science which, above all, teaches us how to govern and direct the state. In this connection, they defined the tasks and significance of the intelligentsia in cultural and political life. They stood for collective cooperation between the intelligentsia and the workers, since they believed that the significance of the intelligentsia lay in an awareness that 'workers and the intelligentsia are natural allies'. They emphasised that only the evolution of the situation itself would demonstrate the real political relationship between the workers and the intellectuals: 'Will the place of the Slovene intelligentsia in the coming political struggle be directly in the ranks of the workers or at least beside them?' They were not interested in the form of struggle, they were only interested in the aim, and that was 'freedom and "existential provision" for physical and spiritual work!'[29]

As Slovene Masarykians came to look for other ways of changing conditions apart from 'small-scale work', however, they turned increasingly towards Social Democracy. They never debated the reasons for merging, and in the correspondence between them no evidence about this has been found. In an article about Masarykians entering the party, Josip Ferfolja[30] wrote that, as a student of Masaryk, he also learned about socialism: 'In practice Masaryk's realism overlapped with socialism, it just did not admit its scientific foundations – Marx's historical materialism – and it directed its activity more towards the strata which stood above the working class.'[31] Only in 1914, with the death of the spiritual leader of the Masarykians, Anton Dermota, did they speak of merger as a necessary step, because if they wanted to be active not only culturally but also politically, practically, and not only theoretically, they had to find a party in which they could implement their programme. It was also important that there was not enough room in Slovenia for two anti-clerical parties, since overall the bourgeoisie and the intelligentsia were numerically too weak to support them.

Although they became loyal members of the Social Democratic Party, the Masarykians never actually renounced their primary principles, thus causing some disagreement with official party policy. The first dispute occurred in 1909 with the passing of the Social Democratic Tivoli Resolution,[32] which they could not accept. The main problem was that the Social Democrats accepted the idea of one common language for all Yugoslav nations and, as at Brno, still only treated the national question as a cultural, not as a political matter. As a result the Masarykians demanded a revision of the Brno national programme. They put forward the Yugoslav idea as the main object of their political work and opposed it to the internationalist standpoint of the official Social Democratic programme.

There were also other divergences, but these were not perceived as being so significant as to prevent cooperation between the Masarykians and the Social Democrats. (In 1917, however, they finally caused a split as the Masarykians decided in favour of a nationalist Slovene policy within an independent Yugoslav state, while the Social Democratic party favoured an internationalist stance and the continuation of the Habsburg Monarchy.) Though the Masarykians joined the Social Democrats, they continued to act as a link between the bourgeois parties and the Social Democrats. In this way they gave their 'movement' a dimension which for Slovenes was entirely new. Despite their complete rejection of historical materialism, they entered the Social Democratic party and thus overcame their conceptual differences in order to achieve their aims. This may appear opportunistic, but working outside the party or establishing their own party did not seem either a practical or an effective solution. The numerical weakness of the intellectuals at that time prevented them from following Masaryk's example (the Realist Party) in founding their own party. The minimal or practical programme of the Social Democrats still allowed them scope, especially since they advocated the broad-based editorial policies of *Naši zapiski*, which made possible cooperation between people of different ideological views. Over the next few years, the Slovene Masarykians revised Masaryk's criticism of Marxism. In addition, they created their own idea of a Slovene type of socialism, which was to be based not on the urban proletariat but on the rural population; they opposed heavy industry in favour of smaller workshops and a national independent economy.

For the Social Democrats, cooperation with Slovene Masarykians helped to win over the intelligentsia. This was probably the reason that they did not especially stress the differences dividing them. There were some individual party members who opposed the Masarykians within the party in the belief they would weaken the revolutionary idea, but this did not prevent further cooperation.

It seems clear, therefore, that in spite of the Masarykians' lack of success in political terms their contribution to the study of Slovene history, literature, social and political issues was very significant. They helped to disseminate progressive ideas among the Slovenes and influenced Slovene youth to become more aware of the importance of educational and social activity in achieving national progress and prosperity.

Some of the liberal Slovenes, members of the Slovene liberal party, who studied in Vienna and Graz, like the Masarykians became very critical of the politics of both Slovene bourgeois parties and the Social Democratic Party. That is why the liberal students' society 'Slovenija' in Vienna split into two groups, the liberal and the national radical. The latter group took over the leadership in the society in 1902. That was the time when these students had already become acquainted both with Masaryk's ideas and the plans and aims of the Slovene Realists. As early as 1904, a group of these students began to publish a monthly paper called *Omladina* (Youth)[33] as the organ of 'national radical youth', which aimed at linking secondary school pupils with university students. This journal inaugurated for the national radicals a period when they were able to implement their motto 'From the nation to the nation', by means of educational and cultural work among the people including lectures, travelling libraries, and the foundation of scholarly libraries;[34] other tasks included a struggle against alcoholism among students; the introduction of pupil self-help; work on the Slovene minority question, and the struggle for a Slovene university. They hoped the fulfilment of these aims would help to solve the national and social questions.

Although the basic programme of the national radical movement, accepted in September 1905 in Trieste, was not as theoretical as that of the Masarykians, the differences were insignificant. The same year they published the main items of their programme in the brochure *From the Nation to the Nation.*[35] The programme was directed above all towards the education and self-education of school pupils and students, since national radicals believed that a thorough reform of the political, as well as the cultural, situation began with the intelligentsia; after awakening the intellectuals it could then extend to the wider masses. To them, national politics meant primarily 'the struggle against indolent people for whom the national question is one of the least concern', and also the struggle against cosmopolitanism or internationalism, for which they reproached the clericals and the socialists. On this last point they fundamentally differed from Masaryk and the Masarykians.

National work, that is, educational and cultural work among the broad mass of the population in order to arouse national consciousness, was designed to help them to achieve the universal emancipation of the Slovene nation, by creating harmony through work and thus achieving the 'Great Slovene Spirit'. They believed that the strongest opponent of these aims was the clerical party. They described it as 'a cosmopolitan movement, which understood the nation only as a religious community and was fighting only for political power.'[36] Like Masaryk and the Masarykians, the national radicals limited themselves to criticism of the Church as an institution and a political factor; they continued to see religion as a personal affair for the individual. In 1907 they unanimously put forward the demand for the separation of church and state and for secular schools. None the less, they accepted a resolution in 1912[37] which stressed the idea that religion, as an individual matter, was only a temporary stage on the way to atheism, which was not achievable under existing conditions. (They were thinking mostly of the Slovene rural population, which was traditionally deeply Catholic.) They saw atheism as their long-term aim, for which Slovene intellectuals had still to fight. The attitude of the national radicals towards religion was obviously also a question of tactics and not just of principles.

By their understanding and treatment of the national question, the national radicals largely distanced themselves from the original views of Masaryk and the Slovene Realists. In the beginning they defined themselves as standing 'at the most resolute national standpoint', which included the awakening of the national spirit by means of national work. In the course of time, their definition, like their work, changed. They placed less emphasis on social and intellectual questions and more on the purely national; in 1909 they defined themselves as a 'reformist pupils' group which intended to regenerate or renew the Slovene intelligentsia in the spirit of *absolute nationalism*'.[38] This caused considerable disagreement within the movement itself. In spite of this nationalistic viewpoint, they forged links with other South Slav youth groups by stressing the need for mutual understanding and cultural cooperation. With the rise of the Yugoslav idea or standpoint, especially after the Austrian annexation of Bosnia and Herzegovina in 1909, they abandoned the notion of Slav unity/reciprocity which had been popular at the beginning. In contrast to Masaryk, they stressed: 'Havlíček was rather narrow-minded when he proclaimed "A Czech, not a Slav". Masaryk's slogan was wider, more far-reaching: "A Man, a Czech, and a Slav". But is it really necessary to put "A Man" in the first place? For the Slovenes, they reasoned, this slogan should sound different since between the Slovene and a Slav is a Yugoslav. Masaryk opposed sterile Slavism, and Slavonic cosmopolitanism. But this does not apply to a Slovene when he calls himself a Yugoslav.'[39] This standpoint prevailed among the radicals, whereas only a few of the most enthusiastic of Masaryk's followers accepted the idea of Neo-Slavism of Slavonic cultural cooperation.

Although the Yugoslav idea was the leading idea in this period the national radicals limited it to cultural and economic cooperation; they still saw the Austria which had been conceived by Palacký as the only possible framework for a solution of the Yugoslav question. They thought of themselves as students and followers of Masaryk, but they largely moved away from his principles including his attitude to Social

Democracy. They reproached it for being internationalist, anti-national, and revolutionary. This is why they did not allow those members who had exceeded the age-limits of their movement to enter the Social Democratic party. In 1909 they tacitly allowed these members to enter the liberal party, though they avoided declaring this as official policy so that the liberals were able to preserve their influence.

In the last two years before the war, a great number of national radicals joined the new movement called 'Preporodovci' (The Rena-scencers). This consisted of Yugoslav nationalists who rejected the idea that it might be possible to achieve national, cultural and economic emancipation in a legal manner by gradual, patient work. They set out to achieve the goal of solving the national question more directly by revolutionary methods and above all outside the framework of the legal struggle and the existing state.

Notwithstanding that a more attractive movement had arisen, the national radicals' official policies did not change. They strongly opposed 'Preporodovci' ideas, and especially their revolutionary tactics in which they saw only 'romanticism and danger'. As a result they lost much of their influence among school pupils. With the beginning of World War I, the national radicals' *Omladina* ceased to be published.

While the Slovene Masarykians in principle remained within the framework of the Social Democratic Party on the ideological positions of Realism, the Slovene national radicals saw Masaryk's ideas as merely the first step towards activating youth and changing conditions, above all among school pupils and students. Over the years they discarded deeper ideological analyses and devoted themselves to practical work and primarily to criticism of Slovene political life. Only when the 'second generation' of Slovene students in Prague had finished their studies in 1909 and 1910, did they try to propagate Masaryk's ideas among the national radicals. They published several articles on Masaryk's thoughts about the national question, Neo-Slavism, political activity and similar issues, but they had little effect on their other activities. The national radicals did not succeed in overcoming party interests; the initial enthusiasm subsided precisely because there was too much compromise and adaptation to the short-term interests of the liberal party.

Although Masaryk's interest in the Slovenes up to 1914 was limited to the framework of the politics of the Austro-Hungarian Monarchy and its relation to the Slavs in general, he inspired Slovene intellectuals by his example and principles. Masaryk's principles represented essentially an intermediate ideology between liberalism and socialism, which contemporary Slovene intellectuals were still prepared to accept. For the majority of those who were dissatisfied but had no clear party affiliation, his principles were suitable and acceptable, mainly because he placed the Realist approach to solving the national and social question above romanticism. Masaryk's Realism was acceptable precisely because it did not aim at the kind of radical change or even revolution put forward by the Social Democratic programme. 'Small-scale work', social reforms, national autonomy, and the idea of evolution still seemed to be a national approach that accorded with the prevailing principles and norms of the Slovene mentality of this era. Even if the influence of Masaryk's ideas among the Slovene intelligentsia and politically active youth was merely transitional, it nevertheless served to heighten national consciousness of alternative approaches in an era when various political possibilities were being explored.

NOTES

1   On the Slovene Masarykians see: Arnold Suppan, 'Bildungspolitische und gesellschaftliche Modernisierung. Die südslawische Studenten an der tschechischen Universität Prag um die Jahrhundertwende und der Einfluss Professor Masaryks', in Richard Georg Plaschka and Karlheinz Mack (eds), *Wegenetz europäischen Geistes: Wissenschaftszentren und geistige Wechselbeziehungen zwischen Mittel- und Südosteuropa vom Ende des 18.Jahrhunderts bis zum Ersten Weltkrieg* (Vienna: Verlag für Geschichte und Politik, 1983).
     A brief note about Slovene students in Prague is to be found in V. Šťastný, 'Ve znamení tzv. pokrokového hnutí', in *Češi a Jihoslované v minulosti* (Prague: Academia, 1975); Dragutin Prohaska, 'Utjecaj T. G. Masaryka na modernu jugoslovensku kulturu' in *T. G. Masaryk Zbornik*, Redaction Jugoslovenska-češkoslovačka liga (Belgrade; Prague: S. B. Cvijanović and Orbis, 1927) pp. 102–68.
2   Count Karl Hohenwart (Prime Minister from 2 February to 27 October 1897), from whose policy the Slovene Conservatives expected some 'language' concessions.
3   Masaryk wrote a short note on this problem: 'Schválení rozpočtu s položkou pro školu v Celji – Sblížení Jihoslovanů a konservativců', *Naše doba*, vol. II (1895) pp. 1018–19.
4   Janko Pleterski, 'Die Badenikrise und die Slowenen', *Die Donau-Monarchie und die Südslawische Frage von 1848–1918* (Vienna: Verlag

der Oesterreichischen Akademie der Wissenschaften, (1978) pp. 65–76, 87–103.

5   Count Manfred Clary was Prime Minister from 2 October to 21 December 1899.

6   The most threatened places were Carinthia and Styria. In Carinthia there were only three Slovene public elementary schools, and 78 German-Slovene, i.e. bilingual, schools.

7   There were only German-Slovene secondary schools in the Slovene territory; the first entirely Slovene *'gymnasium'* was established in 1905 in Ljubljana, but it was a private episcopal school.

8   Vasilij Melik, 'Slovenski liberalni tabor in njegovo razpadanje' (Slovene Liberal party and its decay), *Prispevki za zgodovino delavskega gibanja*, 22 (1982) pp. 19–24.

9   At the founding Congress of the Slovene Social Democratic party in Ljubljana in August 1896, the members decided to name the party 'Yugoslav' in order to collect all South Slav workers within the Monarchy, not only Slovene ones. Therefore they defined the party as Yugoslav Social Democratic Party. The terms 'Yugoslav' and 'South Slav' were identical until 1912, the beginning of the Balkan Wars. After 1913 the term Yugoslav meant that all South Slavs have equal rights for their individual cultures, while politically they should be united in a federation, but without the Bulgarians. Now the term 'South Slav' is used only to define regional or linguistic identity.

10   The situation in Croatia was rather different from that in the Slovene lands. Among other things – apart from a limited franchise – there was no strong Catholic (Clerical) party or any movement equally influential to the Slovene clericals in so many spheres of public life. Another difference was that the Croats were under no compulsion to study in 'foreign' lands; thus their language, culture, and national consciousness was not as threatened as those of the Slovenes. Thirdly, although the pressure of Magyarisation was strong in Croatia, the Slovenes faced the much stronger and more effective pressure of Germanisation.

11   The Croat 'State right' idea was largely accepted by the Slovene People's Party (the Clerical party), which was ideologically close to the Croat Pure Right Party. They both fought for a trialist concept in the Habsburg Monarchy following the Greater Croatian idea. To the Masarykians and national radicals, this idea was unacceptable because they feared Croat dominance, especially in cultural matters, and through this in the language question. This is why they strongly opposed the 'Neo-Illyrian Idea' which spread in 1910 among some Slovene and Croat intellectuals. They advocated the idea of the unification of both languages, Croat and Slovene. For these reasons, the Slovene Masarykians were never drawn to the idea of the Croat 'state right', and to them the ideas of national autonomy and 'natural rights' seemed more appropriate.

12   Matija Murko, 'T. G. Masaryk, *Česká otázka, Snahy a tužby národního obrození*. V Praze 1895' (review), *Ljubljanski Zvon*, 15 (1895) pp. 327–8; Vladimír Foerster, 'Češka književnost II', 'Naše doba-Masarykove *Časové směry a tužby*' (review), *Ljubljanski Zvon*, 15

(1895) pp. 392, 453–4, 518–19 781–2; Ivan Žmavc, 'Masaryk – slovanski filozof', *Ljubljanski Zvon*, 18 (1897) pp. 606–10; Ivan Žmavc, 'Socialno vprašanje', *Ljubljanski Zvon*, 20 (1900) pp. 550–8.

13 *Novo Doba* (Prague) 1898–1899; the editor and publisher was Vice Ilijadica-Grbešić.

14 The majority of Slovene students were constantly suffering from a lack of financial resources so that they had to return home immediately after finishing their studies. For example, Anton Dermota graduated in 1900, but was able to take his doctor's degree in laws only in 1905.

15 'Small-scale work' (*drobno delo* or *práce drobná*) was meant to be widespread educational work among ordinary people, which was one of the items of the Czech Realist programme. B. Hořínek explained that such work should be as much for individuals as for society. Individuals such as school and university teachers, doctors, scholars, and lawyers should claim a 'naturhistorische Weltanschauung'. Society should provide for better schools and libraries and for better general education; *Die Zeit*, No. 16, 19 January 1895, p. 46.

16 *Kaj hočemo – Poslanica slovenski mladini* (What We want – Epistle to Slovene Youth) (Ljubljana: Komisionalna založba L. Schwentner, 1901).

17 *Epistle*, p. 12.

18 Ibid., p. 13.

19 Ibid., p. 18.

20 Ibid., p. 21.

21 Ibid., pp. 22–3.

22 Ibid., p. 25.

23 Ibid., pp. 26–7.

24 Slovene Social Democrats demanded a 'personal principle', which was very similar to Karl Renner's conception, but it was not accepted. The German and the Czech socialists advocated a 'territorial principle' and this was accepted.

25 *Epistle*, p. 31.

26 *Naši zapiski – Socijalna revija* (Ljubljana) 1902–1914. There were approximately 500 subscribers.

27 T. G. Masaryk, 'Socializem in umetnost' (Socialism and Art), *Naši zapiski*, 2 (1903–04), pp. 7–11; 'V boju za vero (V boji o náboženství', *Naši zapiski*, 3 (1904–05), pp. 1–7, 35–8, 51–4, 67–71, 102–4, 135–8; 'O verski svobodi in prostosti prepričanja (O svobodě náboženské a volnosti přesvědčení)', *Naši zapiski*, 2 (1903–4), pp. 129–32.

28 Josip Ferfolja, 'Masarykova praktična filozofija', *Naši zapiski*, 7 (1910) pp. 7–15, 83–8, 110–13, 134–40; Anton Dermota, 'Masaryk in Slovenci' (Masaryk and the Slovenes), *Naši zapiski*; 7 (1910) pp. 247–53.

29 Dragotin Lončar, 'Pomen in naloge slovenske inteligencije' (The meaning and the tasks of the Slovene intelligentsia), *Naši zapiski*, 4 (1906) pp. 113–15.

30 Josip Ferfolja was the only Slovene Masarykian who personally met Masaryk in 1918. As a member of the National Council, he went to Prague to discuss the decisions of the London Pact of 1915, whereby

Italy entered the war on the side of the Allies in exchange for promises of territories in the Yugoslav lands. His meeting with Masaryk was positive; it encouraged the Czech press to report on Italian pressure against Slovenes in the occupied territories. Masaryk advised Ferfolja (and the Slovenes) to fight for Dalmatia and Rijeka (Fiume) rather than for Trieste. This, in fact, was contrary to Slovene national interests as the Slovene minority was rather numerous on the territory of Trieste.

31   Josip Ferfolja, 'Spomini na Antona Dermoto' (Memories of Anton Dermota), *Naši zapiski*, 11 (1914) p. 207; Dragotin Lončar, 'Masaryk in Marx', *Naši zapiski*, 11 (1914) pp. 233–40.

32   The greatly criticised Tivoli Resolution was accepted at the first Yugoslav Social Democratic Conference in Ljubljana, 21–22 November 1909. The participants included Austrian socialists such as Viktor Adler and Karl Renner, the Czechs Bohumír Šmeral and Antonín Brůha, and representatives of the Croat, Italian, and Bosnian Social Democratic parties.

33   *Omladina, Glasilo Narodno radikalnega dijaštva* (Ljubljana: Eksekutiva Narodno-radikalnega dijaštva, 1904–1912; from 1912–1914 in Prague). They had approximately 350 school-pupil and student subscribers, and 250 others.

34   Their 'Znanstvena knjižnica' (Scholarly library) published such valuable works as F. Drtina's *Myšlenkový vývoj evropského lidu*, L. Niederle's *Slovanský svět*, and Lončar's *Socialna zgodovina Slovencev* (Social History of the Slovenes).

35   *Iz naroda za narod* (From the nation to the nation) Ljubljana: Eksekutiva Narodno-radikalnega dijaštva, 1905).

36   Gregor Žerjav, 'Naroden ali klerikalen' (National or clerical), *Omladina*, 1 (1904) p. 2.

37   The resolution was accepted at the national radicals' fourth meeting in September 1912, in Ljubljana.

38   Vekoslav Zalokar's contribution read at the third meeting of national radicals in September 1909, in Ljubljana; *Omladina*, 6 (1909–10) p. 97.

39   Bogumil Vošnjak, 'Masaryk – socijolog in Slovan', *Omladina*, 7 (1910) p. 23.

6 The Fallacy of Realism: Some Problems of Masaryk's Approach to Czech National Aspirations

Eva Schmidt-Hartmann

INTRODUCTION

The Czech political movement known as Realism achieved its lasting influence on Czech political minds not so much by its popularity or even real achievements, as by its association with Tomáš G. Masaryk. There is a widespread interpretation of Masaryk's concept of Realism, which the distinguished biographer and interpreter of Masaryk and his work, W. Preston Warren, puts as follows: 'The term "realism" was employed by Masaryk to put stresses on the diverse factors which any honest person finds he must consider: the material world, the facts of history, the confirmed findings of science, moral values and principles, functional social orders, valid goals . . . For Masaryk, realism meant an opposition to mythology (and all pansubjectivism) in the name of reliable and accurate methodology . . . Better than any other work, however, *The Czech Question* seems to exemplify what "realism" meant to him.'[1] Despite the influence of this interpretation, the following essay intends to challenge it.

While it is true that Masaryk himself presented his notion of Realism in similar terms, if one studies carefully not only what Masaryk said about his intentions, but also how he applied them in practice, serious objections appear to be warranted with respect to the convergence between Masaryk's expressly formulated normative statements on one hand, and the actual content of his written views and ideas on the other. Taking the example of the so-called 'Czech Question' as one significant issue in Masaryk's *œuvre*, the following essay will argue that Realism was an unrealistic concept for grasping open questions in regard to the past and the present of the Czechs, if 'realism', as will be explained below, is understood as an attempt to base actions on a picture of reality with the greatest possible resemblance to real life.

In choosing the term Realism to designate his political philosophy, Masaryk was indebted to the popularity of the term at that time. A search for a realistic approach in various spheres was current in Europe everywhere in the nineteenth century. Particularly in Central Europe, after the preceding periods of excessive religiosity during the period of the Baroque and subsequent optimistic embracing of rationalism under the influence of the Enlightenment, it was commonly assumed that 'realism' might best improve the traditions of the past. In philosophy, the awareness of a fundamental difference between what was perceived as the 'idealistic German philosophical tradition' on the one hand, and the 'empiricist traditions of the Anglo-American philosophy' on the other prompted many authors to search for a synthesis of the two in order to find a realistic approach in philosophy;[2] Masaryk's teacher at the university and a personality whose influence upon Masaryk is evident even long after their ways parted, Franz Brentano (1838–1917), was a prominent representative of this tendency. Among historians, the prevailing so-called romantic historiography was beginning to be challenged by a Positivist scholarly approach to the past. This approach was considered to be more realistic[3] in literature, which was among the spheres of Masaryk's greatest interest. The significance of the concept of realism in the nineteenth century is so well known that here it does not need any further explanation.[4]

But there was also a tradition of a search for realistic policy-making on a scholarly basis in Germany and Austria as represented by August L. von Rochau (1810–73), Johann Kaspar Bluntschli (1808–81) and Albert E. F. Schäffle (1831–1903).[5] It is therefore not surprising that Masaryk should consider the term 'realism' an adequate designation for his own new approach to politics. By using this designation, he can clearly be seen as one thoroughly steeped in the intellectual scene of his time.

There is a popular understanding of what realism means in politics: it is assumed to be an approach which recognises a given situation and clarifies the objectives, then finds the 'appropriate' means and chooses the 'right' method of employing them to change the situation in accordance with the objectives. Masaryk's political philosophy was indebted to this commonsense model: by means of scholarly enquiry he assumed that politicians ought to be able to find the appropriate answers to all problems; by educating people, he hoped to develop a public accessible to rational arguments and therefore ready to support the 'right' policies, and finally, by improving the moral standards of all, the politicians as well as the general public, he believed he could free society from selfishness and, consequently, from conflicting social and political objectives.[6]

Desirable as this state of affairs might appear, the underlying model was employed by Masaryk in too simple a way. His vision of the ultimate state of social and political life was utopian, his presumptions unrealistic: social science provides neither secure knowledge of social and political reality nor means of ascertaining generally valid value judgements; as human beings, politicians as well as the general public perceive and act not only rationally but also emotionally; social and political diversity do not allow for single 'correct' solutions acceptable to all without political compromise; there are far too many options available to any politician when he or she has to decide on a course of action; people's reactions are unpredictable, and so on. In addition, the continuous change of social and political reality requires a continuous dynamic of political reflection and action. As a formulation of a social and political ideal, Masaryk's theoretical conception of politics was indebted to the rationalist optimism of the nineteenth century, which saw politics as an application of 'scientific knowledge' in resolving social and political problems similar to the role played by science in humanity's approach to nature.[7]

With respect to Czech national aspirations, Masaryk's Realism was focused towards history as the main source of knowledge. Obviously, historical knowledge will never establish a final, generally accepted interpretation of any historical development. The question, therefore, of how realistic Masaryk's political approach was in practice, that is how realistic Masaryk's Realism was in respect to the Czech national aspirations, cannot be answered by comparing his views with what we believe the reality to have been. We can, however, reconstruct the picture of reality he himself painted and examine the qualities of his picture; its richness in structure and detail, the presence or absence of elements that we definitely know about; we are able to compare his picture with those painted by his contemporaries; we may study the clarity of his drawing in ways in which various readers and scholars interpret it, and we can, finally, because it is mainly a picture of a people, compare it with our own experience of the human world, even though from a different period. In the following discussion, this kind of analysis will be applied to Masaryk's conception of what he called the Czech Question.

AN HISTORICAL SURVEY OF MASARYK'S REALISM[8]

Founded in 1889 as a group, and in 1900 as a political party, the Realists became a minor but recognisable element on the Czech public scene. The membership of the group underwent substantial changes in the course of time and it never succeeded in voicing its ideas with any force; yet between 1890 and 1914 its voice was continuously heard. Even though there were few prominent names consistently identified with the Realists which are known today, the presence of Masaryk in the group meant a continuity and also a prominence transcending its actual limited political significance. Looking at the context of Masaryk's entire life, it seems strange that he did not find more substantial backing among the Czechs before 1914; yet if it had not been for him, the Realists would not have succeeded in gaining even as little attention as they did at the time.

Originally only three people stood at the cradle of the Realist movement: besides Masaryk they were Josef Kaizl (1854–1901) and Karel Kramář (1860–1937). Although the oldest, Masaryk was neither the most experienced nor the most influential in the group. Kaizl, the nephew of a prominent Czech politician, grew up in Prague, studied there, and travelled widely in Western Europe. He spent three years as a deputy in the Austrian parliament and several years as an official of the state administration in Bohemia before becoming, like Masaryk, a teacher at the Czech University. Kramář, on the other hand, after studies in Prague, Strasbourg, Berlin, and Paris, was able to gain some insight into politics through his father's activities in northern Bohemia before joining his two elder colleagues in the formulation of the Realist political credo. Unlike his two colleagues, Masaryk was an outsider everywhere: in Prague, in the Czech public, but also in Vienna and in the United States of America, his wife's homeland. He was a strong personality who managed to use the detachment of his social and academic position to acquire personal independence.

Even though they were so different from each other, the three politically ambitious Realist intellectuals shared a deep dissatisfaction with the Czech political scene. Not unlike the student group around Engelbert Pernerstorfer (1850–1918) ten years earlier in Vienna, which included such diverse personalities as Victor Adler (1852–1918), Karl Lueger (1844–1910), and Georg Ritter von Schönerer (1842–1921), the Realists did not believe in joining any of the established political parties. They wanted to develop a new kind of politics which would be more closely connected with people, more democratic, and which would allow them to pursue their ideals without compromise.[9] The Realists formulated their own political programme according to their ideals, the so-called Draft of a People's Programme.[10] But it did not take long until they, too, became integrated into Czech political life, just as their Viennese predecessors had entered the Austro-German mainstream.

The three Realists joined the Young Czech Party and, with several dozen other deputies, represented it in the Vienna Reichsrat beginning in 1891, optimistically hoping to impose their own ideas upon the party. While Kaizl and Kramář in fact succeeded in establishing positions for themselves in the Young Czech Party, Masaryk felt rather frustrated after two and a half years and left parliament as well as the party. He described his resignation later on: 'My resignation did not mean that I renounced politics; on the contrary. I wanted to begin from the foundations; I wanted to make a new policy, a policy of the future, and to impress myself on the thought of our people.'[11] By then, he had become the only remaining standard-bearer of what was known as the Realist political movement.

Since 1887, however, the writer and journalist Jan Herben (1857–1936) had established the periodical *Čas*, which became known as the organ of the Realists.[12] The polemics between *Čas* and the daily of the Young Czech Party, *Národní listy*, contributed to the alienation between the Realists and their two previous members turned loyal Young Czechs, Kaizl and Kramář. In the 1890s, *Čas* gradually became the main platform of Realism. Even though Masaryk was closely affiliated with the journal, it was Herben who succeeded in providing the means for the preservation of a continuous Realist political platform. This was all the more important, as the editorship of Masaryk's own journal, the *Athenaeum*, was transferred to Kaizl in 1889 because Masaryk felt unable to continue its publication.[13] In 1893 he nevertheless founded a new monthly journal, *Naše doba*, which, though it was intellectually ambitious, did not exert lasting political influence.[14]

Intellectually, Herben was a disciple of Masaryk's; his contribution to the development of Realism after the first collapse of the Realist group remained limited mainly to organisational matters. This he did successfully, and in 1900 *Čas* became the 'semi-official' organ of the newly founded Realist Party. The continuity of Realism as an intellectual concept, however, remained almost exclusively connected with Masaryk from its very beginning up to World War I. Therefore we can limit the examination of Realism as a theoretical concept of politics to the study of Masaryk's own writings. As a concept of political philosophy, Realism has been elaborated in most detail in respect to the so-called Czech Question, and it is in this respect that the application of Masaryk's normative statements can be best studied.

MASARYK'S PERCEPTION OF AND REFLECTION ON THE CZECH REALITY BEFORE 1914

Usually, the topic of Masaryk's writings is summed up by the term 'Czech Question', and his views on this matter are generally known to students of Czech history. Less familiar nowadays are Masaryk's concrete political efforts and what he actually concentrated on before 1914 as far as the Czech national aspirations were concerned. It is known that Masaryk founded the so-called Realist Party in 1900; yet it is generally unknown what the programme of this party actually envisaged in concrete terms; in fact, the text of the party's programmes are hardly accessible today.[15] Naturally, as Masaryk was a prolific writer and journalist, we can reconstruct various political attitudes on the basis of his daily articles in newspapers and journals. (They were mainly unsigned or written pseudonymously, so there are some difficulties in identifying Masaryk's authorship.) A painstaking historiographical reconstruction of this kind will be avoided in this paper, which is not concerned with the political practice of Realism. The discrepancy between the popularity of Masaryk's ideas on the 'Czech Question' in general and the lack of interest in his political practice before 1914 – with the exception of a few spectacular cases – is, however, noteworthy. This discrepancy might be seen as an expression of a certain disregard for concrete reality and as such, as it will be shown in the following, it might be seen to be an aspect of Masaryk's own intellectual heritage.

Masaryk's book devoted to the Czech Question, *Česká otázka*, was published in 1895, that is when Masaryk was 45 years old, and shortly after he had relinquished his seat in the Reichsrat.[16] Originally, it was published as a series of articles. The author himself presented the book later as a 'hurried piece of work, really only a collection of material.'[17] In spite of this, and even though he clearly stated in his introduction that he did not conceive of the Czech Question in a political sense, but rather as a sociological analysis, Masaryk considered the content of his book as a philosophical basis without which no national endeavours could be successful: 'National politics must receive a fuller content, the notion of nation must be enlarged and deepened according to the principles proposed here.'[18] And in fact, Masaryk repeatedly touched on contemporary political problems in the later passages of the book. Following the first three passages, which were devoted to an analysis of the historical process known as the Czech National Revival, the fourth part of the book dealt with the period 1890–1895, and, in the fifth part, the author evaluated the whole historical process under discussion from the perspective of its implications for the existing political situation. All this means is that, even though there might be some doubts as to the question to what extent the book actually should be viewed as a statement concerning Czech political aspirations as seen by Masaryk, there are weighty reasons to look upon it as such.

As to the content of Masaryk's message, we can recapitulate its popular interpretation by citing once again W. Preston Warren: 'As he saw it, the Czechs must discover through historical analysis wherein their genius consisted, set that for themselves as a guiding conception for internal culture and relations with all other nations, and use realistic methods constantly in its pursuits . . . . The historical continuity of Czech humanitarianism is one of Masaryk's most insistent contentions in opposition to both romantics and static objectivists. In the *Czech Question*, Masaryk traces various stages in the Bohemian 'awakening' and shows how, in Palacký and Havlíček, it found its motive and model in the Hussite Reformation and in the Bohemian Brethren. The earlier 'awakeners' certainly were more immediately connected with the European humanism of their times, but the humanism of the Hussite Reformation was a vanguard of the entire European movement'.[19]

Accordingly, and in compliance with Masaryk's notion of Realism as a concept of 'unpolitical politics', the book does not introduce the assumed Czech political needs in terms usually used in politics. 'Unpolitical politics' was Masaryk's vision of a new kind of politics, which would go as far as to render the existing formal organisation of political life superfluous.[20] The existing plurality of views and groupings was to be replaced by a consensus 'in minds and hearts', and only then, Masaryk believed, 'public criticism and discussion' would emerge and that would amount to 'true philosophical criticism and discussion'.[21] Correspondingly, there are in the book no specific political demands which could be understood as objectives to be presented in parliament or directed to the government. Neither did Masaryk deal with questions common in political philosophy, such as those concerning political power, civil rights, representation, and law. The book is therefore not an analysis of existing political problems of the time; neither is it an historical study nor a treatise on the theory of politics. It was a message directed loosely to all Czechs, and meant to be a new conception of a 'comprehensive general national program'.[22]

Masaryk himself made no distinction between a 'political' and a 'national' programme.[23] Yet at the same time, he aroused confusion by arguing that his 'national' programme was the first and fundamental condition for any successful political solution of what he considered the problem: the 'present crisis'. He presented his 'national' programme as 'intrinsic politics', so that the message of his book must be interpreted as a call to concentrate on issues suggested by him, if the Czechs should cherish any hope of a better future. Very much analogous to his notion of politics in general, where the concern with institutional matters and conflicting interests should be replaced by interest in all-embracing discussions of *Weltanschauung*, Masaryk hoped to replace the Czech concern with politics in the common sense of the word with an interest in the Czech 'national' programme: 'The affairs of the state and of politics are not as important for the nation as it is commonly assumed among us.'[24]

Masaryk does not seem to have been aware of the problems arising from his certainly noble desire to inspire in people a deeper reflection of their social and political doings: focusing their attention on certain questions exclusively, while presenting his perspective as the only desirable one, encouraged the neglect of other aspects: so, for example, by making national identity an issue of politics, Masaryk not only proposed that politics should be reflected in a wider philosophical context, but he also made the philosophical reflection subservient to politics. If politicians were men believing in freedom of expression, as Masaryk envisaged them, this ambiguity might not have mattered much. Yet if we accept that one of the main tasks of politics lies in preventing politicians from misusing power, then Masaryk's conception of a Czech national programme did not provide an adequate framework for people to recognise this task.

With respect to Masaryk's attitude to reality, it is remarkable how little he was concerned with the questions and problems which occupied his Czech contemporaries. His diagnoses of the given situation as 'crises'[25] hardly corresponded to the immediate issues which were discussed by the Czech public. His concentration on general questions of morality, religion, literature, and education will certainly never lose some degree of attraction to people interested in politics, the intellectuals in particular; in this respect, his ideas are timeless. Yet in view of the fact that Masaryk aimed at replacing the common issues of the political debate by new issues of his own interest, he showed a considerable degree of disregard for reality.

And indeed, his contemporaries did not seem to think that Masaryk was offering them answers to the problems they were concerned with, since they did not pay much attention to his Realist movement. This fact has usually been interpreted as an indication of the narrow provincial and short-sighted intellectual standards of Masaryk's Czech contemporaries; the continuous Czech interest in Masaryk's intellectual heritage among subsequent generations was then considered to prove the case. It might be, however, that the initial lack of interest resulted from the weak social and political relevance of his ideas during his pre-1914 career whereas precisely their lack of contact with a concrete historical situation made them timeless in their universal appeal. The question to be answered then remains, to what extent the questions with which Masaryk was dealing in fact concerned problems relevant to subsequent generations or, possibly, to what extent it might have been for other reasons that people have continued to refer to his ideas. The continuous interest might well be motivated by Masaryk's political success as a founder and the first president of Czechoslovakia, and to the lack of concrete contents in his statements, rather than by his treatment of questions relevant for the Czech political experience.

From the perspective of the European political experience of the twentieth century, Masaryk's effort to create a 'comprehensive national programme' hints, however, at one more serious problem. In Masaryk's time, Czech society was a well-developed pluralistic political community which did not show any signs of lacking cohesion, if one does not consider political plurality dangerous. Yet Masaryk's ideas were not intended to represent one particular credo competing with alternative notions. He rather claimed the necessity to replace or reshape other attitudes and ideas: 'Czech politics must cease to be politics.'[26] Together with his general concept of 'unpolitical politics', Masaryk's desire to promote a particular set of ideas concerning all spheres of Czech social life has to be seen as a tendency promoting the concern for the adherence to one particular ideology rather than for the solution of concrete political problems or for the formal rules of political procedure of compromise within society. Masaryk's urge for a 'national programme' appears to correspond very much with a 'felt need', as Michael Oakeshott describes the rationalist tendency to disregard concrete reality and to produce all-embracing recipes of how a society should be changed in accordance to a particular set of ideas. It can be seen as anticipating some modern regimes based on strict adherence to one chosen ideology.[27]

We can, nevertheless, tentatively accept Masaryk's proposition about the significance of the national consciousness for political life in general, and then examine his writings as an attempt to influence the political culture of the Czechs by concentrating on the contents of his concept of Czech national consciousness. How realistic was Masaryk's approach in this respect?

In his studies on this topic, among which the *Česká otázka* occupies a prominent place, Masaryk did not try to assess realistically the existing national consciousness among the Czechs by studying empirical facts. The Realist approach consisted primarily in defining the desirable form and content of Czech national identity, and it only touched upon other publicly voiced thoughts on related issues by assessing their similarities and deviations from the Realist concept. Yet even in using this method, a certain degree of disregard for reality can be discerned in Masaryk's way of dealing with ideas with which he differed. He hardly ever introduced sufficiently what he criticised. Thus Masaryk did not inspire his readers to arrive at their own conclusions but encouraged them instead to accept or to reject his own view in an unreflected emotional rather than rational manner, even if this effect might have contradicted his own intentions.[28]

The focus of the Realist conception of Czech national consciousness was historical self-awareness. Yet at the same time, Masaryk's approach to the past was not through studying the history of the Czechs in order to find some 'roots' of the national identity, hoping to discern in this way more substantial aspects than the study of the present would allow. Instead, Masaryk turned to the past in order to select particular tendencies from it, which appeared to him to offer a desirable orientation for the present. This was very much in accordance with older traditions of European historiography, in which the writing of history was primarily considered as equal to making political statements.[29] Masaryk saw the essence of his Realist approach precisely in looking upon history according to the subjectively defined needs of the present: 'Use the light of the present for looking into the past; it is wrong to believe that it could be done the other way round.'[30] Obviously, no historian can succeed in avoiding personal bias in this respect; yet it is important to note that at the time when historians were beginning to try to overcome the limitations of their subjective bias in scholarly work as much as possible, Masaryk declared the politicising approach toward the past as a desirable norm of the Realist study of the past.[31]

In addition, Masaryk's particular interpretation of Czech history, as he introduced it for inspiration and use in contemporary political life, was extremely restricted in content. I shall outline certain facts concerning Czech history that were largely or completely disregarded by Masaryk, in order to show the highly abstract manner in which he viewed the past and which can hardly be called realistic in any common meaning of the word. Thus the criterion according to which the following points have been chosen is not directed toward the search for historiographical accuracy of the examined interpretation. The following remarks are intended rather to illustrate the way in which Masaryk's political philosophy and his interpretation of the Czech past coincided in neglecting particular aspects of the political reality.

Even though Masaryk did not fully denounce the common Czech claim to the historical rights of the Lands of the Bohemian Crown, that is, the aspiration for a recovery of an independent state legitimated by the former legal status of the Bohemian Lands, he belonged to those who introduced the claim of the natural rights of national self-determination into Czech political discussions around 1900 most forcefully.[32] He criticised the allegedly exaggerated interest of the Czechs in history as expressed by their recalling of the past rights of the Bohemian Crown. By turning the force of argument towards the national self-determination of a people, Masaryk's interest in the past concentrated upon the people. The history of the state of the Bohemian Crown was transformed into the history of the Czech people. This reduction of the content of Czech history in Masaryk's concept has been paid insufficient attention so far both by Masaryk's interpreters and his critics. Ever since the emergence of the Bohemian state, its internal and external developments were so closely connected with the neighbouring German states that no historical study concerned with the Czechs can ever exclude these interdependencies without distorting the picture of the past. Moreover, the population of the state consisted from very early on not only of Czechs, but also of Germans, even though the ethnic mixture of the population varied at different periods. Every interpretation of the history of this state which concentrated exclusively on its ethnically defined Czech aspect naturally reduced the reality unduly, apart from the practical difficulties or even impossibility of distinguishing this aspect from the history of the population of the state as a whole.

The history of the Czech nation cannot be identified with the historical development of the state and its legal and political structures or the social history of its population. It was common and widespread from the mid-nineteenth century onwards to identify the history of the Bohemian Kingdom with the history of the Czechs, and the often cited translation of František Palacký's first edition of *Die Geschichte von Böhmen* (History of Bohemia) into *Dějiny národu českého* (History of the Czech nation) in its later Czech version illustrates this tendency. Yet what were the consequences of such a reduction of historical reality for the historical and political consciousness of the Czech people?

There is a difficulty in identifying the concrete historical manifestation of the Czechs as a nation. Surely, historiography cannot be limited to political history, and particularly in the last few decades various other aspects of the past have been examined more carefully than before, such as social and economic developments. Yet the Bohemian Lands, having been inhabited by an ethnically mixed population, do not allow for any separation of ethnic groups as independent objects of historical research on any other than on the local level in some specific regions.

Masaryk's concentration on the history of the Czechs only perpetuated the widely spread tendencies of the nationalist struggles of his time, which subsequently resulted in the tedious fights about the extent of Czech or German 'national ownership' in the Bohemian Lands and in its history. We nowadays recognise such an approach as unrealistic, as there are no criteria by which the modern ethnic criterion of nationality can be applied to the past. Masaryk's often conciliatory attitude towards the Bohemian Germans in practice could not, however, outweigh the still effective limitation of his conception of Czech history, in which the German-speaking population was not given an adequate place. Thus, the most important manifestation of the Czech achievements in the past, the ancient state of the Bohemian Crown, was reduced in his concept of Czech historical self-awareness from an ethnically plural to an ethnically homogeneous entity that had never existed in reality. Such an approach certainly could not promote the readiness of the Czechs to respect that the national aspirations of the Germans in the Bohemian Lands might be equally as legitimate as those of the Czechs – as Masaryk might have wished in political practice. Nor did it contribute to a sharpening of the sensitivity of the Czech majority either in its perception of the complexities of historical developments or of the political aspirations of minority ethnic groups in general, as the First Czechoslovak Republic manifested so unfortunately.

Further, the history of the Czech people was greatly reduced in the Realist conception, which argued that the development of a particular idea alone, as Masaryk called it, the 'idea of humanity', was worthwhile continuing in the present. Religion, Hussitism, Reformation, national 'rebirth' – these were developments that Masaryk recommended as the ones that should receive attention. As an interpretation of the Czech past, this concept has been criticised in detail many times as simplified and inaccurate.[33] Yet it seems important to note that apart from such criticism, another difficulty of this approach lies in the suggestion that adherence to a particular idea should be the main criterion for the assessment of the significance of contributions to the social, political, and historical life of the Czechs. Reference to other kinds of contributions is lacking and, accordingly, many of the past achievements of the Czech people are negelected, such as, for example, the renown of the ruling dynasties of the Bohemian Kingdom, the great cultural and political expansion of the thirteenth and fourteenth centuries, the sophistication of the social and political structures and commercial achievements of the Czechs in various periods, the cultural attractions of Prague, or the political, economic, educational, and scholarly achievements of the Czechs during the second half of the nineteenth century.

Masaryk's presentation of Czech achievements past and present reduced reality so considerably that his reader not only acquires a false perception of Czech society past and present, but also learns that the complexity of human reality can be largely disregarded. Reducing the notion of national identity to one particular idea – however admirable that idea might be – is unrealistic in the literal sense of the word, and it certainly does not contribute to a sharpening of the individual's perception of complexities in social and political life.

Once again we can tentatively examine Masaryk's concept of the 'idea of humanity' and its content from the viewpoint of considering how it related to reality. Masaryk never presented any study which would systematically spell out the substance of the 'idea of humanity'. His explanations are vague: 'The idea of humanity, the main and guiding idea which leads all Enlightening and Revivalist efforts, is the idea of our Reformation: humanity is simply a different word for Brotherhood in the sense of the Bohemian Brethren and it was with this idea that Palacký created our national program.'[34]

There are hints of personalities and insufficiently defined movements, which are to be seen as protagonists of that idea. Masaryk never made clear what it was that they all shared in common apart from moral appeal, an interest in religion, and concern for people in a populist sense of the word. He never indicated the way in which he arrived at the idea of an historical continuity between the ideas of Jan Hus, the Hussite movement, the ideas of the Bohemian Brethren, and those of the Czech National Revival of the eighteenth and nineteenth centuries. Nor did he present the ideas to which he was referring in any depth. Readers might understand intuitively what Masaryk meant so that they are able to accept or reject it, but there is very little information for those who are searching for a rational understanding of Masaryk's thoughts.

The sentence I have just quoted also proposes an extremely simplified version of humanitarian ideals: 'humanity is only a different word for Brotherhood.' This is such a vague statement that it allows for all kinds of interpretations, and is, as such, free of any concrete content. Additionally, Masaryk suggested a distinction between the content of his idea of Brotherhood and the concept of 'fraternité' as used in the French Revolution, a concept popular in the 1890s: 'Czech humanitarian ideals have their specific historical and factual foundation in our Reformation, not in the French Revolution; liberal humanitarianism is not identical with the humanity of our revolution. Everyone wanting to think and to feel Czech must be aware of this difference.'[35] Once again, the historical reference is used here as an indication of the content of the 'idea of humanity' instead of as an explanation of what Masaryk actually meant; this time, however, we are left with an even vaguer notion.

We are given some hints, when Masaryk referred to contemporary forms of the 'idea of humanity', such as the demands for national equality, the abolition of violence, educational and social reforms, or

democracy.[36] Are we to think that these demands had their origins in
Czech Hussitism? It seems so when reading Masaryk's books and
articles. Surely he did not mean to suggest a direct historical
continuity; yet he certainly offered a highly restricted conception of
the historical developments which contributed to the formulation of
those modern aspirations.

Masaryk disregarded once again the complexity of reality: he
disregarded the struggles and developments within the Roman
Catholic Church before the fifteenth century, the emergence of
secularising and rationalist tendencies in the field of European
scholarship from the twelfth century, the spiritual and political
plurality and developments within the Utraquist Church in Bohemia
and Moravia from the late fifteenth century onwards; he disregarded
fully the traditions of classically orientated humanism emerging in
Italy and reaching Bohemia with great intensity in the sixteenth
century, and the aristocratic political developments in the Bohemian
Kingdom with their failed, yet most interesting, reform attempts of
the early seventeenth century. In addition, it has hardly ever been
noted that Masaryk also paid little attention to the role of British
developments in parliamentary rule or to the significance of the
American Revolution for the development of modern social and
democratic ideals. These are a few hints at the richness of the
historical reality which in Masaryk's writings was reduced to a
simplified picture.

The most explicit presentation of Masaryk's ideals can be found in
a small book entitled *Ideály humanitní*.[37] It is not quite clear exactly
how the 'idea of humanity' relates to the 'humanistic' or 'humanitist'
'ideals'; yet in his book, Masaryk seems to be treating them as
identical.

There are three main tasks which the book seeks to fulfil: to
introduce Masaryk's suppostion as to the nature of history and
society; to analyse selected conceptions of social philosophy such as
socialism, individualism, utilitarianism, pessimism, evolutionism,
Positivism and, finally, Nietzsche's philosophy; and last but not least,
to present the 'First Principles of the Ethics of Humanity'.[38] The last
named task of the book alone will be discussed here.

In summary, Masaryk's ideals can be introduced in the following
list of commands: morality founded in religion should be liberated
from the influence of the churches, and it should reconcile emotions
with reason; thou shalt love thy neighbour as thyself, and the love
should be concentrated upon the nearest fellow human beings; work

for those whom you love; do not love death and martyrdom, and free yourself from the persecutors; liberate yourself from fear; judge and think independently; search for practical, but also general and philosophical, education; do not make any difference between politics and morality; believe in progress; do not postpone anything for the future; do not despise the material world; do not be lazy or excited, and believe only what you can justify. Obviously, this is only a brief extract of Masaryk's text; yet it is sufficient to indicate alone the variety of problems arising when we examine Masaryk's attitude towards reality.

In view of the central role which the 'idea of humanity' played in Masaryk's attempt to formulate a 'national program', there is no reason why we should consider the above ideals as either specifically Czech in their nature, or as ideals playing any special role in Czech political efforts in the past, including Masaryk's own lifetime.

Even if we accept these ideals as a formulation of general moral principles valid for all people at all times, however, we cannot accept Masaryk's formulation as sufficient to be considered a basis of a social and political philosophy. The reason lies mainly in the question which Masaryk hardly considered at all – namely, what happens if people do not behave in such a way, or if they even happen to believe in other norms and values, in other ideals, as undoubtedly is often the case? Masaryk's ideals are directed almost exclusively at individual human beings and their behaviour, without touching upon problems crucial to social and political life, that is, those ensuring that people of different characters and religious beliefs and nationalities, pursuing opposing interests and disagreeing about politics, can live peacefully within one community. The appeal to individuals to change their behaviour in order to resolve political problems certainly was a noble appeal, and would have helped, if people had followed it; yet the historical experience and the tradition of European, and particularly Anglo-American, political philosophy offered grounds for the contemplation of specific issues of social and political reality, which Masaryk did not seem to have recognised, having focused his own social and political philosophy on individual behaviour.

We do not deny the importance of Masaryk's ideals; yet the emphasis which Masaryk gave to them in his notion of politics led to a devaluation of the significance of the institutional structures and procedural rules in political conflicts. The emphasis on the individual qualities and characteristics of the actors in politics, the desirability of which is obviously important, overshadows the need for an independent protection of the weak against the strong. Where this protection is guaranteed, there, and only there, the appeal for general moral improvement of the powerful ruler makes sense and can be seen as a realistic political objective. Without protection, however, the desires for moral improvement and educational or behavioural reforms are illusory. Masaryk's neglect of this aspect of politics might be understood in view of the fact that in Europe before World War I, basic civil rights were generally guaranteed and had deeply penetrated the public consciousness in the countries to the west of Russia. It was only later that they became once again an object of disputes and political struggles, a fact which many of Masaryk's followers failed to recognise after 1945. Reading Masaryk's writings uncritically at the present time will divert one's attention to problems of secondary significance.

CONCLUSION

My examination of Masaryk's approach to Czech national aspirations has shown that Realism was a concept based on such a highly abstract notion of reality that it cannot be called realistic in the common sense of the word. Far from the interpretation cited at the beginning of this paper, which considered Realism as a concept opposing mythology in the name of reliable and accurate methodology, the present analysis suggests that Realism provided a framework for a way of thinking about Czech national aspirations which was orientated towards utopian objectives, based on distorted pictures of real situations, and founded on historical mythology as the focus of the proposed Czech national self-identity.

Masaryk's contention that the Czechs were in need of a 'national programme', his notion of 'unpolitical politics' as the desirable new form of politics; his highly restrictive reference to Czech history; his concentration on one allegedly guiding idea of the Czech past, the idea of humanity; his interpretation of modern humanitarian ideals as emerging from the Czech Reformation, and, finally, his presentation of individual moral commands as the ideals of social and political efforts, all were unrealistic.

Apart from using arbitrarily distorted pictures of reality, Masaryk's Realism as applied to the analysis of Czech national aspirations offered space for a conception of politics which in many ways contradicted European liberal-democratic traditions, and the Anglo-

American traditions in particular. In some ways, also, this might have contradicted Masaryk's probable intentions.

The fallacy of Realism was its exaggerated trust in the force of reason. Masaryk's intentions corresponded to the best human hopes for a better life. Yet because reason is only one part of human reality, a realistic approach can hope to acquire omnipotent 'scientific' knowledge as little as it can hope to change people according to any desirable ideals. Masaryk certainly did not disregard the variety of forces affecting human beings, and Preston Warren is right when he suggests that Masaryk tried to emphasise precisely the broad variety of 'diverse factors which any honest person finds he must consider', as cited above. But because he disregarded the difference between the individual human and the social and political dimensions, Masaryk wanted too much and too little at the same time. He envisaged a society of ideal men and women, and was less interested in the society of fallible and imperfect human beings. His analysis of Czech political aspirations before World War I failed not only to fulfil his intentions, but also to provide a realistic framework of thought about Czech national identity and politics.

Taking into consideration Masaryk's incorporation of Czech national aspirations into a framework of universal human perspectives, the change in his political activities concerning the Habsburg monarchy after the outbreak of World War I can be understood even without knowing in concrete terms the actual political demands that the existing state failed to fulfil. On the basis of his lifelong feeling that the existing social and political order was in a state of deep crisis and probably beyond repair through political reforms, the outbreak of the Great War obviously must have appeared to him as offering a chance for the construction of a new order. Surely, it must have appeared to him as an impulse for action that opened unknown perspectives. In this situation, Masaryk's attitude to Czech national aims changed fundamentally: his notion of the Czech national and political problems as linked to a universal human destiny caused him, in his interpretation of the war, to leave behind 'unpolitical politics' and to opt for a change of the political order through political action that would eventually help change the legal and political framework of his country. His resolve to change the interpretation of Czech national aspirations seems to have been motivated by his assessment of the European and world situations in general, rather than by new insights into the specific Czech situation. Yet, in particular because of the lasting effects of his political activities after 1914, Masaryk's heritage in political philosophy surely deserves more careful reconsideration than it has been given so far.

NOTES

1   Thomas G. Masaryk, *Humanistic Ideals*. Translation and Preface by W. Preston Warren with a Foreword by Hubert H. Humphrey (Lewisburg, PA: Bucknell University Press, 1971) p. 20.
2   Compare Eva Schmidt-Hartmann, *Thomas G. Masaryk's Realism. Origins of a Czech Political Concept* (Munich: Oldenbourg, 1984) pp. 56–64.
3   For an elaboration of this point with particular reference to Czech historiography compare Jaroslav Werstadt, 'Politické dějepisectví devatenáctého století a jeho čeští představitelé', in *Český časopis historický*, vol. XXVI (1920) pp. 1–93.
4   For an interesting and most informative introduction to this field of study, see Stefan Kohl, *Realismus, Theorie un Geschichte* (Munich: Wilhelm Fink, 1977).
5   For the best introduction see *Geschichtliche Grundbegriffe. Historisches Lexikon für politisch soziale Sprache in Deutschland* (Stuttgart: Klett-Cotta, 1978) vol. IV, pp. 865–7.
6   For a detailed analysis of Realism as a concept of political philosophy compare Schmidt-Hartmann, *Thomas G. Masaryk's Realism*, pp. 139–43, 176–96.
7   For details, see ibid.
8   The only attempts at a detailed survey of developments of the Realist movement are the following: Václav Vaníček, 'V počátcích realismu', in *Masarykův sborník* (Prague: 1926–29) vol. II, pp. 289–300; vol. III, pp. 50–72, 122–45, 210–21, 303–29; Jurij Křížek, *T. G. Masaryk a česká politika. Politické vystoupení českých 'realistů' v letech 1887–1893* (Prague: SNPL, 1959); Stanley B. Winters, *Karel Kramář's Early Political Career*, Ph.D. Diss., Rutgers University, NJ, 1966; Schmidt-Hartmann, *Thomas G. Masaryk's Realism*.
9   For an elaboration of the comparable features of the so-called Pernerstorfer Circle and the Realists, see my forthcoming essay 'People's Democracy: the Emergence of a Czech political concept in the late 19th Century', in *Selected Papers Presented at the III World Congress for Soviet and East European Studies*, the volume on East European Politics edited by Stanislav J. Kirschbaum.
10 'Návrh programu lidového' published in *Čas*, vol. IV, no. 44 (1890) pp. 689–94; explanatory notes were published in the following issue of the journal: 'Glosy ku programu lidovému', *Čas*, vol. IV, no. 45 (1890) pp. 705–13.
11 *President Masaryk Tells his Story*. Recounted by Karel Čapek (London: Allen & Unwin, 1934) p. 175.

12 *Čas* was founded in 1886 as a fortnightly by a group of young intellectuals led by Jan Herben, who hoped to provide support for the journal *Athenaeum* in the so-called Battle of the Manuscripts. In 1889 it was transformed into a weekly and financed by a syndicate of intellectuals sympathising with and led by Kaizl, Kramář, and Masaryk, with Herben as the editor. From then on, *Čas* became a platform of the Realists.

13 The *Athenaeum*, a monthly aiming to provide a critical introduction of native and foreign scientific work to the academic public, was founded by Masaryk in 1883. The ownership changed hands several times. The editors were Masaryk and Kaizl. Publication ceased in 1893.

14 *Naše doba* was established in 1893 and edited by Masaryk until 1914.

15 *Rámcový program české strany lidové (realistické)* (Prague: Výkonný výbor české strany lidové, 1900); *Program české strany pokrokové, schválen třetím valným sjezdem strany konaným v Praze 6, a 7.ledna 1912* (Prague: Tisková komise, ČSP, 1912).

16 T. G. Masaryk, *Česká otázka. Snahy a tužby národního obrození*. Originally published as a series of articles in the journal *Naše doba*, as a book first published in Prague (Čas, 1895). The edition used in this paper is the 6th (Prague: Čin, 1948).

17 *President Masaryk Tells his Story*, p. 175.

18 Masaryk, *Česká otázka*, p. 174.

19 Masaryk, *Humanistic Ideals*, pp. 19–20.

20 Compare T. G. Masaryk, *Karel Havlíček: Snahy a tužby politického probuzení* (Prague: Laichter, 1896); the edition used in this study has been the 3rd (Prague, 1920) pp. 452–504.

21 Ibid., p. 504.

22 Masaryk, *Česká otázka*, p. 225.

23 Ibid.

24 Ibid., p. 123.

25 Compare Masaryk's book usually read together with *Česká otázka*: T. G. Masaryk, *Naše nynější krise. Pád strany staročeské a počátkové směrů nových* (Prague: Čas, 1895).

26 Masaryk, *Česká otázka*, p. 165.

27 Compare Michael Oakeshott, *Rationalism in Politics and Other Essays* (London: Methuen, 1962) p. 22.

28 This feature of Masaryk's writing was already observed by Franz Brentano in his comments on Masaryk's doctoral dissertation. See Jaromír Doležal, *Masarykův almanach* (Vienna: Academický spolek, 1925) p. 29.

29 Compare Werstadt, 'Politické dějepisectví', pp. 11–34.

30 Masaryk, *Česká otázka*, p. 68. Similarly on p. 151.

31 This problem of Masaryk's notion of historiography was recognised by a number of his contemporaries, such as Josef Kaizl, Jaroslav Goll and, above all, Josef Pekař.

32 Bohuš Tomsa, *Masarykův zápas o právo přirozené. Příspěvek k ideologii českých politických stran* (Bratislava: Universita Komenského, 1928).

33 On the first Czech critics among Masaryk's contemporaries and their arguments, compare Schmidt-Hartmann, *T. G. Masaryk's Realism*,

pp. 144–62. It is, however, noteworthy that in spite of the continuous criticism, Masaryk's interpretation of the Czech past has remained popular until now and has even, in its main characteristics, been accepted by the orthodox Communist historiography since 1948.

34   T. G. Masaryk, *Jan Hus, Naše obrození a naše reformace* (Prague: Čas, 1896). The edition used here is the 3rd (Prague, 1903), p. 9.

35   Ibid., p. 14.

36   Masaryk, *Česká otázka*, pp. 91, 130, 144, 219, 270.

37   T. G. Masaryk, *Ideály humanitní. Několik kapitol* (Prague: Čas, 1901). The edition used here is the 8th (Prague: Čin, 1946).

38   Ibid., pp. 54–63.

Part 2
Masaryk as Politician and Social Critic

7 T. G. Masaryk and Karel Kramář: Long Years of Friendship and Rivalry

Stanley B. Winters

The relationship between Tomáš G. Masaryk and Karel Kramář (1860–1937) in the quarter-century before World War I forms a significant chapter in modern Czech history. Almost every issue that affected the nation's political fortunes was on their agenda. From the time of their cooperation in the original Realist movement in 1889 until the outbreak of the war they strove, sometimes as allies, often as rivals, to win equal rights, material improvements, and social justice for the Czechs and other minority nationalities in Habsburg Austria.

During those pre-war years the nationalities were girding for political action. In the Bohemian crownlands where the Czechs lived alongside many Germans, the small farmers, agrarian and industrial working classes, and tradesmen were enlisting in militant new parties that arose with the expansion of suffrage and modernisation of society. There was growing discontent with the traditional bourgeois leadership in the Old Czech and Young Czech parties. The moderately liberal Austrian constitutional system, with its aristocratic privileges and authoritarian prerogatives of government, favoured a German centralistic administration that ran counter to Czech demands for fully equal civil rights and national autonomy. These issues, and the vital one of Austrian foreign policy, were at the heart of the political activities of Masaryk and Kramář.

By 1914, when the forward movement of Czech politics seems to have reached a dead end, Masaryk was sixty-four and Kramář fifty-four. A contemporary might justly have observed that their careers were past their zeniths, but with the outbreak of war in the summer of 1914, new opportunities opened for them and the nation. With the war's end in late 1918, Masaryk became president of the new Czechoslovak Republic and Kramář its prime minister. From then until their deaths in 1937, these 'two great old men'[1] created another chapter in their relationship by engaging almost incessantly in heated debates over official policy and personal history.

This paper will deal with their pre-war association, which began in respectful collaboration and ended in open hostility. Their fates first became intertwined in the summer of 1888, when a financial crisis arose in the *Athenaeum*. Masaryk, the journal's founder and editor, had become highly controversial in Prague's academic and intellectual circles. With the *Athenaeum*'s future in question, he resigned as editor to be succeeded by Josef Kaizl (1854–1901), professor of political economy at the Czech university in Prague. Among the nineteen persons appointed to *Athenaeum*'s reorganised editorial board was Kramář, its youngest member and Kaizl's former student. Through Kramář's contacts with Kaizl and the physician-poet Eduard Albert, among others, he was aware of the emerging 'Realist' current that was energised by Masaryk's forthright critical stance towards the dominant cultural ideas and forces in Czech life.[2] Kramář was then living in Vienna, conducting research on the Austrian governmental administration under Maria Theresa in the hope of pursuing a university career, when Kaizl invited him to write for the *Athenaeum*.[3]

Kramář's first meeting with Masaryk probably occurred in December 1888, when the two of them met with Kaizl to discuss their political alliance under the banner of Realism. Kaizl had already held elective office under the Old Czech Party; Masaryk had sounded out the Old Czechs and the Young Czechs with an eye towards a candidacy; and Kramář, too, was politically ambitious.[4] The three agreed to unite with the audacious objective of gaining national leadership by entering one of the existing liberal parties or founding a new one. Being highly conscious of the importance of mass communications they sought a press organ. For several years previously, Kaizl and Kramář had been discussing the founding of a new political weekly; now, at Masaryk's insistence, they settled on *Čas*, a two-year old biweekly edited by Masaryk's disciple, Jan Herben. Their intention was to moderate *Čas*'s polemical tone and highly subjective editorial stance so as to convert it into 'a well-managed publication . . . which would show that our group was indeed a new force.'[5]

In the course of their political activity, Kramář often corresponded with Kaizl and Masaryk and sometimes met with them in Prague and Vienna.[6] He was primarily attracted to the Realist strategy of intellectuals engaging in politics,[7] but the personal factor also intrigued him. Both Masaryk and Kaizl were role models he was striving to emulate. Although he had not been a student of Masaryk's while studying for his doctorate in jurisprudence at the university, he knew about his reputation for sympathy with student youth and that he taught 'practical philosophy'. He was impressed by Masaryk's moral sincerity and honesty, and above all that Masaryk had opened 'the window to Europe' for the Czechs.[8] To be with Masaryk meant to stand at the cutting edge of the young generation against defensive traditionalism and sham patriotism in Czech society. Further, the two shared an enthusiasm for Slavonic, especially Russian, art and culture, although Masaryk was more the scholar-critic and Kramář the observer-aficionado in that regard.[9] Masaryk respected Kramář's journalistic skill, boundless energy, and knowledge of Austrian government and finance, the last being a topic he prudently left to his two colleagues to elaborate in their Realist manifestoes. Kramář regarded Masaryk as 'a more warm, feeling person' than the individually ambitious, 'coldly solipsistic' Kaizl;[10] but while Kramář acknowledged Kaizl's intellectual and political influence upon him, he denied any intellectual debt to Masaryk, whom he regarded as naive in legal and administrative matters and murky, if not a bumbler, in politics.[11]

Even as Masaryk and Kramář were forging their political alliance, they were differing on the most contentious Czech intellectual issue of the time, the 'Battle of the Manuscripts'. To Masaryk, the dispute over the genuineness of the old poems was primarily a moral question that opened an opportunity for national reform and regeneration in line with his growing concept of Realism. His position was that, 'The national honour demands defence – I mean acknowledgement – of the truth and no more, and there is greater morality and courage in acknowledging a mistake than in defending a mistake which the whole nation may share . . . If the manuscripts are fraudulent, they are similarly a symptom of a spirit which we do not seek in our present time.'[12] By coupling this editorial viewpoint with Jan Gebauer's scholarship, Masaryk transformed a literary and philological debate into a public ideological controversy that he hoped would expose long-held, cherished, and presumably false national assumptions.[13] The ensuing tumultuous reaction indeed served his purpose of bringing into the open (in fact, aggravating and reinforcing) the conservatism and prejudice of elements in the Czech cultural and political establishments.

Kramář was studying in the Austrian state archives in Vienna while the Battle of the Manuscripts raged in Prague.[14] Although not involved in the dispute, his reaction to it typifies his pragmatic, politically conscious approach to such symbolic issues. On one hand, he defended the right and duty of scholars to teach freely and search for truth. He hailed the intellectual reassessment stimulated by the controversy as a wholesome development that paralleled the progressive realignments that he felt were then possible in politics. On the other hand, the issue was not simply one of good versus evil, truth versus falsehood, as Masaryk and some of his supporters were arguing. The Manuscripts, even if forgeries, were to Kramář 'a pious fraud' that had served the honourable function of reviving the nation's pride and self-identity after the destruction of its literary heritage during the Habsburg-imposed Catholic Counter-Reformation. While he rejected the caustic denunciation by defenders of the Manuscripts of Masaryk and others who had questioned their authenticity, he believed the poems to have been 'a moral support' with 'a great, truly blessed mission', at a time when the Czech nation badly needed such reinforcement.[15] In Kramář's eyes, the nurture of the nation was the highest good, so certain means to achieve it, even if not ideally true and pure, might still help the national cause.

As for the public uproar that followed Masaryk's intervention in the dispute, Kramář felt that *Čas*, under Jan Herben's direction, by baiting the opposition, was needlessly hurting Realism. He made his participation in *Čas* conditional upon the ending of the polemics over the Manuscripts in its columns.[16] Subsequently, the political aspects of the dispute were cooled by mutual agreement between the Realists and the Young Czech leaders at their merger in December 1890.[17] That was the end of it as far as Kramář was concerned. Masaryk, also, upon withdrawing as editor of the *Athenaeum*, virtually terminated his open involvement with the Manuscripts;[18] but he never fully forgave his detractors from the Young Czech Party; for after he split with the party in 1893 and openly began to attack it, he asserted that the party's abandonment of 'freedom' and its adoption of 'reactionary intolerance and dogmatism' dated from party leader Julius Grégr's attacks on him over the Manuscripts in 1886.[19] Masaryk conceded that Grégr personally had later overcome his prejudices in the affair, but he charged that other Young Czech leaders, and some members of the editorial staff at *Národní listy*, the party's organ, remained unreconciled and were unprepared to accept the merger with the Realists.[20] So, while Kramář was relatively unscathed by the Battle, Masaryk felt it for many years afterward as a searing experience.

Upon joining the Young Czech Party, Masaryk and Kramář worked together more closely than ever before or after. Being novices in parliament and the party,[21] both had to adjust to new routines, and both underwent trying moments at the hands of critics and enemies. Each emerged from his initial years in politics with vastly differing perceptions of what it had meant. After their elections to parliament in March, 1891, they faced – with Kaizl, who also became a Young Czech deputy – three basic tasks: to be loyal Young Czechs, implementing the party's programme and accepting its discipline while pursuing their Realist goal of national regeneration; to defend Czech interests in Vienna while pressing for improved nationality relations and empire-wide reforms; to educate the Czech public on the Realist prescription for securing Czech equal rights with the Bohemian Germans and self-government for the Bohemian crownlands (Bohemia, Moravia, and Austrian Silesia) within a restructured, federal Austria.[22] Indeed, they made some headway on the latter two tasks; but Masaryk could not cope with the first one and in the course of struggling with it, he became separated from Kramář and Kaizl and from the party. At the bottom of this problem lay their differing conceptions of politics.

Masaryk brought to politics pronounced attitudes and perceptions that arose from his university education and socio-philosophical interests, his late arrival in the Prague Czech milieu, his academic professionalism, and his personal idealism grounded in a tutorial, essentially religious morality. Politics to him was neither an end in itself nor a means to any worthy end. He wrote in 1889 to Kramář: 'I don't expect from political activity more appreciable help for our unfortunate conditions', and at the time he rejected entering politics.[23] He had little respect for the Young Czech leaders, terming them 'children, most even brats'.[24] Neither was the selection of the Young Czechs over the Old Czechs for a merger with Realism appetising to him; it was 'a choice not between the devil and the deep blue sea but between two deep grey seas'.[25] When the tide of public opinion turned against the Old Czechs because of their 'Punktation' agreement with the Austrian government and the Bohemian German parties in 1890, he softened his position and said he would work for 'the young ones' but would not do any 'arse-licking'.[26] This indecision, even distaste, at formally affiliating with a political party expressed not only Masaryk's dislike for the Czech liberal brand of politics, but also his belief that political activity *per se*, even if it won some reform legislation, could not produce the fundamental changes in social and spiritual conditions that he desired. Only individual ethical behavior, a striving for moral purity and goodness, not for self-interest or power, could, in the long run, result in an informed, truly rational politics.[27] The way out of the spiritual crisis of the time, in his view, lay in a religious and moral revival, at best a slow process that required proper upbringing and education, literary works of an uplifting sort, and suitable role models to inspire change in human values. True, politics did offer a platform from which one could inform one's fellow citizens of the causes of their 'unfortunate conditions' and prescribe remedies. Proper values, however, are embodied not in party proclamations and platforms, but in the works of creative men and women. 'Literature is our parliament, government, and state', he told an American audience.[28]

It appears that Masaryk was drawn to politics in the late 1880s, despite his lack of confidence in it, by a dearth of other avenues of searching for means of uprooting complacency among his compatriots and prodding them to examine critically the quality and direction of their lives. His university career was in a cul-de-sac; his promotion to a full professorship was blocked; his enemies controlled the academic administration, and his students were organising on their own initiative. Scholarly writing was painstaking; further, he did it in spurts, and since the outbreak of the Battle of the Manuscripts he had settled in a trough where – save for some essays on Slavophilism – his political commentaries and articles on applied criticism predominated over enduring works of scholarly reflection and research. Trade and business held no interest for him, and certainly the ordinary ranks of the civil service did not. While respecting the importance of journalism, scrounging for a living in the politically dominated press was an unappealing poor second choice; the very notion of working to meet externally imposed deadlines was obnoxious, and his experience with publisher Jan Otto's Czech encyclopaedia showed that he was unable to meet them.[29] The Old Czech Party had several notable academics among its leaders (Albín Bráf, economist, Josef Kalousek, historian, Jan Kvíčala, philologist, and others), and this made the party somewhat attractive to him. The nation had venerated its scholars *qua* politicians such as František Palacký and F. L. Rieger. Perhaps through politics, there might even be the chance of a ministerial position in Vienna by means of which his ideas could be realised on a broad scale.[30] In the light of these considerations, Masaryk's entry into politics at the age of forty was not only a reasonable move; it marked also the first stage in his most lasting and fruitful area of activity.[31]

Kramář, in contrast to Masaryk, gave politics his highest priority.

He saw control of state power as the vital goal of politics.[32] His research into eighteenth-century Austrian history taught him the importance of Theresian and Josephinist policies for Bohemia's later development.[33] In Adolf Wagner's seminar on economics at the University of Berlin he had absorbed the *Kathedersozialist* maxim that the state which injures can also be the state which repairs and remedies. Politics, even in a quasi-authoritarian state like Austria, was a means of climbing the ladder of power. By terminating his studies in Vienna and working full-time as a Young Czech politician and deputy, Kramář abandoned his goal of a university career but fulfilled his familial and adolescent predilictions for the party. He was thereby destined to become the first professional, that is full-time, Czech politician. This career was made possible by generous support from his father, a building contractor and factory owner, who provided regular stipends and placed investments in his son's name, and by income derived from Kramář's marriage in 1900 to a wealthy Russian woman.

Masaryk dedicated his public life to educating the Czech nation in his ideals of moral regeneration and social justice, Kramář with equal passion to the causes of Czech liberalism and nationalism. The artist Max Švabinský caught the essence of this zeal when on the occasion of Kramář's fiftieth birthday he wrote: 'I have always respected you very much because you are the only one among the leading politicians who considers politics as his sole love, just as the artist his art. You, the only one, sacrificed your whole life to your profession. You staked everything on one card, you renounced any reserve that could in case of possible failure substitute for it, which always impressed and touched me.'[34]

Right after Masaryk and Kramář joined the Young Czechs, they were busy with drafting the party's platform, campaigning for election to parliament, and, after being elected, attending its sessions in Vienna. In this period Masaryk was contented with the party and optimistic about future prospects.[35] But he was unduly hopeful: by staying for meetings in Vienna he lost touch with Julius Grégr in Prague, with whom he had developed a good rapport, and the party's new platform with its strong Realist imprint meant little to the members ('Very few absorbed it in the bones and blood.').[36] His parliamentary speeches were prepared conscientiously enough, and some impressed hearers with their array of facts and insights; but like most speeches in parliament, they had little practical outcome save for drawing occasional rebuttals. He was not a stirring speaker, although his expressiveness improved toward the close of his two years (April 1891 to March 1893) at the parliamentary session; meanwhile, he was becoming more discursive and prone to generalise.[37] Kramář, the youngest deputy in parliament, was not then the outstanding orator that he was to become later; however, he soon learned where the levers of power were located in the Viennese bureaucracy and made valuable connections. Both men, and other Young Czechs, spoke in parliament on significant issues such as nationality relations, language usage, taxes and tariffs, education, and especially the party's bold new demand for universal equal suffrage. Their arguments were presented in constructive and innovative ways that high Austrian officials were slow to appreciate and understand.[38]

In addition to having their parliamentary speeches communicated to the Czech public through the press, Masaryk and Kramář often wrote commentaries on politics and discussed issues at open meetings.[39] Masaryk was particularly blunt in publicly mentioning matters on which the party had not yet taken a united position. Some of his colleagues felt this to be a breach of party discipline, to which he replied that excessive control over public discussion would weaken the party and inhibit outsiders from supporting it. His bold Strakonice speech of September 1891, which ranged from Austrian foreign policy and Panslavism through 'demogogic radicalism' within the party drew much comment, some unfavourable for airing party problems in the open.[40] Julius Grégr tried unsuccessfully to have the speech condemned as factionalism in the party's executive committee.

Masaryk and Kramář were still close and friendly; they frequently consulted with one another and with Kaizl, but a gulf appeared because of Masaryk's running quarrel with party extremists and writers on *Národní listy*, and Kramář's reluctance to back him in every squabble. Masaryk felt that the party's leaders exercised insufficient control over the newspaper, which sometimes ran items that seemed to him irresponsible and contrary to the party's platform. The dispatches of the newspaper's veteran Vienna correspondent, Gustav Eim, especially irked Masaryk. He charged Eim with misrepresenting his statements in parliament and those of other deputies.[41] In his Strakonice speech and even earlier, Masaryk had recommended that *Národní listy* be replaced as the party's main organ. His major grievance perhaps was that, because of the paper's inaccurate and sometimes sensational reporting, many Young Czechs in Prague were out of touch, and even disagreed, with the actions of the parliamentary deputies in Vienna; consequently, the paper was misleading the public and raising false hopes on what it could expect from parliament. In his view, this was bound to feed an empty radicalism among party regulars, rather than a moderate realism. He could not tolerate such duplicity in others; he was eager for praise that rarely came his way, and he was sensitive to animadversions about his loyalty to the party and fidelity to the Czech national cause from men who should have been his comrades-in-arms.[42]

Kramář was well aware of Masaryk's concerns and sympathised with him. As a fellow newcomer and Realist, and in addition because of his relative youth (he had turned thirty shortly before election), he suffered from similar attacks, but not yet as many as Masaryk. Unjust criticism upset him and he fought back. He survived because he was more realistic than Masaryk in understanding that they were part of a rite of passage, one of the features of an immature, hyper-reactive Czech political-party system to whose reform he had dedicated himself. Above all, he realised what Masaryk did not, that the essence of non-revolutionary politics was compromise and that incremental gains in ordinary times were better than no gains at all.

An equally bothersome problem for Kramář was *Čas*. He accused it of immoderately sniping at *Národní listy* in response to the newspaper's attacks on Masaryk, and because of editor Herben's resentment at having been dismissed from the *Národní listy* staff during the Manuscripts dispute. By engaging in journalistic warfare, *Čas* had become an obstacle to the full assimilation of the Realists into the Young Czech Party.[43] Despite Kramář's complaints, Masaryk refused to rein in Herben on the grounds of editorial freedom, although *Čas* was the Realists' organ, not Herben's, and although he decried that very editorial freedom when practiced by *Národní listy*. Masaryk's desire for a personal medium of expression, as exemplified in *Čas*'s editorial positions and openness to his articles, was dearer to him than party solidarity. He preferred the loyalty of a devoted and obedient follower like Herben to the respect of independent-minded colleagues such as Kramář and Kaizl. He paid the heavy price of losing the trust of his two fellow Realists and of having some of *Čas*'s most disputatious articles, published anonymously or pseudonymously, wrongly attributed to him, thereby further isolating him in the party.

By mid-1892, Masaryk was considering abandoning his deputy's mandate. He told Kramář and Kaizl that he wished to remain in

Prague to be close to his family, the university, and the student youth.[44] At their urging he refrained from taking this step at the time, but he finally made the decision when his intra-party feuds boiled over in the summer of 1893.[45] The culminating event was a bitter controversy with Julius Grégr: the Šromota affair. An inquiry into the controversy by the party's executive committee found that Masaryk had behaved incorrectly, and the committee chastised him in a statement.[46] A month later, on 25 September, he voluntarily surrendered his mandates to parliament and the Bohemian Diet. His withdrawal in the immediate sense was a protest against his treatment by the committee; in the long-range sense it signified that he had lost patience with the party's failure to deal with his accumulated complaints and its slowness to reform its *modus operandi* along the lines he desired.

Until the eleventh hour Masaryk hoped for changes in party policies through actions which had been promised to him by the parliamentary deputies' club chairman Emanuel Engel and by Grégr. His two Realist colleagues refused to join him in surrendering their mandates. Deep down, Masaryk never forgave them for this.[47]

Masaryk's resignation at that juncture (as he later related to Karel Čapek) was probably an impulsive act intended to express his profound discontent, and this applies equally to his withdrawal from the Bohemian Diet, which he had not earlier contemplated. In the event, he soon had second thoughts about what he had done, for his action was widely interpreted as an admission of disloyalty, and this he could not stomach. To prove otherwise, he declared himself a candidate for the two mandates in December 1893, and asked for the party's endorsement in a special election. When this was refused (he was instead promised endorsements for the next general election to each body), he withdrew his candidacies.[48] Another Young Czech was elected from his district. Technically, Masaryk remained a party member and a member of its executive committee, but when he soon launched blistering attacks on the Young Czechs in *Čas* and elsewhere, it was clear that his allegiance to them was over.[49]

These actions in late 1893 climaxed Masaryk's unease and confusion about partisan politics. Four years earlier he had written to Kramář: 'The young [Czechs] are no better than the old [Czechs], and the other way round.'[50] Politics to him being at best a necessary evil, his tenure with the Young Czechs had the character of a self-fulfilling prophecy: either the party marched to his beat or he marched alone.[51] In exchange for leaving politics, however, he was liberated to think and write freely for the first time in years. Having had his first serious involvement in the rough-and-tumble world of practical affairs, he could apply its lessons to furthering his self-appointed mission as enlightener and reformer of the Czech nation.[52]

While Masaryk's political career for the time being was ending, Kramář was drawing closer to Kaizl and both of them to the Young Czech Party. Their hopes of working within it and becoming leaders were crystallising: opportunities were opening because of Julius Grégr's terminal illness, the ageing and retirement of leaders from the older generation, and their own growing expertise and firm commitment to politics. Splitting from Masaryk was a difficult decision for Kramář but a logical one. From conviction he could not follow Masaryk into a strident factionalism via *Čas* or even contribute to *Naše doba*, the new journal of public affairs which Masaryk founded as a successor to the *Athenaeum*.[53] His decision to remain a Young Czech was not simply guided by personal ambition, although that was a powerful factor, or by blind loyalties to the party whose deficiencies he well knew. There existed no other political alternative for a person of his middle-class background and liberal nationalism. He had come to see Masaryk in a rounded sense as a man with weaknesses as well as strengths, with both unattractive and admirable qualities, with narrow character traits as well as lofty ethical principles. He wanted Masaryk as a friend, respected his knowledge and frankness, and hoped to retain his good opinion. He was, however, differing increasingly with Masaryk on basic issues that were to form the substance of their future debates and squabbles: the nature of political 'radicalism', the hairline between compromise and 'opportunism', Czech attitudes towards Russians and other Slavs, justifications for Czech claims to autonomy and self-determination in the Bohemian Crown Lands, Austria's Balkan policy, and the future of the Habsburg Empire and its peoples – as the next two decades were to show.

If Masaryk was intellectually liberated by leaving the Young Czech Party, Kramář was politically and, to a certain extent, psychologically, liberated from Masaryk. For five years, as a Realist and Young Czech, he had stood in the older man's shadow. Being self-assured, proud of his family and north Bohemian heritage, and somewhat vain, Kramář was irritated by seemingly minor occurrences in their relationship.[54] He felt that his first-rate education in Prague, Berlin, and Paris, his travels to Russia and Western Europe, prolific journalism and intensive archival studies entitled him to a greater measure of intellectual regard than Masaryk displayed. (He regretted never having published his study of governmental administration under Maria Theresa, thereby gaining academic recognition as a scholar.) With Masaryk gone, he no longer had to endure his 'professorial' attitude and tutorial corrections to his writings, something the more tactful Kaizl was careful to avoid.[55] Kramář's (and Kaizl's) decision to stay in the party showed that they no longer were Masaryk's 'disciples' or 'children' or 'lambs' but mature men who were capable of defending their positions without him and eventually against him.

One immediate step Kramář took was to end his feud with the journalist Gustav Eim. He knew that, without Eim's support or at least acquiescence, his prospects in the party would suffer. In late 1893 he explored with Eim the idea of forming 'a Slavonic coalition on a democratic basis' in parliament as a means of altering the balance of power there toward the Czechs.[56] As confidence between these two men grew, this grand if ultimately futile conception evolved into a plan in 1896 to get the Austrian premier Count Badeni to grant language concessions in return for Young Czech support of his legislative programme.[57] Masaryk and Eim meanwhile remained bitter foes, each complaining to Kramář about the other's nastiness. Kramář faithfully defended Masaryk against Eim's fulminations, particularly those about the salvos from *Čas* against Eim and *Národní listy*. Placing responsibility for the diatribes on editor Herben, Kramář wrote to Eim: 'Masaryk is angry and he condemns many things, but he does not deserve to be condemned for it . . . Masaryk is also a human being and therefore he is angry.'[58] Even as Eim was suffering from his fatal illness he complained about Masaryk; Kramář replied: 'Masaryk is sincerely sorry for you . . . Masaryk has a kinder heart than you suspect.'[59]

For his part, Masaryk continued to admonish Kramář for what he felt were betrayed ideals by the younger man; for example, he chided Kramář for condemning the Czech youths in the militant 'Omladina' group and for misjudging the meaning of their trial.[60] But as Kramář became increasingly influential in parliament and official circles, Masaryk relied on him to resolve his financial grievances against the university and the Ministry of Public Worship and Education. On several occasions in the late 1890s he explained to Kramář the mishandling ('what they stole from me') of salary, back pay, and increments allegedly due to him because of the long delay in his promised advancement to a full professorship. He asked Kramář to make enquiries and representations in his behalf. Finally, the promotion was announced in June 1896. Since other faculty members were also bringing their problems to Kramář, he became their chief spokesman in Vienna on salaries and working conditions.[61]

Late in 1897 Masaryk suffered from a leg ailment. Kramář, although preoccupied with the turbulence in the aftermath of Count Badeni's resignation as prime minister, found time to console him. In replying, Masaryk deplored their inability to meet for frank talks: 'I see the sadness of our situation just in that, our relationship . . . when two people such as we cannot speak about that which fills their hearts.'[62] Three years later, upon receiving Kramář's announcement of his imminent marriage to his great love, Nadezhda Nikolaievna Chludova-Abrikisova, at the age of forty, Masaryk immediately sent congratulations and wished him 'all that you expect and desired so truthfully and steadily for such long years.'[63] These expressions of warm sentiment were typical of those they sent each other – despite political differences – at times of joy or grief in their lives.

One of the most significant domestic issues that involved Masaryk and Kramář from the outset of their political careers until it was implemented in Austrian legislation and approved by the Emperor on 26 January 1907, was universal suffrage. Both stood consistently in favour of a broadly expanded suffrage, a demand they first advanced in the Realist programme of 1890,[64] but they played variant roles in seeing it to fulfilment. The Young Czech Party had raised the issue earlier but took no concrete action until after its electorial triumph in 1891, after which pressure from the Social Democrats and the 'progressive movement' forced its hand.[65]

Masaryk approached suffrage reform as a means of extending popular control over government. He favoured universal suffrage for elections to both parliament and the Bohemian Diet, but in principle did not believe that a vast increase in the number of voters by itself would bring unalloyed benefits. In keeping with his idea of tutorial leadership in politics, he wanted the new system to be subject to the influence of experts who would use the findings of science and ethics to educate the electorate for responsible participation.[66] While he was a Young Czech deputy he spoke in parliament on the issue; but he favoured only manhood suffrage at the time, feeling that extending the vote to women, a demand advanced by the student 'progressive movement' in 1891, was premature.[67] In 1896, in his book on Karel Havlíček, the Czech democratic journalist from the 1848 era, he cited Havlíček at length in support of universal suffrage as a means of democratising citizenship and reducing the potential threat from revolutionary doctrines among the masses.[68]

The programme of Masaryk's People's Party, founded in 1900, urged universal suffrage not just in elections to parliament but also at all levels of self-government.[69] When the demand for suffrage expansion grew powerfully after the turn of the century, Masaryk lacked a deputy's mandate from which to advocate it; instead, through his writings and public speaking he tried to shape public opinion favourably towards the reform and thereby, incidentally, maintain his links with political allies such as the Social Democrats. In September, 1905, he participated in a mass demonstration on behalf of the franchise.[70] In the following year he hailed the rising public demand for universal equal suffrage as a means of pressuring parliament to act, despite what he described as its domination by reactionary interests from the great landlords and other privileged groups. Yet all the while he seems not to have had much faith in the capacity of universal suffrage to bring about progressive changes; for, as he wrote pseudonymously, 'Whoever expects freedom, populism, and political progress from Austria is a political child.'[71] Such pessimism did not, however, deter him from seeking a seat in the new parliament after the suffrage reform became law. In May 1907, after finishing second in a three-man race on a first ballot, he won a deputy's mandate on a second ballot with Social Democratic support in a district in eastern Moravia. This narrow squeak enabled him to regain a public forum from which his views could be aired throughout the Empire. By 1910, his effective use of parliament for speechmaking had moderated his pessimism sufficiently for him to praise a law cosponsored by Kramář against parliamentary obstruction and for its undisturbed functioning. 'I am for a working parliament. I am for the use of parliament', he told a public meeting early that year.[72]

The intensity of Kramář's involvement in the cause of suffrage reform varied according to Young Czech active interest in the issue and his own estimate of its chances of success. This meant that on occasion he accepted a minor improvement in the electoral system as a step forward towards an eventual major change. But he never deviated from his belief that universal manhood suffrage was essential if Austria were to modernise her government, relieve social and political tensions, and move towards solving her nationalities question. Like Masaryk he spoke often in public and in parliament in support, not only of proposals by the Young Czechs but also of those by other parties such as the Social Democrats, always stressing that only a comprehensive reform could bring a socially just solution.

When his party's commitment to universal suffrage seemed to be waning, he urged that it not abandon the demand 'because that is the entirety of our new policy – its democratisation.'[73] He limited his conception of reform, none the less, to elections to parliament in Vienna and not to the Bohemian Diet in Prague. The Diet was a Young Czech stronghold, the key to the party's strength in the towns and local districts. Kramář and his party colleagues feared that a Diet reform would allow for a great increase in the votes for rival, notably radical, parties such as was occurring in parliamentary elections.[74]

In association with the deputies Adolf Stránský and Bedřich Pacák, Kramář introduced in parliament on 26 September 1905 a proposal for establishing a system of universal, equal manhood suffrage.[75] In November the Emperor asked the premier Baron Gautsch, to proceed to shape enabling legislation to that effect. During the prolonged debate in the months following, it became clear that the Czech parties as a whole would not gain as many added seats as they had hoped, relative to the gains of the German parties, if they were to rally sufficient votes for a reform measure. Further, the Young Czech Party was bound to lose its position as the nation's leader, a status that had anyway been eroding since the beginning of the century. Still, Kramář stayed on course. In 1906 he wrote to the executive committee chairman, Václav Škarda, that, 'It is necessary to tell our people all those things so that, despite the injustice of the electoral reform, [they] do not forget that it is, in spite of everything, a great advancement on the way to justice for our nation . . . I think that such a frank, truthful description of the matter will find a response and understanding among the Czech people.'[76]

Kramář's commitment to a sweeping franchise reform was strengthened by his fear that the Russian Revolution of 1905 might inspire the Austrian working classes to violent action in pursuit of their political demands.[77] Having witnessed revolutionary turmoil on a visit to Russia, he had no illusions that the installation of a parliamentary system by itself could liberalise a backward, authoritarian state in which the monarch held the reins of power. Mindful of Prussia's experience under Bismarck, he wrote in 1906: 'Even the strongest of parliaments is not decisive in the great political questions.'[78] Still, he believed that timely concessions to rising demands from the masses would preserve what he regarded as healthy elements in a social order and permit further progress, as against gambling on last-ditch resistance to any change whatsoever. Hence he strove energetically in his party and parliamentary positions to help secure the democratic suffrage reform in Austria.

The most sensitive and complicated sphere of Masaryk's and Kramář's activity was Austrian foreign policy. Neither man entered politics with any expertise or experience at it. Since the heydays of Palacký and Rieger, no Czech politician had paid it much attention. The disclosure by Bismarck of the provisions of the Austro-German Alliance in February 1888, occurred just as the seeds of Czech political Realism were sprouting. Both men were bent on criticising the alliance publicly (but not their associate Kaizl, who avoided foreign policy in order not to hurt his career prospects). Masaryk's debut in 1891 as an analyst of foreign diplomacy was inauspicious; he dismissed the chances of a Franco-Russian rapprochement on the grounds that 'the Russian tsar will never acknowledge the justification of the French Revolution.'[79] A few weeks later the first formal agreement for Franco-Russian diplomatic consultations was signed, to be followed by a draft military convention between the two powers. But Masaryk began to learn the facts of diplomatic affairs in 1892, when he was elected a member of the Czech parliamentary contingent that participated in meetings of the joint Austro-Hungarian Delegations in Budapest. He visited Bosnia and Herzegovina to gather material for a report critical of the Austrian administration in the two provinces that he delivered in the Delegations.[80]

Masaryk believed that Austria's foreign policy reflected its domestic arrangements of power and decision-making. Foreign policy was a consequence of internal conditions rather than a cause of them.[81] In Austria, this meant the persistence of aristocratic and absolutist institutions that excluded broad public opinion from affecting diplomacy. He distinguished between the aggressive foreign policies of states, especially multinational ones, and the peaceable cultures of their constituent nationalities. This freed him to criticise Austrian foreign policy rather boldly, according to the principle that large, strong states had no inherent right to oppress and exploit weak ones or lesser nationalities. In November 1892, he characterised the Triple Alliance as a vehicle for imperial German aggrandisement that could lead to the Germanisation of Austria.[82] Along similar lines, Kramář and Gustav Eim, the other chief Czech speakers on foreign policy in the 1890s, attacked the Triple Alliance as inimical to Austria's independence and a threat to her historic role as a haven for her Slavs against external (mainly German) chauvinism. Kramář's strategy of opposition was outlined as early as 1889: The Czechs lacked the strength to affect Austrian foreign policy at the time; therefore resistance to it would be 'entirely sterile' until the nation had reinforced its position to the point at which it constituted a real force in Austrian affairs.[83] This point, in Kramář's estimation, seems to have been reached in the later 1890s.

After Kramář's election to the Delegations in 1896, his involvement with foreign policy issues increased. His forays, and those of Masaryk and Eim, into a sphere that traditionally and constitutionally belonged to the Emperor and his close advisors opened the way for other Czechs to deal with Austrian diplomacy; but none of their colleagues dealt so forcefully with the issues as those three. Kramář was virtually insulated from official reprisals for his comments – in peacetime at least – by his immunities as a parliamentary deputy. Masaryk had certain privileges as a tenured university professor, but he discreetly reserved his strongest statements to the times when he held a parliamentary seat.

After the crisis of 1897 over Count Badeni's language ordinances had revealed the extent of imperial Germany's commitment to support the Austrian Germans against the demands of Austria's Slavs for civil equality, Kramář began a major effort to persuade European opinion that the Czech Question was not a minor internal Austrian problem but one of great international importance. In articles published in England and France, he dramatically portrayed the dangers posed by Pan-Germanism to the hard-won gains of Austria's Slav peoples and to Austria's very survival as a sovereign entity.[84] A Germanised Austria would mean her inevitable incorporation into the German Reich, thereby upsetting the European balance and facilitating German economic and military penetration of the Near East. Fortunately for Europe, he wrote, the Czechs, 'planted in the heart of Europe, in the midst of an ocean of German influence', form 'a barrier that prevents the German flood from swamping all from the North Sea to the Adriatic.'[85] While such verbal flourishes brought Kramář no credits in Berlin or Vienna, they cast him as the chief spokesman for Czech interests in Austria, and they drew attention especially in France to the Czech struggle for equality with the Germans and Magyars of the Empire.

The above analyses by Masaryk and Kramář were aimed not at weakening Austria but at reorientating her foreign policy to prolong her tenure as a European power. Both men advocated good relations with Serbia, whose strivings for an outlet to the Adriatic they supported, and both urged Austria to avoid provocations that might stir a conflict with Serbia and her Russian ally and thus throw Austria deeper into Germany's militaristic embrace. Masaryk was concerned not merely that Austria should adhere to principles of justice and morality in its policy towards small nations and states; he also did not want German interests to block Czech commercial ventures in the Balkans. Kramář, a personally wealthy man with connections to Czech banking and industry, wished to preserve the Balkans as a field for Czech economic expansion.[86] He relied – overoptimistically – on cordial Austro-Russian relations to restrain the German *Drang nach Osten*. Convinced that the Austro-German alliance buttressed German political and cultural superiority within Austria, he sought to deflate the appeal of Pan-German agitation by reducing Czech-German tensions in Bohemia. In 1912 and 1913 he worked tirelessly to negotiate a Bohemian compromise between the two nationalities on such matters as the official language of administration and the fiscal responsibility of each nationality for education and public services. The failure of the Czechs and Germans to reach agreement was no fault of Kramář's, who several times saved the negotiations from collapse by his tactical skill. Masaryk played a relatively minor role in the negotiations because he held no seat in the Bohemian Diet and his parliamentary mandate was from a Moravian district; yet he served with Kramář and others in a small group of party leaders that presented proposals to the government in accord with changes in the Czech bargaining position. One such proposal was to have serious results, and that was on 17 May 1912, when the Czechs deputies' club led by Kramář and Masaryk presented five points to the government of the premier, Count Stürgkh, as the basis for further discussions with the Germans. Soon after, the negotiations broke down because of escalating Czech demands, the outbreak of the first Balkan War, and dwindling German support for a settlement.[87]

Kramář's zealous sponsorship of the Neo-Slav movement in the first decade of this century marked the peak of his Empire-wide prominence but brought few lasting results. As one of Neo-Slavism's spiritual fathers, he committed himself heavily to it after the Young Czechs had lost ground in the general parliamentary elections of 1907. Their numerical strength dwindled from fifty-three to twenty-one deputies and was surpassed by that of the Agrarian Party and the Czech wing of the Social Democrats. The time when his party could claim to speak for the whole nation was gone, and with it Kramář's hope to be the national spokesman, although he still ranked with a small group of politicians at the top. Neo-Slavism offered him an opportunity to retain the spotlight in addition to promising fulfilment of his life's dream of close inter-Slav cooperation. He repeatedly affirmed Neo-Slavism's non-political orientation and goals; but the movement entailed the cooperation of Austrian and Russian subjects and thus aroused official suspicion in both countries. Kramář wisely avoided espousing an uncritical Russophilism or a cultural Pan-Slavism that would advance the religious and linguistic aims of Slavophile Russian chauvinists. Much as he respected and in some ways romanticised aspects of Russian life, he knew the country's weaknesses and was, as a Czech patriot, unready to surrender the Czech cultural heritage to Russia or any other power.[88] All too soon, the fragility of his hopes from Neo-Slavism was exposed through actions of the European powers, such as the crisis over the annexation of Bosnia and Herzegovina by Austria and renewed Russian oppression in the Polish kingdon.

Masaryk apparently intended to participate in the Prague Neo-Slav Congress of July 1908 (his name is listed in the programme booklet among the Czech representatives), but he changed his mind when informed that the question of Russo-Polish relations, on which he wanted to speak, would not be on the agenda. The leading role at the Congress was played by Kramář, as chairman of the Slavonic Committee of the Czech National Council.[89] That fact, plus the large number of Young Czech participants, may also have soured Masaryk. Later he excused his abstention as having foreseen that nothing substantial would result from the meeting; it would have been impractical for him to have worked with the Russian Neo-Slavs because, in his view, they were ignorant of conditions among the Czechs and Poles and of the true state of Polish-Ukrainian relations.[90] Nonetheless, the programme of Masaryk's Progressive party in 1912 espoused a Neo-Slav goal when it urged the strongest cultivation of 'mutual cultural and economic relations with the Slavonic peoples'; and he was not averse to meeting in Petrograd with leading Russian Neo-Slavs when conducting research on Russian literature and philosophy for the book he was preparing on these subjects.[91] In the book, which appeared in German in 1913, Masaryk dismissed Neo-Slavism as 'a fiasco', an understandable but peremptory judgement at variance with the observations of some later scholars.[92]

During his Neo-Slav years, Kramář pursued a two-edged strategy in parliament that led to contradictory results. On the one hand, he warned that if Austria's recklessness drew her into a war 'for Germany's greatness',[93] she should not count on the willing support of her Slavs in such a conflict. In this regard he was a forceful and prophetic speaker. On the other hand, in keeping with the Young Czech 'positive policy', he backed specific measures that eased Austria down the slope leading precisely to such a war; for example, he initially supported the Bosnian annexation, assuming that Russia had given prior approval. Afterwards, he turned against his long-time acquaintance, the foreign minister Count Aehrenthal, for allegedly having deceived him about obtaining the Russian foreign minister Izvolsky's consent for the action. Forced to choose between two versions of the event, he picked the Russian. Even so, he thereafter rallied vital Czech votes for increases in the Austrian military budget and for reform of the law on conscription as part of the Defence Bill of 1912. His justification – and the great majority of Czech deputies voted with him – was that a militarily prepared Austria would not have to depend upon German support as it had in the annexation crisis (Oct. 1908–March 1909). He also claimed that the Czech nation derived substantial benefits from its loyalty to the state through budgetary allocations in Bohemia and Moravia for public works, civil service jobs, schools, and cultural facilities that otherwise it might not have received.

Kramář's strategy indeed brought specific benefits of that sort, and they were by no means negligible in improving the quality of life for many people; but the central government's financial pinch due to its defence programme made them smaller than was hoped; besides, there was great competition for these allocations from other parts of the Empire. The military reforms which Kramář supported also had their negative effects: they increased the domestic influence of the army command; they strengthened centralising forces in the state administration at the expense of regional autonomy; they embittered Serbia and alarmed Russia. Kramář's vote for the Bosnian annexation, moreover, angered Václav Klofáč, leader of the Czech National Socialist party, who opposed the annexation as illegal and whose party launched anti-militarist demonstrations in Prague and other Czech cities.[94]

Masaryk acknowledged Austria's authority to annex the two provinces; he dissented from the clumsy manner by which it was done.[95] He had long been interested in South Slav developments, and like Kramář had no wish to see Austria involved in a war with Serbia. Always alert to unearth cases of official wrongdoing, his noteworthy interventions in the Zagreb treason trial of May 1909, and the Friedjung affair of late 1909 and 1910 proved of enormous long-run importance to his later career. These actions earned the plaudits of Klofáč and the Czech anti-militarist camp; they enhanced the respect in which he was held by South Slav leaders, and they drew positive attention abroad through the reporting of H. Wickham Steed and Robert W. Seton-Watson. Masaryk's persistence as a self-righteous crusader in unpopular causes and for probity in government was winning him a special niche in Czech public life.

The final phase in the pre-war relationship between Masaryk and Kramář coincided with the year 1914. The year opened with tense and abrasive rivalries among the Czech political parties as they jockeyed for advantage against each other, while negotiating a compromise with the Bohemian Germans and conducting business with the government. The Austrian premier Stürgkh sought to resolve the Czech-German strife in order to make a smooth passage in parliament for his military reforms and public works programme. In July 1913, he prorogued the Bohemian Diet because of German obstruction of its agenda. The Germans were protesting against Czech efforts to alter the system of Diet elections to the disadvantage of the Germans. Because the Diet, through its executive council (*Zemský výbor*), was the only Crownland body constitutionally authorised to fund essential public services, a fiscal crisis arose. The handling of Crownland finances was thereupon delegated to a government-appointed administrative commission. Protesting against the Diet's suspension, and angered by Kramář's help in bringing the administrative commission into being, the Czech National Socialists and the Agrarian party, supported by Masaryk's Progressives (he was their lone parliamentary deputy) and a small group of 'independents' from Bohemia and Moravia, began to obstruct parliament in December 1913, under the slogan of 'Bez českého sněmu – žádná říšská rada' (Without the Bohemian Diet – no Reichsrat).

The Young Czechs and the Czech Social Democrats abstained from this obstruction. They hoped thereby to keep the Stürgkh government from lining up unalterably with the Bohemian Germans in the compromise negotiations.[96] Unable to proceed with his legislative programme, Count Stürgkh prorogued parliament on 31 January 1914, leaving both Bohemia and Austria without functioning organs of representative government. (This also left the deputies without per diem payments for attendance at the sessions of parliament.) He was prepared to govern by emergency decree under Article 14 of the Law No. 141 of the Constitution until parliament could be reconvened.[97] The patience of the Austrian ruling circles with the seemingly endless nationality conflict in Bohemia was wearing thin, while passions and petty calculation prevailed among many politicians in the Czech camp.

Kramář was a linchpin (another was Bohumír Šmeral, leader of the Czech Social Democrats) in the moderate approach that was dividing the Czech parties in their resistance to the government. By keeping a bridge open for negotiations with the Bohemian Germans, he was, according to his critics, keeping Count Stürgkh from pressing the Germans to accept the Czech terms for a compromise. The Czech Progressives (Masaryk's Realists) and the National Socialists, seeking to discredit Kramář and his party, launched a press campaign through their chief organs *Čas* and *České slovo*, charging that Young Czech officials in lesser towns were corrupt. Failing to arouse the public on this issue, they stepped up their campaign by accusing Young Czech leaders with having accepted 20 000 crowns in 1907 from secret funds to start up *Den* as a journalistic rival to the militant *Národní listy* and as a mouthpiece for the Kramář wing of the party.[98]

Národní listy conceded that a Young Czech official – Josef Fořt, not Kramář – had indeed accepted the proffered money but denied that it had been used for any improper purpose. Then, several days after the German parties had definitively withdrawn from the compromise negotiations and hopes for a settlement had collapsed, *Národní listy* counterattacked. On 4 March 1914 it published a report that accused Karel Šviha, chairman of the National Socialist parliamentary deputies' club, with being a paid informer for the Austrian state police.[99] Thus began the sensational 'Šviha affair' which was to preoccupy Czech politicians and the public through the spring and summer of 1914. It had profound repercussions among leading figures in Czech politics, and poisoned the nation's atmosphere as World War I began. And it darkened relations between Masaryk and Kramář for years to come.

The crux of the affair was the charge that Šviha, a prominent member of the foremost Czech oppositional and antimilitarist party, was secretly providing reports to the police on the activities and plans of his party colleagues, and perhaps on those of other parties, too. In the furious journalistic battles that ensued, Kramář's Young Czechs and Šmeral's Social Democrats stood against Klofáč's National Socialists and Masaryk's Progressives. Each side heaped abuse on the other.[100] Šviha sued Servác Heller, the responsible editor at *Národní listy*, for libel. A 'trial' was arranged, to be presided over by six Czechs chosen by the Czech National Council. Šviha was represented by attorneys Václav Bouček, a close associate of Masaryk's and a Realist, and Rudolf Traub, an eminent legal scholar, also a Realist. Servác Heller was defended by the Young Czech attorney and publicist, Alois Rašín. Witnesses from the various political parties included Masaryk, Kramář, Klofáč, and Antonín Švehla (who was one of the six judges), among others. No one from the Austrian state police testified; the idea was to have the Czechs handle their own messy affairs.

The decision rendered by the tribunal was that Heller was wrong to publish the article, and had offended Šviha by its appearance, but that he had not libelled Šviha because it was proven during the proceedings that Šviha had indeed been an informer in the pay of the police.[101]

At first blush it would seem that Masaryk had no reason to become involved in the case or in the trial, since he was not a National Socialist and he had no direct evidence to provide. The National Socialists, however, were his political allies in the 'radical coalition' with his Progressives and other small parties; and he had gathered scraps of information by talking with persons on the periphery of the affair. He saw an opportunity to kill several birds with one stone by assailing the procedures used to charge Šviha and by decrying the evidence against him as flimsy, meanwhile avoiding a direct assertion that Šviha was innocent. This tactic was bound to embarrass Kramář and the Young Czechs, and infuriate the editors at *Národní listy*, his old *bête noire*. It would cement his relations with the National Socialists and advance his reputation as a defender of unpopular causes against the avalanche of ignorant mass opinion that accepted Šviha's guilt on the basis of newspaper charges even before a trial was held. Masaryk later observed that he came to believe that Šviha's activities were linked to someone higher in the official hierarchy than the local police commandant, and that he wanted this brought out.

There is no doubt that Masaryk was embarrassing and embittering the Young Czechs with his repeated onslaughts and others written by *Čas*'s staff when the affair was at its height. He questioned why the editor of *Národní listy*, who received the information about Šviha's connection with the police (at the time it was the late Josef Anýž) as early as 1911, did not immediately act on it but instead sanctioned the electoral alliance between the Young Czechs and Šviha's National Socialists for the parliamentary elections of that year. In effect, he was charging a Young Czech coverup of the scandal until convenience dictated that they reveal its details. By intervening, Masaryk gained in National Socialist esteem,[102] but he paid a high price. Šviha, faced with overwhelming evidence of his linkage with the police, resigned his mandate to parliament on 14 March. Masaryk was perceived as defending a traitor to the nation, not a principle;[103] so the cost to him was probably greater than that incurred in his previous crusades, if only because this was an issue that the average person could clearly understand.

True to his style, Masaryk had entered the Šviha affair, as Klofáč's biographer comments, 'by nobody summoned and nobody asked'; and he provoked reactions of which that by historian Josef Pekař, that he was either 'a lunatic or a knave', may have been typical of many others.[104] His commitment reinforced his links with the National Socialists but severed those with other parties and left him politically isolated.[105] Finally, Masaryk wounded Kramář as he had never done before, and at the most critical moment in their careers, as the coming months were to prove. The wound seems to have occurred during a period of strong feeling between them, perhaps due to the accumulated grievances of many years, the parlous state of Czech affairs, and their inability to find any basis for cooperating on the major issues of the day.

The testimony offered by Masaryk at the 'trial' of Šviha of 13–15 May 1914 was surprisingly unappetising. It was rambling, disjointed, based on hearsay and innuendo, and alleged that Kramář lacked self-discipline and was even indiscreet. (Kramář was not present when Masaryk testified.) Masaryk also cast aspersions on the good sense of the Czech people as a whole in the face of Austrian police surveillance and intelligence activities.[106] Only the Realist attorney Bouček's timely intercessions kept Masaryk from making a complete fool of himself under Alois Rašín's sharp questioning. In the weeks following the 'trial', as the journalistic warfare continued, Masaryk's *Čas* seemed more eager to discredit Kramář and the Young Czech party than to develop a complete picture of the affair,[107] although that was his avowed intention.

The Šviha affair, and Masaryk's eccentric role, shook Kramář deeply. Whatever the weaknesses in his public image as painted by critics in 1914 – his baronial life style, his admiration for things Russian, his quest for the middle road, his defence of upper-class interests, his reliance upon Austria as a Czech shield against Germandom – he was a man of his word, he said what he thought (sometimes too bluntly for others to accept), and he had never sold his soul for a governmental position; he was generally respectful of Masaryk, and his personal selflessness and devotion to the nation were unquestioned.[108] As he said in December 1915 at his trial for treason before an Austrian military court, the Šviha affair 'threatened my personal situation and the whole [Young Czech] party.'[109]

Only shortly before the affair erupted, he had met with Masaryk at the insistence of friends, but they achieved only a minor reconciliation. After the 'trial' he decided to sever all contact with Masaryk because of 'the personal, very hard to forgive, personal attacks' on him.[110] None the less, responding to appeals by colleagues, including Masaryk's ally, the State Rights Progressive party leader Karel Baxa, he met once more with Masaryk (probably in late June or early July 1914) to discuss the Šviha affair. It was a very difficult time for Kramář because his mother was terminally ill with cancer. When he began to assure Masaryk that the party's moves for unmasking Šviha 'were quite pure', Masaryk attacked him 'in an unheard of manner'. From then on Kramář refused to speak to Masaryk, even when he was forced by the other party chairmen to attend a meeting later in 1914 at which Masaryk was present. A final effort to bring the two together came to naught.[111] Not only was Kramář averse to a reconciliation; Masaryk himself, even before the Šviha affair, had no genuine interest in one. He told the poet J. S. Machar that no complete reconciliation with Kramář on the level of their previous friendship was possible and, further, that he did not care much for Kramář.[112]

When Masaryk left Prague in December 1914, for the last time until the war's end, he apparently wished to invite Kramář to go abroad with him. In this decisive moment, Masaryk's rationality triumphed over his past grievances; Kramář's presence would have helped convince European colleagues and statesmen that the Czech parties were united in their attitude toward an Entente victory. Masaryk, a man of peace, had no wish for the war to erupt, but he had sensed that 'something was in the air'; he welcomed it as a release from personal tensions and a way out for the Czechs in dead-end Austria.[113] From foreign contacts he realized that the war could be a long one. He had neither faith nor hope in a speedy Russian victory over Austria that would 'liberate' the Czechs. Facts, plus his strength of will, pointed towards a long stay abroad to work for Czech independence.[114] Kramář, like Masaryk, foresaw vast changes in the map of Europe resulting from the war; but whereas Masaryk analysed it as a contest for European hegemony between two vast imperial agglomerations, Kramář saw it as a racial and cultural struggle between Slavdom and Germandom.[115] A German victory would mean the most difficult of times for the Czechs with all their past gains wiped out; a Slav – meaning Russian – victory would give them the chance to live a full life. Having faith in Russian arms, he opted to remain in Bohemia, with his wife and property, so that he could be at hand to welcome the Russian armies when they reached Prague. His miscalculation may be called the triumph of sentiment over reason.

By leaving Austria Masaryk burned his bridges home for four long years. His gamble was to pay off, but the bridge of friendship to Kramář was never repaired. After the war, Kramář reminded Masaryk how seriously the older man had offended him in the Šviha affair. Masaryk answered: 'I don't recall what I said against you in the Šviha affair. I judge that it was not as serious as you say. But these are *de facto* individualistic, petty things; we did not split apart because of them. We estranged ourselves because you were with the Young Czechs and I was against them. I gladly admit that I wronged some people, and perhaps I wronged the whole movement. Of course, I think these disputes and animosities benefited everybody, but I admit that was not my goal. I admit that I was more personal than necessary. On the other hand, you were not right when you defended the party.'[116]

This exchange of views, coming seven years after their bitter encounters of 1914, and twenty-eight after Masaryk left the Young Czechs and Kramář gave up Realism, shows how profoundly interconnected the personal and the political were in their memories. In the quarter-century of their political activities surveyed here, neither escapes unsullied; both were intensely human, amazingly energetic, and totally committed to their causes. No other figure in the Czech political milieu from that time approaches their stature. Masaryk is no doubt reduced here in the heroic qualities accorded him in the deferential historical writing during his presidency and since his death, but is still much larger than life. To his associates in politics he was difficult to get along with; he was often insensitive to others' concerns, not out of any meanness of spirit but perhaps because of the high standards he set for himself, his moral certitude, his impatience with detail, his focus on his reforming mission. He was not a team player, the first requisite for conventional, pluralistic politics; but he attracted a small, devoted group of like-minded persons, and he retained Kramář's respect for longer than is usually thought. His practical achievements in the political activities covered here were rather modest.[117] His true distinction in the pre-war era lay in other spheres and events. Kramář, whose contributions have usually been ignored, underplayed, or derided, comes across more positively than he has been portrayed in most writings. His labours, and their results, at helping to build liberal institutions and national pride, at helping people solve problems and at professionalising politics, deserve recognition. Within the historical setting of conditions among the Czechs of the Habsburg Empire in its late decades, his actions were as true to his interests and character as Masaryk's. His enemies in the post-war era, the national search for scapegoats, and the simplifications of historians who came later have given him an undeservedly poor image.

The final word belongs to Vlastimil Klíma (1898–1987), perhaps the last surviving leading member of Kramář's political party under the inter-war republic, who achieved a certain perspective in his memoirs of that time when he completed them in May 1976. Writing of the reconciliation between Kramář and Masaryk in their final, ailing months, and of their deaths so close together in 1937 – Kramář on 26 May, Masaryk on 14 September – he said: 'These "two great old men" began in public life side by side and then reconciled themselves, but it was too late. Between them lay whole lives filled with contradictions, different fates, and also mutual struggles. Man is a world unto himself; not even with the ordinary individual is it possible to surmise what thoughts, impressions, feelings, and sentiments are running through his head. How then is it possible with quite extraordinary individuals, when even they are seized by that "eternal human"'.[118]

NOTES

1 The phrase 'two great old men' comes from Vlastimil Klíma, 'Hrst vzpomínek na politiku mezi dvěma válkami', Archiv Národního Muzeum v Praze (henceforth ANM), manuscript, p. 235. All citations to unpublished materials used here are made with grateful acknowledgement to the responsible archival officials.

2 The broadest surveys of political Realism are Václav Vaníček, 'V počátcích realismu', *Masarykův sborník*, II (1927) pp. 282–322; ibid., III (1929) pp. 50–72, 122–45, 210–21, 303–29; and Jurij Křížek, *T. G. Masaryk a česká politika. Politické vystoupení českých 'realistů' v letech 1887–1893* (Prague: SNPL, 1959).

3   Kramář held a doctorate in public law from the Czech university in Prague (1884) and studied economics and political science abroad thereafter. In 1886 he published *Das Papiergeld in Österreich seit 1848*, a study of Austrian monetary policy. Essays written for the *Athenaeum* helped his standing as an expert on finance and public administration.

4   Hermann Bahr, *Selbstbildnis* (Berlin: Fischer, 1923), p. 176. Letter of F. L. Rieger to Marie Riegrová, 30 Jan. 1887, cited in Bohumil Němec, Antonín Pimper and Vojtěch Holeček (eds), *Sborník Dra Karla Kramáře* (Prague: Pražská Akciová tiskárna, 1930) p. 277.

5   Karel Kramář, *Paměti*, 2nd ed., (ed.) Karel Hoch (Prague: Pražská Akciová tiskárna, 1938) p. 109. Oskar Butter, 'Masaryk novinář', *Masarykův sborník*, VI (1932), esp. 394–8. On Kaizl's journalistic skills see Josef Kaizl, *Z mého života*, 3 vols. (ed.) Zdeněk V. Tobolka (Prague: J. Vilímek, 1909–14) II, pp. 218–19.

6   Křížek, *T. G. Masaryk a česká politika*, pp. 83–92. Kaizl, *Z mého života*, II, 391–625 *passim*. This same ground is recently covered in Jaroslav Opat, *T. G. Masaryk v Čechách v letech osmdesátých (1882–1891)* (Prague: Typescript, 1985) pp. 248–59.

7   Kramář, *Paměti*, p. 85. Kramář's father, an active Young Czech, frowned on his son's association with Realism and favoured his direct entry into the Young Czech party.

8   Ibid., p. 94. Kramář adds, 'even though he shattered more than was necessary'.

9   T. G. Masaryk, *Slovanské studie Slavjanofilství Ivana Vasil. Kiřejevského* (Prague: Bursík a Kohout, 1889; 2nd ed. 1893). T. G. Masaryk, K. Kramář, D. P. Makovický, Zd. Nejedlý a K. Velemínský, *Československé vzpomínky na Jasnou Poljanu* (Prague: B. Kočí, 1925) pp. 5–24. Karel Kramář, 'Dojmy z Ruska', *Čas*, vol. V (1891) pp. 5–6, 22–4, 52–5, 69–72, 84–5.

10   Kramář, *Paměti*, p. 83.

11   Ibid., p. 84. Kramář's denial of Masaryk's intellectual influence is belied by his response to Masaryk in many of his publications in later life. I am indebted to Hans Lemberg for citing convincing examples of this from their relationship. In the memoirs cited here, written at the end of his life, Kramář bitterly denigrates Masaryk's political acumen; but see also the testimony of Josef Fořt, Young Czech radical and later Austrian Minister of Commerce, no great admirer of Kramář, in characterizing Masaryk: 'An unusually gifted, almost a genius of a philosopher, but on the subject of politics he cannot possibly be taken seriously. His vagueness, his aimless, haphazardly connected opinions aroused and strengthened in me the impression that he is not suitable for politics, especially the Czech brand.' *Proces dra Kramáře a jeho přátel*, Zdeněk V. Tobolka (ed.) 5 vols. (Prague: the editor, 1918–20), III/i, p. 201.

12   T. G. Masaryk, 'List redaktora Athenaea ... [J. Gebauerovi]', *Athenaeum*, vol. III (1885–86) no. 5, pp. 164–68.

13   Theodor Syllaba, *Jan Gebauer* (Prague: Melantrich, 1986) pp. 64–77, the most recent treatment of the philological aspects, credits Gebauer with the most constructive role in the controversy. On Masaryk's probable motives for entering the controversy, see Simon Rosengard

Green, *Thomas Garrigue Masaryk: Educator of a Nation*, Ph D dissertation, University of California at Berkeley, 1976, pp. 373–5. On the historical significance of the Manuscripts dispute, see Richard Georg Plaschka, 'Um Könighofer Handschrift und Funktion der Geschichte', *Österreichische Osthefte*, 27 (1985) pp. 419–38; also Milan Otáhal, 'The Manuscript Controversy in the Czech National Revival', *Cross Currents*, 5 (1986) 247–77; and J. Opat, *T. G. Masaryk v Čechach v letech osmdesátých*, pp. 154–216.

14   This circumstance enabled him to claim that he had underestimated the intensity of the storm created by Masaryk's notorious editorial article in the *Athenaeum*; Kramář, *Paměti*, pp. 92–3. Kramář implies that had he known all the facts, he might not have joined with Masaryk in political Realism two years later. Here also see Albín Bráf, 'Mé styky s T. G. Masarykem', *Paměti*, 5 vols., ed. Josef Gruber (Prague: Vesmír, 1922–24), I, pp. 17–18.

15   Kramář, *Paměti*, p. 80. Idem, 'Mladá generace', *Čas*, vol. VI (1892) p. 578.

16   Kramář to Kaizl, 18 Nov. 1888, in Kaizl, *Z mého života*, II, p. 481n. *Čas* was aggravating the controversy with barbs against Masaryk's critics.

17   The announcement of the merger in *Národní listy*, 20 Dec. 1890, stipulated that the Manuscript question would henceforth be restricted to purely scholarly discussions in which 'all sides will enjoy full freedom of enquiry and thought'; Vaníček, 'V počátcích realismu', *Masarykův sborník*, III, p. 328.

18   Masaryk's last published mention of the controversy, save in passing, was 'Spor rukopisný', *Naše doba*, vol. III (1895–96) no. 10, pp. 957–8.

19   T. G. Masaryk, *Nynější krise a desorganisace mladočeské strany* (Prague: E. Beaufort, 1903) p. 34. Julius Grégr was titular head of the Young Czech Party and major owner of *Národní listy*. In 1886 he permitted scurrilous articles attacking Masaryk and his colleagues to appear in the newspaper, and he wrote a pamphlet in the same vein.

20   T. G. Masaryk, *Politická situace. Poznámky ku poznámkám* (Prague: Čas, 1906) pp. 9, 13, 26. These comments, delivered by Masaryk in rebuttal to Kramář's earlier assertion that Masaryk was bitter at the party's handling of the dispute, do indeed reveal his bitterness. Kramář, *Poznámky k české politice* (Prague: Bursík a Kohout, 1906) p. 9, originally raised the issue.

21   Masaryk was elected to the Reichsrat in March 1891, and to the Bohemian Diet in December 1891; Kramář to the Reichsrat also in 1891, to the Diet in 1894. Masaryk was named to the Young Czech party's executive committee upon its merger with the Realists and Kaizl to its board of trustees. Kramář, who was chosen for no party position, felt slighted by these arrangements; Kramář, *Paměti*, p. 262.

22   The Realists' 'draft programme' for Empire reform appears in *Čas*, vol. IV (1890) no. 44, pp. 689–94. Kramář's contribution to Realist political thought is commended in Eva Schmidt-Hartmann, *Thomas G. Masaryk's Realism. Origins of a Political Concept* (Munich: Oldenbourg, 1984) pp. 101–5. For Masaryk's activities in Moravia, see Jiří Malíř, 'Poměr moravské lidové a národní strany svobodomyslné

(mladočeské)', *Časopis Matice moravské*, 104 (1985) no. 1–2, pp. 55–78. Also, *idem*, *Vývoj liberálního proudu české politiky na Moravě: Lidová strana na Moravě do roku 1909* (Brno: Univ. J. E. Purkyně, 1985) pp. 178–81 *passim*.

23   Letter of Masaryk to Kramář, 19 June 1889 in Kramář, *Paměti*, p. 144. On Masaryk's 'aversion to politics', see Roman Szporluk, *The Political Thought of Thomas G. Masaryk* (Boulder, CO: East European Monographs, 1981) p. 49. Szporluk notes (p. 104) 'Masaryk's relative lack of concern for and appreciation of politics in general'. On Masaryk's search for a political affiliation see Otakar Odložilík, 'Enter Masaryk: A Prelude to his Political Career', *Journal of Central European Affairs*, 10 (1950) no. 1, pp. 21–36.

24   Letter of Masaryk to Kramář, 8 Aug. 1889 in Kramář, *Paměti*, p. 151.

25   Ibid., 16 May 1890, p. 212.

26   Ibid., 6 July 1890, pp. 215–16.

27   Szporluk, *The Political Thought of Thomas G. Masaryk*, pp. 64–79; Schmidt-Hartmann, *Thomas G. Masaryk's Realism*, pp. 75–86.

28   Quoted in Draga B. Shillinglaw (ed.), *The Lectures of Professor T. G. Masaryk at the University of Chicago, Summer 1902* (Lewisburg, PA: Bucknell University Press, 1978) p. 113.

29   Stanley B. Winters, 'Jan Otto, T. G. Masaryk, and the Czech National Encyclopedia', *Jahrbücher für Geschichte Osteuropas*, 31 (1983) no. 4, pp. 516–42.

30   Kramář, *Paměti*, p. 337. Kramář recalls that Masaryk had expressed eagerness to become a cabinet minister in order to represent the Czechs in government and overcome Young Czech isolation from official circles. See also Emil Ludwig, *Defender of Democracy. Masaryk Speaks* (London: Ivor Nicholson and Watson, 1936) p. 91.

31   Green, *Thomas G. Masaryk: Educator of a Nation*, p. 403.

32   For appraisals of Kramář's political activities see E. Denis et al., *Dr. Karel Kramář k šedesátým narozeninám* (Prague: Ženský svět, 1920); Kamil Krofta, *Politické postava Karla Kramáře* (Prague: Chytil, 1930), a cogent evaluation; V. Škarda et al., *Karel Kramář k padesátým narozeninám* (Prague: Český čtenář, 1910); Stanley B. Winters, *Karel Kramář's Early Political Career*, Ph D dissertation Rutgers University, 1966, pp. 581–93.

33   Kramář, *Paměti*, p. 65.

34   Letter of Švabinský to Kramář, 26 Dec. 1910, ANM Kramář Papers, 2–3, 503–4. Arne Novák, commenting on Švabinský's striking full-length portrait of Kramář, remarked 'the elegant tribune of the old school . . . aware equally of himself and the effects of his conduct . . . the clever debater . . . with unending readiness to pursue action and the weak point of his opponent'; see Max Švabinský, *Hlavy známé i neznámé. Padesát portretů se studií Arna Nováka* (Prague: Štenc, 1928) p. 27.

35   Masaryk, *Politická situace*, pp. 11–12.

36   Ibid., p. 27.

37   Masaryk's speeches in this era covered 250 pages in the record and each averaged about forty-five minutes; Kramář's filled 108 pages and each averaged twenty minutes. On Masaryk's career in the Reichsrat

see Schmidt-Hartmann, *Thomas G. Masaryk's Realism*, pp. 105–16; also Jiří Kovtun, *Slovo má poslanec Masaryk* (Munich: Jadrný, 1985), which reproduces translated excerpts from Masaryk's speeches with a sketch of his career. On Kramář's parliamentary activities: Winters, *Karel Kramář's Early Political Career*, pp. 233–354. On the overall Czech efforts in parliament see Bruce M. Garver, *The Young Czech Party 1874–1901 and the Emergence of a Multi-Party System* (New Haven, CT: Yale University Press, 1978) pp. 154–9.

38 Josef Penížek, *Česká aktivita v letech 1878–1918*, 2 vols. (Prague: Český čtenář, 1929–32) II, pp. 117–24, mentions Kramář's outstanding speaking ability. Also Ernst Birke and Kurt Oberdorffer, *Das böhmische Staatsrecht in den deutsch-tschechischen Auseinandersetzungen des 19. und 20. Jahrhunderts* (Marburg/Lahn: Elwert, 1960) p. 106; and Otto Urban, *Česká společnost 1848–1918* (Prague: Svoboda, 1982) p. 481. Although Kramář never held a government position, his influence within the higher bureaucracy was considerable; see Hermann Münch, *Böhmische Tragödie. Das Schicksal Mitteleuropas im Lichte der tschechischen Frage* (Brunswick: Westermann, 1949) pp. 577–9.

39 In the great tradition of Czech political journalism, three-quarters of the Czech parliamentary deputies wrote for newspapers; see Owen V. Johnson, 'Unbridled Freedom: The Czech Press and Politics, 1918–1938', *Journalism History*, 13 (Winter, 1986) no. 3–4, p. 100.

40 Garver, *The Young Czech Party*, pp. 161–2. The Strakonice speech appears in *Čas*, vol. V (1891) no. 39, pp. 622–24. For analyses of it, consult Schmidt-Hartmann, *Thomas G. Masaryk's Realism*, pp. 109–11; and Miloslav Trapl, *Masarykův program* (Brno: Zář, 1948) pp. 169–70.

41 Masaryk disliked Eim, whom he termed an intriguer, 'a neurotic, a sceptic', as much as he ever hated anyone; Masaryk, *Politická situace*, p. 16; also Karel Čapek, *Hovory s T. G. Masarykem*, Complete Edition (Prague: Fr. Borový a Čin, 1937) p. 107. See the favourable appraisal of Eim in Garver, *The Young Czech Party*, pp. 106–7. Eim, a Young Czech parliamentary deputy, leaked confidential decisions of the deputies' club to *Národní listy*, to the dismay of the Realists.

42 In Prague, according to Masaryk, 'a quarrel became a heresy'; letter of Masaryk to Kramář, 8 Aug. 1893, ANM Kramář Papers, 2–3 6374; also Kramář, *Paměti*, p. 342.

43 'Herben's underground work', Kramář complained in his *Paměti*, pp. 374, 376–7. See also letter of Kramář to Kaizl, 20 Oct. 1892, in Kaizl, *Z mého života*, III/i, p. 201n. Kramář was offended that *Čas* featured the speeches of Masaryk and Kaizl over his. Herben describes *Čas*'s sectarian, moralistic tone in his *Kniha vzpomínek* (Prague: Družstevní práce, 1935) pp. 447–50. See also Szporluk, *The Political Thought of Thomas G. Masaryk*, p. 95.

44 Letter of Masaryk to Kramář, 28 Aug. 1892, in Kramář, *Paměti*, p. 343.

45 Masaryk's break with the Young Czechs is often depicted in the older literature as a far-sighted move, but this simplifies the circumstances and considers the event only retrospectively. The memoirs of Kaizl, *Z*

mého života, III/i, pp. 10–309 *passim* are essential but insufficient. Kramář, *Paměti*, pp. 264–387, is important but coloured by the disappointments of his later years. In English the most comprehensive account, is Winters, *Karel Kramář's Early Political Career*, pp. 355–96.

46　The committee stated that Masaryk's 'behaviour and its consequences damaged the prestige and welfare of the party'; Winters, ibid., pp. 380–1. For the circumstances in the Šromota affair see also the citations above in n. 45. Zdeněk V. Tobolka, who personally knew many of the main personalities, assigns the basic responsibility for Masaryk's isolation in the party to 'the tactlessness and vehemence of Professor Masaryk, who, despite his lofty spiritual qualities, did not know how to behave in such a way as to calm distrust towards his person'; see his *Politické dějiny československého národa od 1848 až do dnešní doby*, 4 vols. (Prague: Československý kompas, 1932–37) III/i, p. 62.

47　Letter of Masaryk to Kramář, 15 June 1921, ANK Kramář Papers, 2–3 6466, where Masaryk writes, 'We became estranged because you were with the Young Czechs and for them and I was against them.' Masaryk's attacks on the Young Czech party exceeded in vitriol any he directed against other Czech or German parties. On the promise made to Masaryk about imminent party reforms, see his letter to Kramář, 1 Aug. 1893, ibid., 2–3 6371–74.

48　During these negotiations Masaryk wrote to a constituent, 'I know also that it is not [between] me and the party but me and Dr. Grégr.' Letter of Masaryk to Chlum, n. d. (probably 23 or 24 Dec. 1893), in *Masarykovy listy z r. 1893* (Jihlava: Chlum, 1930) p. 25. Also letters of Masaryk to Engel, 20 and 23 Dec. 1893, Literární archiv Památník národního písemnictví (hereafter LAPNP), Engel Papers; and telegram of Eim to Engel, 28 Dec. 1893, ibid. Masaryk might not have wanted to challenge this decision because he preferred to run in an uncontested election with party endorsement.

49　Masaryk's exit from the Young Czech party is usually dated from the surrender of his mandates, but this is incorrect; for example, see Paul Selver, *Masaryk* (London: Michael Joseph, 1940) p. 161; also Urban, *Česká společnost 1848–1918*, p. 429. It is probable that Masaryk remained a party member for some years after 1893, perhaps as late as 1899. Vladimír Sís, *Karel Kramář 1860–1930: Život a dílo, Skizza* (Prague: 'Základ Dra Karla Kramáře a Dra Aloise Rašína', 1930) p. 85, says the party congress in Nymburk in 1894 settled the question of Masaryk's 'secession', but this probably applied only to his official party positions. As late as 1896, Masaryk was identifying with the party, for he wrote to Kramář on 8 March 1896, 'You are the only one who binds me to the party. If you were not there, I would write more frequently and appear more frequently in a different way'; ANM Kramář Papers, 2–3 6396–99. Jan Herben, *T. G. Masaryk*, 4th ed. (Prague: Sfinx – B. Janda, 1938) p. 54, states that Masaryk remained a Young Czech until 1899; so does Butter, 'Masaryk novinář', *Masarykův sborník*, VI, p. 398.

50　Letter to Kramář, 29 Jan. 1889 in Kramář, *Paměti*, p. 120.

51　When Masaryk's former publisher and employer Jan Otto learned in

1891 that Masaryk had been endorsed as a Young Czech candidate for parliament, he predicted: 'Either he'll lead them or break them up'; see Bráf, *Život a dílo*, I, pp. 25–6.

52 On this mission see Green, *Thomas G. Masaryk: Educator of a Nation*, pp. xxv–xxvi, 316–17.

53 Masaryk hoped that income from *Naše doba* would reduce his need for outside lecturing. In refusing to join *Naše doba* Kramář proved more prescient than Kaizl, who agreed to collaborate but later withdrew along with the historian Jaroslav Goll and other Realists. Kaizl, *Z mého života*, III/i, pp. 280n., 292, 326–7. The *Athenaeum* had folded in 1892.

54 For one thing, Masaryk addressed Kramář as 'Dítě' (child), not only in letters but also in public in the presence of other deputies (Kramář, *Paměti*, pp. 272–3). For another, Masaryk was praised mistakenly for a series of articles on Realist policy which Kramář wrote using pseudonymous initials; Masaryk never disclaimed authorship and Kramář kept silent (*Proces Dra Kramáře a jeho přátel*, II, p. 239. Also, Urban, *Česká společnost 1848–1918*, p. 430.

55 'He has to correct every manuscript, even superfluously, he has to find fault in everything in a professorial manner'; letter of Kramář to Kaizl, 21 June 1893 in Kaizl, *Z mého života*, III/1, p. 255n. On Masaryk's 'arrogance' see Green, *Thomas G. Masaryk: Educator of a Nation*, p. xiii. On his 'self-righteousness and combativeness' see Václav Černý, 'The Essence of Masaryk's Personality and What TGM Means to Us Today' in Milič Čapek and Karel Hrubý (eds) *T. G. Masaryk in Perspective. Comments and Criticism* (New York: SVU Press, 1981) p. 109.

56 Letter of Kramář to Eim, 7 Nov. 1893, LAPNP Eim Papers; yet earlier in that year, Eim had accused Kramář of 'unjust attacks' and 'spreading stupid gossip' about him; letter of Eim to Engel, 17 Jan. 1893, ibid.

57 Letter of Kramář to Eim, 26 Dec. 1896, ibid.

58 Ibid., 2 Feb. 1894. Masaryk was then being savagely attacked in Young Czech publications for his open criticism of the party.

59 Ibid., n.d. (probably Jan. 1897). Eim died one month later.

60 Letter of Masaryk to Kramář, 3 March 1896, ANM Kramář Papers 2–3 6397.

61 Ibid., 6398–9. Hearing about his impending promotion, Masaryk wrote: 'I must consult with you and learn about the situation from you.' On the same topic, see also ibid., 26 April 1898, ANM 2–3 6402–03. On Kramář's role as intermediary, see Václav Král, *Zdeněk Nejedlý a Gollova škola* (Prague: Univerzita Karlova, 1986) p. 120.

62 Letter of Masaryk to Kramář, 14 Dec. 1897, ANM Kramář Papers, 2–3 6400.

63 Ibid., 25 Sept. 1900, ANM 2–3 6406. On Kramář's marriage, see Karel Hermann and Zdeněk Sládek, *Slovanská politika Karla Kramáře* (Prague: Academia, 1971) pp. 12, 44. Kramář recognised the transient nature of Masaryk's sentimentality; *Paměti*, p. 263.

64 *Čas*, 4 (1890) no. 44, p. 693.

65 Jan Havránek, *Boj za všeobecné přímé a rovné hlasovací právo roku 1893* (Prague: Academia, 1964) pp. 21, 35. Urban, *Česká společnost*

1848–1918, pp. 420–1, 450–2.

66   Szporluk, *The Political Thought of Thomas G. Masaryk*, pp. 75–6, but also p. 149.

67   Speech of 20 March 1893, reprinted in part in Kovtun, *Slovo má poslanec Masaryk*, esp. pp. 89–90. Karen J. Freeze, *The Young Progressives: The Czech Student Movement 1887–1897*, Ph D dissertation Columbia University, 1974, pp. 109.

68   T. G. Masaryk, *Karel Havlíček. Snahy a tužby politického probuzení*, 3rd. ed. (Prague: Jan Laichter, 1920) pp. 392–9. As late as 1913, in his *Russland und Europa*, Masaryk expressed extreme distaste for violence and revolution; Szporluk, *The Political Thought of Thomas G. Masaryk*, pp. 129–30.

69   Garver, *The Young Czech Party 1874–1901*, p. 304. Upon re-entering the Reichsrat on 20 June 1907, Masaryk repeated this demand for Diet reform.

70   Oldřiška Kodedová, 'Boj pražského dělnictva za všeobecné hlasovací právo v letech 1905–1907', *Příspěvky k dějinám KSČ*, 12 (Oct. 1960) p. 95.

71   S. [Masaryk], 'Všeobecné právo hlasovací a česká demokracie', *Naše doba*, vol. XIII (1906) p. 163. Masaryk denied that the winning of universal suffrage was the result of popular mass movements but rather of the Emperor's wishes, according to Bohuslav Šantrůček, *Masaryk a Klofáč. Srovnávací studie* (Prague: Melantrich, 1938) p. 328.

72   Ibid., p. 357.

73   Letter of Kramář to Eim, 14 Aug. 1894, LAPNP Eim Papers.

74   Kramář's major speeches in parliament on suffrage reform appear in *Stenographische Protokolle über die Sitzungen des Hauses der Abgeordneten des österreichischen Reichrathes* as follows: XI Session, 17 Jan. 1893, p. 8605; 6 April 1894, p. 12, 841; 14 Dec. 1894, p. 16, 345; 21 April 1896, pp. 24, 250–3. On his attitude toward diet reform, see the letter of Count Thun to the premier Count Stürgkh, 8 Sept. 1913, cited in F. B. M. Fowkes, *The Policy of the Habsburg Monarchy towards the Bohemian Question 1913–1918*, Ph D dissertation University of London, 1967, p. 86.

75   Malíř, *Vývoj liberálního proudu české politiky na Moravě*, p. 131.

76   Letter of Kramář to Škarda, 23 July 1906, LAPNP Škarda Papers. Also William Alexander Jenks, The Austrian Electoral Reform of 1907 (New York: Columbia University Press, 1950), pp. 38, 163, 170. Kamil Krofta had great praise for Kramář's efforts towards suffrage reform; see B. Němec, A. Pimper and V. Holeček, (eds), *Sborník dra Karla Kramáře*, p. 254.

77   *Stenographische Protokolle*, XVII Session, 30 Nov. 1905, pp. 32, 469–70. Also Urban, *Česká společnost 1848–1918*, pp. 523–4.

78   K. Kramář, 'Ruské problémy (politické reformy)', *Nová česká revue*, vol. II (1905) no. 4, p. 253.

79   Č. P. [Masaryk], 'Kronštadtské slavnosti', *Čas*, vol. V (1 Aug. 1891) no. 31, pp. 489–91.

80   'Řeč deleg. prof. dr. T. G. Masaryk proslovena o bosenské správě a okupační politice . . .' *Národní listy*, 37, no. 291, 21 Oct. 1892. Excerpts are in Kovtun, *Slovo má poslanec Masaryk*, pp. 54–61.

81 Oskar Butter, 'Zahraniční politika T. G. Masaryka,' *Zahraniční politika*, (1939) no. 4, pp. 124–42. Also his speech on conditions in Bosnia and Herzegovina in parliament, 16 June 1893, excerpted in Kovtun, *Slovo má poslanec Masaryk*, pp. 104–10.

82 *Stenographische Protokolle*, XI Session, 18 Nov. 1892, pp. 7, 859.

83 L. E. [Kramář], 'Situace', *Čas*, vol. III (10 Aug. 1889) no. 33, pp. 537–40.

84 Kramář's statements drew European attention; see for example his 'Europe and the Bohemian Question', *National Review*, 40 (Oct. 1902) no. 236, pp. 183–205; 'L'Avenir de l'Autriche', *Revue de Paris*, vol. I, pt. 1 (1 Feb. 1899) no. 3, pp. 577–600; also, Pavla Horská, 'Česká otázka v Rakousko-Uhersku 1897–1914 ve světle zpráv francouzských zastupitelských úřadů', *Československý časopis historický*, 15 (1967) no. 3, pp. 449–60.

85 'Europe and the Bohemian Question', p. 204. Kramář's imagery resembles that used by Old Czech leader F. L. Rieger in a notable speech of 26 June 1880 in the Bohemian Diet.

86 Masaryk's view is in his Delegations' speech, 22 Feb. 1911, cited in Jurij Křížek, 'Česká buržoasní politika a "česká otázka" v letech 1900–1914', *Československý časopis historický*, 6 (1958) no. 4, p. 646n. The excerpts in Kovtun, *Slovo má poslanec Masaryk*, pp. 179–87, do not include this point. Also Karel Herman, 'Novoslovanství a česká buržoasie', in Václav Čechan (eds), *Kapitoly z dějin vzájemných vztahů národů ČSR a SSSR*, 2 vols. (Prague: NČSAV, 1958–60) I, esp. 304–5.

87 Testimony of Count Thun, *Proces dra Kramáře a jeho přátel*, III/ii, p. 126. Frank E. Norgate, *The Internal Policies of the Stürgkh Government November 1911–March 1914: A Study in a Holding Action*, Ph D dissertation, New York University, 1978, pp. 225–30, 273–4.

88 On Kramář's Slavonic feelings see Kramář, *Paměti*, pp. 235–6; idem, 'Řeč posl. dra Kramáře při odhalení pomníku F. Palackého dne 1. července 1912 o 11. hod. dopl.', ANM Kramář Papers (typescript), p. 12; Stanley B. Winters, 'Austroslavism, Panslavism, and Russophilism in Czech Political Thought, 1870–1900', in Stanley B. Winters and Joseph Held (eds), *Intellectual and Social Developments in the Habsburg Empire* (Boulder, CO: East European Quarterly, 1975), esp. pp. 183–7.

89 He succeeded the Young Czech Josef Herold, who died in April 1908.

90 Herman, 'Novoslovanství a česká buržoasie', pp. 278–9. Paul Vyšný, *Neo-Slavism and the Czechs 1898–1914* (Cambridge University Press, 1977) p. 95. Křížek, 'Česká buržoasní politika a "česká otázka"', p. 645, n. 96.

91 Dmitrij Vergun, 'Setkání prof. T. G. Masaryka s ruskými neoslavisty', in M. G. Michějěv et al. (eds) *Zahraniční Rusové Československu 1918–1928* (Prague: n.p., 1928) pp. 137–44.

92 See, for example, Milada Paulová, *Dějiny Maffie. Odboj Čechů a Jihoslovanů za světové války 1914–1918*, 2 vols. (Prague: Unie, 1937) I, pp. 41–2; Vyšný, *Neo-Slavism and the Czechs 1898–1914*, p. 248. Cf. Garver, *The Young Czech Party 1874–1901*, p. 269. On the position of the Progressive Party, see *Program české strany pokrokové. Schválen třetím valným sjezdem strany konaným v Praze 6. a 7. ledna 1912* (Prague: Tisková komise ČSP, 1912) pp. 13–14.

93   '... eine Politik *ad Germaniae gloriam* zu machen'; see *Stenographi-sche Protokolle*, XX Session, 24 Nov. 1909.

94   Jan Havránek, 'Der tschechische Pazifismus und Antimilitarismus am Vorabend der Ersten Weltkrieges', in Gernot Heiss and Heinrich Lutz (eds), *Friedensbewegungen: Bedingungen und Wirkungen* (Vienna: Verlag für Geschichte und Politik, 1984) pp. 114–35. On Klofáč, see the sketch in Garver, *The Young Czech Party 1874–1901*, pp. 295–8.

95   Vyšný, *Neo-Slavism and the Czechs 1898–1914*, p. 132.

96   Tobolka, *Politické dějiny československého národa*, III/ii, p. 588.

97   Parliament was recalled on 5 March and again dissolved on 16 March 1914.

98   *Den* was preceded by *Nová politika*, financed by Kramář in 1906. The Kramář wing of the Young Czech Party did not gain ownership of *Národní listy* until 1910, when the newspaper was purchased from the Grégr heirs by the Pražská akciová tiskárna, a stock corporation in which Kramář held 1/20 of the shares. See *Proces dra Kramáře a jeho přátel*, II, p. 111. Also *Národní listy 1861–1941. Jubilejní sborník* (Prague: Pražská akciová tiskárna, 1941) pp. 71, 93–7.

99   *Národní listy*, 54, no. 61, 4 March 1914.

100 The complicated affair and its sensational charges and countercharges may be followed in pamphlets printed by the political parties and their newspapers in 1914: *Zločin a odsouzení dra Švihy*; *Dr. Karel Šviha národně sociální zrádce národa. Dokumenty a úvahy*; *Švihova zrada a její význam pro český politický život*; *C. k. policejní špicl dr. Karel Šviha, předseda klubu poslanců národně sociálních na radě říšské*; *Zrádce dr. Karel Šviha před porotou: Stenografický protokol*. Secondary literature is sparse: Paulová, *Dějiny Maffie*, I, pp. 70–6; Herben, *T. G. Masaryk*, pp. 124–5; Josef Linek, 'Podstata Švihovy aféry', *Novinářský sborník*, 9 (1964) pp. 431–6; Šantrůček, *Masaryk a Klofáč*, pp. 401–9; and more recently the concise summary, Jan Galandauer, 'Bohumír Šmeral a Švihova aféra', *Sborník k dějinám 19. a 20. století ČSAV*, 6 (1979) pp. 155–69, and reprinted in *idem*, *Bohumír Šmeral 1880–1914* (Prague: Svoboda, 1981) pp. 258–66.

101 Faced with overwhelming evidence of his contacts with the police, Šviha resigned his deputy's mandate at his party's request on 12 March 1914. A later revelation, the validity of which is not proven, is that Šviha sent his reports directly to Archduke Franz Ferdinand but was paid by the Prague police for his services; also that he possibly entered into his collaboration through the intermediaryship of no less a person than Klofáč himself.

102 Šantrůček, *Masaryk a Klofáč*, p. 408.

103 'The plain fact that Šviha maintained relations with officials of the state police, supplied them with information, and received payment is indisputable'; Galandauer, *Bohumír Šmeral 1880–1914*, p. 262. Masaryk refers briefly to the affair in his *Světová revoluce. Za války a ve válce 1914–1918* (Prague: Čin a Orbis, 1928) p. 12. This passage is omitted from the English version, *The Making of a State*. See also his mention in Čapek, *Hovory s T. G. Masarykem*, p. 125.

104 Letter of Pekař to Goll, 22 May 1914, cited in Král, *Zdeněk Nejedlý a*

Gollova škola, p. 169. See also Šantrůček, *Masaryk a Klofáč*, p. 408, for other reactions.
105 Král, *Zdeněk Nejedlý a Gollova škola*, pp. 168–9.
106 *Zločin a odsouzení dra Švihy*, pp. 68–9.
107 'Náš postup v aféře Švihově', *Čas*, 28, no. 170, 20 June 1914; no. 172, 22 June 1914.
108 On testimonials to Kramář's character see *Proces dra Kramáře a jeho přátel*, III/i, pp. 3, 136, 139, 169, 218,; III/ii, pp. 71, 73.
109 Ibid., II, p. 142. Even Zdeněk Nejedlý, in his caustic attack on Kramář after Kramář's dismissal as prime minister by Masaryk on 7 July 1919 conceded, 'His political purity is untouchable'; Zdeněk Nejedlý, *Dr. Kramář. Rozbor politického zjevu* (Prague: Fr. Borový, 1920) p. 60.
110 *Proces dra Kramář a jeho přátel*, II, p. 238.
111 Ibid, p. 142; III/i, p. 46; IV/ii, p. 6. Edvard Beneš implies that Kramář was stubborn in refusing to meet before Masaryk left for Western Europe. As quoted by Beneš (twenty years later), Masaryk called Kramář's attitude, 'Nonsense. Now we have more important things to take care of.' Edvard Beneš, *Světová válka a naše revoluce*, 3 vols. (Prague: Čin and Orbis, 1935) I, pp. 35–6. This passage is omitted from the English version, *My War Memoirs* (London: Allen & Unwin, 1928).
112 Letter from Masaryk to Machar, n.d., *Proces dra Kramáře a jeho přátel*, III/ii, p. 112.
113 Masaryk, *Světová revoluce*, p. 10. This passage is not in the English edition. A physician who testified at Kramář's treason trial, Eduard Šubrt (a member of the Young Czech party), said that Masaryk in 1914 was 'from the medical standpoint a man mentally overworked, weakened, and burned out'; *Proces dra Kramáře a jeho přátel*, III/i, pp. 111–12. Masaryk told Karel Čapek that he had long anticipated something like the war, that 'something was in the air'; Čapek, *Hovory s T. G. Masarykem*, p. 141.
114 Reliable guides to the situation in the Czech camp when the war broke out are Karel Pichlík, *Zahraniční odboj 1914–1918 bez legend* (Prague: Svoboda, 1968) pp. 11–42; and Z. A. B. Zeman, *The Break-up of the Habsburg Empire 1914–1918: A Study in National and Social Revolution* (London: Oxford University Press, 1961), especially pp. 14–23, 73–85.
115 Kramář's editorial entitled 'Světová válka' appeared in *Národní listy*, 54, no. 211, 4 Aug. 1914. Masaryk's commentary was published first in *Čas* and then supplemented with statistics and printed as 'Válka', *Naše doba*, vol. XXI, no. 11 (20 Aug. 1914) pp. 961–79. I wish to thank Antonie van den Beld for providing me with a copy of Masaryk's article.
116 Letter of Masaryk to Kramář, 15 June 1921, ANM Kramář Papers, 2–3 6465–66.
117 A basically positive estimate of the catalytic role played by Masaryk's Progressive (Realist) party in the more fluid political-party constellation in Moravia, especially from 1906 onwards, is offered in two important articles by Jiří Malíř: 'Počátky politického realismu na

Moravé', *Časopis Matice moravské*, 106, no. 1–2 (1987) pp. 73–93; *idem*, 'Působení politického realismu na Moravě v letech 1906–1914', ibid., no. 3–4, pp. 202–27.

118   Klíma, 'Hrst vzpomínek na politiku mezi dvěma válkami', pp. 297–8.

8 The Slovakophile Relationship of T. G. Masaryk and Karel Kálal prior to 1914

Thomas D. Marzik

When World War I broke out in 1914, few contemporary political observers could have predicted that by the war's end the Czechs of Austria and the Slovaks of Hungary would find themselves in an independent Czechoslovak state. Yet in 1914 two Czechs – a school-teacher publicist and a professor-politician – did foresee the possibility of such an eventuality. Shortly after mobilisation was declared, Karel Kálal told his wife that an independent Czech state with Slovakia would result from the war, and in October in the editorial offices of the Prague newspaper *Čas* he outlined the southern border of Slovakia, including Bratislava as the capital.[1] Also in October, T. G. Masaryk confided to Robert W. Seton-Watson in Rotterdam his plan to restore the historical Bohemian Kingdom, to which would be added the Slovak districts of Hungary.[2]

At that time, the speculations of these two Czechs might have seemed preposterous; but both men had prior to 1914 contributed towards bringing the Czechs and Slovaks closer together and preparing a basis for the future Czechoslovak state. Masaryk was the only major Czech public figure who had taken a serious interest in the Slovaks and had influenced Slovak political life; Kálal on the other hand was the single most active Czech propagator of Czech-Slovak cooperation and unity. Their work on behalf of the Slovaks led Masaryk and Kálal at the beginning of the century to a brief but significant collaboration, which has not yet been adequately examined.

Masaryk's relations with Slovakia before 1914 are fairly well known.[3] The crucial factor in that relationship was Masaryk's ethnic background: his father was a Hungarian Slovak,[4] and Masaryk had spent his childhood in Moravian Slovakia, the transitional zone between the Czechs of Moravia and the Slovaks of Hungary. As a result of this, Masaryk could never forget the Slovaks. Beginning in 1888, he made a practice of taking his summer vacations with his family in Bystrička, a village near Turčiansky Svätý Martin in north central Slovakia, where he made contact with Slovak cultural and political leaders and acquainted himself with Slovak conditions firsthand.

By the end of the 1880s, Masaryk had come to realise that the Slovaks might be helpful to the Czechs in the struggle against Austro-Hungarian Dualism. He explored the possible importance of the Slovaks with his Young Czech colleagues,[5] continued to follow developments in Slovakia, and later used *Naše doba* to publish information on the Slovaks. Opposing the conservative, Russophile character of the Slovak national leadership, based in Turčiansky Svätý Martin, Masaryk sought out potential allies among Slovak students in Prague who had been influenced by his teaching and his writings on Czech national problems, especially *Česká otázka* (1895).

A group of Slovak students, led by Vavro Šrobár, eventually responded to Masaryk's initiatives. In 1898 they founded an oppositional journal, *Hlas*, which gave its name – 'Hlasist' – to the movement in Slovakia which arose from it. Masaryk provided the journal's basic programme,[6] which was in large part the application of the methods and goals of his Realism to the Slovak situation.[7] Although the Hlasist movement was not solely responsible for the rejuvenation of the relatively stagnant Slovak political life at the end of the nineteenth century,[8] it did help to create an alternative to the Martin leadership. Furthermore, the Hlasists and their followers constituted a core of Czechophile Slovak intellectuals who were to cooperate with Masaryk and other Czechs in building the Czechoslovak state once it was founded.[9]

Unlike Masaryk, whose interest in the Slovaks was a subsidiary and occasional concern, Karel Kálal (1860–1930) saw his 'life mission' in serving the cause of Czech-Slovak reciprocity.[10] Kálal's long Slovakophile career spanned a critical period in the modern history of Czech-Slovak relations,[11] from the increase of Czech interest in the Slovaks in the late 1880s and early 1890s through the establishment of Czechoslovakia.[12] During this time probably no Czech learned more about the Slovaks, wrote more about them,[13] or worked harder for closer relations between them and the Czechs than Kálal.

Born in Rakov u Bernatic in southern Bohemia on 9 January 1860, Kálal was by profession a schoolteacher. In 1885 he became an instructor at a boy's middle school in Frenštát pod Radhoštem in eastern Moravia, a post at which he remained until 1904. From then until 1914 he served as the director of girls' commercial academies, first in Velké Meziříčí (1904–06) and then in Písek (1906–14). At the outbreak of World War I, he opted for early retirement and moved to Prague. From October 1917 to October 1918, he delivered at least 120 lectures in Bohemia and Moravia calling upon the Czechs to liberate Slovakia. In December 1918 Kálal was appointed to the Czechoslovak Ministry of Education and National Culture, where he was assigned responsibility for all vocational schools in Slovakia. He moved to Banská Bystrica in 1920 to organise adult education programmes throughout Slovakia. In 1922 he became director of a commercial academy in Banská Bystrica, a position from which he was forced to resign at the end of that year because of ill health. Kálal then returned to Prague, where he lived until his death on 5 August 1930, at the age of seventy.

Kálal's interest in the Slovaks was first awakened by Slovak tinkers who came to his village during his youth.[14] In 1885 he visited Slovakia for the first time, and until 1907 he returned there every summer. His intimate friendship with a Protestant schoolteacher and publisher in Ružomberok, Karol Salva, became the basis of his future Slovakophile activities. Realising from his own experiences in Moravia the importance of primary education in spreading Czech national consciousness, he decided to promote Czech-Slovak reciprocity among Czech and Slovak schoolteachers. Kálal won Czech subscribers and contributors for Salva's foundering pedagogical journal, *Dom a škola*, and organised meetings between its Czech and Slovak collaborators. This work led eventually in 1896 to the establishment in Prague of the Českoslovanská jednota, which was to become the main Czech institutional vehicle for strengthening cultural and economic ties with the Slovaks in the prewar period.[15]

In 1897 Kálal began to wage a public relations campaign in the popular Czech periodical *Osvěta* designed to reach a wide Czech audience and inform it systematically about the Slovaks and Slovakia. Among the topics covered were: 'O československé vzájemnosti' (1897); 'O mad'arisaci Slovenska' (1898); 'O budoucnosti Slováků' (1899); and 'O působení židů na Slovensku' and 'Jak působí na Slovensku zemané' (1900). It was especially these articles in *Osvěta* which helped to establish Kálal as an acknowledged authority on Slovak affairs and as one of the most effective advocates of Czech-Slovak reciprocity in Czech public life by the turn of the century.[16]

It is not clear exactly when or how Kálal first came into contact with Masaryk. The earliest letter from Masaryk to Kálal preserved in the Kálal Papers in the Literární archív Památníku národního písemnictví at Staré Hrady dates from 27 January 1897 and does not indicate the origin of their relationship. Kálal had possibly initiated contact with Masaryk while he and Karol Salva were seeking contributions for their *Sborník československý. Od Šumavy k Tatrám*, a collection of articles by Czech and Slovak authors intended to demonstrate the existence of a common Czechoslovak literature.[17]

In the second half of the 1890s, Kálal's emphasis on the importance of Czech-Slovak cultural reciprocity reflected the views of the Realist organ *Čas*, the Czech weekly which carried the most information on Slovakia.[18] Occasionally *Čas* included references to Kálal's Slovakophile activities and writings.[19] Furthermore, Kálal's collaboration with Salva in *Dom a škola* and the newspaper *Slovenské listy*, which to a limited degree embodied elements of Hlasism *prior* to the founding of *Hlas*, his amicable personal relations with the Hlasist leaders Šrobár and Pavol Blaho, and the mutual public support expressed by Kálal and the Hlasists for one another, confirmed Kálal as a prominent Czech ally of the Masaryk-inspired Hlasist movement.[20]

In the light of Kálal's growing reputation as a Czech expert on the Slovaks, whose outlook was compatible with that of *Čas* and of his connections with the Hlasists, it is not altogether surprising that the paths of Masaryk and Kálal would cross. Their first meeting took place in Bystrička, Slovakia, in the summer of 1897, when Dušan Makovický, Kálal's good friend and a former student of Masaryk's, brought Kálal along on a visit to the vacationing Masaryk family.[21] Late in the summer of 1900, Kálal apparently wrote to Masaryk in Bystrička requesting another meeting. Masaryk informed him that he, too, wanted to speak with Kálal 'about Slovak affairs and some joint work' and suggested that they met in Těšín (Teschen) on 12 September 1900.[22] During their discussion, Masaryk asked Kálal to undertake two important projects: to write a pamphlet which would expose the Magyarisation of the Slovaks to the outside world, and also a critical appraisal of the Slovak leadership in Martin for *Naše doba*.

Kálal's previous study of Magyarisation in *Osvěta* provided the basis for the first project, but it took a long time before it was fully realised. Kálal produced a manuscript; Masaryk amended it and wrote a short addition,[23] had it translated into German (a language Kálal did not know), and arranged for its publication, with financial support from the Československá jednota. Not until 1903 was it published anonymously as *Die Unterdrückung der Slovaken durch die Magyaren*. This work was one of the first attempts in a major European language to publicise the ongoing campaign of the Magyarisation of the Slovaks and to seek support for the Slovak national cause beyond the borders of Bohemia and Austria.[24] It was cited in Thomas Čapek's *The Slovaks of Hungary* (1906) and Robert W. Seton-Watson's *Racial Problems in Hungary* (1908), the single most important publication on the Slovaks in the English language prior to World War I.[25] Revised and updated editions of the work were published in Czech in 1907 and 1908 under the title *Vyhubit. Obraz slovenského utrpení* and under the pseudonym 'R. Targo'. Slovak, Magyar, and English editions were also planned but were never realised; most of *Vyhubit*, however, was translated into Russian and printed in a Russian newspaper by Andrei Sirotnin, a friend of Dušan Makovický's.[26] As a result of Masaryk's initiative and considerable assistance, Kálal's Slovakophile efforts were thus able to reach an international public which knew almost nothing about the existence of the Slovaks, let alone their struggle for national survival against Magyarisation.

The other project took much less time to accomplish. Prior to his meeting with Masaryk, Kálal had usually focused in his Czech publications on the oppression of the Slovaks by forces over which they had little control, primarily Magyarisation and the economic and political activities of the Jews and gentry. He had generally refrained from openly criticising the Slovaks themselves, in part because he was an extremely sensitive person and possibly feared incurring the wrath of certain Slovak leaders. He was therefore reluctant to accept Masaryk's second request. But Masaryk succeeded in winning Kálal over to one of the basic tenets of Czech Realism. In Těšín, according to Kálal, Masaryk had

> said literally: 'Nothing can help Slovakia except criticism.' This statement filled my soul; I thought that in addition to criticism Slovakia needed something else. Returning home on the train I kept meditating on the statement until I formed my own definition: Criticism is seeking truth, and I added from the Scripture: Truth liberates and saves. From that time on I wrote more critically about Slovakia, of course, always in the belief that I was serving the truth.[27]

The result of Kálal's change of heart was the series entitled 'O věcech slovenských. Úvahy a kritiky', which appeared anonymously[28] in the first five numbers of Volume VIII of *Naše doba* from October 1900, to February 1901.

The target of Kálal's criticism was the very top rank of Slovak society: the tiny band of cultural and political leaders who directed the Slovak National Party and its official organ, *Národnie noviny*, in Turčiansky Svätý Martin. He singled out for special scrutiny Svetozár Hurban-Vajanský, a poet, novelist, and journalist of considerable talent whose ideas had shaped the Slovak national movement in the 1880s and 1890s. Following in the tradition of L'udovít Štúr, who after the failure of the 1848–49 Slovak rising had turned to Pan-Slavism, Vajanský was an ardent Russophile. Since he believed that the Slovaks were too few and powerless to change their political fortunes within the Magyarising Hungarian Kingdom, he placed all hope in Russia as a *deus ex machina* to rescue the Slovaks from extinction. In the meantime, the main goal of the intelligentsia was to preserve Slovak national identity, primarily through the cultivation of the Slovak language and literature. Vajanský's élitist, passive, authoritarian political romanticism and Russophilism had already been challenged by Masaryk's Hlasist followers and other Slovak oppositional elements. It was also at the crux of Kálal's own condemnation of the official Slovak national leadership.

Kálal's first complaint centered on Turčiansky Svätý Martin itself. The fact that this small town had become the cultural capital of Slovakia was in his view a fatal mistake. Only a large city with a sizable population, with industry, trade, and cultural institutions, could serve as a national spiritual powerhouse.[29] As alternatives, Kálal suggested either Trnava in western Slovakia or even Budapest, with its relatively large Slovak population.

In the editorial policy of *Národnie noviny*, Kálal could discern no well-defined political programme beyond recording the attacks of Magyarisers on nationally conscious Slovaks. Not only did the Martin editors fail to provide initiative, personal example, and plans for controlled national work, but they even wrongly castigated those, like the Hlasists, who had the temerity to do so. They also lacked concern for the moral education of the nation and completely underestimated the importance of the common people in national life.

Kálal chided the Martin leadership for outmoded, unrealistic, and counter-productive romanticism, characterised by useless gestures of political martyrdom and reliance on salvation from the outside.[30]

Aiming particularly at Hurban-Vajanský, he claimed that his newspaper articles, filled with passion, invective, and lament, offered no new thought, practical advice, or ethical stimulus to their Slovak readers. And he probably did more harm to than good for the Slovak cause by his brutal verbal assaults on the Magyars. Vajanský was a 'political bully' who depended on force rather than humane behaviour to defend the Slovak nation against its Magyar oppressors.[31] Especially unforgiveable for Kálal, the Czech Slovakophile, was Vajanský's negative attitude towards Czech-Slovak reciprocity. He denied his readers information about the Czechs and Czech culture; predicted that the Czechs would be swallowed up by the Germans; opposed the sending of Slovak students and apprentices to the Bohemian Lands; and vilified Czech Slovakophiles.

Kálal insisted that the Martin leadership's almost obsessive opposition to criticism and competition was a barrier to Slovak national renewal; and he welcomed such new publications as *Hlas* to break it down.

The moral degeneration of the Slovak intelligentsia was another serious defect which Kálal found in Slovak society. He lambasted most of the intelligentsia for their epicurism, laziness, frivolity, neglect and exploitation of the common people, and in particular for their arrogant, gentry-like attitude, which separated them from the Slovak masses and left those masses bereft of sound moral direction.[32] Kálal even attacked the Slovak Catholic clergy,[33] whom he judged to be either indifferent to the national cause or accomplices of Magyarisation. The majority were concerned with impressing the Slovak people with their exalted priestly status and they identified respect for themselves with piety. Slovak Catholics were less advanced than their Protestant co-nationals, whose own clergy, Kálal indicated, were also not above reproach.

Having condemned the Martin leadership for its lack of a definite programme and for its moral deficiencies, Kálal offered his own prescription to cure the Slovak nation's ills. His basic premise was:

> The aim of every nation is to raise itself *morally, culturally and educationally, economically, and socially* (politically). It is necessary to work in all directions, for each one is supported by the other. Of course, morality and enlightenment are first; it is necessary to begin there, not at all with politics.[34]

In placing the stress on raising the cultural and ethical levels of the people as the pre-condition for successful political action, Kálal was proceeding in his proposals for the Slovaks on a fundamental premise of Masaryk's own Realist programme.[35]

With regard to morality, Kálal's principle was, 'Let everyone first purify himself, his family, from there go to the community and the nation.'[36] The chief moral evils which the Slovaks had to wipe out were alcoholism,[37] prostitution, and business corruption.

Not surprisingly, schoolteacher Kálal maintained that the education of the Slovak masses was to be given a very high priority.[38] This was feasible because the elementary schools were still for the most part in the hands of the Slovaks themselves, but the intelligentsia would first have to abandon their traditional disdain for elementary education. Kálal suggested that school buildings be improved, teachers' salaries be raised and perhaps even augmented by national subventions (just as Magyarising teachers were compensated by the Hungarian government), and proper teacher training be given special attention. A solid pedagogical journal and lectures by the intelligentsia at teachers' meetings would help train qualified teachers.

For Slovak students, Kálal recommended that a children's periodical be sponsored by the national leaders in order to develop an early interest in reading; a library should be placed in every school, with suitable reading matter for adults, and large numbers of Slovak students should be enrolled in Czech schools in bordering Moravia, which would compel the Magyars to set up Slovak secondary schools in Slovakia.

According to Kálal, an adult education programme for Slovak peasant workers would also be needed. Inasmuch as non-political lectures in Slovak were not prohibited by Hungarian law, Slovak priests and teachers had an obligation to instruct the people by those means. It was of crucial importance that massive quantities of uplifting and inexpensive reading material be made available.[39] Especially well suited for this purpose were the selections of Czech literature which Slovaks could easily read, such as those issued by the Matice lidu and other Czech sources. The establishment of several more presses would help to provide almanacs, calendars, and local periodicals. Popular historical works, maps of Slovakia, and reliable geographical and topographical manuals were also needed.

Kálal's recommendations for building the local economy included the formation of grocery cooperatives and credit associations. Periodical literature should extensively review Czech publications on economic matters. The sons of Slovak farmers should be sent to agricultural schools in Moravia, apprentices to Czech artisans, and students to Czech commercial academies. Finally, small businesses specialising in the products of Slovak folk culture should be organised.

Recognising the extremely weak political situation of the Slovaks *vis-à-vis* the powerful and aggressive Magyar establishment, Kálal opted for a very cautious, moderate political approach. The most realistic political goal for the Slovaks was 'equality of rights' in Hungary, and he advised the Slovak leaders to substitute that for the demands of the Memorandum of the Slovak Nation of 1861, which called for the creation of an autonomous Slovak region in Upper Hungary.[40] Instead of provoking the Magyars with insults and impossible demands, Slovak politicians should confront the Magyars with the facts on how Slovaks were being treated, and compare those facts with the existing laws. Where the laws operated in such a way as to deny equal rights to the Slovaks, then the Slovak spokesmen should point out how incompatible those laws were with natural rights and a humane viewpoint and ask for redress.

Kálal's 'foreign policy' recommendations for the Slovaks were simple: They should maintain and increase friendly relations with the other non-Magyar nations in Hungary. Of course, cultural unity with the Czechs should be promoted. It would not be necessary for the Slovaks to turn their backs on Russia, but the fantasies about beneficient Russian intercession on Slovakia's behalf should be abandoned. Finally, they might try to gain access to the throne in Vienna, perhaps with the help of the Bohemian and Polish nobility, to bring their plight to the attention of their sovereign.

The last plank of Kálal's programme consisted of small-scale political activities realisable within the existing restrictive Hungarian-dominated framework. Among them would be for the Slovak political leaders to prepare the common people in a systematic and sustained manner for the election of Slovak national candidates for the Hungarian parliament. Characteristically, Kálal concluded his article by stressing the need of the Slovaks for Czech assistance: he suggested that a meeting of Slovaks and Czechs be called to develop action programmes for the Slovaks and also for 'Czechoslovak cultural reciprocity'.

The response from Martin to Kálal's onslaught in *Naše doba* was entirely predictable. Before the series had run its course, there appeared in the 4 December 1900 issue of *Národnie noviny* the first instalment of a lengthy rebuttal entitled 'Odpoved' Našej dobe' from the acerbic pen of editor Jozef Škultéty, Vajanský's closest collaborator.[41] Throughout this spirited defence, Masaryk was savagely assailed, and 'O věcech slovenských' was condemned for its errors, lies, distortions, slanders, naivety, and gross ignorance of Slovak personalities and conditions. The fire-storm in Martin did not subside with the end of Kálal's article in February. To Kálal's immense discomfort, at the beginning of June, *Národnie noviny* carried an announcement that he was the real author of the *Naše doba* series.[42]

Kálal derived slight consolation from Masaryk's reactions to the whole matter. Masaryk printed a notice in *Naše doba* in which he expressed satisfaction with the 'gratifying' and 'salubrious' commotion which the article had stirred up, especially in Slovakia. He denied having written a single line; and although he admitted that there were some quite minor and insignificant points which were not entirely true, and which he did not have time to rectify before publication, he declared that the article was accurate.[43] Shortly thereafter, Masaryk acted as an intermediary between Kálal and Detvan, the Slovak students' society in Prague, which requested permission to have the series reprinted in pamphlet form.[44]

The publication of 'O věcech slovenských' helped to make unbridgeable the rift between the Martin Slovaks on the one hand and the Hlasists and their Czech supporters on the other.[45] Henceforth Kálal was ranked by the Martin leaders along with Masaryk and the Czech Realists as an enemy of the Slovaks.[46] He lost the confidence and goodwill of some of his Slovak friends,[47] and his own efforts to promote Czech-Slovak reciprocity in Slovakia were definitely crippled.

While Professor Masaryk revelled in public controversy, the schoolteacher from Frenštát was severely stung by it. As a result of the notoriety and other adverse effects which followed from his writing 'O věcech slovenských', Kálal may indeed have had second thoughts about Masaryk's injunction concerning the necessity of criticism for Slovakia – or at least Masaryk's type of criticism. In his published reminiscences about his relations with Masaryk, Kálal never mentioned his role in the *Naše doba* series. The cause of this deliberate omission was a detectable bitterness which could have been in part attributable to Masaryk himself. Shortly before his death in 1930, Kálal penned two sets of notes with regard to his *Naše doba* venture which are contained in his papers. In the second (May 23), he suggested that the article not be republished in his collected writings because of its 'sharpness'. In the first (May 13), he directed that if the article were to be reprinted 'only after Masaryk's death', it should be made clear in an introduction that it was written at Masaryk's behest and that although Masaryk himself did not write it, he '*sharpened* [italics mine] several words.' It is impossible to determine the veracity of Kálal's claim. But Kálal presumably regretted having fulfilled Masaryk's request to write 'O věcech slovenských' and held Masaryk responsible for the disastrous personal consequences of his having done so.

Masaryk and Kálal met again on at least four other occasions prior to 1914. In December 1901, when Kálal delivered an important lecture on the Slovaks in Prague, sponsored by the Českoslovanská jednota, Masaryk was there. Masaryk was also present along with Kálal at two gatherings of prominent Czechs, who included the venerable František Ladislav Rieger, which related to Slovakophile concerns.[48] It is possible that Kálal had already become a member of Masaryk's Realist Party, for he had also intended to address a group of the party's followers during his visit to Prague.[49] Masaryk's adoption of the natural rights theory, along with the inclusion of consideration of the plight of the Hungarian Slovaks in his party's platform,[50] has been interpreted as an indication of Masaryk's pre-World War I commitment to the union of the Czechs and Slovaks.[51] Kálal assumed that Masaryk

> had in mind by means of natural rights the unification of Bohemia with Slovakia. What follows from natural rights follows from natural reason: If the Czechs and Slovaks are one nation, they have the right to live in one state. Except that it was not yet the right time to make such a declaration.[52]

Although Kálal never verified that assumption in his subsequent correspondence or meetings with Masaryk,[53] he remained for a time an active member of the Realist Party, perhaps because it was one of the few Czech political parties which took special notice of the Slovaks.

Most probably, however, it was the general ideological affinity between Kálal and Masaryk that explains Kálal's party membership. Kálal maintained that, although spiritually he was closest to Tolstoy,[54] he had eventually been attracted to Masaryk: 'To love the nation *by means of a moral life and work*, that was extraordinarily to my liking as an educator. I got to know this substance of Realism fully only from [Masaryk's] "Jak pracovat?"'[55] Much of Kálal's thinking actually mirrored that of Masaryk. This is evident from Masaryk's choice of Kálal as a collaborator; as he confided to Kálal in early 1901, 'You see what I am striving for in *Naše doba*; I know that you understand it and that is the reason why I shall always call upon you to help.'[56] Furthermore, 'O věcech slovenských' was generally assumed to have been written by Masaryk himself. It is true that in an exchange of letters with Masaryk in 1903, and even in his contribution to the Masaryk *Festschrift* in 1910 Kálal objected to the Realist Party's (and Masaryk's) lack of popular appeal and excessively harsh critical approach.[57] His collaboration with Masaryk, however, was based not only on their shared Slovakophilism; Kálal was also very much a Czech Realist.

Masaryk's correspondence with Kálal diminished after 1903, when *Die Unterdrückung der Slovaken* was finally published and Masaryk's involvement in Slovak affairs had already abated. (His last summer vacation in Slovakia was in 1901.) Masaryk attempted to elicit from Kálal further contributions to *Naše doba* on other subjects (such as alcoholism and religion) and wanted him to suppply regular reports on Slovak affairs for the journal.[58] Although Kálal discussed such possible articles in his letters to Masaryk and even apparently provided him with some material, which he requested Masaryk to keep confidential,[59] it is not clear whether Kálal published anything else in *Naše doba*. On the other hand, *Čas* issued Kálal's booklet *Slováci. Stručný rozhled po době minulé i přítomné*; and both *Čas* and *Naše doba* continued to report on Kálal's Slovakophile activities and publications.

Masaryk remembered and appreciated his prewar collaboration with Kálal. As Czechoslovak president in 1922, he granted Kálal a gift of 10 000 Kč towards recuperation from a serious illness;[60] and upon Kálal's final retirement in 1923 he thanked him for his service to the nation, assuring him that 'Slovakia is especially grateful to you for your revivalist endeavours and for your cultural and educational activity.'[61]

The Masaryk-Kálal Slovakophile relationship constituted a minor but significant episode in the history of Czech-Slovak relations in the period preceding World War I. Through the efforts of these two men, the Slovaks and their precarious economic and cultural situation received attention outside Hungary and as far away as Western Europe. Concern for the welfare of the Slovak people was demonstrated in print, not only to the Czech public but to the Slovaks as well. In so far as Czechs played a positive role in assisting the Slovaks in their struggle for national survival against Magyarisation, the parts Masaryk and Kálal played must be acknowledged.

In his postwar *Světová revoluce*, Masaryk claimed that, 'Both Slovaks and Czechs knew that I had always stood for Slovakia; that as a Slovak by origin and tradition, my feelings are Slovak, and that I have always worked, not merely talked, for Slovakia.'[62] The precise validity of that claim has been debated by Masaryk's idolators and detractors. While it is true that Masaryk's interest in the Slovaks before 1914 was not as constant and intense as some have maintained, none the less his Slovakophile relationship with Kálal proves that it was a serious concern of Masaryk and that Masaryk exerted himself on its behalf.

Masaryk's influence on the Slovaks themselves through the Hlasists was crucial, mainly because of its consequences for the establishment of a Czechoslovak state in 1918. If Masaryk had lacked some sort of following in Slovakia, it would have been more difficult for him to realise the unification programme he developed during the war. With regard to Masaryk's influence on Czech opinion concerning the Slovaks prior to 1914, it must be admitted that other Czechs did more than he to publicise the need for Czech-Slovak reciprocity and unity. What is significant about the Masaryk-Kálal relationship is that it shows that one of the most important Czech Slovakophiles – Karel Kálal – whose views on the Slovaks did much to shape Czech perceptions of the Slovaks before 1914, was a representative of Masaryk's Realism. In that specific respect, Masaryk's influence on the Czech Slovakophile movement prior to 1914 was more extensive than it might have seemed.

NOTES

1   Karel Kálal, 'Moje slovenské tajemství,' *Kúpelné listy z Trenčianských Teplic*, vol. V, no. 1 (22 May 1927) p. 3.
2   R. W. Seton-Watson, *Masaryk in England* (Cambridge University Press, 1943) p. 44.
3   An annotated survey of the literature (including primary sources) is to be found in Ludwig von Gogolak, 'T. G. Masaryk's slowakische und ungarländische Politik. Eing Beitrag zur Vorgeschichte des Zerfalls Ungarns im Jahre 1918', *Bohemia: Jahrbuch des Collegium Carolinum*, vol. IV (1963) pp. 219–27. See also Thomas D. Marzik, 'T. G. Masaryk and the Slovaks, 1882–1914', in *Columbia Essays in International Affairs: The Dean's Papers, 1965*, ed. by Andrew W. Cordier (New York: Columbia University Press, 1966) pp. 155–74.
4   On this point and doubts raised – chiefly by Willy Lorenz – about Masaryk's natural father, see Thomas D. Marzik, 'Masaryk's National

Background', in Peter Brock and H. Gordon Skilling (eds), *The Czech Renascence of the Nineteenth Century* (University of Toronto Press, 1970) pp. 241–2 and Willy Lorenz, 'Die Sternstunde ging vorbei: Wer war Thomas Garrigue Masaryk?' in *Monolog über Böhmen* (Vienna: Verlag Herold, 1964) pp. 112–42. Unless convincing evidence can be found to prove Lorenz's conjecture that Masaryk was the illegitimate son of Nathan Redlich, it would be prudent in this matter to be guided by the old Roman principle *Pater est quem nuptiae demonstrant*.

5   See Karel Kramář, *Paměti*, 2nd. ed., ed. Karel Hoch (Prague: Pražská akciová tiskárna, 1938) pp. 111–13 and also von Gogolak, 'T. G. Masaryk's slowakische und ungarländische Politik', pp. 195–7.

6   An outline of Masaryk's specific suggestions is to be found in Vavro Šrobár, 'Vliv Masarykov na Slovákov', in E. Beneš et al. (eds), *T. G. Masarykovi k 60. narozeninám* (Prague: Grosman a Svoboda, 1910) pp. 190–3.

7   See Štefan Janšák, *Život dr. Pavla Blahu. Slovenské národné hnutie na prahu XX. storočia*, 2 vols. (Trnava: Spolok sv. Vojtecha, 1947) I, pp. 129–30.

8   A critical evaluation of the Hlasist movement can be found in Ján Bodnár, 'Ideové základy hlasizmu', in Elena Várossová (ed.) *Prehľad dejín slovenskej filozofie* (Bratislava: Vydavateľstvo Slovenskej akadémie vied, 1965) pp. 301–34. For an appraisal of earlier and perhaps more important non-Hlasist sources of opposition in which the role of Slovak Catholic populism is emphasised, see Pavla Vošahlíková, *Slovenské politické směry v období přechody k imperialismu* (Prague: Academia, 1979).

9   Šrobár, for example, became the 'Minister Plenipotentiary for the Administration of Slovakia' in 1918.

10   Kálal, *Prúdy*, vol. V, no. 9–10 (1914/published 1919) p. 544.

11   For an excellent historiographical survey of Czech-Slovak relations in general, see Jiří Malíř, 'Problematika česko-slovenských vztahů v 80. a 90. letech 19. století v dosavadní české a slovenské historiografii', in *Sborník prací filozofické fakulty brněnské university*, vol. XXV–XXVI (1976–1977), 'Řada historická 23–24', pp. 237–59.

12   Although the importance of Kálal has been acknowledged in all studies of pre-World War I Czech-Slovak relations, no critical monograph has been devoted to him by Czech or Slovak professional historians. Only three minor works have been published on Kálal. Alois Zbavitel, his former student and disciple, wrote two of them: *Karol Kálal vo službe ľudovej výchovy na Slovensku* (Trnava: 'Nové Slovensko', 1927) and *Karel Kálal ve službách československé jednoty* (Prague: Mazáč, 1929). The third is Ján Hamaliar and František Loubal (eds), *Sborníček k sedmdesátým narozeninám lidovýchovného pracovníka spisovatele Karla Kálala* (Brno: 'Kroužek oddaných žáků, 1930). Although containing valuable factual information, these publications are rather hagiographical. The only study in English is Thomas D. Marzik, 'Czech Relations with the Slovaks: The Slovakophile Writings and Activities of Karel Kálal, 1885–1900' (Unpublished Ph D dissertation, Columbia University, 1975).

13 A bibliography of Kálal's Slovakophile writings which was published in 1910 alone covers eight pages (Kálal, 'Karla Kálala literární práce slovenofilská. Seznam článků a knih', *Naše Slovensko*, vol. III, no. 5–6 (1910) pp. 216–24). All told, Kálal published thirty separate Slovakophile works (half of which were didactic fiction) and hundreds of articles. His most important Slovakophile writings were collected and reprinted in six small volumes and in two editions: *Karla Kálala spisy slovákofilské* (Prague: Mazáč, 1928 and 1930). His articles appeared in a wide variety of Czech publications (including *Národní listy*, *Čas*, *Osvěta*, *Naše doba*, *Slovanský přehled*, and *Ottův slovník naučný*) and covered a broad range of fields (including journalism, pedagogy, economics, politics, history, and geography).

14 Kálal, 'O kraji a lidu drátenickém', *Osvěta*, vol. XXIX, no. 8 (1899) p. 677.

15 On this organisation, see Vladimír Kulíšek, 'O činnosti a významu Českoslovanské jednoty před vznikem ČSR', *Historický časopis*, vol. X, no. 3 (1962) pp. 351–68.

16 One of the more important Slovakophiles influenced by Kálal's *Osvěta* articles was the Czech literary historian Albert Pražák. See his 'Dík Karlu Kálalovi', in *Sborníček k sedmdesátým narozeninám lidovýchovného pracovníka*, p. 56. These articles had an indirect international effect as well, for they were used as sources in the preparation of two of the earliest American publications in English dealing with the Slovaks: Thomas Čapek, *The Slovaks of Hungary: Slavs and Panslavism* (New York: The Knickerbocker Press, 1906) pp. xv, 197; and Emily Greene Balch, *Our Slavic Fellow Citizens* (New York: Charities Publication Committee, 1910) pp. 96, 495. The editor of *Osvěta* was Vácslav Vlček, a bitter intellectual foe of Masaryk since the Battle of the Manuscripts of the later 1880s.

17 František Pastrnek, president of the Českoslovanská jednota, and a noted Slavist, served as intermediary between Kálal and Masaryk in this regard. See Pastrnek's letters to Kálal of 25 January, 30 January and 4 February 1896 (Kálal Papers, Literární archív Památníku národního písemnictví-Staré Hrady). Masaryk did not write an article for the *Sborník*.

18 Zdeněk Urban, *Problémy slovenského národního hnutí na konci 19. století* (Prague: Universita Karlova, 1972) p. 147.

19 See, for example, K. Sch., 'Pro Slovensko – pro nás', *Čas*, vol. XIV, no. 88 (27 July 1900) p. 2.

20 On the Kálal-Salva relationship with the Hlasists, see Marzik, 'Czech Relations with the Slovaks', pp. 188–99.

21 Kálal, 'Masarykovo učenie o práve prirodzenom', in *Slovensko Masarykovi*, ed. by Jozef Rudinský (Prague: 'Vydalo pod protektorátom slovenskej odbočky Československej národnej rady v Bratislave', Literárne–vedecké nakladateľstvo Vojtecha Tilkovského, 1930) p. 75.

22 Letter of Masaryk to Kálal, 3 September 1900, Kálal Papers.

23 This was the last part of the second edition, 'Die Magyarische Staatsidee – Die Magyaren und die Freiheit', pp. 9–12. This passage is marked off in red pencil and identified as Masaryk's contribution in the

copy of the pamphlet in the Library of the National Museum in Prague, a gift of Kálal's first son, Miroslav Kálal.

24   Albert Pražák, 'Karel Kálal', *Bratislava*, vol. IV (1930) p. 493.

25   Čapek, *The Slovaks of Hungary*, p. xi, and Scotus Viator [Seton-Watson], *Racial Problems in Hungary* (London: Constable, 1908) p. 519. (Curiously, *Die unterdrückungen* [sic] *der Slovaken durch Magyaren* is listed with R. W. Seton-Watson as its author in Robert Joseph Kerner, *Slavic Europe. A Selected Bibliography in Western European Languages* (Cambridge, MA: Harvard University Press, 1918) p. 220.) Upon the urging of Jan Herben, Seton-Watson visited Kálal in Písek in 1907 and received from him a copy of *Die Unterdrückung der Slovaken*. See letter of Herben to Kálal, 11 May 1907, Kálal Papers and Kálal, '25 rokov slovákofilom', *Slovenský denník*, vol. III, no. 3 (6 January 1912) p. 3.

26   Josef Rotnágl and Valentin Bulgakov. *S Tolstým. Památce Dušana Makovického. K 80. výročí jeho narození* (Liptovský Svätý Mikuláš, 1946) p. 51.

27   Speech of Kálal at the Národní rada Československa in Prague on 7 March 1930, as printed in *T. G. Masaryk, president Československé republiky. K jeho 80. narozeninám* (Prague: Národní rada Československá, 1930) p. 13. See also letter of Kálal to Masaryk, 14 September 1900, Masaryk Archive, Archiv Ústavu marxismu-leninismu ÚV KSČ in Prague.

28   At the time, the article was considered by many to have been the work of Masaryk himself. Anton Štefánek, 'Masaryk a Slovensko', in Miloš Weingart (ed.) *Sborník přednášek o T. G. Masarykovi* (Prague: Orbis, 1930) p. 238. Most of the article was reprinted, with a reservation about Masaryk's actual authorship, in J. B. Kozák et al. *Masarykova práce. Sborník ze spisů řečí a projevů prvního presidenta československé republiky k osmdesátým jeho narozeninám* (Prague: Státní nakladatelství, 1930) pp. 128–44. Kálal never publicly admitted that he was the author; however, the article's style and specific content, the correspondence between Masaryk and Kálal, and a note in the Kálal Papers written in his own hand on 13 May 1930 prove that 'O věcech slovenských' was the work of Karel Kálal.

29   Masaryk made a similar point about the Slovaks' lack of an urban national capital in his lecture to Slovak students in Budapest on 23 February 1911. 'Problém malého národa', *Prúdy*, vol. II, no. 6 (1911) p. 242. Martin in 1900 had about 2900 inhabitants.

30   On Masaryk's own condemnation of romanticism and martyrdom, and for his attitude towards 'práce drobná' (everyday small deeds), see his *Jak pracovat? Přednášky z roku 1898* (Prague: Čin, 1926) pp. 16–26.

31   This reflects a cardinal point of Masaryk's humanitarian programme. Cf. Antonie van den Beld, *Humanity: The Political and Social Philosophy of Thomas G. Masaryk* (The Hague: Mouton, 1975) p. 45. For a sample of Masaryk's own extremely critical appraisal of Vajanský, see his review of Vajansky's novel *Kotlín* in *Naše doba*, vol. IX, no. 1 (1901) pp. 66–9.

32   The moral dimension in the relationship between the intelligentsia and

the common people was an important element in Masaryk's influence on the Hlasists. See Branislav Štefánek, 'Masaryk and Slovakia', in Milič Čapek and Karel Hrubý (eds), *T. G. Masaryk in Perspective: Comments and Criticism* (New York: SVU Press, 1981) p. 212.

33 Like Masaryk, Kálal had been born a Roman Catholic but he eventually became a member of the Evangelical Reformed Church; he was a militant anti-clerical. See the letter in which he told Masaryk: 'I see your mission chiefly to help the nation *substantially* get out of the Catholic mire' and urged him to write a popular pamphlet explaining why he had left the Catholic Church. Kálal to Masaryk, 23 June 1903, Masaryk Archive.

34 'O věcech slovenských', *Naše doba*, vol. VIII, no. 5 (1901) p. 338. Italics in original.

35 See Eva Schmidt-Hartmann, *Thomas G. Masaryk's Realism: Origins of a Czech Political Concept* (Munich: Oldenbourg, 1984) p. 163.

36 'O věcech slovenských', p. 338.

37 A fanatical teetotaller, Kálal claimed that he had a role in converting Masaryk to abstinence. See his 'Abstinenství T. G. Masaryka', *Čechoslovák*, vol. IV, no. 5 (15 May 1930) p. 177. Masaryk referred several times to the subject in his correspondence with Kálal, and in his message of condolence to Kálal's widow, Anna, he mentioned that he valued especially Kálal's 'fight against alcoholism and his work for Slovakia.' (Telegram dated 5 August 1930, Personal Archive of Dušan Kálal, Kálal's second son [hereafter cited as Dušan Kálal Archive].)

38 The emphasis on formal education in national life was one of Masaryk's most significant and constant themes. See, for example, his *Česká otázka. Snahy a tužby národního obrození*, 7th ed. (Prague: Melantrich, 1969) p. 153.

39 Masaryk apparently also felt the need for such publications. See the undated Czech document, neither in Masaryk's nor Kálal's handwriting, entitled 'Prof. Masaryka návrhy k programu pro lidový list slovenský', in the Kálal Papers (see note 17).

40 Kálal's stress on the 'equality of rights' for the Slovaks can be related to Masaryk's own references, especially in *Česká otázka*, to the renewal of Palacký's programme for the reformation of Austria into a federal state of the nationalities on that basis. Jozef Butvin, 'Vonkajšie otázky politiky slovenskej maloburžoázie na prelome storočí (1895–1904)', *Československý časopis historický*, vol. XXXII, no. 4 (1984) p. 554.

41 *Národnie noviny*, vol. XXXI, no. 143. The other instalments were published in vol. XXXI, nos. 145, 147, and 148; vol. XXXII, nos. 11, 13, 15, 17, 18, and 20.

42 Jozef Škultéty, 'Tie články Našej doby', *Národnie noviny*, vol. XXXII, no. 64 (4 June 1901) p. 1. It is not clear whether the Martin editors ascertained or merely guessed Kálal's authorship.

43 M. [Masaryk], 'Věci slovenské', *Naše doba*, vol. VIII, no. 6 (1901) p. 480.

44 See Detvan's minute book for the meeting of 8 June 1901; p. 57, Detvan Papers, Archiv University Karlovy in Prague, and letter of Masaryk to Kálal, 1 July 1901, Kálal Papers. The pamphlet appeared

under the title '"Věci slovenské" články z "Našej Doby"', vydal s doslovom pôvodcovým vo zvláštnom odtiska pražský spolok "Detvan" u Teslíka' (Skalice, 1901).

45   Andrej Mráz, *Jozef Škultéty* (Turčiansky Svätý Martin: Matica slovenská, 1933) p. 98. Also, see Jozef Butvin, 'Česko-slovenské vzťahy koncom 19. a začiatkom 20. storočia (1880–1914)', in *Zborník filozofickej fakulty Univerzity Komenského. Historica*, vol. XXIX–XXX (1978–79) pp. 30–1.

46   One example of this hostility is the blistering charge from Martin that 'The gossips of Masaryk, Kálal, nasty *Čas*, and others have directly poisoned our brotherly relations.' 'Po slavnostiach', *Národnie noviny*, vol. XXXIII, no. 93 (12 August 1902) p. 1.

47   The most important casualty was perhaps the Reverend Andrej Kmet', the indefatigable Slovak botanist-archaeologist, and founder of the Muzeálná slovenská spoločnost', whose previous cordial relationship with Kálal was severed in 1901. See his extremely bitter letter to Kálal of 2 April 1901, Kálal Papers.

48   Kálal, 'Dr. F. L. Rieger a Slovensko. Vzpomínka', *Příloha Národní politiky*, vol. XLVI, no. 64 (4 March 1928).

49   Letter of František Pastrnek to Kálal, 29 November 1901, Kálal Papers.

50   See Article VIII of the party's 'Všeobecný program politický', as reprinted from *Čas* (April 1900) in *Masarykova práce*, p. 126 (see note 28).

51   Paul Selver, *Masaryk: A Biography* (London: Michael Joseph, 1940) pp. 192–3.

52   Speech of Kálal at the Národní rada československá, 7 March 1930, p. 11. That Masaryk's concern for the Slovaks as part of the Czech nation was a possible motive for his espousal of the natural rights theory is also suggested by George J. Kovtun, 'Thomas G. Masaryk's Road to Revolution', in *T. G. Masaryk in Perspective*, pp. 149–150 and Schmidt-Hartmann, *Thomas G. Masaryk's Realism*, p. 174.

53   Kálal, 'Masarykovo učenie o práve prirodzenom', p. 77.

54   Kálal, 'Kálal o sobě', *Rozpravy Aventina*, vol. IV, no. 35 (1928–29) p. 348.

55   Kálal, [Vzpomínka], in Edvard Beneš et al. (eds), *T. G. Masarykovi k šedesátým narozeninám*, 2nd ed. (Prague: Čin, 1930) p. 378. 'Jak pracovat?' was first published in *Hlas*, vols. 1–2 (1898–99). For another comment by Kálal concerning the influence on him of Masaryk and Realism, see his *Mravný národ, silný národ. Výbor článků a přednášek z doby válečné a poválecné* (Prague: Mazáč, 1931) p. 160.

56   Letter of Masaryk to Kálal, 10 February 1901, Kálal Papers.

57   See letter of Masaryk to Kálal, 6 July 1903, Kálal Papers and Kálal, [Vzpomínka], in *T. G. Masarykovi k šedesátým narozeninám*, 2nd ed., pp. 378–9.

58   Kálal managed to convince a pro-Realist Slovak Protestant minister, Ladislav Novomestský, to perform this task instead of himself, claiming that he was too burdened with writing articles on Slovakia for other Czech publications. Novomestský was a contributor to *Naše doba* from 1903 to 1910. See letter of Kálal to Novomestský, 18 December 1902,

as quoted by Ján Hamaliar, 'Miesto K. Kálala medzi našimi slovákofil-
mi. [9. ledna 1860–4. srpna 1930]', *Prúdy*, vol. 14, no. 7 (1930) p. 437.

59 See letter of Kálal to Masaryk 10 June 1901, Masaryk Archive (see
note 27).
60 Curiously, Kálal at first refused to accept this grant and had to be
persuaded by Přemysl Šámal, chancellor of the Chancellery of the
President, not to return it. Letter of Šámal to Kálal, 12 September
1922, Kálal Papers.
61 Letter of Masaryk to Kálal, 6 December 1923, Dušan Kálal Archive.
62 Thomas Garrigue Masaryk, *The Making of a State: Memories and
Observations, 1914–1918* (London: Allen & Unwin, 1927) p. 209;
Světová revoluce za války a ve válce 1914–1918, 2nd ed. (Prague: Čin
and Orbis, 1933) p. 256.

9 Masaryk and the Trials for High Treason against South Slavs in 1909

Arnold Suppan

When Thomas Garrigue Masaryk, Professor of Philosophy at the Czech section of the Charles-Ferdinand University in Prague, spoke in the Chamber of Deputies of the Austrian Reichsrat on 14 May 1909 on behalf of the South Slavs, his action no longer created the sensation as it once might have. The socially committed Czech teacher had become acquainted with the South Slavs and learnt Serbo-Croat while studying in Vienna in the 1870s. In 1891 he had attended the banquet of a Slav student conference in Prague with the Istrian deputy of the Reichsrat, Vjekoslav Spinčić, and in 1892 he had participated in an important meeting of Slav students in Graz. As a Young Czech deputy in the Reichsrat, he had been elected in 1892 to the Austrian delegation that discussed common affairs with Hungary and, on 18–19 October 1892, he had delivered his first major speech on Bosnia and Herzegovina. In it he criticised the policy of the Finance Minister Benjamin von Kállay, who supervised the administration of these two occupied regions.[1]

The fact that Masaryk intervened in 1909–10 in the Zagreb trial for high treason, the Friedjung trial, and the Vasić trial may be attributed to four motives. First, in Zagreb and Vienna, leading politicians of the Croatian-Serbian Coalition (Hrvatsko-srpska koalicija) who were directly or indirectly involved were his former students. The procedure at the political trials ran contrary to Masaryk's historical-philosophical, sociological, and ethical positions. His political criticism had long been directed against the Hungarian nationalities policy in Croatia-Slavonia (against Croats and Serbs) and in Upper Hungary (against Slovaks). Finally, Masaryk had been analysing foreign affairs since 1892–93 and criticised the drifting apart of Austro-Hungarian foreign and domestic policy and the false policy toward Serbia. After the annexation of Bosnia and Herzegovina on 5 October 1908, he began to question the diplomacy of the 'Minister des k.u.k. Hauses und des Äußern,' Aloys Lexa Count Aehrenthal.[2]

MASARYK AS MENTOR OF THE SOUTHERN SLAVS

Around 1890 only about 900 Slovenes, Croats, and Serbs were studying at the universities of the Danube Monarchy, most of them in Vienna, Zagreb, and Graz, and only a few in Budapest, Prague, and Innsbruck. In the period up to 1914 Zagreb became the most important university for the South Slavs of the Monarchy, and the number of South Slavs at the Czech university in Prague increased from three to one hundred and fifty-four.[3]

This South Slav trend towards the leading Czech academic institution was instituted in joint meetings of Slav students in Prague, Vienna, and Graz, beginning in 1891. Czech and South Slav students exchanged their journals and endorsed common resolutions to federalise the Habsburg Empire. From 1893 onwards Stjepan Radić (1871–1928) became the most important student agitator. He created a bad impression on the authorities at commemoration ceremonies, meetings, and demonstrations, declared 'Pereat Khuen' in 1893, and was sentenced to penal servitude. Expelled from Prague University in 1894, he burnt a Hungarian flag on Jellačić Square in 1895 on the occasion of the Emperor's visit to Zagreb, with the declamatory call, 'Long live the Croatian King Francis Joseph I! Honour to Jellačić! Hungarian withdrawal!'

Radić and fifty-three other demonstrators were punished and removed from Zagreb University; a campaign of help by members of the independent National Party (Obzoraši) helped them to procure new permission to study at the Czech university in Prague from the summer semester of 1896 onwards. This first generation of South Slav students in Prague also attended lectures on 'practical philosophy' given by Professor Masaryk; they edited the monthly *Hrvatska misao*, and formulated their 'Što hoćemo' in its first issue: On the one hand, the economic, social, cultural, and political powers of the South Slavs were still weak, so a national conflict between Croats and Serbs only endangered the development necessary for the country and its population. On the other hand, the unity of Croats and Serbs, a policy of social reforms, and the democratisation of political life were necessary preconditions for a new kind of politics in Croatia-Slavonia.[4]

Because the postal transport of *Hrvatska misao* to Croatia-Slavonia was forbidden, the second-year edition in 1898 was published under the title of *Novo doba* with the nationally very accentuated nationalistic subtitle, 'List sjedinjenje hrvatske, srpske i slovenačke omladine za politička, socijalna i književna pitanja'. Not only were the Slovenes Ivan Žmavc and Anton Dermota members of the editorial staff, but also the Croatian-Slavonian Serb Svetozar Pribićević, later a member of the Croatian-Serbian Coalition, and after 1918, Minister of the Interior and Minister of Education of the Kingdom of Serbs, Croats and Slovenes. After the German nationalist Badeni riots in November 1897, South Slav students in Vienna and Graz shouted: 'Away from Vienna! Away from Graz! Let us study in Prague!' This increased the influx to the Czech university. Among South Slav secondary-school students, Czech began to be learnt more intensively, and at the turn of the century a second generation came to Prague, among them the future outstanding literary critic Milan Marjanović, the later Dalmatian politician Josip Smodlaka, and the Slovene Social-Democrats Anton and Etbin Kristan. The Slovene students in particular now studied under Masaryk and soon formed the group of the 'Masarykovci.' A third South Slav generation finally formed in Prague in 1907.[5]

What were the most important political and ideological components of Masaryk's influence on the South Slav students in Prague between 1896 and 1908? The Prague groups learned for the first time about French and Russian social and political sciences and began to break away from the hitherto dominant influence of German culture. Furthermore, the South Slavs realised the importance of a nation's economic resources in its national struggle, and saw the necessity to establish well-developed economic and social organisations. Masaryk himself drew his students' attention to the need for the intelligentsia to work more intensively for the broad mass of the population. The South Slavs had heard Masaryk's criticism, too, that the Young Czechs incorrectly clung to the Bohemian 'Staatsrecht' and so began to question the Croatian 'Staatsrecht'. The students had also heard Masaryk's criticism of clericalism and, in their home country, they began to resist the dominant influence of the Catholic church on Slovenes and Croats. Above all, in Prague the Croatian, Serbian, and Slovene students saw the necessity for co-operation against German cultural expansionism, whereupon they uncritically applied the concept of German '*Drang nach Osten*', particularly dreaded by the Czechs, to their own regions. Admittedly only the Slovenes were directly threatened, whereas for Croats and Serbs, the Hungarian and Italian expansionist tendencies were more to be feared.

Finally, it must not be overlooked that the South Slavs' university training led them to adopt many avant-garde academic and artistic ideas and instilled in them new expectations concerning, for example, the standard of living, working conditions, social collaboration, and political participation. Masaryk's courses and lectures played no small part in disseminating these ideas.[6]

MASARYK'S FUNDAMENTAL HISTORICAL-POLITICAL AND SOCIOLOGICAL POSITIONS

At the heart of Masaryk's academic and political interests was human existence, 'true man', the 'truthfulness of life'. As his critical point of departure to analyse this problem of life, he chose the experience of the 'non-identity' of man: the dichotomy between inner conviction and external action, the denial of the self in the face of other people. Masaryk immediately applied these concepts to the field of politics: he criticised this inner conflict in people who embodied authority and from whom moral integrity could be expected.[7]

In the mid-1890s, Masaryk published the following historical-philosophical studies: *Česká otázka*, *Naše nynější krise*, and *Jan Hus*. Masaryk also tried to interpret humanitarian behaviour and action in the historical context. So 'humanism', 'reformation', 'Realism', and 'anthropism' represent central concepts in his thinking. From his studies of the sources and personalities of Czech and Slovak history, he elaborated a series of concepts: a humane Slav civilisation (Josef Dobrovský); the idea of fraternity (Jan Kollár, Pavel Josef Šafařík, František Palacký, Karel Havlíček-Borovský) and humanity as the aim and programme of the nation (idem). Masaryk's conception of history was, in his own words, 'preparation for political activity', directions for political action. Admittedly, some of his constructions, in particular his thesis of the direct link between Hussitism and the National Revival did not withstand scholarly criticism. Josef Pekař, Jaroslav Goll's most important pupil and the preeminent Czech historian in the early twentieth century, expressed the sharpest criticism in 1912:

> We realised . . . that Professor Masaryk, wherever he deals with historical questions, works and judges one-sidedly and doctrinarily . . . a lack of a sound method, a lack of scepticism and sharp criticism, a lack of careful heuristics are, in our scholarship, worse evils than a lack of philosophical or sociological opinions[8]

Zdeněk Nejedlý, one of the leading Masaryk scholars, inferred from Masaryk's philosophy of history that he believed that a politician had to know the limits of history and the limits of human development. With justification, the philosopher Milan Machovec objected that Masaryk had not constructed a pattern of thought of his own, indeed had not even tried to explain socio-economic upheavals. On the other hand, Masaryk had criticised erroneous viewpoints like historicism or 'mysticism in history' and proposed new ways of looking at things; for instance, he prompted his contemporaries to correct their image of history with open minds and to attain an 'authentic awareness of history'. The success of his sequence of ideas, Hussistism – Humanity – Democracy, at the end of the World War I seemed to prove Masaryk right.[9]

It is not the scholarly value of Masaryk's awareness of history that is under discussion in our context, however, but his political and social activism: in the decades before World War I, Masaryk was the antagonist and critic of nationalists, chauvinists, and anti-Semites, at the same time convinced of the mission of a democratised and federalised Danube and Balkan area. Only a structure of states organised along such lines could offer protection against social and legal insecurity, against the imperialistic aspirations of a Great Power, against privileges and cabinet politics, against censorship and 'relative' constitutionalism. In a series of trials and affairs – the Polná trial for ritual murder, the Wahrmund Affair, the Zagreb trial for high treason, the Friedjung trial – Masaryk appeared as an implacable enemy of despotism, bondage, and ideological terror, as a champion of democracy and freedom. Machovec defines Masaryk's conception of freedom as follows: 'Freedom also for the opponent's opinion, respect for the opposition, protection for a minority's rights to existence and full development. . . .'[10]

MASARYK AND THE ZAGREB TRIAL FOR HIGH TREASON

Since the murder of the Serbian king and the change of dynasties in Belgrade in 1903, a foreign policy conflict had been smouldering between Austria-Hungary and Serbia which found expression in disputes over customs duties, loans, shipments of artillery, and railway projects. Parallel to this, a more domestic level of conflict involved discussions over the 'New Course' of the Croatian-Serbian Coalition in Croatia-Slavonia and the question of Pan-Serbian propaganda among the Serbs of the Danube Monarchy. In December 1907, and April 1908, both the Hungarian Prime Minister Alexander Wekerle and the Austro-Hungarian Foreign Minister Aloys Aehrenthal discussed the Serbian problem in the Joint Council of Ministers. Both politicians finally agreed 'that as long as the annexation [of Bosnia and Herzegovina] has not taken place, subversive movements will not cease in South Slav territory.'[11]

Upon Foreign Minister Aehrenthal's orders to the Croatian Banus Paul Rauch on 26 March 1908 to gather material on Serbs guilty of high treason for later use, there followed the publication of denunciatory articles ('Finale' and 'Revolutionäres Statut' of the 'Slovenski Jug') and the arrest of fifty-three Serbian businessmen, traders, teachers, priests, civil servants and farmers at the beginning of August 1908 – all members of the Serbian National Independent Party (Srpska narodna samostalna stranka). Serious violations of legal norms occurred during their month-long detention pending trial. Almost ten months were to pass before the public prosecutor Accurti published his bill of indictment on 12 January 1909 and had it distributed as a supplement to the official gazette *Narodne Novine*. The charge of high treason according to Paragraph 58(c) of the penal code for Croatia-Slavonia was raised against Adam Pribićević and fifty-two comrades. It imputed to the accused direct or indirect contact with the Belgrade political association 'Slovenski Jug', which allegedly advocated the liberation and the political, social, national, and cultural unification of all South Slavs; the propagation of the idea of the Pan-Serbian state in the Kingdoms of Croatia-Slavonia and Dalmatia and in Bosnia and Herzegovina; the unleashing of a general revolution in these territories; the separation of these territories from the Austro-Hungarian Empire with the aid of the Serbian and Montenegrin armies, their incorporation into the Kingdom of Serbia, and the creation of a Serbian state under Peter I Karadjordjević.

The accused were charged with having undertaken activities, partly public and partly secret, performed either individually or in association, and carried out by means of intrigues and machinations, provocation, agitation and sedition, letters, printed matter and graphic presentation of treacherous ideas, advice given and actions of their own; secret-society activity and planning, which were aimed at separating the Kingdoms of Croatia, Slavonia and Dalmatia and Bosnia and Herzegovina 'from the uniform body and territorial expanse of the Austro-Hungarian Monarchy, at the same time threatening or at least endangering this state from abroad, but also directed towards provoking a rebellion or civil war in the interior'.[12]

The indictment was to a degree based on a denunciatory article written by a certain Djordje Nastić and published in German in Budapest on 31 July 1908, and in Serbo-Croat in Zagreb on 1 August. It was based also on the ostensible 'Provisorisches Statut' of the 'Slovenski Jug' which had the aim of liberating the South Slavs – this was published in the appendix to Nastić's pamphlet. As it later transpired, this 'statute' resembled the statutes of the national Serbian organisation 'Narodna odbrana', which was founded in December 1908, after the annexation, and which sought to unite all forces against the supposed unsurper, Austria-Hungary. In its specifics, the justification of the indictment contained many totally untenable assertions such as that: the population of the territory of the Kingdom of Croatia-Slavonia, including the section professing the Greek Orthodox faith, had known nothing about even the name of Serbia until a few years before; the population with Greek Orthodox beliefs who had immigrated from Bosnia had come under the name merely of 'Vlasi', a term denoting 'of Romance origins'; until a short time before, the population professing the Greek Orthodox faith had not known 'church' banners and 'church' arms; it was only priests who had made these emblems popular, introducing 'Serbian' banners and 'Serbian' arms; the Cyrillic alphabet was said to be a Serbian characteristic and had not been known to the population until a short time previously.[13]

Interpellations against this bill of indictment were made in the Hungarian Parliament and the Austrian Reichsrat, and the synod of bishops of the Serbian Orthodox Church protested against the charges. The Imperial War Ministry ordered XIII Corps headquarters in Zagreb to find out whether there were cases 'of the demoralising influence of Pan-Serbian propaganda on the discipline of the Imperial Army'. Deputies of the Croatian-Serbian Coalition, many of them former pupils of Masaryk's, now requested him to take a closer look at the trial for high treason in Zagreb. Masaryk went to Zagreb on 13 April 1909 to gain a personal impression of the trial and travelled on to Belgrade on 22 April to gather information there.[14]

As early as 7 May 1909, Masaryk called for a vote of urgency in the Chamber of Deputies, supported by sixty-seven Czech, Ukrainian, Slovene, Croatian, and Serbian deputies. He demanded that the annexation committee analyse the evidence presented at the Zagreb trial for high treason, evidence alleging the existence of a ramified treasonable separatist movement in the southern territories of the

Empire. If the annexation had been motivated by Pan-Serbian propaganda, he said, it was the duty of parliament, purely for humanitarian reasons, to examine this. The deputy of the German People's Party, Julius Sylvester, doubted whether Masaryk was really supporting the Serbs for humanitarian reasons. The Christian Social from Tyrol, Professor Michael Mayr, stressed that the trial was an autonomous affair of Croatia and that decency demanded no interference. Following Foreign Minister Aehrenthal's advice, the Prime Minister Richard Bienerth questioned the competence of the Austrian Reichsrat: 'According to the principles and provisions of our constitution, exclusively court authorities are authorised to track down treasonable movements in our sovereign territory; politics must not interfere in legal matters.'[15]

The Dalmatian-Croatian deputies Frano Ivanišević and Juraj Biankini spoke as seconders of Masaryk's motion. Finally the Social Democrats also voted in favour of Masaryk's emergency motion so that, in all, one hundred and sixty-seven deputies supported the motion and one hundred and thirty-two opposed it. The motion did not, however, gain the necessary two-thirds majority. Yet the calculations of Masaryk and the deputies of the Croatian-Serbian Coalition partly succeeded, because the Hungarian and Croatian press treated reports from the Austrian Reichsrat as immune and did not exclude them from their pages. This press policy circumvented the fact that during the trial in Zagreb there was a censorship 'in no way inferior to the Russian'. The Zagreb trial for high treason therefore became internationally known, not least for the reason that the Serbian Foreign Ministry invited many British, French, German and Italian journalists to Zagreb.[16]

Masaryk justified his emergency in two lengthy speeches in the Reichsrat on 14 and 18 May 1909. He began on a decidedly dramatic note: 'Gentlemen! Fifty-three gallows are to be erected, those are more than Russian conditions . . . fifty-three defendants . . . if you add the families, that amounts to 200 to 300 people to whom hundreds more are closely attached, so that 1000 people are certainly involved in the trial . . .'[17]

So, 'from a purely humanitarian viewpoint', according to Masaryk, the Austrian parliament had to deal with this trial, especially as it might touch off national passions anew in the Austrian 'half' of the Empire, which was in the midst of a conflict among the nationalities. The point of departure of the trial was the so-called 'Revolutionäres Statut' of Djordje Nastić, from which it was inferred that in the

Monarchy's southern region, a treasonable separatist movement was already organised along the statutory lines, and that not only in Hungarian and Croatian territory but also in Slovenia. Further, a pamphlet had been published by a certain 'Austriacus' in Cilli with the title: *Von Laibach bis Belgrad, serbische Umtriebe in Südöster- reich*, in which members of the Reichsrat were denounced, namely, the chairman of the Slovene People's Party, Janez Krek, and the leader of the Slovene liberals, Ivan Hribar.[18]

Masaryk criticised the 'blatant and malicious distortions of the facts' caused by the denunciations of the *agent provocateur* Nastić; he blamed the president of the court and the examining magistrate for grave personal misdemeanours, but he was also in a position to refute some serious charges analytically. He said that the concept 'Serbian Church' was justified as a *terminus technicus*, since the patriarch in Sremski Karlovci bore the official title 'Serbian Patriarch'. According to the Croatian-Slavonian law of 1887, the Cyrillic alphabet was to be used for official purposes in every community with a Serbian majority and the learning of the Cyrillic alphabet was compulsory at school. King Peter's picture could be bought by anyone at fairs and many vendors 'were certainly not aware of the political significance of these pictures.' But in the districts of Bohemia bordering on Bavaria and Saxony, there were also many pictures of neighbouring monarchs, and that, according to Masaryk, struck no one as high treason.[19]

Masaryk had, however, researched the legal background to the charge of high treason less carefully. He was merely of the opinion that the concept no longer appeared in the *Österreichisches Staats- wörterbuch* drafted by Ernst Mischler and Joseph Ulbrich, but that it was still valid in Hungary and Croatia. Indeed, according to the Austrian penal code, only the crime of 'Landesverrat' existed, whereas the Hungarian Criminal Code of 1878 differentiated be- tween 'Hochverrat' and 'Staatsverrat'. The legal basis for the indict- ment in the Zagreb trial for high treason was the neo-absolutist Austrian penal law of 1852, which was still in force in Croatia- Slavonia. According to its Paragraph 58:

> The crime of high treason is committed by whoever undertakes something
> a) harming or endangering the person of the Emperor as regards body, health or liberty or intending to prevent him from using his right to rule; or
> b) aimed at bringing about a violent change in the form of government [since 1862 also in the constitution];

c) intended to separate one part of the body or territory of the Austrian Empire or to bring about or increase a threat to the state from abroad or directed at provoking an uprising or a civil war in the interior; whether this happen publicly or secretly, is committed by individuals or groups in the form of conspiracy, exhortation, agitation, sedition, word of mouth, in writing, print or in graphic representation, advice or deed, with or without the taking up of arms, in the form of secrets or plots communicated for such purposes, seditious activity, recruitment, espionage, abetting or whatever other action for such a purpose, even if it had been unsuccessful.[20]

In the indictment Masaryk could not find the precise wording that might indicate whether the fifty-three Serbs were being accused of crimes against the sovereign as 'Hochverrat' or 'Landesverrat'. So most of the defendants did not know which form of high treason they were supposed to have committed, although they faced the death penalty for it. Nevertheless, Masaryk overlooked the fact that the charges were formulated expressly in connection with Paragraph 58(c), even if the wording was rather vague. At the end of August 1908, the retired Croatian-Slavonian senior civil servant (Sektionschef) Aleksander Badaj expressed his views on the problems of high treason and denunciation in a letter to the Banus Rauch: 'It is of the least credit to the [Croatian] legislator when he makes people guilty of high treason without conclusive necessity.' The limits of high treason were 'flexible' in the old Austrian penal law still in force in Croatia. High treason was interpreted as having been committed even when 'the only preparations for it had become facts'. Moreover, the Zagreb trial for high treason was based on the testimony of a person who was a 'criminal' and a 'denouncer', but who had been assured of immunity by the penal law. The charges also branded 'nationalities of the Monarchy hitherto always loyal to king and country with the stigma of high treason'. So Badaj considered this criminal case 'as difficult from the legal viewpoint, politically critical and, at any rate, disastrous for the country'.[21]

Masaryk's assessment of the situation was even more drastic: 'The so-called trial for high treason in Zagreb is bluntly an exemplary case of the old school of politics and its interpretation of historical events and developments.' Politically speaking, it belonged to the epoch of aristocracy and aristocratic absolutism. The aristocratic court diplomats and their illusion that the views and actions of the few potentates and their helpers were all-important were beginning to lose influence in the running of society; yet the belief that politics was increasingly based on observation of the masses and on science was still subject to public debate. In Austria-Hungary, many remnants of aristocratic absolutism had survived, especially in foreign policy, and were expressed in constitutional terms in the joint ministries separated from parliamentarianism and in the unspecific incorporation of the delegations.[22]

MASARYK ON THE FRIEDJUNG AND VASIĆ TRIALS

On the first anniversary of the annexation of Bosnia and Herzegovina, on 5 October 1909, the court in Zagreb passed its sentence – twelve years' penal servitude for the brothers Adam and Valerijan Pribićević and severe terms of imprisonment of between five and eight years for thirty other defendants.[23] Meanwhile, in Vienna, another trial was being prepared concerning the Pan-Serbian propaganda. As early as 25 March 1909, the eminent historian Heinrich Friedjung published an article with the title 'Österreich-Ungarn und Serbien' in the *Neue Freie Presse* which referred to documents the Ballhausplatz had made available to him. This article made grave charges against the Serbian dynasty, the Serbian government, and their alleged allies in the Croatian-Serbian Coalition, blaming the deputies Svetozar Pribićević, Edo Lukinić, Franko Potočnjak, and Frano Supilo directly for having been bribed by Serbia. In the *Reichspost* in November 1908, the editor-in-chief, Friedrich Funder, had published German translations of five Serbian documents tending in the same direction. The deputies under the leadership of Frano Supilo (1870–1917) from Dalmatia sued Friedjung and the *Reichspost*, although the suit was really directed at the Foreign Minister, Count Aehrenthal.[24]

Although expert testimony provided by the dynastic, court, and state records office in Vienna, and dating from 8 October 1909 exposed the signatures under documents of the 'Slovenski Jug' as forgeries, Friedjung, who never saw the 'originals' himself, continued to believe in the authenticity of the material, which had been drawn up by the Serbian confidant Milan Stefanović (Vasić) at the Austro-Hungarian embassy in Belgrade. At the beginning of the trial on 9 December 1909, he submitted 'Aktenstücke zur großserbischen Bewegung in Österreich-Ungarn.' Funder also presented a similar collection, among other things a cash order from the senior Serbian civil servant Miroslav Spalajković to Supilo. When the testimony of the Belgrade university professor, Božidar Marković, proved the minutes of the 'Slovenski Jug' to be forgeries and when Spalajković's statements similarly exposed other documents, however, the trial threatened to become a scandal for the Ballhausplatz. The president of the court appealed to Joseph Baernreither, a member of the upper chamber, and to the parliamentary deputy Masaryk to bring about a compromise. When Friedjung declared he would make no further use of these documents, Supilo and the Croatian-Serbian Coalition withdrew their suit. This moral victory for the Croatian-Serbian deputies soon had important consequences in Zagreb. On 1 April 1910 the 'Septemviraltafel' quashed the verdict of 5 October 1909.[25]

In the delegation sessions of 8 and 11 November 1910, Professor Masaryk took critical stock of Count Aehrenthal's policy and of the Belgrade embassy:

> Count Aehrenthal has always listed two reasons for the necessity of the annexation: first the introduction of the constitution in Turkey . . . ; secondly the Pan-Serbian revolutionary movement. . . . Both arguments are invalid, the second is not an argument at all, but a falsehood . . .

> A Pan-Serbian movement such as that with which Count Aehrenthal caused such alarm has never existed. That is proved by the double-dealings of the Zagreb trial for high treason; it is proved by the sorry outcome of the Friedjung case . . . Count Aehrenthal has the great diplomatic merit of having fabricated a revolutionary *actio in distans* – the forgeries of his Belgrade embassy and his reactions to these forgeries have not saved the provinces, but made Austria-Hungary ridiculous throughout the Balkans, among the South Slavs, and in the whole of Europe.[26]

The political outcome was even graver. After 1909, Serbia became a centre of different revolutionary and nationalist societies, and in the South Slav territories of the Empire, the idea of Yugoslavia began to spread among the young.

NOTES

1   On the relations between the Czechs and the South Slavs see Václav Žáček (ed.), *Češi a Jihoslované v minulosti. Od nejstarších dob do roku*

1918 (Prague: Academia, 1975); Milada Paulová, 'Tomáš G. Masaryk a Jihoslované', in *Československo-jihoslovanská revue*, vol. 7 (Prague, 1937) pp. 241–87; Jaroslav Šidak, 'Československo-južnoslavenski odnosi', in *Enciklopedija Jugoslavije*, vol. 2 (Zagreb: Leksikografski zavod, 1956) pp. 557–71.

2   See Seton-Watson, *Die Südslawische Frage im Habsburger Reiche* (Berlin: Meyer & Jessen, 1913); Ludwig Bittner, Alfred F. Pribram, Heinrich Srbik, Hans Uebersberger (eds), *Österreich-Ungarns Außenpolitik von der bosnischen Krise bis zum Kriegsausbruch 1914. Diplomatische Aktenstücke des österreichisch-ungarischen Ministeriums des Äußern* (Vienna-Leipzig: Österreichischer Bundesverlag, 1930) vol. I; Rene Lovrenčić, *Geneza politike 'Novog kursa'* (Zagreb: Liber, 1972).

3   Ernst Pliwa, *Österreichische Universitäten 1863/64 – 1902/03* (Vienna: Tempsky, 1908); *Spomenici u povodu proslave 300-godišnjice sveučilišta u Zagrebu* (Zagreb: Školska knjiga, 1969); Jan Havránek: 'Die Studenten an der Schwelle des modernen tschechischen politischen Lebens', in *Acta Universitatis Carolinae – Philosophica et Historica*, vol. IV (Prague, 1969) pp. 29–52; Gustav Otruba, 'Die Universitäten in der Hochschulorganisation der Donaumonarchie. Nationale Erziehungsstätten im Vielvölkerreich 1850 bis 1914', in *Student und Hochschule im 19. Jahrhundert* (Göttingen: Vandenhoeck and Ruprecht, 1975) pp. 89–138.

4   Vlastimil Šťastný, 'Ve znamení tzv. pokrokového hnutí', in *Češi a Jihoslované*, pp. 488–510; Bogdan Krizman (ed.), *Korespondencija Stjepana Radića* (Zagreb: Liber, 1972) vol. I pp. 25–70; Lovrenčić, *Geneza politike*, pp. 40–2; *Hrvatska misao*, vol. I (Prague, 1897).

5   Václav Burian, 'Slovinci na universitě Karlově', in *Slovanský přehled* (Prague, 1948) vol. XXXIV, no. 3–4, pp. 140–51; Mirjana Gross, 'Nacionalne ideje studentske omladine u Hrvatskoj uoči svjetskog rata', in *Historijski zbornik* (Zagreb, 1968–69) vol. XXI–XXII, pp. 77–9; Anton Dermota, 'Masaryk a Slovinci', in *T. G. Masarykovi k šedesátým narozeninám* (Prague: Grosman and Svoboda, 1910) p. 37; Karel Herman, 'Styky v období neoslavismu', in *Češi a Jihoslované*, pp. 563–7.

6   Lovrenčić, *Geneza politike*, pp. 43–5; Arnold Suppan, 'Bildungspolitische Emanzipation und gesellschaftliche Modernisierung. Die südslavischen Studenten an der tschechischen Universität Prag um die Jarhrhundertwende und der Einfluß Professor Masaryks', in vol. I Richard G. Plaschka and Karlheinz Mack (eds), *Wegentz europäischen Geistes* (Vienna: Geschichte und Politik, 1983) pp. 303–25.

7   Josef Král, 'Masaryk filosof a sociolog', in *Sborník přednášek o T. G. Masarykovi* (Prague: Orbis, 1931) pp. 3–24; Milan Machovec, *Thomas G. Masaryk* (Graz, Vienna, Cologne: Styria, 1969) pp. 92–3.

8   Masaryk, *Česká otázka. Snahy a tužby národního obrození* (Prague: Renn, 1895); *idem*, *Naše nynější krise. Pád strany staročeské a počátkové směrů nových* (Prague: Renn, 1896); *idem*, *Jan Hus. Naše obrození a reformace* (Prague: Čas, 1896); Josef Pekař, 'ad Vančura', in *Český časopis historický*, vol. XVIII (Prague: 1912) p. 29; Josef Pekař, *Masarykova česká filosofie* (Prague: Historický klub, 1912); see

Richard G. Plaschka, 'Um Königinhofer Handschrift und Funktion der Geschichte', in *Österreichische Osthefte*, vol. XXVII (1985) p. 428.
9   Zdeněk Nejedlý, *T. G. Masaryk* (Prague: Melantrich 1931) vol. I/ii pp. 226–7; Machovec, *Masaryk*, pp. 135–6.
10 Kamil Krofta, 'Masaryk und unser politisches Programm', in *Masaryk – Staatsmann und Denker* (Prague: Orbis, 1930) pp. 25–50; Machovec, *Masaryk*, pp. 22–9; see T. G. Masaryk, *Die philosophischen und sociologischen Grundlagen des Marxismus* (Vienna: Carl Konegen, 1899).
11 Dimitrije Djordjević, *Carinski rat Austro-Ugarske i Srbije 1906–1911* (Belgrade: Istorijski institut, 1962); Andrej Mitrović, *Prodor na Balkan i Srbija (1908–1918* (Belgrade: Nolit, 1981); Mirjana Gross, *Vladavina Hrvatsko srpske koalicije 1906–1907* (Belgrade: Institut društvenih nauka, 1960); Haus-, Hof- und Staatsarchiv Wien [HHStA], Protokolle des Gemeinsamen Ministerrates 1907/08, Kart. XL/306, 1 Dec. 1907, 30 April 1908, 19 Aug. 1908.
12 On the preparations of the trial for high treason and the arrests and the interrogations see Mirjana Gross, 'Hrvatska uoči aneksije Bosne i Hercegovine', in *Istorija XX veka* (Belgrade: Institut društvenih nauka, 1962) Zbornik radova, vol. III, pp. 37–9; Scotus Viator (=R. W. Seton-Watson), *Absolutismus in Kroatien* (Vienna, Leipzig: Stern, 1909); 'Obtužnica, koju je kr. državno odvjetničtvo u Zagrebu dne 12. sječnja 1909. podiglo protiv A. Pribićevića i 52 druga radi zločina veleizdaje' – Supplement to *Narodne Novine*, no. 12, 12 Jan. 1909.
13 Georg Nastić, *Finale* (Budapest, 1908). There is a German translation of the 'Provisional Statute' in the *Berliner Monatschefte*, 12 (1930) pp. 1142ff. In the *Pester Lloyd* on 12 August and 23 August 1908, official denials were published that neither Banus Rauch nor prime minister Wekerle nor foreign minister Aehrenthal – not to mention the king – had had anything to do with the arrests.
14 The deputy Djuro Šurmin in *Agramer Tagblatt*, 11 Feb. 1909; 'Einsichtsstück' of the Imperial War Ministry, no. 1826, 8 April 1909 in HHStA, PA XIX, Serbien 80, Liasse XII/4.
15 *Stenographische Protokolle des Abgeordnetenhauses des österreichischen Reichsrates*, vol. 1 (Vienna, 1909) pp. 1128–40; private letter of Aehrenthal to Bienerth, Budapest, 9 May 1909 in HHStA, PA XIX, Serbien 80, Liasse XII/4, no. 1835; Masaryk, *Der Agramer Hochverratsprozeß und die Annexion von Bosnien und der Herzegowina* (Vienna: Carl Konegen, 1909) pp. 1–5.
16 Masaryk, *Hochverratsprozeß*, pp. 4–5; see *Le Procès d'Agram et l'opinion européenne* (Paris, 1909); *The Times*, 2 Dec. 1908, 12 Feb. 1909, 1 March 1909. Bogdan Medaković, chairman of the Serbian Independent Party, had already contacted the Serbian consul Petović in January 1909 in the course of the sessions of parliament in Budapest, and had asked that the Serbian Foreign Minister Milovanović be asked to induce the Serbian government to mobilise the foreign press for the Zagreb trial. Milovanović thereupon ordered the Serbian ambassadors in the capitals of Europe, particularly Vesnić in Paris and Popović in St Petersburg, to ensure that as many foreign journalists as possible came

to Zagreb. The editorial staff of some French newspapers even received subsidies from the Serbian embassy in Paris. Milovanović not only used his reserve funds, he also tried to enliven things with the news that, under the circumstances, death sentences might be expected in Zagreb. In the Belgrade *Samouprava* he characterised the Zagreb trial as a second Dreyfus affair. (Diplomatski Arhiv Saveznog Sekretarijta za inostrane poslove (DASSIP) Beograd, Političko odeljenje, Pov. br. 2, 6 Jan. 1909, Pov. br. 62, 8 Jan. 1909, Pov. br. 206, 26 Jan. 1909, Pov. br. 270, 31 March 1909, Pov. br. 314, 5 Feb. 1909; Miloš Boghitschewitsch, *Die auswärtige Politik Serbiens 1903–1914* (Berlin: Brücken–Verlag, 1929) vol. I, doc. no. 62.)

17 Masaryk, *Hochverratsprozeß*, p. 7.
18 See Joseph Maria Baernreither, *Fragmente eines politischen Tagebuches. Die südslawische Frage und Österreich-Ungarn vor dem Weltkrieg* (Berlin: Verlag für Kulturpolitik, 1928) p. 135.
19 Masaryk, *Hochverratsprozeß*, pp. 20–2.
20 *Das Strafgesetz über Verbrechen, Vergehen und Übertretungen vom 27. Mai 1852*, 18th ed. (Vienna, 1897). §58 (c) was reinforced by §59 (b) of the penal code, which included the death penalty, too.
21 Letter of Dr. Badaj to Banus Rauch; note of Rauch to Aehrenthal, 29 Aug. 1908; HHStA, Kabinettsarchiv, Geheimakten, Karton 26.
22 Masaryk, *Hochverratsprozeß*, pp. viii–ix. 'In conclusion I can say: a Serbian or Serbo-Croatian irredentism in the territory of Hungary, Croatia, Slavonia, and in the territory inhabited by the Slovenes, does not exist, nor has it ever existed. And it does not occur to the Serbs in Belgrade to pursue Pan-Serbian propaganda in Austria, simply for the reason that they are culturally and financially ill-equipped to do so.' Masaryk, *Hochverratsprozeß*, p. 65; see Waltraud Schuster, *Der Agramer Hochverratsprozeß* (Phil. diss. University of Vienna, 1979).
23 'Osuda kr. sudbenog stola u Zagrebu u kaznenoj parnici kr. državnog odvjeništva u Zagrebu proti Adamu Pribićevića i 52 druga radi zločinstva veleizdaja označ. u §-u 58. k.z.' (Zagreb, 1909) p. 8.
24 See Seton-Watson, *Die südslawische Frage*, pp. 233–4; H. Wickham Steed, *Through Thirty Years* (London: Heinemann, 1924) vol. I, pp. 308–9; Friedrich Funder, *Vom Gestern ins Heute. Aus dem Kaiserreich in die Republik*, 3rd ed. (Vienna, Munich: Herold, 1971) pp. 342–3.
25 *Österreich-Ungarns Außenpolitik*, vol. II, no. 1752, 1851, 1894; Seton-Watson, *Die südslawische Frage*, pp. 243–317; *Die Zeit*, 22 Dec. 1909; 'Obustava kaznenog postupka, proti Adamu Pribićeviću i dr., radi zločinstva veleizdaje' (Arhiv Hrvatske Zagreb, Kralj. ministar hrv.-slav.-dalmatinski, br. 322/1910); letter, R. W. Seton-Watson to Heinrich Friedjung, 25 Dec. 1909, *R. W. Seton-Watson i Jugoslaveni. Korespondencija 1906–1941* (Zagreb, London: Liber, 1976) vol. I, p. 65.
26 T. G. Masaryk, *Vasić – Forgách – Aehrenthal. Einiges Material zur Charakteristik unserer Diplomatie* (Prague: Čas, 1911) pp. 77–8; see also T. G. Masaryk, *Rakouská zahraniční politika a diplomacie* (Prague: Čas, 1911).

10 Masaryk and Czech Politics, 1906–1914

Bruce Garver

This chapter emphasises Masaryk's work as the founder and leader of the Czech People's, later Progressive, Party; as advocate of a more democratic and 'progressive' Czech nationalism, and as a critic of rival Czech political movements and of shortcomings in Czech and Austro-Hungarian society, education, and government. It touches upon Masaryk's scholarly publications about politics, religion, and history only to the degree necessary to indicate the great extent to which they not only conditioned his politics and expectations of continued 'national revival', but were in turn informed by his political activities and concerns. The chapter also briefly discusses Masaryk's role as a spokesman internationally for the rights of small nations, with a view to understanding how this activity logically and effectively complemented his efforts in Austria-Hungary to 'democratise' politics, promote Czech national solidarity and self-help, encourage freedom of conscience and speech, and promote social reform.

The chapter consists of three parts. The first examines Masaryk's role in the founding of the Czech People's Party (1900) and in its reorganisation and development as the Czech Progressive Party from 1906 to 1914, with emphasis on continuity as opposed to change in party programmes and tactics. The second part discussed Masaryk and the Progressive Party in their relations with other Czech political parties and with the Habsburg authorities, and emphasises those domestic social, political, and religious disputes in which Masaryk figured prominently as a critic of 'feudal' institutions, dominant social classes, and prevailing prejudices. The third demonstrates how Masaryk emerged in the years 1909 to 1914 as the leading opponent in word and deed of Austro-Hungarian imperialism abroad and authoritarianism at home; it also indicates how Masaryk never ceased to be a forthright critic of Czech society, politics and character, and how in the years 1911 to 1914, he continued his efforts to persuade all Czechs that their future national welfare required not only continued hard work and good citizenship, but also the implementation of such reforms as the emancipation of women, universal suffrage at all levels of government, and greater educational opportunities for, and increased political participation by, workers and farmers. The paper concludes with an assessment of Masaryk's importance as a national leader in the years 1906 to 1914, as he, an 'outsider', moralist and scholar in Czech politics became one of the few Czech politicians known and respected in the world arena. The Czech nation did not then lack ambitious and articulate advocates of the Czech national interest or of the interests of a specific sex, class or religion. What it found unusual, and initially unpalatable, in Masaryk was that he was a foe of injustice and advocate of reform who insisted that he acted first out of moral imperative and secondly, if at all, out of political expediency, and he was a 'Realist' whose 'Realism' obliged him to try to make people and institutions better than they were rather than to accept them as they were. This man wanted to emancipate workers without embracing Marxism, liberate women without promoting feminism, and educate the young without celebrating youth. In both his 'humanity programme' before 1900 and his increased advocacy of 'democracy in politics' thereafter, he stressed those qualities, aspirations, and interests all human beings have in common regardless of class, age, sex, or nationality.

Among recent scholarly monographs, my chapter is most indebted to works by Roland J. Hoffmann, Eva Schmidt-Hartmann, Roman Szporluk, Otto Urban, and my own study, *The Young Czech Party, 1874–1901, and the Emergence of a Multi-Party System*.[1]

PART I

The General (Rámcový) Programme issued upon the founding of the Czech People's (Realist) Party (ČSL/Česká strana lidová [realistická]) on 31 March 1900, emphasised national solidarity and social, political and educational reform, and was based on Masaryk's views of Czech history and politics as expressed in his seminal theoretical works of the 1890s.[2] This 107-page Programme and the appended 90-page proceedings of the first Party Congress discussed all the issues that Masaryk would more specifically address during the next six years and that would condition the enlargement by merger of the ČSL in October 1905 and its reorganisation at the Pardubice congress of January 1906 into the Czech Progressive Party (ČSP/Česká strana pokroková).[3] Its founding followed a decade in which Masaryk had entered politics as a Young Czech in 1890, only to break with that party at the end of 1893 and emerge in the last half of the decade as that party's most outspoken and perspicacious critic. His decision to become the principal founder and leader of the ČSL in 1900 arose only partly from his disillusion with the Young Czechs' inability to implement their political agenda of the nineties, which included language legislation and other moderate reforms. To a greater degree, this decision grew, first, out of his desire to create an independent party as an instrument with which he and reform-minded colleagues could most effectively influence the policies of the leading 'bourgeois' parties and, second, out of his conviction that the Young Czechs, like their Old Czech predecessors, were tied to an antiquated and unrepresentative political system, given their alliance with the Conservative Large Landowners and their unwillingness to support women's suffrage or even suffrage in local, district and provincial government for men without property or higher education. In a series of speeches from 1895 to 1906, all later published, he thoroughly exposed that system's inadequacies and the unfitness of the Young Czechs to represent the interests of the Czech people. Instead he called for the reordering of Czech politics on the basis of 'natural' as opposed to 'historical' State rights, and for the establishment of universal suffrage and a truly representative government at every level, responsible neither to the Habsburgs nor to the privileged strata of society, but to all citizens, regardless of sex, class, nationality or creed.[4]

Though the ČSL's demands for equal educational and economic opportunities for all citizens did not call for any redistribution of property, its advocacy of extensive social legislation in addition to educational reforms brought its desiderata much closer to those of the Social Democrats than to those of any 'bourgeois' party. The General Programme also reflected Masaryk's profound disenchantment with the justice and viability of the Habsburg state, a conviction that he had reached after the Young Czech political debâcle at the end of the nineties, and that only grew deeper as the Habsburg authorities and the aristocracy demonstrated, in his view, their increasing incapacity to manage domestic or foreign affairs honestly, efficiently and in the interests of all citizens. The enlarged (185 pages), almost entirely new, and much more specific Programme of the Czech Progressive Party of 1912 that he helped write and edit reflected his increasing disillusion with the Habsburgs, the aristocracy, and the privileged classes of Czech society, and reaffirmed not only his programme for political democratisation but also a call for the Czechs to help defend the interests of other small nations, and to work to achieve the greatest possible cultural and political independence.[5]

The remarkable consistency and continuity from 1881 to 1914 in Masaryk's work as a teacher and scholar and in his understanding of history, society, and religion, contrasts markedly with his often changing political views and tactics, changes attributable in part to changing circumstances and in part to his attempts to improve those circumstances in accordance with his principles and his understanding of the past and the present. In fact, during those years, Masaryk's political career developed in at least three fairly distinct phases. The first, alluded to above, began with the Manuscripts controversy and encompassed the 1890s, during which Masaryk first joined and then (in 1893) left the Young Czech party to become its most formidable critic, in part by developing his 'humanity programme' and redefining 'the Czech Question'. The second phase beginning with the founding of the ČSL in 1900, saw Masaryk's participation in myriad political and religious controversies, and ended with the reorganisation of the inadequate ČSL as the ČSP in 1906, at a time of worsening political crisis in Austria-Hungary just before the introduction of universal male suffrage for elections to the lower house of the Reichsrat. The third phase, the subject of this paper, encompasses the nine years of Masaryk's leadership of the Czech Progressive Party (ČSP) in that brief period of limited mass male participation at one level of Cisleithanian politics. During this period, Masaryk gave greater emphasis than before to foreign affairs. His deepening interest in and understanding of Russia and the United States led him increasingly to view Czech problems and prospects in an international perspective. His growing concern over the increased aggressiveness of Austro-Hungarian and Imperial German foreign policy prompted him to support both radical and progressive patriots among the South Slavs and the Slovaks and to become the most outspoken and one of the best informed critics of Austro-Hungarian foreign and domestic policies.

The decision by Masaryk and his colleagues to enlarge the ČSL by merger in 1905, and to reorganise it and rename it the ČSP in January 1906, arose to a limited extent from internal and to a much greater extent from external causes. Internal party divisions included ideological and personality disputes typical of all Czech parties and one public scandal, the Herben affair of 1902 that included embezzlement charges – later dropped – against Jan Herben, editor of *Čas*, the party's unofficial newspaper. More important was the disaffection and later the defection of some of the ablest younger party members, like historian and editor Zdeněk Tobolka and sociologist Emanuel Chalupný, who chafed under Masaryk's unsystematic management and were attracted by the prospects for cutting a larger figure in another more powerful party.[6] On the positive side, in May 1905, the ČSL was joined by the Progressive Citizen's Club for Pardubsko and Chrudimsko under the leadership of Alois Hajn. These new members brought not only the newspaper *Osvěta lidu* but also new talent and some new ideas to the ČSL. Noteworthy among the latter was an unequivocal commitment to women's emancipation.[7]

At least three external causes for reorganisation can be identified. First was the 1905–1906 campaign for universal male suffrage, led initially and principally by the Social Democrats, but they were joined eventually by the 'bourgeois' parties, first of which was the ČSL. This campaign persuaded the Emperor to agree in October 1906 to introduce universal male suffrage in the January 1907 elections to the lower house of the Reichsrat, thanks in part to concern about the spread of the Russian Revolution of 1905, and in part to hopes – unrealised – that such suffrage would diminish the representation of nationalistic reform-minded parties and increase that of *kaisertreu* clerical and agrarian movements.[8] Secondly, anticipation of this new franchise led in 1906 to the reorganisation of the Czech Agrarian party and all Czech 'bourgeois' parties, as the liberal wing of the Agrarians under Antonín Švehla prevailed and endorsed universal male suffrage, as the National Socialists accented youth, as the State Rights Radicals and Radical Progressives combined to form the State Rights Progressives, and as the Young Czechs, with Václav Škarda and Karel Kramář as their principal spokesmen, touted a new 'positive politics' and suggested that their reorganised and slightly enlarged party would be the logical leader of a coalition of all Czech parties except the Social Democrats.[9] Anticipating such reorganisation by its rivals, the ČSL undertook its reorganisation first, in order to remain competitive. Thirdly, the serious internal social and political problems in the Bohemian Lands that had prompted the founding of the ČSL in 1900 were in 1906 no closer to resolution or alleviation, thus requiring Masaryk's and his colleagues' rededication of time and energy to politics.

In the light of the internal party dissension and defections up to 1906, Masaryk recognised the need to clarify party organisation, delegate greater authority as well as responsibility, broaden the party's base of support, continue to improve party finances, and regularise party administration on a continuous basis through the creation of a permanent Secretariat. The first two objectives were implemented in 1906, and the third became an ongoing task, made somewhat easier by the reorganised party's decision to admit women as full members, electing one to a high party office, and running two as candidates in the 1908 Bohemian Diet elections. Achieving the fourth objective was facilitated by the establishment late in 1905 of the Progressive Cooperative (Družstvo Pokrok) to print all party periodicals, pamphlets, placards and monographs. The fifth task was completed in August 1907.[10]

The party held a total of three congresses before the outbreak of World War I, the first in January 1906, the second in June 1908, and the third in January 1912.[11] Evident from the first congress up to July 1914 was Masaryk's willingness to profit from his and others' mistakes, and to attract able and independent-minded associates who took over enough of the day-to-day burdens of party managements to allow him to concentrate on what he did best – teaching, writing, public speaking, and handling the most delicate political negotiations at home and abroad. Though Masaryk remained the dominant personality in the ČSP, it never became, as the ČSL almost did, a one-man show. Masaryk clearly understood that without a party and without the help of his colleagues, especially František Drtina and Alois Hajn, he could not have achieved the success that he did achieve in his many pre-war political endeavours.[12]

A profile of Progressive Party leadership in 1906 and in 1912 shows educators and women present in small numbers but in a greater proportion than in other Czech parties. Lawyers and other professional occupations predominated in the ČSP as they did in other bourgeois parties, the National Socialists to some degree excepted.[13] Given its radically progressive programme, especially its advocacy of suffrage extension and women's and workers' interests, the party had little chance of winning any elections under class voting in local and district or curial voting in provincial self-government. Beginning in 1907 when universal male suffrage obtained in lower-house Reichsrat elections, the party understood its chances of winning elections would be increased wherever it could conclude electoral agreements with one or more compatible parties.

Becoming a mass political party had not been among the expectations of Masaryk and other founders of the ČSP, but they had expected that they could best influence other 'bourgeois' parties to adopt some Progressive views only if Progressives were to have the independence of judgement and action that came with control of their own party. Masaryk's experience as a Young Czech representative in the Reichsrat from 1891 through 1893, and his increasing disenchantment with Young Czech objectives and tactics from 1894 to 1906, persuaded him that he could not effect the reforms he desired by associating with a party where leadership and policy-making responsibility would never be his. Given his reservations about Marxism and his 'bourgeois' occupation, he could never exercise leadership in Social Democracy, despite his humble origins and general agreement with Social Democratic political and cultural aims. His goal was not, as some detractors claimed, to be the big fish in a small pond but to acquire the forum outside of his classroom and the press that he believed necessary if he were to have any chance of effecting the reform of Czech politics and society that he desired.

So few changes had occurred in the relationships between the ČSL and the other Czech political parties from 1900 to 1906, and so explicitly had the General Programme discussed these relationships past and present, that the Progressives at their inaugural party congress of 21 January 1906 decided that an extensive review and redefinition of these relationships was unnecessary, save for cursory reference in the Concise (Stručný) Programme of 1906 to those crises and conflicts that since 1900 had demonstrated the soundness of the party's first estimation of its opponents.[14]

A comparison of the General Programme of 1900 as amended in 1906–08 with the 1912 Programme of the Czech Progressive Party clearly indicates both continuity and change in Masaryk's and the party's political views and tactics in the first six years of mass male participation in Cisleithanian politics. The two programmes well reflected Masaryk's expectations for social, political, and educational reform, not only because he composed large parts of these programmes and helped edit the rest, but also because the General Programme was based on his scholarly and philosophical writings, and the 1912 Programme reflected the content of his political speeches and scholarly publications during the first decade of the twentieth century. Before extensively examining the issues which Masaryk and the Progressives defined more explicitly, discussed more thoroughly, and advocated more forcefully in 1912 than in 1906–08 or 1900, let us survey briefly the considerable continuity in political theory and practice between the General Programme and the 1912 Programme.

Masaryk and his Progressive colleagues based their 1912 Programme in large part upon the view of history and politics Masaryk had defined in his seminal works of the nineties, summarised in the General Programme of 1900, and reaffirmed by the Concise Programme of 1906 and the *Organisační řád* of 1908.[15] The 1912 Programme sought, as Masaryk did in his publications, to stimulate Czech national self-confidence and self-help, to diminish Czech acceptance for better or for worse of the inevitability of Habsburg rule, and to reduce the influence in politics both of Catholicism and its liberal antithesis, Czech free thought. In its historical world-view, this programme elaborated upon and slightly modified František Palacký's vision of the Czech past, while in politics it revealed its debt to Karel Havlíček, especially in its efforts to 'democratise' Czech political life, curtail aristocratic privileges, and stand up to the authoritarian Habsburg state. Between 1906 and 1912, Masaryk and the Progressives had thus given increasing emphasis to political 'democratisation' without repudiating the 'humanity programme' of the 1890s.

Continuity from 1900 to 1914 is also remarkable in the relationship between the ČSL/ČSP and the other Czech political parties. In the General Programme, Masaryk and his associates went to great lengths to distinguish their platform and tactics from those of the already established Czech parties, in part because the ČSL was the last of five new Czech parties to appear in the multi-party system that emerged from 1898 to 1900, upon the break-up of the majority Young Czech coalition party that had exercised hegemony in Czech politics during the 1890s.[16] The ČSL, as the smallest as well as the newest Czech party, had the difficult task of persuading the electorate of the need for supporting a third small party of the intelligentsia. Furthermore, Masaryk and his colleagues clearly wished to demonstrate the extent to which their party had developed an interpretation or 'philosophy' of Czech history and politics that, in its reformulation of Bohemian State rights and in its greater emphasis on achieving political democratisation and social reform consonant with Christian charity and belief in the equality of souls, was more comprehensive, 'progressive', and clearly formulated than the programme of liberalism and 'historical' Bohemian State rights – rights 'not worth a tinker's fart' – advocated by all other 'bourgeois' parties except the Radical Progressives, some of whose adherents under Alois Hajn would help transform the ČSL into the ČSP in 1906.[17] This ČSL interpretation, in its complexity and universality, both rivalled and offered an alternative to the Marxism of the Social Democrats and to the Catholic worldview of the clerical parties. Finally, the leaders of the ČSL wished to demonstrate to other Czech political parties the desirability of promoting Czech national solidarity by incorporating into their party platforms something of Masaryk's and the ČSL's political 'philosophy', a concept that, as Roland J. Hoffmann suggests, is perhaps best defined as a political 'ideology'.[18] This effort by Masaryk and the ČSL to persuade opposition leaders and the general public to support 'progressive' proposals for reform reflected Masaryk's endorsement of the multi-party system as one well suited to the free expression, representation, and reconciliation of various class and occupational interests in Czech society.[19] Masaryk and the ČSL (later ČSP) leadership thus had no expectation that their party would ever become as large or powerful as the Young Czech or Agrarian parties. Rather Masaryk saw the ČSL/ČSP and their programmes as an antidote to the excesses of Young Czech nationalism, liberalism and materialism, and as a means of influencing the 'bourgeois' parties to strengthen the Czech nation by promoting 'progressive' measures.[20] The extent to which the ČSP fulfilled this expectation from 1906 to 1914 through conflict and cooperation with other Czech parties will be discussed in the second part of this chapter.

Masaryk's work in Czech politics from 1900 to 1914 was coloured by his belief, based primarily upon his perception of growing collaboration between clerical and reactionary forces in Austria-Hungary, France, and Russia, that political democratisation required the reform of organised religion to the extent that religious values, notably the golden rule – respect for the dignity of every individual – should become the foundation for such democratisation, and that established churches should cease to be handmaidens of authoritarianism and religious intolerance. More specifically, at this time religious issues primarily preoccupied Masaryk for many reasons. First, this preoccupation was a logical continuation of his deep interest in religion, ever since he had asserted in *Suicide as a Mass Phenomenon of Modern Civilisation* (1881) that religious faith, principally by increasing every believer's self-respect and sense of social responsibility, was the best antidote to self-destruction. Just as his *Czech Question* (1895) followed Palacký in positing a religious basis for Czech nationality, so did his *Social Question* (1898) contend that implementing social reforms or making revolution without reference to Christian values risked the perpetration of injustices comparable to those the Social Democrats rightly wished to abolish.[21] Second, not only had the Hilsner affair demonstrated to

Masaryk that religious intolerance and anti-Semitism were more deeply embedded in Czech and German society than he had thought, but he was persuaded that he must give high priority to combating clericalism after noting how most German clericals had made common cause with German nationalists in the 1897 riots against the Badeni language ordinances, and how Czech clericals had either applauded or ignored the perpetrators of the Polná ritual murder libel. Third, militant clerics initiated most of the incidents from 1903 to 1911, including the Rumpler, Juda, and Wahrmund affairs, in which Masaryk became their foremost opponent and as a consequence of which he published most of his short articles on religious questions.[22] Fourth, the organisation of clerical political parties in Austria-Hungary in the 1890s in accordance with *Rerum novarum* and their increasingly strident political activity after 1897 worried Masaryk as the harbinger of clerical attempts to realign Czech politics by forging a Clerical-Agrarian-Old Czech-Conservative Large Landowners coalition.[23] Fifth, Masaryk and the ČSP faced the clerical party as their principal adversary in their two successful campaigns for his election to the Reichsrat. Sixth, Pope Pius X's condemnation of Modernism in *Pascendi Dominici gregis* in 1907 marked the demise of a Catholic reform movement with which Masaryk was much in sympathy and that he had hoped might correct many of the shortcomings he and the Modernists discerned in the Catholic Church.[24] Finally, Masaryk increasingly turned his attention to religious and related political issues abroad, especially in France as a result of the Dreyfus Affair, in Russia as an outgrowth of his study of the 1905 Revolution and the ensuing reaction, and in the United States as a consequence of his having been invited to address American Unitarian-Universalist convocations and to lecture at the University of Chicago.[25]

Explicit in Masaryk's principal theoretical works and implicit in the General Programme of the ČSL and the 1912 Programme was his conviction that necessary improvements in economic productivity and efficiency would not – given the authoritarian and imperialistic character of the Habsburg Monarchy – automatically bring equally desired social and political reforms. So was his belief that achievement of political democratisation, greater national autonomy, and improved public services and social welfare would increase the opportunity for every citizen to lead a freer and more productive life. Hence the importance he always attached to basing all political and social systems on Christian values and on improving education at all levels for adults as well as for youth. Propagation of these values among citizens would encourage them to behave decently towards one another, just as additional education would make them more likely to exercise their civic responsibilities and elect honest and public-spirited representatives. Given Masaryk's puritanical outlook and his flair for conducting moral crusades, his fellow Realists of the early nineties had good grounds for calling him 'pastor', and not surprisingly he toyed briefly in 1900 with the idea of naming the ČSL, which was soon to be formed, 'the fellowship of Czech brethren' in honour of the Unity of Bohemian Brethren, whose ideals he so much admired, and as an indication that he expected the infant party to be much like a religious fellowship.[26]

Masaryk's Christian view of human fallibility and propensity to do evil did not dissuade him, as it did for most aristocrats and intellectuals in Austria-Hungary, from consistently endorsing the social reforms advocated by Social Democracy or from lambasting the pretensions of the aristocracy and upper middle classes to rule in the interests of the commonweal as well as in their own. On the contrary, Masaryk's understanding of Christian fellowship reinforced his conviction that all people, regardless of class, sex, or nationality, were equal in the eyes of God, and therefore ought to have equal opportunities for education and employment and an equal voice in determining who would manage the affairs of state. In this sense, his advocacy of social legislation, his denunciation of superstition and religious intolerance, and his wish to limit the arbitrary exercise of Imperial authority also flowed logically out of, while differing in emphasis and detail from, his 'humanity programme' of the nineties. So did his contention that such reforms were only the first step towards establishing a better life for all citizens, and that Czechs should work at improving themselves individually and collectively and hold no one else primarily responsible for their individual ills or national shortcomings.[27]

PART II

The development and limited changes from 1906 to 1912 in Masaryk's and the ČSP's political goals and tactics are well illustrated by the differences in politics advocated or in the objectives emphasised between the 1900 General Programme, as amended in 1906 and 1908, and the 1912 Programme of the Progressive Party. As noted above, the continuity and similarities between the Programmes are more striking than their differences, in large part because Masaryk and his colleagues regarded the 1912 Programme as the reaffirmation of the worldview and broad political principles expressed by the General Programme. They also, in the light of their experience in politics and what they perceived to be a worsening political situation at home and broad, intended the 1912 Programme to be a modification, amendment, and expansion of the General Programme. In its broad view of domestic and foreign issues, the 1912 Programme differed from its predecessor primarily in taking into account not only Masaryk's perception of growing German and Austro-Hungarian militarism and imperialism but, in addition, his slightly changing views of Czech history and politics and of the difficulties in implementing democratisation, which would be reflected in forthcoming essays such as *Democracy in Politics* and *The Difficulties of Democracy*.[28]

In its organisation and content, the 1912 Programme differed from the General Programme in discussing all specific issues much more explicitly and at greater length, and in saying much less about the party's understanding of Czech history and politics and its relationship to other parties. The first difference reflected Masaryk's and his colleagues' better understanding of, and consequent ability to, define and discuss contemporary issues. The second difference reflected the fact that authors of the 1912 Programme had no need to restate at length the General Programme's worldview, which they had already in large measure endorsed. A third difference arose from the fact that the authors of the General Programme often looked back to the nineties and the turbulent origins of the ČSL, whereas the authors of the 1912 Programme looked forward to a dangerous and uncertain future and as a consequence gave far greater emphasis to at least six different objectives than did any earlier programme. These objectives, all intended to advance the interests and solidarity of Czech citizens, regardless of sex or social class, were (1) women's emancipation; (2) reform and democratisation of self-government (*samospráva*) at every level; (3) the concomitant expansion and improvement of public education, with emphasis on adult and continuing education as well as universities and primary and secondary schools; (4) the application of modern, especially electrical, technology to transportation and public power; (5) the adoption of recent improvements in medicine and public health, and most importantly, (6) the need for the Czech nation, understood in the context of 'the problem of the small nation' generally, to achieve to the greatest possible degree its political independence.[29]

In advocating the first two reforms, Masaryk and the ČSP expressed views much like those of Social Democracy, and differed from the Young Czechs and Agrarians, who opposed both reforms, and from the State Rights Progressives, who favoured only the first. Because all Czech parties emphasised improvements in public education and the establishment of a Czech university in Moravia, the ČSP distinguished itself on this issue primarily in the clarity and thoroughness of its discussion and, like the Social Democrats, in emphasising adult and continuing education and equal educational opportunities for women.[30] The increased interest by Progressives and their opponents in the fourth and fifth objectives is explained by the fact that much in electrical technology, as in improved medicines and public sanitation, was of very recent origin, and that in rebuilding its railways and urban transportation systems to include recent advances in technology, Austria-Hungary was somewhat behind France, Germany, Great Britain, and the United States.[31]

The 1912 Progressive Programme contended that women should be granted equal opportunities with men in politics, education and employment, and, much more specifically than the General Programme of 1900, indicated what steps should be taken to achieve this goal. The General Programme, while advocating women's emancipation in principle, had equivocated on the questions of women acquiring equal employment opportunities and fully participating in all aspects of public life.[32] This change in the party's attitude was promptly reflected in its *Organisační řád* of 1908, and appears to have been brought about in part by Alois Hajn and other East Bohemian Radical Progressives, after they joined the ČSL in 1905, and in part by Masaryk's and other party members' growing realisation that the democratisation of politics required full equality for women.[33] In his inaugural Reichsrat speech of 20 July 1907, Masaryk advocated women's suffrage as a reform consonant with the values of democracy and social justice, and as a means of improving the honesty and responsiveness of government by making voters of citizens noted for their concern with morality, temperance and a healthy family life. From then through 1914, Masaryk more explicitly endorsed women's emancipation in several short essays on the 'woman question' and in most of his more general political treatises.[34] On women's, as on religious and social, issues he had long been strongly influenced by his reform-minded American wife, Charlotte Garrigue Masaryk, who, incidentally, had joined the Social Democratic party in 1905 because it alone among Cisleithanian parties at that time endeavoured to treat women equally with men.[35]

Beginning in 1907, the ČSP became the second Czech 'bourgeois' party not only to advocate but also to provide equal rights and opportunities to women, the first having been the Radical Progressives and the third, in 1908, the State Rights Progressives. On 2 June 1907, at a meeting of the ČSP Board of Trustees, women for the first time joined the party with privileges and duties of membership identical to those of men to the extent then permitted by Cisleithanian law. At this meeting, the Trustees also elected Olga Stránská to the party's Central Executive Committee.[36] The list of ČSP candidates in the February to March 1908 elections to the Bohemian Diet included two women, Karla Máchová and Marie Tůmová, the first Czechs of their sex to run for this public office. These women ran, respectively in Prague-Holešovice and Vysoké Mýto, not with the expectation of winning but as a first step in persuading male voters that women belonged in politics.[37]

Masaryk's and the ČSP's discussion in 1912 and 1913 of the degree to which, and means by which, Czechs might some day achieve political independence, paralleled similar and contemporaneous discussions by the Czech State Rights Progressives. This issue's place of prominence (it was printed in italics) in the 1912 ČSP Programme; the sense of urgency with which it was presented, and the extent to which it anticipated Masaryk's subsequent work for Czechoslovak independence, justifies quoting Masaryk's comments on 'political independence', part of his longer discussion of 'the problem of the small nation and state'.

Palacký did not consider possible the political independence of the Czech state because of its small area and population and its interior location; he was therefore satisfied with trying to achieve a federalised Austria that would guarantee equal rights for all of its nations. But, the development of politics, as history teaches us, leads to the organisation of greater and larger states. Imperialism is the battle-cry of our times. Therefore the problem of the small state and nation has arisen. *This, the problem of Czech politics, is how to secure our cultural and national independence through political independence and, of course, to what extent this political independence and the independence of other nations may be realised.*[38]

In Masaryk's opinion, the ČSP stood in the Czech political

spectrum between Social Democracy and the left 'bourgeois' parties, that is to say to the left of centre in that spectrum, being more like the former in its advocacy of social reform and equal political rights for all citizens, and more like the latter in the occupations, social class, and educational attainments of its members, and in its emphasis upon Czech national interests, national unity, and support for Czech ethnic minorities in predominantly German-speaking areas. The ČSP addressed the interests of self-employed business people and farmers, and of citizens in the learned professions and civil service, primarily by encouraging the promotion of economic opportunities and prosperity, and the improvement of education, transportation and other public services. The party expected to cooperate with both Social Democrats and moderate to left-leaning 'bourgeois' parties on projects of mutual concern, as it tried to wean all 'bourgeois' parties away from their adherence to 'historical' Bohemian State rights, and persuade them to support legislation to increase state responsibility for social welfare, and to admit industrial and agricultural workers to full partnership in choosing representatives to provincial, district, and local self-government.[39] Such a democratisation of politics and implementation of social reform appeared to the ČSP to provide the best means of facilitating cooperation between different social classes and different nationalities, and thereby gradually decreasing those unproductive and potentially violent nationality conflicts, especially between Czechs and Germans, that had long adversely affected the political stability of the Habsburg Monarchy, and given the Habsburgs and the privileged classes so many opportunities to divide and rule.

Ideologically, Masaryk's criticism of Marxism differentiated the ČSP from the Czech Social Democrats, just as his supplanting 'historical' by 'natural' Bohemian State rights distanced the ČSP from other 'bourgeois' parties, including the Agrarians. Masaryk's and the ČSP's adversarial relationship with the Young Czechs from 1900 to 1914 was based principally on the following objections: (1) the undemocratic character and policies of the Young Czech party, given its control of unrepresentative district self-government in Bohemia and its frequent cooperation since 1894 with the Conservative Large Landowners in the Bohemian Diet and the Reichsrat; (2) its unrelenting opposition to Social Democratic demands for extensive political and social reform; (3) its 'positive' relations with the authoritarian Habsburg state, especially reprehensible when the party did not protest at the occupation of Bosnia-Herzegovina in 1908; (4) its unwillingness to criticise Tsarist Russian autocracy or its friends among the anti-Dreyfusards in France; (5) its materialistic liberalism and indifference to religious questions not pertaining to politics, and (6) its continued pretensions to speak for and lead the Czech nation in spite of all the above.[40]

Masaryk was especially concerned about the development of the Agrarian Party, the largest of the Czech parties in popular support after Social Democracy, lest it be tempted to enter or re-enter an alliance with the Young Czechs and Conservative Large Landowners, or, less likely but worse, come to terms with the clerical parties in an electoral alliance that would dominate the Moravian Diet and approach a majority in the Bohemian Diet. In his proposals in March 1908 for a 'new formation of Czech political parties', Masaryk placed the Agrarians on the right of a Progressive grouping of Czech parties that included the Young Czechs in the centre and the State Rights Progressives and the ČSP on the left.[41] Best of all would be to create a partnership of Czech parties that would include the Agrarians and perhaps the Social Democrats, and exclude only the Clericals, Old Czechs, and Conservative Large Landowners of the right.

Up to 1909, Masaryk criticised the National Socialists, as he had criticised the Agrarians, for 'opportunism'. Ideologically, he and the ČSP differed primarily from the National Socialists and State Rights Progressives by giving primacy to achieving national autonomy on the basis of 'natural' as opposed to 'historic' Bohemian State Rights, and in taking a more positive view of the Social Democratic political agenda. Furthermore, Masaryk compared unfavourably to his own ideology of Czech history and politics what he perceived to be the 'disorganised, poorly thought out and opportunistic' policies of his rivals, without, of course, ever closing the door to possibilities of cooperation in support of mutual goals. Noteworthy in light of the cooperation that occurred from 1909 to 1914 is the recognition in the General Programme of 1900 of the National Socialists and the predecessors of the State Rights Progressives as parties managed by 'opportunistic but energetic leaders of good will.'[42]

Changing Czech party relationships in the years 1907 to 1914 saw the ČSP and Masaryk draw closer to the Social Democrats on issues of social welfare, women's emancipation and anti-imperialism, and through electoral agreements with them in 1907 and 1911, Masaryk was twice enabled to win election to the Reichsrat. The relationship became somewhat closer after the Czech Social Democrats formally separated from Austrian Social Democracy to run a separate slate of candidates for the Reichsrat in 1911, primarily as a consequence of disagreement on nationality questions. The ČSP also joined forces with the National Socialists and the State Rights Progressives, in opposition to certain arbitrary Imperial actions, from the occupation of Bosnia-Herzegovina in 1908 to the issuance of the St Ann's Patent of July 1913, actions that were not opposed by the Young Czechs. With regard to the occupation of Bosnia-Herzegovina, these three political parties were also joined by the Social Democrats, with the National Socialists conducting the most vigorous public demonstrations against the occupation including an 'anti-militarist' campaign in the summer of 1908 that directly attacked recruitment for the Imperial army. True to form, the Habsburgs quashed the campaign and meted out stiff jail sentences to the ringleaders. In part as a consequence, the National Socialists and the ČSP, despite many differences in political ideology and tactics, reaffirmed their willingness to cooperate in parliamentary opposition to certain Imperial domestic and foreign policies, a cooperation that had begun with the two parties joining in December 1907 to oppose the renewal of the decennial Austro-Hungarian customs agreement.[43]

In May 1914, Masaryk and the ČSP found themselves at loggerheads with all the Czech parties except the National Socialists in the Šviha affair, whose repercussions were brief and inconsequential only because of the outbreak of the World War in July. The Young Czechs, on incomplete evidence, had charged Karel Šviha, a prominent National Socialist deputy and officer, with having been a paid police informer. Masaryk suspected, correctly as it later turned out, that Šviha had been, even worse, a direct informant of Archduke Franz Ferdinand who, unwilling to pay Šviha out of his own pocket, had arranged for him to be paid with police funds. Masaryk attempted to persuade the parties involved to withhold public judgement of Šviha until all incriminating and other evidence might be obtained, and Šviha's conduct precisely accounted for. Only then should any information or opinion concerning that conduct be publicised. Masaryk's action, widely interpreted as aid to a traitor, aroused much antagonism, even among the Social Democrats. In objecting to any public trial of Šviha, Masaryk was apparently trying to smoke out the Franz Ferdinand connection, and almost certainly sought not only to minimise the unpleasant consequences of the affair for the Czech National Socialists, then his political allies, but, by taking the offensive, to try to prevent his old opponents, the Young Czechs, from reaping great benefits from Šviha's indiscretion. Though Masaryk argued that he acted out of principle – defending a colleague convicted by political opponents before all the evidence was in – and in order to get at the truth about the affair, he soon found himself, as in the nineties, widely denounced as a meddler and troublemaker.[44]

As noted earlier, Masaryk and the ČSP measured their success, not in the number of elections won, but in their ability to influence the policies and attitudes of other Czech parties. When the ČSL and ČSP ran candidates, they usually did so with little prospect of success but with every prospect of advertising their party's views and increasing slightly their number of adherents. The ČSL participated in only two elections, those to the Bohemian Diet in October 1901, in which it did poorly, and later in a special election to fill a vacant seat in the fourth or rural curia of that Diet, in which the ČSL candidate, Dr. Štemberk, surprisingly obtained a larger number of votes in the first round than any other candidate, only to be beaten in the run-off election by a coalition of Agrarians, Clericals, and German parties.[45]

The ČSP entered slates of candidates in three elections, those to the Reichsrat in 1907 and 1911, and to the Bohemian Diet in January 1908. Because the latter involved curial voting, the ČSP, like the Social Democrats, had little or no chance of winning, but none the less ran ten candidates, including two women. Of these ten, only Dr. Jindřich Štemberk was elected, but because of poor health he soon resigned his mandate. Masaryk, running in Prague against the popular Young Czech, Jan Podlipný, garnered only slightly less than half the vote in the first and in the run-off elections.[46]

In Reichsrat elections the ČSP had more success. Of its nine candidates in Bohemia in 1907, Professor František Drtina alone was victorious and then only after winning a close run-off election. In the 1911 elections, he lost his seat. Masaryk, the sole ČSP Reichsrat candidate in Moravia, won in 1907 and 1911 in the Valašsko district, thanks to the support of the Social Democrats in the run-off election of 1907 and in the general election of 1911. He had chosen to run in this east central Moravian district against the advice of those ČSP members who preferred that their party's leading spokesman remain in Bohemia. He had done so principally because of his extensive personal connections and the favourable political circumstances in Valašsko, and because he recognised he stood little chance in Bohemia against a Young Czech, Nationalist Socialist, or State Rights Progressive candidate in any middle-class district, and likewise little chance against a Social Democrat or an Agrarian in a proletarian or rural district. Consequently he chose a Moravian district of farms and small towns in which no one social class predominated and in which the Social Democrats, the party most likely to support him, could not on their own elect a candidate. Valašsko met these requirements. It also had the largest Protestant minority – but still very small – of any Czech-speaking electoral district, a situation that was bound to help Masaryk, whose Protestantism would be a handicap wherever he ran. Masaryk was also helped by the fact that the Clerical Party had so much influence in Valašsko that other Czech parties would have to form an electoral coalition if they wished to prevent a Clerical victory.[47]

In both the 1907 and 1911 campaigns in Valašsko, Masaryk revealed himself to be a tireless and outspoken campaigner who demonstrated that he understood how to translate his theories of political democracy into practice. He also came better to understand the importance of teamwork and the delegation of responsibility in politics, something he had not always so well appreciated, either as a Young Czech in the early nineties, or in his leadership of the ČSL during its first few years. From the start in Valašsko, he had the support of respected and influential professional people – doctors, grammar-school masters and lawyers – who did most of the work in organising and running his campaigns. He also enjoyed the backing of the Social Democrats, who, fearing a Clerical victory and appreciating Masaryk's endorsement of many Social Democratic goals, threw their support behind him in the run-off election of 1907 and ran no one against him in the election of 1911. Finally, Masaryk made himself seen and heard throughout the district and, as one would expect, proved adept at clearly presenting his views and proposals to voters from all walks of life and persuading most of them of his genuine interest in their welfare. Valašsko demonstrated what the First Czechoslovak Republic would confirm: Masaryk, among the Czech intellectuals who had entered politics in the 1890s, was one of the few who best made the transition from curial to democratic politics.[48]

Consistency was evident from 1900 to 1914 not only in the ČSL/ČSP's relations with other Czech political parties, but in its critical stance towards the institutions and the domestic and foreign policies of the authoritarian Habsburg state. At the same time, the party's members understood that this state was likely to survive quite a while, despite its resistance to change, and that working for its reform, however unlikely, was to be preferred to attempting its overthrow by a revolution that would have almost no chance of success in times of peace. Being reasonable men and women of good will, Czech Progressives wished to avoid war, and did not until July 1914 rule out all intentions of ever cooperating with the Habsburg authorities, just in case those authorities might someday prove amenable to instituting long overdue reforms. But, in criticising the unrepresentative nature of self-government as well as in exposing the often harsh and capricious actions of the Imperial administration, the ČSL General Programme clearly identified the reactionary and authoritarian character of the state, a character attributable primarily to its increasingly serving 'the interests of incompetent *feudalism* along with those of finance capital'. Those feudal aristocrats, the Conservative Large Landowners, were working 'to exercise their unjust influence to use the state to serve their own personal and family ends.'[49] The state was certainly authoritarian to the extent that the civil bureaucracy was accountable only to the Emperor or to his judicial appointees, and periodically ruled by decree or proclaimed martial law in its 'efforts to rule above parties'.[50] Masaryk often criticised this character of the state in public speeches, notably at Velim in 1901 and in his remarks of September 1905, where, as the only 'bourgeois' politician at a Social Democratic rally in Prague, he attacked aristocracy and clericalism as pillars of the Habsburg state.[51] Alone among Czech critics of Austro-Hungarian authoritarianism and among the advocates of Czech cultural and political autonomy, Masaryk undermined the ideological foundations of the Habsburg Monarchy, not only in the name of 'democratisation' and national self-determination, but in the name of religious values and of the 'humanity' and 'dignity' of every individual as well. Principally because Masaryk attacked Catholic clericalism from Protestant, as opposed to liberal and anti-clerical, convictions, he appeared to some contemporaries as he now appears to some scholars, as an old-fashioned puritanical, pre-French-Revolution radical reformer.[52]

Masaryk's relative unpopularity among Czech voters in contrast to the respect he had earned abroad is partly explained by his fair-minded approach to contemporary domestic political questions. He never suggested that all Czech actions or goals were good or that whatever served German or Habsburg interests was bad. He often disconcerted his opponents by attacking injustice wherever he saw it, in Czech as well as in German society, as in the Hilsner and Wahrmund affairs, in Czech party politics, as in the Šviha affair, and in Habsburg foreign and domestic policies, as in, respectively, the

Zagreb trials and the St Ann's Patent. Though he became one of the severest critics of imperial policies and actions, he recognised that most civil servants, regardless of nationality or religion, were persons of competence and good will. The task, as he and the Progressives defined it, was to make both the imperial and self-governmental bureaucracies subject to the popular will, as determined by a majority vote of all citizens regardless of sex, nationality, or class. If government could thus be constituted and persuaded to advance political, educational and social reform, and the rights of national and religious minorities, Masaryk expected nationality and class conflicts to diminish, as every citizen came to enjoy equal political liberties and economic and educational opportunities.

PART III

Just as the ČSP from 1906 to 1914 acquired a broader outlook and clarified its objectives, so did its principal spokesman T. G. Masaryk. His intellectual interests continued to reflect, as they also conditioned, his actions in the political arena. Having clearly and forcefully criticised Young Czech opportunism in many publications up to 1907, Masaryk afterwards returned only occasionally to this subject, primarily in Reichsrat debates and other public speeches, to reaffirm his opposition to a policy that, whatever new names like 'positive politics' it might assume, was but a variation on the traditional Old Czech-Young Czech policy of working through established unrepresentative institutions and with officials of the authoritarian state to gain 'one crumb at a time'.[53] Similarly, Masaryk and his clerical opponents had fought hammer and tongs through many debates from the Hilsner Affair, to the Lutvinov versus Juda case. Neither in court nor on the hustings had clerical reactionaries succeeded in intimidating Masaryk, that honest and deeply religious man whom they persisted in denouncing as a God-forsaken despoiler of youth. Facing relentless clerical opposition in the university, in the press, and in the Reichsrat, Masaryk had set forth his views on religion and his religious understanding of the Czech question in a series of works on religion from 1894 to 1905.[54] After 1906, Masaryk fought his principal battles against clerical obstruction and intolerance on behalf of Ludwig Wahrmund in 1908, and in his 1907 and 1911 electoral campaigns. In the Wahrmund case, as in the Hilsner and Juda cases, the injustice done to an individual was not Masaryk's foremost concern. As usual, the more petty-minded of his 'patriotic' Czech opponents did not understand the pertinence to Czech interests of Masaryk's defence of a German Catholic Modernist teacher temporarily removed from his classroom in the distant Tyrol. In Masaryk's view, Wahrmund's dismissal was more than a threat to academic freedom, without which no Czech or any other university in Austria-Hungary could maintain an international reputation. Wahrmund's dismissal, though initiated by clerics with closed minds, also met acquiescence from officialdom, not only from self-governmental bodies in the Tyrol but from the premier, Baron Beck, and his government, thus indicating to Masaryk the unwillingness of the Austro-Hungarian authorities to defend the intellectual integrity of higher learning. Equally deplorable in Masaryk's view was the indifference of the Young Czech and other Czech parties, who, in order to continue to collaborate politically with Beck, took no interest in Wahrmund's plight or the consequent danger of increased clerical influence in Beck's or any successor government.[55]

Though unsuccessful in winning Wahrmund's reinstatement, Masaryk eloquently exposed at home and abroad Austrian clerical censorship and the unwillingness of Austro-Hungarian officialdom to uphold academic freedom. The Wahrmund affair also heightened Masaryk's perception of a growing ambition and intolerance in clerical parties, which was most colourfully embodied by the rabble-rousing anti-Semitic and anti-Czech mayor of Vienna, Karl Lueger, and certain to be encouraged by Franz Ferdinand d'Este once he succeeded to the throne. Masaryk's study of the 1905 Revolution in Russia further confirmed his fears that clerical reactionary governments might come to prevail in Austria-Hungary, for he had seen the extent to which church and state had cooperated in undoing many of the reforms conceded by the Tsar in 1905 to the Russian revolutionaries.

In *The Spirit of Russia*, published in two volumes in 1913, Masaryk also most penetratingly and thoroughly continued his examination of the religious dimensions of personality, literature, nationality and politics, this time in a Russian context.[56] Pertinent to an understanding of Masaryk's career in Czech politics is the extent to which *The Spirit of Russia* clearly reveals (1) Masaryk's continuing advocacy of political democratisation and social reform; (2) his efforts to place private and public life on surer moral foundations, and (3) his practice of looking for the best in people, whatever their religion or nationality, without ignoring or excusing the worst. As Masaryk had tried during the eighties and nineties to define Czech national character and objectives through the study of outstanding Czechs of religious, humanitarian, and, by his definition, democratic convictions, so he based his study of Russia primarily on the writings and deeds of those Russians who stood in the forefront of literary, religious, and philosophic achievement. Just as Masaryk had balanced his exposition of Czech inadequacies with a plea for brotherhood, civic-mindedness and Christian charity, so he balanced his strong antipathy towards Tsarist autocracy with an examination of Russian thought and imagination that managed not only to convey enlightened criticism but also a genuine appreciation for Russian arts and letters, and for what Westerners could learn from the Russian experience about their own opportunities and shortcomings. Finally, Masaryk's disappointment at the triumph of reaction – theocracy, autocracy, and aristocracy – over revolution in Russia after 1905, paralleled his growing concern over analogous efforts by reactionary forces in Austria-Hungary to stifle political democratisation, the emancipation of women and the national self-fulfilment of the non-German and non-Magyar peoples. Logically, as one would expect, just as Masaryk sympathised – critically, to be sure – with the reformers and revolutionaries in Russia, so he increasingly came to support by word and deed the advocates of democracy and social reform in the Habsburg Monarchy and the Balkans, to the extent that by 1910 he had emerged as the leading critic of Austro-Hungarian authoritarianism at home and imperialism abroad.

In Masaryk's view, the Habsburg Monarchy's growing irresponsibility and aggressiveness in foreign affairs after 1906 was not only encouraged by Imperial Germany, but further abetted at home by the absence of ministerial responsibility to a popularly elected parliament, and by a class system that systematically discriminated against workers, small farmers and women in favour of the landed aristocracy and the upper middle class. The Monarchy's imperialism abroad and authoritarianism at home fed one another. The denial of equal language and voting rights to small nations at home in the Monarchy, especially in Hungary as opposed to Cisleithania, went hand in hand with the attempts from 1906 to 1914 to thwart the independent development of the small nations of the Balkans. Just as the wave of strikes and demonstrations from 1906 to 1907 in Hungary, culminating in the Černová 'massacre' of October 1907, prompted Masaryk to establish closer ties with reform-minded Slovak politicians and educators, so did his appearance in the Zagreb trials of May 1909 strengthen his already close association with Croatian, Slovene, and Serbian leaders favourably disposed to Yugoslav unity. The Zagreb trials, the Friedjung trial, and the Vasič case enabled him to demonstrate to the world that an Austria-Hungary bent on aggression – the annexation of Bosnia-Herzegovina – would not hesitate to violate international compacts – the 1878 Treaty of Berlin – or the civil liberties of its subjects – by attempting to convict them on the basis of forged evidence. Here authoritarian traditions, especially the absence of public accountability, encouraged the mendacity, servility and arrogance all too evident in the conduct of some Austro-Hungarian officials.[57]

Masaryk's and the ČSP's involvement with Russia and the smaller Slav nations differed markedly from that of the Young Czechs, the National Socialists, and the Social Democrats, the only other Czech political parties with extensive international connections. Through their association with Austrian Social Democracy and with the Second International, Czech Social Democrats were primarily involved with comrades from the more industrialised countries, none of which besides the Bohemian Lands and Lower Austria were in East Central Europe. Masaryk vehemently rejected the Neo-Slavism that Karel Kramář and the Young Czechs began to propagate in connection with their hosting a Slav Congress in Prague in July 1908, to commemorate the sixtieth anniversary of the famous Slav Congress of 1848, and continued to propagate through their participation in a follow-up Congress in Sofia in 1910.[58] He did so primarily because Kramář had formulated Neo-Slavism in part in order not to embarrass Tsarist Russia, either in calling attention to Imperial Russian discrimination against Poles and Ukrainians, or the suppression of liberties granted in the wake of the 1905 Revolution. Masaryk, unlike the Neo-Slavs, believed that were the Czechs to realise greater civil liberties and political autonomy, they would out of fairness, consistency, and expediency have to support every small European nation that pursued similar goals. To believe, as Kramář did, that the Czechs or any other small nation might eventually persuade an authoritarian imperialistic state, be it Habsburg or Romanov, to advance the national interests of any small nation was a delusion that could only retard the achievement of that freer and more prosperous society that the Young Czechs professed to want. Kramář, in his Neo-Slavism as in his parliamentary leadership of the Young Czech party, believed in working for reform within existing political institutions and without unduly antagonising established authorities or offending popular prejudices. Kramář, like Masaryk, stressed national self-help and self-reliance in political and economic development, but unlike Masaryk and the ČSP, he usually opposed Social Democratic political objectives, and did not hesitate to court or accept imperial patronage if such patronage seemed likely to advance particular Young Czech objectives.[59]

Masaryk's advocacy from 1908 to 1914 of the rights of small nations as opposed to Neo-Slavism – or 'warmed-up Pan-Slavism' as he once called it – encouraged closer Czech ties with the Ukrainians and South Slavs, and did not foreclose, as did Neo-Slavism, greater Czech interest in the Polish question or better relations with the Poles. Though Masaryk, given his strongly anti-clerical outlook, humble origins, and close associations with Social Democrats and Ukrainians, was hardly *persona grata* in upper-class Polish circles, he did, as did few Czechs, somewhat resemble typical Polish revolutionary leaders of the later nineteenth and early twentieth centuries in temperament, with his deeply felt religious convictions and his dedication to national independence.[60]

Through his continuing participation in Czech and Cisleithanian politics, and his increasing collaboration with South Slavs, Ukrainians, and Slovaks, Masaryk came to see by 1912 that the Habsburg Monarchy was becoming less and not more susceptible to reform, and increasingly a threat not only to world peace but to the goals he held so dear – political democratisation, national self-determination, and social reform.[61] No finer testimony either to Masaryk's dedication to these ideals or to his breadth of vision and depth of understanding can be found than the sixty testimonial essays written by colleagues at home and abroad for publication in a volume dedicated to Masaryk on his sixtieth birthday in March 1910. This volume also testifies to the esteem and admiration Masaryk won, not only through his courage and intellectual achievements, but also through a warmth of personality more evident in interpersonal relationships than in his writings or in his words and actions in public forums.[62]

Masaryk was among the few Czech politicians before 1914 who acquired a broad understanding of foreign affairs and established close relationships with leading politicians abroad. Like his colleagues Václav Klofáč and Karel Kramář, he cultivated good relations with politicians and opinion-makers among the Slav and other nations of Eastern Europe, but, unlike his colleagues, he chose to associate primarily with liberal as opposed to conservative circles in

Imperial Russia, with radical as well as moderate elements among the South Slavs, and with leading academics and journalists in Great Britain and the United States.[63] Thanks in part to his two lecture tours to the United States in 1902 and 1907, Masaryk had also acquired considerable influence among American Czech immigrant communities. Because most Czech-Americans were of peasant or working-class origins, and advocates of American democracy, many of them found Masaryk's political views much more congenial than those of any other Czech political movement in Bohemia. Czech-Americans who expressed reservations about Masaryk's politics included staunch Catholics, a few of the many Social Democrats, and those militant free-thinkers whose attitudes were not at all to Masaryk's liking.[64]

Masaryk's concern about the dangerous course of Austro-Hungarian authoritarianism and imperialism, a concern expressed in most of his political statements from 1909 to 1913, was amply confirmed within two years. By the St Ann's Patent of 26 July 1913, the Habsburg authorities suspended elective self-government in the crownland of Bohemia, a high-handed action reminiscent of events in 1851, 1868, and 1893, which was taken primarily in response to the German nationalists who, adamant in their refusal to accept majority rule, had obstructed the Bohemian Diet and thereby invited the rule of appointed civil officials.[65] In July 1914, Austria-Hungary, under German pressure, declared war on Serbia and then followed Germany into the ensuing World War that at home soon led to the suspension of the Reichsrat, further curtailment of civil liberties, and mass arrests. When Masaryk left Austria-Hungary for the last time in December 1914, he was well prepared by his work in Czech politics, and as a Czech spokesman known abroad, to understand the enemies he would face and allies he would need, in order to lead to victory the revolutionary movement that would help overthrow the Habsburgs and establish an independent Czechoslovakia.

NOTES

1   Roland J. Hoffmann, *T. G. Masaryk and die Tschechische Frage: Die nationale Ideologie und politische Tätigkeit T. G. Masaryks bis zum Scheitern des deutsch-tschechischen Ausgleichsversuchs vom Februar 1909* (Ph D dissertation, University of Tübingen, 1984). Eva Schmidt-

Hartmann, *Thomas G. Masaryk's Realism* (Munich: Oldenbourg, 1984) concentrates on developments up to 1900. Roman Szporluk, *The Political Thought of Thomas G. Masaryk* (Boulder: East European Monographs, 1981) covers Masaryk's entire academic and political careers. Otto Urban, *Česká společnost, 1848–1918* (Prague: Svoboda, 1982) is the most comprehensive, informed and recent Marxist study of the period. It discusses Masaryk in the context of Czech social, economic and political developments, though surprisingly says very little about Masaryk from 1897 to 1914. Other noteworthy recent Czechoslovak studies of Masaryk include Milan Machovec, *Tomáš G. Masaryk*, 2nd ed. (Prague: Svobodné slovo, 1968), Jan Patočka, *Dvě studie o Masarykovi* (Toronto: Sixty-Eight Publishers, 1980), and Zdeněk Šolle, 'Masarykova idea československého státu', *Dějiny a současnost*, vol. 10, no. 6 (1968) pp. 14–21. Bruce M. Garver, *The Young Czech Party, 1874–1901, and the Emergence of a Multi-Party System* (New Haven: Yale University Press, 1978) discusses Masaryk's political career primarily during the years 1890 to 1907 in the context of Czech and Cisleithanian political history.

2   *Rámcový program české strany lidové (realistické)* (Prague: Renn, 1900), 208 pp. including the index and pp. 108–97, which contain the agenda and minutes of the Constituent, or Founding, Congress of the ČSL. This programme was supplemented and slightly modified by the *Organisační řád české strany pokrokové* (Prague: ČSP, 1908). On events leading up to the party's founding, see also Jan Herben, *Kniha vzpomínek* (Prague: Družstevní práce, 1935) pp. 447–50.

3   Alois Hajn, *Život novinářův, 1894–1930: Výběr článků, feuilletonů, řečí, a projevů* (Prague: Orbis, 1930) is the best documentary collection on the history of the ČSL and the ČSP. Pp. 176–81, 'Ustavení české strany pokrokové', discuss the Pardubice Congress. Also excellent is Emanuel Chalupný, *Vznik české strany pokrokové: historické vzpomínky dle původních pramenů* (Tábor: Kubíček, 1911), and *Úvahy politické* (Prague: Přehled, 1911), especially pp. 11–86 and 154–61.

4   T. G. Masaryk, *Právo přirozené a historické* (Prague: Cas, 1900) is Masaryk's most detailed exposition of the subject.

5   *Program české strany pokrokové: schválen třetím valným sjezdem strany konaným v Praze 6. a 7. ledna 1912* (Prague: Tisková komise ČSP, 1912), 192 pp. including the index.

6   Detailed sources on the Herben affair and the problems of the ČSL include Zdeněk Tobolka, *Politické dějiny čsl. národa*, vol. III, part 2: *1891–1914* (Prague: Čsl. Kompas, 1936) (pp. 282–90 deal with the founding of the ČSL through to the Herben affair); Jan Herben, *T. G. Masaryk: život a dílo presidenta osvoboditele*, 4th ed. (Prague: Sfinx/ B. Janda, 1938) in pp. 90–4 discusses the first years of the party but not the affair in which Herben was involved. Chalupný, *Vznik ČSP*, pp. 17–21; Hoffmann, *Masaryk und die Tschechische Frage*, pp. 247–51 and Hajn, *Život novinářův*, pp. 169–71, are much more explicit.

7   Hajn, *Život novinářův*, pp. 150–75.

8   On suffrage extension, see William A. Jenks, *The Austrian Electoral Reform of 1907* (New York: Columbia University Press, 1950); Tobolka, *Politické dějiny*, III, 2, pp. 416–61; and Oldřiška Kodedová

et al. (eds), *Prameny k revolučnímu hnutí a ohlasu první ruské revoluce v Českých zemích v letech 1905–1907*, 2 vols. (Prague: Čsl. Akademia Věd, 1959, 1962), a documentary collection.

9   Karel Kramář, *Poznámky o české politice* (Prague: Bursík a Kohout, 1906) and T. G. Masaryk, *Politická situace: poznámky ku poznámkám* (Prague: Čas–Beaufort, 1906) are the principal sources for the Kramář-Masaryk debate on 'positive politics' and other issues on which the ČSP and the MČS disagreed in the years up to and including 1906.

10   On ČSP reorganisation, see *Program ČSP*, pp. 179–81; Alois Hajn, *Život novinářův*, pp. 181–7; and Tobolka, *Politické dějiny*, III, 2, pp. 451–5. The most complete discussion of some of the problems to be addressed will be found in *Česká strana pokroková a její ustavující valný sjezd dne 21. ledna 1906 v Pardubicích: příspěvek ku poznání jejího programu* (Pardubice: ČSP, 1906), the report on the founding ČSP Congress.

11   *ČSP a její ustavující valný sjezd* for the first congress; *Program ČSP 1912*, p. 183, on the second congress; and *Program ČSP 1912*, *passim*, for the third congress.

12   Karel Čapek, *Hovory s T. G. Masarykem* (Prague: Čs. spisovatel, 1969) pp. 107, 118–19; Hajn, *Život novinářův*, pp. 1'/8–9. František Drtina, the only ČSP candidate ever elected to the Reichsrat from Bohemia, was the principal author of the thorough and informed proposals for educational reform in the 1912 party programme, *Program ČSP 1912*, pp. 72–126. Some of his many scholarly publications on education are collected in *Reforma školství: Soubor statí* (Prague: Laichter, 1931), and *Universita a učitelstvo: Soubor statí* (Prague: Laichter, 1932).

13   Herben, *T. G. Masaryk*, pp. 92–3; *Program ČSP*, pp. 182–3.

14   *ČSP a její ustavující valný sjezd*, *passim*; Hajn, *Život novinářův*, pp. 181–4.

15   T. G. Masaryk, *Česká otázka: snahy a tužby národního obrození* (Prague: Čas–Renn, 1895); T. G. Masaryk, *Naše nynější krise: pád strany staročeské a počátkové směrů nových* (Prague: Čas–Renn, 1895); T. G. Masaryk, *Karel Havlíček: Snahy a tužby politického probuzení* [1896], rev. 2nd ed. (Prague: Laichter, 1904); and T. G. Masaryk, *Otázka sociální: Základy marxismu filosofické a sociologické* (Prague: Laichter, 1898). The last is available in abridged form in English translation as *Masaryk on Marx: An Abridged Edition of the Social Question: Philosophical and Sociological Foundations of Marxism*, ed. and trans. Erazim V. Kohák (Lewisburg: Bucknell University Press, 1972).

16   Garver, *The Young Czech Party*, pp. 245–76, 'The Constitutional Crisis of 1897–1899', and pp. 277–308, 'The Young Czechs and the Successor Parties'.

17   'Not worth a tinker's fart' was Edvard Grégr's comment in 1876 on the value of Bohemian State Rights in his *Naše politika: Otevřený list panu dru. Fr. L. Riegrovi* (Prague: Grégr a Dattl, 1876) p. 10. The Czech phrase literally says 'not worth a pipe of tobacco'. T. G. Masaryk appropriated this phrase, giving due credit to its author, in his debates

on the value of 'natural' as opposed to 'historical' Bohemian State rights.

18 Hoffmann, *T. G. Masaryk und die Tschechische Frage*, is the best source on this question. I have followed Hoffmann's practice of referring to Masaryk's 'ideology' as opposed to 'philosophy' of 'the Czech question', believing with Hoffmann that 'ideology' is more descriptive of what Masaryk was attempting to create than 'philosophy'.

19 Čapek, *Hovory s Masarykem*, pp. 109–10. Hoffmann, cited in note 18 above.

20 *Rámcový program*, pp. 70–95.

21 T. G. Masaryk, *Sebevražda hromadným jevem společenským moderní osvěty* (Prague: Laichter, 1904). This work first appeared in German in 1881 and in English in 1970 (University of Chicago Press). Masaryk, *Česká otázka*, and Masaryk, *Otázka sociální*.

22 Masaryk's religious works from this era include the series of articles first published in *Naše doba* from 1896 through 1898 and later reissued as a book titled *Moderní člověk a náboženství* (Prague: Laichter, 1934); *V boji o náboženství* (Prague: Laichter, 1904); *O svobodě náboženské a volnosti přesvědčení* (Prague: ČSL, 1904); *Přehled nejnovější filosofie náboženství* (Prague: Aug. Smetana Society, 1905); *Zrcadlo katechetům* (Prague: Čas, 1906); and *Inteligence a náboženství* (Prague: Čas, 1907), a speech delivered in Hradec Králové (Königgrätz) in Oct. 1906.

23 T. G. Masaryk, 'Otevřený list urozenému pány, panu baronovi dr. F. L. Riegrovi v Praze', *Čas*, 2 Nov. 1901.

24 On Czech Catholic Modernism, see Miloslav Kaňák, *Z dějin reformního úsilí českého duchovenstva* (Prague: Blahoslav, 1951), and Josef Svozil, 'Z historie Katolické Moderny České', *Česká Demokracie*, 3 (1911); 138–43, 177–9, and 191–8.

25 T. G. Masaryk, *Americké přednášky*, 2nd ed. (Prague: Čin, 1929); and *The Lectures of Professor T. G. Masaryk at the University of Chicago, Summer 1902*, trans. and ed. Draga B. Shillinglaw (Lewisburg: Bucknell University Press, 1978). The first work includes all the 1907 lectures.

26 'Pastor' is most often found in the Kramář-Kaizl correspondence published in Josef Kaizl, *Z mého života*, 3 vols., ed. Zdeněk V. Tobolka (Prague: Vilímek, 1909–1914). On 'the fellowship of Czech brethren', see Herben, *T. G. Masaryk*, pp. 90, 102.

27 T. G. Masaryk, *Ideály humanitní: Několik kapitol* (Prague: Čas, 1901); T. G. Masaryk, *Jak pracovat?* (Prague: Čin, 1926), a work first published in serial form in 1898–99 in *Hlas*, vols. I–II.

28 Masaryk's views on militarism and imperialism are expressed in the short pamphlet: *Dnešní politická situace dle názoru Prof. T. G. Masaryka* (Prague: Jaroš, 1911), pp. 3–4. T. G. Masaryk, *Demokratism v politice* (Prague: Studentská revue, 1912); and T. G. Masaryk, *Nesnáze demokracie: Dvě úvahy* (Prague: Pokrok, 1913).

29 *Program ČSP 1912*, pp. 15–21, on the sixth point. The others are noted in notes below.

30 *Program ČSP 1912*, pp. 70–1, 88, 112–15.

31 *Program ČSP 1912*, pp. 51–3.

32   *Rámcový program*, pp. 11, 38, 64, 135; *Program ČSP 1912*, pp. 5, 24, 70–1, 75, 112–13.
33   Garver, *The Young Czech Party*, pp. 301–2.
34   T. G. Masaryk, 'Čeští voličove!' *Čas*, 26 Jan. 1908. The 20 July 1907 speech is cited in note 39 below.
35   On the probable influence of Charlotte Garrigue Masaryk, see Szporluk, *Political Thought*, pp. 30–2; Čapek, *Hovory s Masarykem*, p. 119.
36   Františka Plamínková et al. (eds), *Masaryk a ženy: Sborník k 80. narozeninám prvního presidenta Republiky československé T. G. Masaryk* (Prague: Ženská národní rada, 1930) pp. 123–5.
37   *Program ČSP 1912*, pp. 182–3.
38   *Program ČSP 1912*, p. 15.
39   *Rámcový program*, pp. 71–87, 174–84. Masaryk addressed 'the Czech question' and related questions of Czech national identity and development in almost all the works he published from the 1890s to 1914. Noteworthy in this respect, besides the many works already cited in notes 4, 9, 15, 23, 27 and 28 above, and in 41, 51, and 56 below, are: *Národnostní filosofie doby novější* (Jičín: Holvek, 1905); his Reichsrat speech of 20 July 1907, reprinted as *Řeč posl. T. G. Masaryka v debatě o zatímním rozpočtu* ... (Prague: Čas, 1907); one of his most thorough criticisms of Young Czech Party policies, *Nynější krise a desorganisace mladočeské strany: Organisujme se ku práci* (Prague: Čas, 1903); *Student a politika* (Prague: Studentská Revue, 1909); *Demokratism v politice* (1912); *V čem je význam Karla Havlíčka: Přednáška* ... (Pardubice: Osvěta lidu, 1906); and an essay, first published in 1897–98 in *Naše doba*, entitled *Palackého idea nárida českého* (Prague: Grosman a Svoboda, 1912). All of these works complement the discussion of Czech nationality and national reform in the *Program ČSP 1912*.
40   T. G. Masaryk, *Politická situace: Poznámky ku poznámkám*, passim.
41   T. G. Masaryk, 'Politické strany a nové formace: řeč posl. T. G. Masaryka na schůzi v Typografické besedě 22. března 1908', *Čas*, 24–25 March 1908. Masaryk, 'Čeští voličové!'
42   *Rámcový program*, pp. 75–6.
43   Emil Špatný, *Český antimilitarism: Kus historie a trochu vzpomínek* (Prague: Melantrich, 1922); and Bohuslav Šantrůček (ed.), *Buřiči a tvrci: Vzpomínky, úvahy, kus historie, životopisy* (Prague: Melantrich, 1947) pp. 193–9, both discuss the anti-militarist campaign and its consequences. Masaryk, by advocating social reform and encouraging the intelligentsia to look out for the workers' interests, would appear to resemble the German 'academic socialists' (*Kathedersozialisten*); but the similarity between these academics and Masaryk is as limited as that between the ČSP and the small, reform-minded Social-Political party (Sozialpolitische Partei) of Vienna. This is so because the Austrian party emphasised social reform from above, whereas Masaryk and the ČSP sought to achieve reforms principally from below, in partnership with the Social Democrats. Masaryk took this position because, first, he was less sanguine than any Viennese about the willingness or ability of state authorities to appreciate, much less act in, the interests of the underprivileged, and second, he believed that the authorities would not concede reforms unless faced with mass

popular pressure organised and directed by parties of the working class, a pressure desirable in any event to achieve that 'political democratisation' necessary to improve the honesty and responsibility of government in the Dual Monarchy.

44 Čapek, *Hovory s T. G. Masarykem*, pp. 117–18, and Herben, *T. G. Masaryk*. discuss Masaryk's part in the Šviha affair. Tobolka, *Politické dějiny*, III/2, p. 594, surveys the affair but not Masaryk's part in it.

45 *Program ČSP 1912*, pp. 182–3.

46 The totals from the Masaryk-Podlipný contest, with the number of run-off votes in parentheses, are as follows: Jan Podlipný, 1280 (1104), and T. G. Masaryk, 732 (582). *Program ČSP 1912*, pp. 182–3.

47 The principal sources on the two campaigns in Valašsko are Stanislav Jandík, *Masaryk na Valašsku* (Prague: Volné myšlenky, 1936), the most detailed and informed monograph; and Jaroslav Dorazil et al., *Hrst vzpomínek na dobu poslanecké činnosti T. G. Masaryka na Valašsku* (Valašské Meziříčí: Sokol, 1935), a lengthy collection of memoirs by persons associated with Masaryk's electoral campaigns.

48 A more recent account of Masaryk and the Social Democrats in Valašsko is B. Kučera, 'O spojenectví sociální demokracie s Masarykem při říšských volbách v roce 1907', *Časopis Matice moravské*, vol. LXXIII (1955), pp. 166–73. See also Richard Fischer, *Pokroková Morava, 1893–1918*, 2 vols. (Prague: Cesta, 1937), vol. II, pp. 242–3.

49 *Rámcový program*, p. 91.

50 Ibid.

51 T. G. Masaryk, *Naše politická situace* (Prague: ČSL Beaufort, 1901), is the Velim speech. The September speech is reported in detail in *Čas* of 25 Sept. 1905, the day after Masaryk delivered it.

52 See, for example, Urban, *Česká společnost*, pp. 443–4.

53 Garver, *The Young Czech Party*, pp. 311–19.

54 T. G. Masaryk, *O klerikalismu a socialismu* (Valašské Meziříčí: Politický spolek pokrokový, 1907); *Věda a církev* (Prague: Pokrok, 1908); and T. G. Masaryk and Fr. Drtina, *Za svobodu svědomí a učení* (Prague: Pokrok, 1908).

55 T. G. Masaryk, *Freie wissenschaftliche und kirchlich gebundene Weltanschauung und Lebensauffassung: Die kirchenpolitische Bedeutung der Wahrmund-Affäre* (Vienna: Carl Konegen, 1908).

56 T. G. Masaryk, *The Spirit of Russia*, 2 vols., trans. Eden and Cedar Paul, 2nd ed. (London: Allen and Unwin, 1955). The third volume appeared as *The Spirit of Russia*, vol. III, edited by George Gibian and translated by Robert Bass (London: Allen and Unwin, 1967). The German edition, *Russland und Europa* (Jena: Eugen Diedrichs, 1913), was the original. Pertinent to the discussion that follows in the text of the paper are: references from the English edition to a critical evaluation of aristocracy and absolute monarchy as obstacles to reform, vol. I, pp. 196–8; a concise definition of 'democracy', vol. II, pp. 508–9; comments on democracy vs. theocracy, ibid., pp. 506–7; and on the importance of the 1905 Revolution: 'The interest in the Russian revolution does not attach solely to the political aspect of the question. The philosopher of history sees in the revolution the great religious and ethical problem of the age. This is a matter upon which

we may learn something from the Russians.' Ibid., p. 565.

57   T. G. Masaryk, *Vasić–Forgách-Aehrenthal: Einiges Material zur Char-akteristik unserer Diplomatie* (Prague: Čas–Beaufort, 1911). This work contains facsimiles of some of the documents at issue in the trials.

58   The most recent and most thorough study is Paul Vyšný, *Neo-Slavism and the Czechs, 1898–1914* (Cambridge University Press, 1977). Masaryk, though critical, may have attended the 1908 Congress.

59   My brief mention of the Masaryk-Kramář relationship owes much to my discussions with Stanley B. Winters, his critical observations on this paper, and my reading of his published works. Citations to some of his works, and more of my views, will be found in Garver, *The Young Czech Party*, especially pp. 264, 304–19, 364, and 549. Personal animosity exacerbated relations between Masaryk and some of the Young Czechs, whom he had opposed primarily on political questions, notably Gustav Eim and Jan Vašatý and, to a lesser degree, Kramář and Tobolka.

60   A discussion of Masaryk and the Polish question is beyond the scope of this paper. Masaryk's most detailed observations on Polish politics, primarily in Galicia, may be found in his Reichsrat speech of 25 May 1908, *Stenographische Protokolle über die Sitzungen des Hauses der Abgeordneten des österreichischen Reichsrathes*, XVIII Session, 75th meeting, pp. 4887–95. The principal scholarly source on Czech-Polish relations in the late nineteenth and early twentieth centuries is Václav Žaček, (ed.), *Češi a Poláci v minulosti*, vol. II: *Období kapitalismu a imperialismu* (Prague: Academia, 1967).

61   *Program ČSP 1912*, pp. 15–34.

62   Edvard Beneš, František Drtina, František Krejčí, and Jan Herben (eds), *T. G. Masarykovi k šedesátým narozeninám* (Prague: Grosman a Svoboda, 1910). For example, pp. 25–8, 35–8, 177–94, 223–30, and 275–313, emphasise personal relationships.

63   The most recent of many works that discuss Masaryk abroad before and during World War I is Hugh and Christopher Seton-Watson, *The Making of A New Europe: R. W. Seton-Watson and the Last Years of Austria-Hungary* (Seattle: University of Washington Press, 1981), especially pp. 46, 52, 109–11, 123–5, 141–3, 153–4, 213–14, 317–18, 324–5, and 400–3.

64   T. G. Masaryk 'Svobodomyslní Čechové v Americe', in *Naše doba*, vol. 10 (1902–03), pp. 1–7. Bruce Garver, 'Czech-American Freethink-ers on the Great Plains, 1871–1914', pp. 147–69 in *Ethnicity on the Great Plains*, ed. Frederick C. Luebke (Lincoln: University of Nebras-ka Press, 1980); reference to Masaryk and freethinkers is on p. 165.

65   One of the best short studies that trace Masaryk's political career through the period 1895 to 1920 is Jaroslav Werstadt, *Od 'České otázky' k 'Nové Evropě.' Linie politického vývoje Masarykova* (Pra-gue: Klecanda, 1920). See also Miloslav Trapl, *Vědecké základy Masarykovy politiky: pokus o soustavný výklad Masarykovy politické sociologie* (Brno: Zář, 1946); and *idem, Masarykův program: Demok-racie-socialismus česká otázka* (Brno: Zář, 1948). To be sure, Czech politicians also contributed to the provocation of German obstruction in the Bohemian Diet, to the extent that they sought political

representation for the Czechs that would reflect the Czech preponderance in Bohemia as a whole, equality of the Czech language with German in the internal as well as external service of the civil bureaucracy, and adequate protection for Czech minorities in the predominantly German-speaking areas of Bohemia. But, save for some of the Young Czechs and Czech Agrarians, Czech politicians generally did not view the circumvention of representative self-government by imperial decree, as in the St Ann's Patent, with the same equanimity as did the German 'bourgeois' parties, who expected favourable treatment from an Imperial bureaucracy whose principal managers in Cisleithania were of German nationality.

11 Masaryk and the Women's Question

Marie L. Neudorfl

The movement for women's emancipation in Czech society up to 1914 increased significantly in the decades before World War I.[1] Until the 1880s it mostly evolved around campaigns to establish a greater number of private secondary and specialised schools for girls, and around literary efforts to depict faithfully the life of women in various strata of Czech society. Although the middle class of better educated women, especially writers and wives of politicians, formed the core of endeavours for the intellectual elevation of Czech women, they were significantly assisted by a number of Czech politicians, intellectuals, and wealthy citizens.[2] By the 1890s the women's emancipation movement had become more widespread and better organised, and its major goals were more clearly formulated than in previous decades. It also acquired a partly political character.[3] Although its impact on society became considerable, the women's movement has been largely ignored as a topic of a serious historical investigation. The relevant works, including those dealing with the involvement of Thomas G. Masaryk, are scarce, are written in Czech, and were published before World War II.

Masaryk has been recognised by modern Czech historians as the most influential male intellectual of the movement, and he was considered as such by prominent female personalities of the time. His courage in talking openly, his appealing ideas, personal integrity and happy family life, including his participation in bringing up four children, made women see him as a trustworthy figure.[4] His slogan 'Let women be put on equal footing with men culturally, legally, and politically' ('Žena budiž na roveň postavena muži kulturně, právně i politicky'), became the motto of *Ženská revue*, a women's journal that began publication in Brno in 1905.[5] In the same year, Zdenka Wiedermannová-Motyčková wrote in *Čas*: 'The name Masaryk has and always will have a significance in the women's movement such as women seldom assign to men.' In 1910 she claimed that by 1905 his views had prevailed in the women's movement in Moravia.[6] But women also complained that only a handful of men truly accepted these views in their private lives.[7]

Masaryk's essential ideas relating to man-woman relationships were already formulated in the early 1880s.[8] His mature views on the women's question were expressed in numerous articles in *Čas* and *Naše doba*.[9] In the latter there are articles related to the question of women's emancipation in other countries. In the 1890s and 1900s, Masaryk delivered a considerable number of lectures on this subject, many of which were published. As a Young Czech deputy in the Reichsrat in 1891–93, Masaryk fought for equal educational opportunities for women, because he believed this to be the most effective means of raising their status and of increasing men's respect for them as well as their own self-respect. Moreover, he believed that better education for women and the greater independence they would derive from it would benefit the whole of society.[10]

Masaryk's views on the women's question were developed in harmony with his broader philosophical and political opinions and beliefs, but they were never divorced from his personal observations and life experience. His happy relationship with his affectionate, deeply religious, but ambitious and strong mother were probably at the root of his sensitivity to women's lot. His approach to the women's question was essentially pragmatic: once he had gathered what he considered to be sufficient evidence for the equality of women with men in their capacity for intellectual, moral, emotional, and religious growth, his interest focused on the practical consequences of these findings: the need for public influence, implementation of changes directed towards the improvement of women's situation in education, political rights, their general status and their roles as wives and mothers. Masaryk emphasised the need to encourage and cultivate increased cooperation between men and women in the family and in public life. According to his daughter Alice, Masaryk's concern with the need to change widespread public attitudes towards women developed under the influence of his wife Charlotte (1850–1923) and her 'pragmatic American way' of thinking: 'If it is so, what are you going to do to put it right?'[11] As a musician she was partly educated in Europe, and her interest extended to literature and philosophy. Her intelligence and sternness were equally attractive to Masaryk as her beauty. According to Masaryk, his wife's ideas on women's roles in family and society were most influential in formulating his thinking on female emancipation. Masaryk also acknowledged that his lecture 'Polygamy and Monogamy' was mainly the work of his wife. She translated John Stuart Mill's *Subjection of Women* into

Czech and dedicated it to the self-understanding of Czech women.[12] Charlotte was an active participant in Masaryk's scholarly work and in fact read all his manuscripts.[13]

Involvement with the campaign for women's emancipation was a direct result of Masaryk's belief in democracy and progress. He understood these concepts in the broad sense, involving respect for human beings as multidimensional creatures at their roots:

> The struggle to invigorate and elevate the energy of human beings and the feeling of personal responsibility, to cultivate their faculties and to place every individual on equal terms, is modern. Equality is not identity: all individuals should have a chance to develop normally, and all their good, positive virtues should be used also for the benefit of the whole [community]. It is modern to struggle for the removal of privileges of some classes – the stronger classes should participate in work for the benefit of the weaker.[14]

The establishment of democracy and social justice and the spiritual and moral advancement of humanity were the major goals of Masaryk's political work. People who were politically, economically or intellectually advantaged had, in his view, a moral obligation to strive for betterment of the underprivileged. Socially weaker groups such as women cannot, for whatever reasons, rightfully be excluded from the process of democratisation, and thus from equally contributing to overall progress and from sharing its fruits. Although Masaryk was far from underestimating the importance of economic development, he severely criticised economic liberalism and Marxism for their overemphasis on the economic dimension of human life, and for ignoring the importance of spiritual and moral qualities. He believed that changes in women's economic and political status had to be accompanied by a changed morality and different social attitudes, especially on the part of men, if a new form of exploitation was not to take place.[15]

Since Masaryk increasingly realised that the political situation in the Austrian Empire was unfavourable to substantial improvement through political and legal channels, he used opportunities such as lectures, speeches and publications to educate and influence public opinion. Today, the appeal of Masaryk's views on women's emancipation lies in his unorthodox assertion that the 'women's question' is equally a 'men's question' of complex social and moral ramifications. The focus on the equal 'modernisation' of men and women was a consequence of these views. While he was critical of traditional male privileges, he was equally critical of fashionable trends which made human contentment and health dependent mainly on sexual satisfaction. He kept a close watch on literature, particularly on French, German, and Russian authors, and on some widespread medical views, because of their influence on young people and their tendency to promote escapism instead of teaching how to prevent problems and how to face and solve existing ones. Some social problems of the time were, as he put it, 'veiled in general silence': prostitution and its resulting diseases, alcoholism, suicide, illegitimacy, and long working hours.

Prostitution was widespread, especially in Prague, and in 1912 Masaryk mentioned how prevalent syphilis was among students.[16] Masaryk devoted much attention to prostitution, which he saw as partly arising from economic need, but more as a visible sign of moral decadence in society and as a source of incurable disease, which had disastrous consequences also for the offspring of those involved with prostitutes or prostitution. Furthermore, his criticism was directed not only at the women involved; he also placed blame on the male population and the general atmosphere. His initial frank treatment of what was, in the 1880s, an unmentionable topic, caused a public furore in 1884: one self-styled Czech patriot, having obtained a copy of his university lectures, proceeded to petition several ministries, the Academy of Sciences, and high-ranking politicians to strip Masaryk of his academic position for alleged corruption of students.[17] At the beginning of the 1900s in Bohemia, over ten per cent of children were illegitimate,[18] and in Prague itself forty-eight per cent.[19] Their lot was much worse than that of legitimate children, although the lot of children of working mothers was far from ideal. Women, who made up one-third of Czech industrial workers, worked an eleven-hour day.[20] Suicide and mental disturbances were relatively frequent among all married women, and were usually the result of marital abuse.[21]

Masaryk's argumentation for women's emancipation proceeded from the belief in male-female equality and in the benefits of increased cooperation between men and women in marriage and in public life. Recognition of the physical and psychological differences between the sexes made him aware that equality did not mean identity, that differences were not a sign of superiority of one sex over the other, but rather of their complementary nature. His strong belief in the possibility of cooperation rather than in a master-slave relationship, which he saw was frequently the case, was tempered by the knowledge that many changes would have to take place in men's attitudes. He had no illusions about the difficulties involved.

Masaryk had formulated his ideas on the conditions for a satisfying marital life as early as 1881 in his book on suicide, and he changed them very little over the years:

> Marriage can have a wholesome influence only if the marriage results from a true affection and proves and confirms this affection, and if married life is rational and moral: this is not a result of marriages, but must rather be brought into marriages. Marriage improves one's ways, but it, in and of itself, does not make for good in all things. Marital happiness and its beneficial influences, above all, depend upon the intellectual and moral attributes of the people concerned and is regulated by certain places, certain times, and to a great degree by the economic conditions of the country, since married life also requires bread . . . *Today marriage has little or no beneficial influence, perhaps may even have a harmful one.*[22]

Masaryk's understanding of love was far removed from the romantic vision of his time: to him it meant to work for others, especially for those in need. An essential prerequisite for a productive life was good health, secured by leading a pure life, good physical and mental hygiene, and avoidance of potentially harmful activities, such as drinking and prostitution.[23]

Masaryk devoted considerable effort to the analysis of obstacles which prevented women from gaining a position of equality and responsibility in society. He blamed in part the low moral standards of the time: lack of religious faith, the premature sexual awakening of children because of pictures, theatres, taverns and newspapers; and lastly, the failure of families, schools and churches to provide adequate moral instruction. He placed even greater emphasis on altering the traditional perception of women as intellectually inferior beings whose purpose was to serve men, since he believed this was a reform which individuals could undertake on their own through a genuine effort to treat women as equal beings. He cricitised double moral standards, which he saw to be harmful: men's abuse of women's economic dependency together with the tendency to escape their emotional and family responsibilities; the lack of adequate educational opportunities for women, as well as the lack of public concern and debate about the entire 'women's question' in the sense of their social, political and family status, and the absence of opportunities for intellectual and economic advancement.

He noted religious attitudes based on biblical interpretation as causes of the traditional belief in women's inferiority. He did not question the practices of the past, when survival, especially because of numerous wars, made it necessary to have many children, and to place the burden of their raising and of maintaining the household entirely on the shoulders of women: but he considered the biblical attempt to solve the 'sharp opposition between nature and morality' by subordinating women to men to be inadequate and even harmful in modern things, when the relatively advanced economic conditions, scientific discoveries and medical progress made all forms of privileges unjustified and obstacles to social emancipation.[24] In public lectures, Masaryk elaborated on the fact that the concept of love as we know it today, as an emotional and spiritual relationship between husband and wife, is absent in the Old Testament, where the ideal is that of a hard-working wife in a rigid, patriarchal family.[25]

The changes brought about by the teachings of Christ and St Paul became the basis of the Christian Church's teaching. The substantial differences between the teachings of Jesus and Paul were of considerable interest to Masaryk. The rigid views of Paul, with which Masaryk disagreed, had prevailed over Christ's compassionate understanding of human nature, and had gradually became official Church doctrine. Masaryk disagreed with Paul's contempt for women and assertion of male superiority; these ideas are nowhere to be found in the teachings of Christ, who did not promote virginity as superior to marriage, who acknowledged the right to marry and, in Masaryk's view, who approved the right to divorce in cases of infidelity.[26] Paul considered woman the weaker vessel, created not directly from God but from a man. The devaluation of women found in the epistles of Paul, together with the belief in the virginity of the Mother of God, were significant factors in the Church's uneasy attitude to women. The confusion of purity and chastity with physical intactness, the glorification of the soul and mistrust of the body, the high value placed on celibacy and asceticism, all, according to Masaryk, had resulted in a double standard of morality with disastrous consequences on relationships between men and women. He believed that extreme hostility toward the body was a major source of many men's perverse attitude towards sexual relations, which separated coitus from emotional and psychological needs and desires.[27]

Masaryk favoured the Augustinian concept of marriage as physical and spiritual union, but he was fearful of contemporary views such as that of the influential Italian priest St Alfons Liguori (1696–1787),

who reduced the purpose of marriage to procreation and the preven-
tion of lust. He felt such views constituted a threat to morality, and he
attempted to foster an awareness on the part of his readers and
audiences that traditional teachings did not necessarily apply to the
requirements of modern life. Masaryk was a firm believer in dynam-
ism in marriage, the striving for spiritual growth and unity which
would provide plentiful resources for pure, intimate and happy
relations, including sexual relations. He claimed that a man could be
more noble and pure in marriage than outside of it because it was not
the body but the relations between body and spirit that really
mattered.[28] He considered sensuality without love destructive, a
source of great disappointment for women who tended to lose all
their optimism in marriage and often became apathetic.[29] He thought
that less emphasis on sexuality would also be of benefit to women and
children. Forced pregnancies, resulting in the high number of illegal
abortions and high illegitimacy, had detrimental consequences for
women's physical and mental health, and were serious social
problems.[30] They also had damaging consequences for children.

Masaryk criticised certain contemporary trends which he considered to have rather a dubious influence, especially on young people,
who tended to take imaginative literature as a source of knowledge
and insight into real life. Some of modern literature depicted or even
glorified men's irresponsible and immoral attitudes towards women,
worshipping sexual intercourse and seeing women as targets of male
desire. Authors such as Zola, Musset, Goethe, Artsybashev and
Strindberg earned strong criticism from him.[31] Masaryk recognised
them as great artists and never questioned their right freely to express
themselves, but he objected to their narrow perception of life and
their lack of constructive thinking, which he felt were signs that they
did not really understand life, particularly women, family matters,
and children. Masaryk objected to the scepticism and denial of love
and emotions deeper than sensual passion which he found in the work
of Musset. He was equally critical of Zola's interest in what he felt
was abnormal behaviour, such as prostitution, brutality and perversity, and privately he suspected Zola of being incapable of strong
feelings of erotic sensuality. He judged Zola's books to be mere
exercises in shocking the reader. Masaryk also questioned Goethe's
Gretchen and other female characters, for these women seemed to be
puppets. It was Masaryk's opinion that Goethe had probably never
understood women. Masaryk considered these authors prisoners
trapped in their excessive preoccupation with physical aspects of life

by the old prejudice of the strict division of body and soul. His main complaint against them was that if they could ignore healthy feelings and needs, and see love only as a sensual experience, they must lack insight into human life. Since Czech literature traditionally served as a source of knowledge about the life of people in various social strata, Masaryk was aware that these translations were in need of different perception, and he tried to pinpoint the shortcomings in the way they tried to reflect life.

Since Marxism was gaining ground in the 1890s among politically involved youth, Masaryk also elaborated on the opinions of Friedrich Engels on marriage, especially the idea of free love. He argued that Engels's explanation of monogamy as a consequence of the concentration of wealth was an absurd oversimplification, and that his idealisation of working-class marriage was far removed from the unpleasant reality. He placed Engels in the category of conservative writers who had not yet shed their beliefs in the supremacy of sexual instincts. Masaryk saw love as a complex relationship and insisted on the need for responsible sexuality, lest it degenerate into a destructive instinct. Although he was not blind to the many problems facing contemporary families, Masaryk believed that at its best the family could provide children with a sense of security and well-being, and a climate for the development of a satisfying intimacy between men and women. Since Marx and Engels had ignored the importance of moral values, love, and mutual caring in human life, including marriage, Masaryk found their doctrines distasteful.[32]

Masaryk responded quickly to a younger generation's attempts to find direction in the maze of contemporary ideas on relations between men and women. *Nové proudy*, a bimonthly journal which began publication in February 1893, annoyed him particularly with its intellectual immaturity and tendency to vindicate free love and divorce on the grounds of boredom. Its idea that emotions, often confused with love, are completely independent of mind and will did not harmonise with Masaryk's complex understanding of marital relations. He especially questioned the writer's silence over the 'consequences of love', namely, children.[33] August Bebel (1840–1913) seemed to have a great influence on the views expressed in *Nové proudy*. Masaryk pointed out the lack of evidence for Bebel's 'pseudo-scientific view' that divorce and free love would solve a number of serious problems. He ridiculed Bebel's idea that creative genius needed free love because sexual restraint was harmful to health. In Masaryk's view, Bebel ignored the human need for moral principles and failed to grasp the complexity of marital relations. Masaryk considered premarital sexual relations to be hazardous to one's health and a barrier to development of openness, trust, and responsibility in future marriage. He felt that young people were searching in vain for some comprehensive philosophy of life, and since in his view Czech intellectuals and writers had provided none, they were turning to foreign sources of frequently dubious influence. Adherence to intellectual fads rather than reasoned choice seemed to be the motivating factor in *Nové proudy*'s easy dismissal of some ideas and acceptance of others. In the slightly revised version of the article that he used in *Naše nynější krise*, Masaryk explicitly connects morality, humanity and democracy, since he cannot see how humanity could be advanced without freeing women from men's excessive sexual desires (often resulting in too many children and women's overwork), and liberating men from slavery to their instincts.[34]

Masaryk valued highly several Czech writers for their honest attempt to capture reality in all its complexity, including the suffering of women and the tragedy of relationships between the sexes. According to Masaryk, Karel Hynek Mácha, Božena Němcová, Jan Neruda, and J. S. Machar did not perceive women as inferior to men and maintained a healthy balance in their ethical outlook on male-female relations. They helped the reader to understand life more deeply, and encouraged emotional and ethical growth and the search for truth.[35] Masaryk's perception of the role of literature was perhaps too narrow and demanding. It was, however, consistent with the Czech literary tradition, and it was justified in light of the existence of so few channels through which people could learn about themselves and others, as well as the fact that Masaryk always viewed adequate knowledge as the basis of progress.

Masaryk considered the fulfilment of one's emotional and intellectual needs – provided they were not perverted and destructive – a source of great satisfaction and strength. He attempted to show that the traditional suppression of women's needs and potential was no longer justifiable. In his essays he outlined conditions that would improve cooperation and understanding in marriage. Women should carry a lighter work-load and be free to pursue their education. They should also communicate more with men concerning their needs, whereas men should become more involved in activities which they traditionally avoided, child-raising and domestic work especially, since the benefits of modern society, including shorter working hours and long periods of peace, allowed them greater participation in family life.

Masaryk summarised his views on intimate relations between men and women in 1899 in his lecture, 'Mnohoženství a jednoženství' (Polygamy and Monogamy).[36] He complained that the subject of his lecture was an unusual topic for public discussion, but he felt it was very important to discuss it. He set his topic into a broad framework, and as in his other works he was critical of the Church's fear and ignorance in talking about relevant issues, and its tolerance of the widespread belief that sexual sins were of a physical rather than a spiritual nature. He considered modern tendencies like excessive individualism, the call for free love, and the move away from religion as well as ignorance of women's dignity and needs equally harmful. Masaryk welcomed the spread of the belief in the equality of sexes, and assumed that equal opportunities in education and, partly, in the job market would quickly follow. He considered choice essential to women's self-esteem, even if most still chose to be homemakers and caregivers; there was nothing wrong with such a decision, provided it was the result of a genuine choice. Marriage should not be only a vehicle for economic security and social acceptance; for while Masaryk saw women's economic independence as necessary for their emancipation, he warned that it should not become a green light for an even greater irresponsibility on the part of men, and possibly of women.

Masaryk's major argument centred on his persuasion that contemporary society lived in polygamy, which stood in the way of more satisfying and fulfilling relations between men and women because of its psychological consequences and health hazards. He was particularly critical of young men's premarital sexual experiences, since they gave very little chance for positive emotional growth or for a feeling of responsibility for a serious relationship. He again attacked the widespread belief that sexual restraint was unhealthy, and the fact that boys received so little guidance in this respect when growing up. Too many young people who had to marry while very young were incapable of properly bringing up their children, unprepared for marriage, and unable to develop a mutually satisfying relationship. Masaryk believed that abstinence before marriage was a greater guarantee of happiness in marriage than the opposite, since it gave the couple a better chance to know each other and to develop a trusting and secure relationship. Since monogamy was the norm for women, and their deviations from it, with the exception of prostitution, did not seem frequent, Masaryk urged that the double standard be abandoned: 'Every man should have sexual relations only with one woman and every woman with one man and these should be marital relations.' Masaryk saw a satisfying sexual relationship as an integral part of the overall fulfilling relationship and one's ability to cultivate it. Although Masaryk occasionally elaborated on the importance of children's upbringing and the role of mothers and fathers, he did not discuss in specific terms how emotional maturity and responsibility should be taught, or how to encourage desirable character traits; however, he mentioned that the example of parents was extremely important because children learned by observing and imitating their parents.[37]

Since the issue of equality was at the centre of the women's question, Masaryk devoted considerable attention to demonstrating women's equality with men: whatever intellectual inferiority persisted on the part of women he explained as the result of historical conditions which did not provide women with equal opportunities.[38] In his view the traditional glorification of women as gentler, more moral beings, emotionally orientated, and weaker intellectually and physically, constituted merely 'foxy phrases' used by men to justify their domination and use of women. He found it distressing that the average man saw marriage as the end of his spiritual aspirations and was satisfied with having obtained a good servant. Behind the theoretical idealisation of women he saw a 'chase after money and comfort, a chase after a cook, lover, nurse and housekeeper in one person.'[39] The situation was aggravated by the perception of women as being more suited by nature to be the primary care-givers to their children, while fathers avoided their parental responsibilities by laying claim to their 'right' to rest after work. Masaryk considered the custom of going to the pub, the favourite place of escape for Czech men, to be of potential harm to children and a major cause of overwork for women. In his view, there was generally very little attempt to understand women's needs, especially in the emotional and intellectual spheres: 'political practices, capitalism, medical theories, neo-Romantic literature, religion and even science' all reinforced prevalent attitudes.[40]

Masaryk continued to blame the Roman Catholic ideal of asceticism, with its 'special Jesuit sensuality', as preventing men from being morally pure and honest and maintaining a truly gentlemanly, loving and cooperative attitude towards women. He also disagreed that the abilities and intelligence of mothers and wives were less than those of men; bringing up children well and keeping house, usually with very limited means, were in his view more strenuous and mentally demanding than work in an office, university or church. Masaryk insisted that even if women were physically weaker, it was immoral to use and exploit this weakness for men's advantage. The crucial point of his outlook seems to be his belief in the need and possibility to cultivate those personality features which assist constructive behaviour, including cooperative relations between men and women.

Masaryk was unsure of the most effective means to change deep-seated attitudes towards women, seeing that the problem was ignored by the politicians as well as the Church. He suggested trying self-help in the hope of involving as many women and men as possible in efforts at educating themselves with the help of lectures, schools, families and associations of various kinds, to discuss and spread general awareness of all related problems as a prerequisite for discarding antiquated ideas.[41] The division of work in the modern era provided realistic possibilities for women to become involved in activities outside the home, especially in education and public affairs. Masaryk was particularly concerned with middle-class women, since they had more time and means to advance themselves and to contribute to society. Masaryk thought that women should not be kept away from public activities in the name of family life, because to do so would be to restrict their horizons and prevent them from developing their full potential. Masaryk refused to accept the most common arguments against women's emancipation: that women were too weak to compete, and that competition would threaten men. In Masaryk's vivid descriptions, the empty life of upper-class girls comes across as much more exhausting than any competition in the work place. Most lower-class women worked anyway for economic reasons. He viewed the situation of farmers' wives as closest to economic equality because the division of work on farms was to a significant degree established by tradition; women's work was indispensable for maintaining a farm, and it was as such socially and legally recognised.[42] Masaryk considered most urgent the need to help girls from the lower classes, because they received a poor education and their chances of economic security through marriage were very slim. He urged women to become involved in public and political life, initially at least through their husbands. This involvement, in his view, was indispensable if greater social justice were to be won through the legislative process. Masaryk continually emphasised that emancipation should not be confused with imitating men; smoking, drinking, and similar behaviour could do women no good, but would only conceal those phenomena which traditionally stood in the way of cooperation.

Masaryk had great hopes for various associations and social clubs which united people with common interests and gave the less privileged, including women, a chance to raise their voices in public and cooperate with men. Teachers and some political parties were probably most advanced in this respect. He felt it very encouraging that 'modern' Czech men and women had already begun to cooperate more closely for the improvement of women's lot, although the number of such men was not yet great.

Part of Masaryk's contribution to greater understanding between men and women was his active participation in the Czech temperance movement, of which he was a founding member in Moravia. He saw alcoholism especially in Moravia as a serious obstacle to the improvement of the quality of family life. His heavy emphasis on the detrimental influence of alcohol on health, both physical and mental, as well as its needless waste of time and money, culminated in 1912 in the publication of his pamphlet on alcoholism.[43] To a large extent he agreed with the analysis made by the temperance movement of alcoholism as a problem caused by economic and social conditions, yet he also insisted on its power to cause, in consequence, even greater economic hardship, sometimes leading to pauperisation, as well as a range of associated problems: physical and psychological disorders, degeneracy among alcoholics' offspring, an increase in criminal behaviour, and the brutalisation of the alcoholic, particularly of his intellectual and moral state. Consequently, Masaryk considered alcoholism a significant problem, one which he diagnosed as the immediate gratification of a powerful urge to escape life and as having destructive effects on all those involved, especially wives and children.[44]

Masaryk appealed to educated people, who he thought should be more knowledgeable and responsible, to set a good example to others in avoiding alcohol as much as possible. He accused doctors, lawyers, teachers and even the clergy of tolerating alcohol and thus setting a bad example to youth, who often failed to develop respect for their elders. Escape to alcohol encouraged men to shirk their duties and responsibilities, especially towards their families, and was a serious obstacle to satisfactory family and marital relations. He argued that the biblical injunction to 'honour thy father and mother' needed to be complemented by 'respect the soul of your child'.[45] Masaryk was aware that abstinence alone would not solve the problem of rehabilitating a person spiritually and morally; it would only provide one of the necessary preconditions, and it would provide involved women with more humane conditions.[46]

On the whole, Masaryk saw spiritual and moral improvement through individual initiative as a practical approach towards changing some negative realities. He considered human beings capable of continual development in all important areas of thcir lives, but as weak, though not necessarily evil, and in need of seeing the sense and purpose of their efforts. Cooperation and the Christian conception of love could be powerful when used to achieve this goal, provided people were encouraged by those in a position of greater knowledge and authority. To show that he shared some of his most important ideas with significant contemporary European thinkers, he occasionally referred to Nietzsche, Björnson, Tolstoy, Dostoyevsky and others. It was not a coincidence that Masaryk saw a social and moral component to the women's question and insisted that it involved men equally as much as women, because without the substantial cooperation of men, significant improvements in the status and situation of women were impossible. Changes in personal values and attitudes had to be accompanied by changes in the legal status of women, their access to equal education, and their equal civil and political rights. Such changes could not be achieved other than through the legislative process, which was partly dependent on public opinion.

When Masaryk was elected a deputy to the Reichsrat in March 1891, he became very active in discussions on social and educational issues, which usually raised the women's question. His political views had been presented to the public previously in *Čas*, and to a great extent were incorporated into the programme of the National Liberal Party (Národní strana svobodomyslná, the Young Czechs) when it was joined by the Realist group, of which Masaryk was the senior member.[47] Improved educational opportunities and women's suffrage was a part of this programme.[48] Despite frequent discussions in the Reichsrat on social issues, no significant social legislation became law (with the exception of the creation of a workers' curia for voting purposes). An eleven-hour working day applicable for both sexes and instituted in 1884 remained unchanged, despite increasing demands to further limit working hours.[49]

To show the urgent need for certain reforms, Masaryk published in 1900 in *Naše doba* an article by Josef Gruber on the overall situation of women in Austria.[50] The article revealed alarming statistics. It showed that most women worked outside the home at some point in their lives, but most of them neither possessed basic skills nor had the opportunity to obtain practical training, since the government paid only 156 000 crowns a year to all schools for females, as opposed to 8.22 million crowns for boys' secondary schools. The situation in Bohemia was probably better than that in most other parts of the Empire because Czech women activists, notably writers such as Eliška Krásnohorská, Karolína Světlá or Marie Palacká-Riegrová, succeeded with the help of sympathetic male patriots and politicians in establishing an admirable, if still inadequate, network of private secondary schools for girls. Unfortunately, the major objective of the women's movement, the inclusion of girls' secondary schooling into the governmental system, was not achieved under the Monarchy, though some important improvements were made.[51] Masaryk was in the forefront of those who struggled for these changes.

In the early 1890s, opposition to women's education was still strong, but support increased in parliament and in the daily press. The press occasionally provided space for women activists, who rejected the idea that women should not be more than mothers and wives, and therefore did not need education. This argument was based on the assumption that women did not have to work. But lower-class working women lacked education and so were qualified only for the most tedious, laborious and low-paid jobs. Since these women often had children, working hours were an extremely important issue for them. Moreover, single-parent families were increasing, and were completely dependent on women's work.[52] In the 1890s the women's emancipation movement extended its struggle to the political arena by demanding the right to vote.[53]

In his parliamentary speeches, Masaryk frequently dealt with issues related to the improvement of women's lot.[54] He concentrated especially on justifying better educational opportunities for women. In his October 1891 speech he boldly spoke in favour of permitting women to study in some university faculties. His concern for women was often linked with other issues. Although he considered improvements through the legislative process important, he tried to influence the workers' attitude towards women as well as the direction of the workers' movement by speaking at their public meetings, including meetings of women workers. The governmental authorities were cool towards Masaryk's activity: he was prevented from speaking at one of the largest rallies of working-class women (700 attended) in Prague in 1892, when the arrival of police ended the gathering.[55] Lecturing to workers was another way Masaryk contributed to their education. He was the first university teacher to give lectures for workers, beginning with an 1893 address to the workers' association 'Dělnická beseda českoslovanská', and he volunteered to teach at the Workers' Academy in Prague when it was established in 1896. He insisted that the Academy should be available to women as well, and that practical courses be established especially for them.[56] Typically, ethical and social considerations were an important part of his lectures.

Although during Masaryk's first term in the Reichsrat women gained no substantial concessions, increased public pressures and the continual attention which the press paid to women's efforts brought results in subsequent years. The most important was that by the end of the 1890s women were permitted to study in some university faculties, and a small number of girls could study at male secondary schools as special students. (They were not supposed to form more than 10 per cent of classes.)

From 1894 onwards Masaryk followed the women's question carefully in *Naše doba*, exposing conservative views and bringing up arguments and evidence in favour of women's emancipation. Comparisons with other countries were a frequent way of showing shortcomings on the part of the Czech male population as well as on the part of the Viennese government. In the first issue of *Naše doba*, Masaryk presented impressions from his trip to the United States. The greater degree of equality in American male-female relationships, together with the perception that men there were generally involved in household work and bringing up children, impressed him very much.[57] When the Austrian Minister of Education, Baron Gautsch, argued that the state secondary schools were not suitable for girls' physical nature and that he could see no reason why they should study at universities (although he admitted that women might be of equal intelligence with men), Masaryk compared these policies with those in other countries.[58] For many years, opponents of women's admission to university studies had emphasised the dangers of women competing in the job market. Masaryk argued that women who were not able to support themselves had to be supported by their fathers or relatives, a duty which in turn forced men to work harder and longer hours. Since by regulation all women in government jobs (and often in jobs requiring them to deal with the public) had to be unmarried, the number of competing women could never become great. Although Masaryk was not in favour of this regulation, he did not see much chance for its abolition in the near future. *Naše doba* kept its readers informed about improvements in the women's situation in the Empire and elsewhere. The periodical wrote appreciatively about the decree of the Ministry of Education that permitted women with successful final examination results at a state grammar school to become special students at the Faculty of Arts in Prague and three years later at the Faculty of Medicine as regular students.[59]

In occasional lectures at girls' schools, Masaryk encouraged girls to continue their education at the university level. He described his positive experiences with female students at the Faculty of Arts, where women, in some respects, treated their studies more seriously than men.[60] He was even willing to give regular lectures at the Girls' Academy in Brno, and asked its principal, Zdenka Wiedermannová-Motyčková, to specify preferred topics.[61] However, he refused in 1903 to become 'honorary' speaker at the summer school for women teachers, arguing that teachers have to learn from each other and develop greater respect for themselves, and to have less admiration for those a step ahead socially and academically. He frequently advised teachers to form their own organisations to help boost their strength and pride in their profession.[62]

From 1905 on, *Naše doba* included two special columns, 'Ženská otázka' (The Women's Question), and later 'Ženské hnutí' (The Women's Movement), renamed 'Ženská hlídka' (Women's Watch) in 1910 and edited by a female editor, Olga Stránská-Absolonová. This latter column discussed urgent questions such as employment, servants, education, emancipation, human rights, prostitution, unemployment amongst women, legal protection and insurance, suffrage, the insufficient cooperation of men in women's emancipation, marital problems, and similar topics.[63] When the Girls' Academy established a new women's journal, *Ženská revue*, in 1905, Masaryk became an occasional contributor, but he was unable to recommend a good book reviewer for the journal, since in his view, all those whom he knew had to a lesser or greater extent an 'unhealthy' perception of women. He advised the journal to cultivate its own female reviewer. Masaryk also urged that the journal, which was published in Brno, become more widely available, particularly in Bohemia.[64]

While Masaryk never tired of promoting equality between women and men, and remained faithful to his ideas on the women's question throughout his life, he gradually became critical of certain tendencies in the emancipation movement. In 1897 he expressed disappointment with the Women's Convention in Prague, describing it as fashionable but not serious. The fact that it took place without the participation of men and that no discussion followed speeches was, in his view, a serious barrier to future attempts to solve urgent problems.[65] To condemn the whole movement, however, because of a few negative aspects would have been, he felt, a wrong decision. He continued to emphasise the possibility of choice for women in their lives as the most important goal of the movement, and recognition of women's equality with men as a precondition of any improvement in intellectual, legal, economic, ethical and other areas.[66]

In conclusion, Masaryk understood the women's question as part of broader problems, especially social and moral ones. His major criticism was directed against the educational, political, and legal inequality of women in comparison with men, but also against the prevailing attitudes of men towards women and family life. These attitudes, nourished by the belief in women's inferiority, disregarded women's emotional and intellectual needs and potential, and chiefly promoted their exploitation. Masaryk tried to show that such attitudes were unjustified, not only in the light of women's overall abilities (which he considered substantially equal to those of men) but also in the light of modern developments, which would not benefit from sacrificing the various positive potentials of women. He directly linked women's emancipation to the issue of democratisation of society, and to progress generally. Moreover, traditional attitudes prevented men from developing more fulfilling, satisfying marital and family relations, and contributed to the misery of both sexes. He considered the struggle for greater cooperation between men and women in families and almost all other spheres as an important component of women's emancipation which should interest men and women equally.

In other words, Masaryk believed that the struggle for institutional changes in women's status and rights had to be integrated with changes in personal attitudes and values. The establishment of equal educational opportunities for women was an immediate goal. He was convinced that the whole of society would gain from the public involvement of women. Since the chances for substantial changes in the political and educational systems under the Habsburg Monarchy were extremely slim, Masaryk placed great stress on self-help, beginning with changes in personal attitudes on the part of individual men, greater initiative on the part of women, and the establishment of various associations with clubs which would enable free discussion of important issues as well as debate over practical action. A first step towards true understanding would be a greater openness and sincerity about problems facing men's and women's relationships. He believed that individuals and society as a whole would benefit from more satisfactory and constructive human relations, especially in marriage. And he tried to inspire men and women to pay greater attention to their development by a conscious effort from childhood throughout their whole lives to triumph over aspects of human nature which were adverse to humanity. His effort to identify major social, intellectual, psychological, religious and economic obstacles standing in the way of women's advancement was a unique phenomenon in Central Europe at that time. And the fact that Masaryk accompanied it with practical suggestions on how to make positive changes in spheres which were within reach of the average person, provided his ideas with considerable public impact.

While the process of clarifying the goals and means of the women's movement culminated in the 1890s, Masaryk had been, as we have seen, indirectly involved in it since the mid-1880s, and he remained active almost until World War I. It is not easy to estimate the degree of his influence on the Czech public or any specific groups, but considering that Masaryk was the only Czech male intellectual systematically concerned with the women's question for almost three decades, the impact of his ideas must have been significant. Even before 1910, he was appreciated by some women activists as the most influential personality in this sphere. The fact that he expressed an awareness of the varying needs of women in different social strata is particularly important. Partly because of Masaryk's activity before 1914, many Czech women found relatively little resistance to their efforts at their advancement among prominent Czech men, and they moved with relative ease up the political ladder after 1918.[67]

NOTES

1　I would like to thank Barbara Reinfeld, New York Institute of Technology, for her helpful comments and suggestions. I would also like to express gratitude to the Lending Division of the National Library, Ottawa, for their excellent services and good will during my research in the winter of 1985–86.

2　Woman writers such as Eliška Krásnohorská, Karolina Světlá, and the wives of Czech politicians, the most devoted being Marie Palacká-Riegrová, were a core of the women's movement in the 1860s and 1870s. The Realist literary trends of this period served as a significant source of public information on the economic, social, and emotional situations of women, and they encouraged sympathy and concern with the less privileged, including both women and men. The neo-Romantic trend of the following decades was partly counterbalanced by new sources of information and communication such as newspapers, journals, public lectures and interest groups. The emancipation movement of Czech women, while more significant than a similar movement in Germany, was never as well-organised as the one in England. There is no comprehensive study on this movement of Czech women before 1914.

3   From the beginning of the 1890s, women struggled for voting rights, but without success, despite some support from Czech political parties. In 1907, when the universal male suffrage was introduced in Austria and the nobility lost many political privileges, aristocratic women lost the voting rights which they had enjoyed for centuries.

4   Jaroslav Kopáč, *Dějiny české školy a pedagogiky v letech 1867–1914* (Brno: Universita J. E. Purkyně, 1968) pp. 93–7. F. F. Plamínková: 'Žena budiž rovnoprávna muži', in *Masaryk a ženy. Sborník*. (Prague: Ženská národní rada, 1930) pp. 31–3. Plamínková, an active member of the Czech emancipation movement since the 1890s, became a parliamentary deputy for the Czechoslovak National Socialist Party during the Czechoslovak Republic. She was executed in 1942 during the German occupation of Bohemia and Moravia.

5   Plamínková, *Masaryk a ženy*, p. 33.

6   Zdenka Wiedermannová-Motyčková, 'Prof. Masaryk a ženské hnutí na Moravě', in E. Beneš (ed.), *Sborník T. G. Masarykovi k 60. narozeninám* (Prague: Grosman a Svoboda, 1910) pp. 127, 260. Also in *Masaryk a ženy*, pp. 126–7.

7   Plamínková, *Masaryk a ženy*, p. 33. It is not easy to specify the extent to which Masaryk's views on women's emancipation were shared by other Realists. In 1895 the daily press remarked, however, that the Czech intelligentsia were 'leaning toward the Realists', 'Z Prahy (Realisté a naše literatura)', *Plzeňské listy*, vol. XXXII, no. 53, 2 May 1895. In 1892 the radical youth periodical *Neodvislost* accused the Realists, since they were influential among intellectuals and students, of stifling radicalism among these groups. 'Radicalismus a realismus', *Čas*, vol. VII, no. 1 (7 January 1893) pp. 2–4.

8   Thomas G. Masaryk, *Suicide and the Meaning of Civilisation*, trans. William B. Weist and Robert G. Batson, with an Introduction by Anthony Giddens (University of Chicago Press, 1970) pp. 27–34, 81–4, 106. (First published in German, *Der Selbstmord als sociale Massenerscheinung der Modernen Civilisation* [Vienna: Konegen, 1881].) Masaryk formulated more detailed views in his 1884 lectures on practical philosophy, 'Přednášky o praktické filosofii'. These lectures are unpublished, but in 1884 they were litho-printed, and became available to interested readers outside the university. Some ideas on the topic of women's emancipation are presented by Zdeněk Franta (ed.), *T. G. Masaryk, Mravní názory*, 2nd ed. (Prague: Státní nakladatelství, 1925) pp. 136–44.

9   A brief view of most of these articles in *Naše doba* is Kamil Harmach: 'Ženská otázka v Masarykově Naší době', *Masaryk a ženy*, pp. 139–73.

10   'První literární orgán pokrokového hnutí', *Čas*, 7, no. 15 (15 April
      1893). Also published as part of the *Naše nynější krise*, (Prague: Čas,
      1895); 'Otázka ženská: Volná láska', in *Otázka sociální* (Prague: Čin,
      1898) pp. 83–97; [1] *Mnohoženství a jednoženství* (Prague: the author,
      1899), originally a lecture given in 'Domovina', an association for the
      protection of morally sick women and girls (Spolek pro záchranu
      hynoucích dívek a žen), on 7 March 1899; [2] 'Moderní názor na ženu',
      a lecture for students in the Girls' Academy in Brno in 1904; [3]
      'Postavení ženy v rodině a ve veřejném životě', a lecture for the
      Association of Czech Ladies in Chicago (Jednota českých dam) in
      1907, in *Americké přednášky*, (Chicago: Výkonný výbor Svazu svobo-
      domyslných v Chicagu, 1907) pp. 57–61; [4] 'Žena u Ježíše a Pavla', a
      lecture to the Czech Women's Association (Ženský klub český), on 9
      December 1910, in *O ženě*, 2nd ed. (Prague: Čin, 1929) pp. 25–42.
      [These above lectures (1–4) are reprinted in *Masaryk a ženy*]; 'Hlavní
      zásady ethiky humanitní', in *Ideály humanitní* (Prague: Melantrich,
      1968) pp. 55–61; first published in 1901. 'Boj proti prostituci', a lecture
      at the meeting of the Czech Progressive Party Club in 1907, in *Čas*, vol.
      XI, 1906, no. 330 and 332. A detailed excerpt is in Franta (ed.), *T. G.
      Masaryk, Mravní názory*, pp. 144–8. *Přechod ze střední školy na školu
      vysokou*, a lecture for students in 1912 (Prague: Studentská revue,
      1913, vol. IX). Masaryk's other relevant works are mentioned in notes
      below. The most important of Masaryk's parliamentary speeches
      bearing on the women's question are: 'O sociální otázce', 26 June 1891,
      published in *Národní listy*, vol. XXXI, no. 191, 10 July 1891; 'O
      úkolech české politiky školské', ibid., no. 202, 21 July 1891; and
      especially significant is his speech on 30 October 1891, 'Říšská rada',
      ibid., no. 304, 31 October 1891.
11   'Je-li tomu tak, co budeš dělat, aby se to napravilo?' Alice G.
      Masaryková, *Dětství a mládí. Vzpomínky a myšlenky* (Pittsburgh:
      Masaryk Publication Trust, 1960) p. 97.
12   T. G. Masaryk, *Mnohoženství a jednoženství*, 2nd ed. (Prague: Kočí,
      1925) pp. 6–7.
13   Charlotta G. Masaryková, *Listy do vězení* (Prague: Žikeš, 1948). In her
      introduction, Alice Masaryková says (p. 5) that her mother faithfully
      followed Masaryk's work, read all his manuscripts, and discussed them
      with him. Masaryk appreciated throughout his life the moral and spiritual
      strength of his wife and her influence on his personality and work. Their
      marriage was happy and both of them considered their intimate relations
      'sacred'; they both disliked jokes about intimate marital relations. Jan
      Herben, *Masarykův rodinný život*, 7th ed. (Prague: Borový, 1937)
      pp. 24–7. When he was twenty-seven, Masaryk wrote about the positive
      influence of women on his emotional development and the formation of
      his character to his friend Zdenka Šemberová. It is apparent from these
      letters that he perceived the emotional aspect of life very seriously, aware
      of its constructive and destructive potential for human beings. Detailed
      excerpts from these letters are in ibid., pp. 9–14. The influence of the
      family and the environment on Masaryk when growing up is described,
      for example, in Karel Čapek, *Hovory s T. G. M.*, 7th ed. (Prague:
      Československý spisovatel, 1969) pp. 9–50. Recollections of his family

life are in *Alice Garrigue Masaryk, 1879–1966*, compiled by Ruth Crawford Mitchell (Pittsburgh, PA: University of Pittsburgh, 1980) pp. 19–40.

14 Masaryk, 'Moderní názor na ženu', in *Masaryk a ženy*, p. 61.

15 In this respect Masaryk vigorously opposed Friedrich Engels and others who wanted to make women 'equally immoral with men', instead of improving general morality. *Otázka sociální*, pp. 93–7.

16 Masaryk, *Přechod ze střední školy*, pp. 10–12. Masaryk knew the situation of university students relatively well. He was one of those rare professors who maintained close personal relations with students (frequently inviting them even to his home). Statistical data on syphilis among the Czech population seem to be unavailable.

17 In 1906, when Masaryk delivered a lecture on the same topic, he was pleased with the sizable audience and remarked that the response of 1884 could not repeat itself.

18 In 1905 in Bohemia 11.46 per cent of children were illegitimate. Břetislav Foustka: 'Ochrana dětství a mládí', in Z. V. Tobolka (ed.), *Česká politika*, 5 vols. (Prague: Laichter, 1906–13) V, p. 126.

19 Harmach, 'Ženská otázka', *Masaryk a ženy*, p. 163.

20 Lev Winter, 'Dělnické zákonodárství rakouské', *Česká politika*, vol. IV, pp. 862–3, 871. One third of the Czech industrial class were women, i.e. 178, 261. Ibid., pp. 862–3.

21 Masaryk, *Suicide and the Meaning of Civilization*, pp. 33–4, 106.

22 Ibid., p. 34.

23 Masaryk, 'Žena u Ježíše a Pavla', *O ženě*, p. 42.

24 T. G. Masaryk, *Modern Man and Religion* (Translation of *Moderní člověk a náboženství. Jak pracovat?* and *Ideály humanitní*), trans. Ann Bibza and Václav Beneš, with a preface by Vasil K. Škrach (Westport: Greenwood Press, 1970) p. 152. Masaryk, 'Žena u Ježíše a Pavla', in Masaryk, *O ženě*, pp. 25–42.

25 The most detailed discussion is 'Žena u Ježíše a Pavla', in Masaryk, *O ženě*, pp. 25–42.

26 Ibid.

27 Ibid. A substantial part of 'První literární orgán pokrokového hnutí', in *Čas* (1893) and a chapter 'Otázka ženská: Volná láska', in *Otázka sociální* are devoted to this issue.

28 Masaryk, 'Žena u Ježíše a Pavla', *O ženě*, p. 40.

29 Masaryk's review of Machar's collection of poems '*Zde by měly kvést růže*', *Naše doba*, vol. II, no. 12 (1895) pp. 1131–4.

30 Masaryk, 'Přednášky o praktické filosofii', *Mravní názory*, pp. 97–8., 140–2. A good discussion on social and criminal consequences of illegitimacy is in Foustka, *Česká politika*, vol. V, pp. 124–8.

31 Masaryk, 'Zolův naturalismus', *Naše doba*, vol. III, no. 1 (1895) pp. 1–16; no. 2 (1895) pp. 120–38; no. 3 (1895) pp. 220–32; no. 4 (1896) pp. 289–301; no. 5 (1896) pp. 423–37. 'Moderní člověk, a náboženství. Moderní titanism. Nemoc století (Alfred de Musset)', *Naše doba*, vol. V, no. 1 (1897) pp. 33–42. 'Moderní titanism. A de Musset: nemoc století', *Naše doba*, vol. V, no. 2 (1897) pp. 142–57. 'Goethův Faust: Nadčlověk'. Ibid., no. 5 (1898) pp. 385–95; no. 6 (1898) pp. 481–92; no. 7 (1898) pp. 585–99. 'Saninism', *Naše doba*, vol. XVII, no. 1 (1909)

pp. 31–7.

32 Masaryk, *Otázka sociální*, 7th ed. (Prague: Čin, 1948) pp. 83–97.

33 Masaryk, 'První literární orgán pokrokového hnutí', in *Česká òtázka*. *Naše nynější krize* (Prague: Čin, 1936) pp. 330–9.

34 Ibid., pp. 341–2.

35 Masaryk, 'Moderní názor na ženu', in *Masaryk a ženy*, pp. 64, 68 – Masaryk's review of Machar's poems, *Zde by měly kvést růže*. [Masaryk is wildly wrong about Mácha and Neruda, in Robert B. Pynsent's judgement. Editor's note.]

36 Masaryk, *Mnohoženství a jednoženství*.

37 From the 1890s, Masaryk does not elaborate on the use of contraceptives as he did in 1884, when he condemned their use as unhealthy and immoral and as robbing the marital relationship of true responsibility and affection. Masaryk, 'Přednášky o praktické filosofii', p. 97–8, in *Mravní názory*, p. 142. Originally, Masaryk was in favour of large families (probably due to Tolstoy's influence), but gradually he came to consider smaller families as more beneficial to the proper upbringing of children and to mother's health. Although Masaryk and Charlotte had five children (one died as an infant), Charlotte became sick after the birth of the second child, and on the advice of her doctor avoided physical work for the rest of her life.

38 Masaryk, 'Moderní názor na ženu', in *Masaryk a ženy*, especially pp. 62–5.

39 Ibid., p. 65.

40 Ibid., pp. 61, 65.

41 Masaryk, *Mnohoženství a jednoženství*, pp. 24–6.

42 Masaryk's concern, related to the economic situation of women, was mainly directed towards women living in urban areas. On the legal position of farmers' wives see *Česká politika*, vol. IV, pp. 87–9.

43 On 11 September 1905 Masaryk addressed workers in a lecture on alcoholism in the Workers' House in Vsetín, Moravia; *O alkoholismu*, 2nd ed. (Prague: Pokrok, 1908). *O ethice a alkoholismu* (Prague: A. Klíčník 1912). A detailed extract of the latter pamphlet is in *Mravní názory*, pp. 148–56.

44 Masaryk, *O ethice a alkoholismu*, pp. 16–17. In 1910 Zdenka Wiedermannová-Motyčková acknowledged that the temperance movement had brought excellent results in Moravia, where alcoholism was traditionally a greater problem than in Bohemia. Wiedermannová-Motyčková, 'Prof. Masaryk a ženské hnuti na Moravé', in *Masaryk a ženy*, p. 126.

45 Masaryk, *O ethice a alkoholismu*, p. 16. See also Masaryk, *Ideály humanitní*, pp. 57–8.

46 Masaryk himself gave up drinking alcohol in the 1880s (most probably due to Tolstoy's example). He continued to use it medicinally when in danger of catching a cold or flu. Herben, *Masarykův rodinný život*, pp. 38–9, 59.

47 'Návrh programu lidového', *Čas*, vol. IV, no. 44 (1 November 1890) pp. 689–94. The programme of the National Liberal (Young Czech) Party was published, as 'Celostátní prohlášení mladočeské strany k českému národu', *Národní listy*, vol. XXXI, no. 53, 22 February 1891.

48 After Masaryk parted from the National Liberal Party in 1893, he became even more active in the emancipation movement, while the party became less involved; however, most Czech political parties later gradually became supportive of women's demands.

49 Although the catastrophic health record of working women was well known, the most common argument in the Reichsrat against further reduction of working hours was that to limit hours meant an imposition on personal freedoms. Masaryk tried to show the advantages of an eight-hour working day in a pamphlet *Osm hodin práce* (Prague: Čas, 1901).

50 Josef Gruber, 'Organisace ženského vyučování odborného', *Naše doba*, vol. VII, no. 10 (1900) pp. 721–32. The article was based on a book by the Advisor of the Ministry of Education, Dr. Franz von Ritter, *Der weibliche Fachunterricht und dessen Organisierung mit Rücksicht auf die praktische Bedürfnisse des Lebens* (Vienna, 1900).

51 By the late 1890s female students were allowed to become special students in grammar schools, and gradually in other schools as well. Alice Masaryk describes her experience of Czech secondary and university education in *Alice Garrigue Masaryk 1879–1966*, pp. 31–54.

52 Pavla Maternová, 'Emancipace a Minerva', *Národní listy*, vol. XXXII, no. 32, 1892.

53 F. F. Plamínková mentions that the struggle for equal voting rights evolved into an organised movement in 1904, and that it was successful. She particularly appreciated the fact that generally Czech men and most political parties supported women. F. F. Plamínková, 'Několik poznámek o práci československých žen', in Masaryk, *O ženě*, pp. 14–15. Although women never gained suffrage under the Monarchy, a loophole in the law was used in 1908 and a woman candidate, Marie Tůmová, was elected to the Bohemian Diet for the Czech Progressive Party by three-quarters of male voters in Vysoké Mýto. Masaryk wholeheartedly supported her candidacy. *Masaryk a ženy*, p. 120.

54 See note 10.

55 Masaryk, 'O sociální otázce', *Národní listy*, vol. XXXI, no. 202, 10 July 1891. 'Veřejná schůze dělnických žen a dívek', *Národní listy*, vol. XXXII, no. 110, 19 April 1892. 'Dělnická akademie', *Naše doba*, vol. IV, no. 2 (1896) pp. 137–48.

56 'Přednášky pro dělníky', *Čas*, vol. VII, no. 50 (16 December 1893), pp. 790–1.

57 'Ženská otázka v Americe a v Čechách', *Naše doba*, vol. I, no. 1 (1894) pp. 42–6.

58 'Ženská otázka v lékařství'. This quotes from an unspecified article in *Rozhledy* on legislation improving the situation of women in England, France, Russia, Sweden, and Denmark. In *Naše doba*, vol. I, no. 1 (1894) p. 80. 'Ženské studium ve Vídni a v Budapešti', ibid., vol. III, no. 3 (1895). In Hungary women obtained permission to study at the Faculties of Arts and Medicine, but under very strict conditions.

59 'Vyšší vzdělání žen v Rakousku', *Naše doba*, vol. IV, no. 7 (1897) p. 670; 'Ženy a studium lékařství', ibid., vol. IV, no. 7 (1897) pp. 632–7; 'Ženské hnutí', ibid., no. 4 (1897) p. 379; 'Universitní studium dam', ibid., no. 6 (1897) p. 569; 'Prokroky žen v Americe v posledních 20

letech', ibid., no. 4 (1897) p. 381; 'Ženy připuštěny k řádnému studiu mediciny', ibid., vol. VII, no. 1 (1900) p. 79.

60   'Odpověd' Prof. T. G. Masaryka na dotazník o vyšším ženském studiu', 'Z archivu Dívčí akademie v Brně'; the letter is without a date, but it seems to be from around the turn of the century. See *Masaryk a ženy*, p. 115.

61   'Z dopisu Zd. Wiedermannové-Motyčkové', *Masaryk a ženy*, 115–16. Masaryk's lecture 'Moderní názor na ženu' was given in 1904 in this school.

62   Ibid., p. 116.

63   A review of these topics is in Harmach,'Ženská otázka v Masarykově Naší době', *Masaryk a ženy*, pp. 139–73.

64   Ibid., p. 120. Since 1896 there was *Ženský obzor*, a women's periodical for social issues, politics, and literature, published in Prague. Masaryk welcomed this periodical, especially because it was published in cooperation with men. 'Ženský obzor', *Naše doba*, vol. III, no. 6 (1896) p. 574. But later it became more entertaining than educational.

65   'Zemský sjezd', *Naše doba*, vol. IV, no. 9 (1897) pp. 826–9. There is no author, but Harmach, 'Ženská otázka', in *Masaryk a ženy*, p. 159, ascribes the article to Masaryk.

66   Masaryk summarised his views in 1907, in a lecture to the Association of Czech Ladies in Chicago: 'Postavení ženy v rodině a ve veřejném životě'. Although Masaryk discussed the situation of Czech women in the Bohemian kingdom, his call for women's participation in political life was also aimed at his American audience.

67   A very brief review by an anonymous author on Masaryk's involvement in Bohemia is in 'Prof. Masaryk a ženské hnutí v Čechách', *Masaryk a ženy*, pp. 121–5. A similar review on his influence in Moravia was written in 1910 by Zdenka Widermannová-Motyčková; 'T. G. Masarykovi k 60. narozeninám', in *Masaryk a ženy*, pp. 125–7.

12 Masaryk and the Russian Question against the Background of German and Czech Attitudes to Russia
Hans Lemberg

Thomas G. Masaryk is generally considered to be the outstanding figure responsible for directing Czech political orientation towards the West and towards Anglo-American values in particular. In view of this fact, it may seem surprising that so far as quantity is concerned, the greater number of Masaryk's writings – apart from his works on the historical and philosophical interpretation of the political existence of the Czech nation – is devoted to the Russian Question.[1] Masaryk's *Russland und Europa* (*The Spirit of Russia*), published in German shortly before World War I, has been considered by no less an authority than Jaroslav Bidlo to be the culmination of his academic life-work.[2] The question arises, therefore, whether Masaryk, then in his sixties, was beginning to develop a new profile in the second decade of the twentieth century, and to gain an international reputation as one of the great specialists in Russian affairs. This paper seeks to shed some light upon this particular role of Masaryk's – his relationship to the Russian Question against the background of German and Czech attitudes to Russia.

1. MASARYK'S *RUSSLAND UND EUROPA*

Let us recall some well-established facts: Masaryk's interest in Russia dates back to his youth; it was nurtured among other factors by the wave of Slavonic feeling and enthusiasm engendered during the 1860s by the Czech national movement. Masaryk soon learned to read Russian.[3] From the 1880s onwards, he frequently reviewed Russian publications and discussed critically some topical Russian problems in brief articles which appeared in various journals, mainly in *Čas* and *Naše Doba*.[4] However, Russian affairs were certainly not the main focus of his academic activity. The only monograph which can be considered to belong to this aspect is his study on the Slavophile I. V. Kireyevsky, which was published in 1889 but did not attract much attention.[5] It formed Volume One of a projected series entitled 'Slovanské studie' (Slavonic studies), but apart from this no further volumes were ever published.[6]

After a period of over twenty years, during which he devoted his scholarly and journalistic activities mainly to philosophy, and to producing writings of more or less fundamental importance on the basic questions of Czech politics, the publication in 1913 of his voluminous work on Russia marks a surprise development in the direction of his political *œuvre*. Once again, this work formed the basis of a new series under the general title *Russland und Europa. Studien über die geistigen Strömungen in Russland, Erste Folge* (Russia and Europe. Studies on intellectual trends in Europe, Series No. 1). The individual title of both volumes is *Zur russischen Geschichts- und Religionsphilosophie. Soziologische Skizzen* (Russian historical and religious philosophy. Sociological sketches). This pedantic German title was so cumbersome that it is not surprising to find it omitted from the translations of the work into Czech,[7] English,[8] Italian[9] and Serbo-Croat[10] which appeared after 1918.

The confusion is increased by the fact that the first half of Volume One bears the heading 'Part One – problems of Russian historical and religious philosophy'. In reality, this part consists of about 180 pages devoted to a survey of Russian history with an annotated bibliography for the German reader. Part One contains practically no trace of the promised philosophy. Part Two, which begins at about the middle of the first volume under the title 'Sketches on Russian historical and religious philosophy', continues until the end of the second volume and contains an author-orientated outline of the development of Russian political and philosophical literature in the nineteenth and early twentieth centuries from the viewpoint of intellectual history.

Considering this complex and involved statement of the book's contents, it is small wonder that not every reader noticed that the work was incomplete. As the foreword points out, Masaryk's work on Russia was intended to focus on an interpretation of Dostoyevsky;[11] one of the contemporary reviewers thought this would be the second part (Folge 2) of *Russland und Europa*, perhaps in two further volumes.[12] Indeed, the existing two volumes of 1913 contain very little about Dostoyevsky.[13] During Masaryk's lifetime, there were occasional hints which indicated that he had actually prepared the third volume and that it already existed in manuscript form, but was not yet ready for printing; only a preview to the contents was published in the thirties.[14] We know that Volume Three did not appear until 1967, and then only in the English translation of a Czech translation of the original German version. It was heavily edited with whole portions omitted.[15] Thus, Masaryk's envisaged monumental work *Russland und Europa*, of which both (or all three) volumes were to constitute probably just the First Series, was destined to remain unfinished.

This chapter is not intended to be a comprehensive study of Masaryk's opus on Russia, which, if one includes the unpublished volume, is nonetheless his largest single work. Instead, it will focus attention on the role of Masaryk's book and some of his other statements on Russia against the background of German and Czech attitudes to that country. This approach can possibly lead to a more differentiated appreciation of Masaryk's significance as an expert on Russian affairs than previous literature, be it of the polemical or mainly panegyric type, has managed to convey.

The significance of the work, generally referred to under the not quite correct title *Russland und Europa*, and called *The Spirit of Russia* in the English version, lies basically in the circumstances surrounding its genesis. In 1902 Masaryk treated the subject in the course of the Crane lectures, which he was invited to give at the University of Chicago.[16] Three years later, like many of his contemporaries, he was deeply influenced by the first Russian Revolution. The extent of the repercussions of this revolution on the Habsburg monarchy have, as yet, still not been fully recognised.[17] Masaryk appears to have paid special attention to the circumstances surrounding the revolution. Those parts in the opening historical section of *Russland und Europa* which deal with contemporary events contain criticism of the deplorable state of affairs in Russia, criticism which, in its intensity, is rivalled only by the disturbing articles written by Henry Wickham Steed and R. W. Seton-Watson about the nationalities problem in Hungary and published in Great Britain before 1914.

The impulse for the publication of this monumental work on Russia stems from the meeting between Masaryk and the well-known German publisher Eugen Diederichs (1867–1930), who eventually published it in 1913. Masaryk and Diederichs carried on a correspondence beforehand, and also had a series of extended meetings at

Bad Schandau in Saxony[18] near the Bohemian border, where Masaryk and his family were staying in the summer of 1912. Since Masaryk's last journey to Russia had taken place more than twenty years earlier,[19] he decided to travel there once more in the summer of 1910 in order to complete his final preparations for the book. Diederichs, who was accustomed to visiting the countries discussed in the books published by his firm, also made a journey to Russia after having sought advice from Masaryk on contacts there as well as places to visit.[20]

2. MASARYK'S BOOK ON RUSSIA AND ITS GERMAN PUBLIC

Although Masaryk's book is based on a series of English-language lectures (in Chicago, 1902) as well as Czech lectures which he held at his university in Prague[21] in 1906 and 1907, it was nevertheless written for a German public and published in the German Reich. Its significance becomes more apparent on consideration of the situation regarding the advancement of knowledge of Russian affairs in Germany at this period. Only a decade earlier, in 1902, the first step towards institutionalising the scholarly study of Russia and its affairs had been undertaken, with the foundation of a Chair for East European history at the University of Berlin; the Vienna Chair came five years later.[22] The year in which Masaryk's book on Russia was published also saw the foundation of the 'German Society for the Study of Russia', which had as its objective the dissemination of scientifically-researched knowledge about Russia among a wider public.

During the nineteenth and the first years of the twentieth centuries, a few important pioneering works had also been written in the German language on the history and contemporary politics of the Russian Empire, which shared a long geographical border with the new German Reich and the Austro-Hungarian Empire. However, these books had either appeared several decades ago, like the Westphalian Baron Haxthausen's book, or they no longer corresponded to recent knowledge and research on Russian affairs. It is easy to understand, therefore, why Masaryk's book became an instant publishing success and attracted widespread attention. Masaryk's name suddenly became familiar in political circles in the Reich, which up to that time had never heard of this Prague professor of philosophy and representative of a small party in the Viennese Reichsrat.

In the same year, a parallel work to Masaryk's *Russland und Europa* was published. It was written by the newly appointed Professor Extraordinarius for East European History at the University of Berlin, the National Liberal Otto Hoetzsch[23]: *Russland. Eine Einführung auf Grund seiner Geschichte 1904–1912*. The composition of this book bears a similarity to that of Masaryk's insofar as it also contains an introductory survey of Russian history. In the following, principal, part of the book, however, Hoetzsch places the main emphasis on providing information about the political institutions and conditions prevailing in Russia, and discusses their development during the decade of the Revolution.

In contrast, Masaryk is concerned in the second half of his work with using the history of ideas to construct an explanation of the present. The concepts of social history and religious history which he used in the title are rather different in meaning from the modern use of these terms. Masaryk's method of evaluation is similar to that of most of his other publications.[24] In a forceful style, he links his highly selective observations and interpretations drawn from the historical and philosophical and even belletristic literature of a certain country or people in such a way that the result is the explanation of the respective nation as a whole. As a consequence of this method, Masaryk often comes perilously close to the conception of a national character, a notion which he himself regarded very critically. Most striking is Masaryk's identical general application of (or his abstraction from) the history of Russia as a model also for the history of Austria-Hungary or Bohemia: in both of them he stresses the conflict of two leading principles: of theocracy and democracy.[25]

Evidently neither Masaryk nor Hoetzsch knew anything of the other's book on Russia before these were actually published. After 1913, however, both books appear to have played a unique role as sources of information for the German public, and they were the only detailed accounts of the subject available. Right up until the 1940s, Masaryk's work in particular was considered to be the sole complete survey of Russian thought and ideas available in Western languages.[26] The work eventually came to possess a certain autonomy of its own insofar as opponents of Czechoslovakia ignored the fact that its author was the country's president at that time, and they continued to regard the book highly.

A third book that manifestly set out to explain the Russian

'character', although in a manner which was more superficial than factual, and tended towards the mythological, was Karl Nötzel's book *Die Grundlagen des geistigen Russland*, published in 1917. Nötzel was able to use the ideas and material of Masaryk's great work. He explicitly refers to it in his preface.

Nötzel offered his book to the same publisher who had accepted Masaryk's work. Eugen Diederichs was a famous name in the German publishing world. He considered it his duty not merely to publish books, but also to raise the general standard of political education and to help form a German élite with a definite intellectual and political orientation.[27] The organ used to propagate these ideas was the periodical *Die Tat* (The Deed), edited by Diederichs. The circle of readers and contributors which *Die Tat* attracted, the so called 'Tatkreis', consisted of a wide spectrum ranging from National Conservatives like Paul de Lagarde or Arthur Möller van den Bruck to the National Bolsheviks.

Admittedly, the fact that Masaryk had his work published by Diederichs does not allow us to conclude that he was close to the 'Tatkreis', even if Masaryk had himself published an article in *Die Tat* in 1913, which evidently served as a hidden sales promotion for his two-volume book: It is a word-for-word repetition of the book's introduction, only with an inversion: The end of the introduction served as the central part of the article.[28] Nevertheless, an investigation into the reception of Masaryk's work on Russia inevitably leads to a consideration of the readership attached to the Diederichs publishing house. This aspect of the question has tended to be overlooked. Some years ago, Hans Hecker analysed the ideas and conceptions of the 'Tatkreis' concerning Eastern Europe, thereby drawing attention to the fact that, during the first three decades of this century, Russia played a very important role in the thinking of German intellectuals.[29]

In the opinion of the 'Tatkreis', the rationalistic civilisation of Western Europe stood in contrast to the 'Osten' (a special German concept of Eastern Europe),[30] which they considered tending towards the irrational, but still of vital significance. Between these two poles stood the German people, whom the 'Tatkreis', in its search for a German role in Central Europe, was inclined to assign to the 'Osten'. The Russians, however, already occupied the leading position in the region. It was this section of the German public which eagerly sought not only information about Russian intellectual history, but also the approaches to its interpretation. At that time, the works of Dostoyevsky attracted vivid interest, followed by those of Tolstoy. Masaryk's book, which was intended to be an interpretation of Dostoyevsky, met these expectations perfectly, even if it did not finally fulfil his objective.[31]

Consequently, Masaryk's book was reviewed in a wide range of German learned and also literary journals.[32] Not all of the reviews were clearly positive; there was some criticism of Masaryk's lack of organisation in his text and of his intricate display of Russian philosophy,[33] which, by the way, was severely criticised in itself for its juvenile, eclectic and irrelevant character, from a Western and Central European point of view.[34] On the other hand, Masaryk gained for the most part a good reputation, even when, soon after the first reviews had come out, his role in World War I made it advisable for the reviewers not to be too positive about an author possibly guilty of high treason.[35] His *Russland und Europa* was then and later of high standing among German readers, including those who did not share his political ideas and who also objected to his roles in the Czech national movement and as President of the Czechoslovak Republic. There have been rumours that during World War I, 'certain high officials of the German Foreign Office kept the book for permanent reference on their table'. In contrast, R. W. Seton-Watson reports that, until 1916, he possessed the only copy of this book in Britain.[36] Eugen Diederichs, who esteemed Masaryk as the 'Slav's Friedrich Naumann',[37] continued his correspondence with Masaryk throughout the World War. They also continued to exchange letters after Masaryk had already become president.

3.   RUSSIA: MASARYK AT THE CROSSROADS

Up to the time he published *Russland und Europa*, Masaryk's reputation as a scholar lay in quite a different area. The academic subject he taught was philosophy. His publications were mainly concerned with the existence of the Czech nation and the 'Czech Question'. From 1907 onwards, Masaryk had once again won a seat in the Reichsrat after a prolonged absence. It was not possible for him to play an important role in the wider context of the Austro-Hungarian monarchy since he was only a representative of a minor party, even though his courageous initiatives repeatedly attracted attention.

It belongs to the realm of non-factual history to speculate what would have been Masaryk's path if World War I had not broken out just a few months after the publication of his book on Russia, and if his career had not followed a most unexpected path in 1918. The sudden turn of events makes it impossible to answer this question. How would Masaryk's newly established international reputation as an expert on Russia have developed outside the Habsburg monarchy, if world history had continued along more peaceful lines? One can presume that in all likelihood the third volume of *Russland und Europa* would have been completed. Masaryk was an energetic writer, and he had a good working relationship with his publisher. Most probably, Masaryk would have become one of the most important experts on Russia, at least from the perspective of the German Reich.

On the other hand, the question can be posed as to why, even after 1918, Masaryk did not complete and publish the third volume of his book on Russia which was so central to this work as a whole. After he had accepted the office of president of the newly established Czechoslovak Republic, the burden of his political activities and official duties was certainly great. But it is not as if Masaryk had ceased at all to publish during the twenties. His *Světová revoluce* (published in Britain as *The Making of a State*) and several essays, some of which appeared under a pen name, prove that even during the period of his presidency he was active in continuing his intellectual work. Moreover, in his new position he was no longer just a pre-war professor working away on his own (staff assistants for professors were unheard of in the humanities and arts faculties at that earlier time). With a large staff now at his command, and with improved and recently founded libraries in Prague, including those with Russian works, at his disposal, he was certainly in a position to finish his manuscript and prepare it for publication if he had so desired. What, then, prevented Masaryk from completing his work, which was already so far advanced? Had he himself already become aware of the weaknesses inherent in the conception of the whole of the third volume?[38]

The most important reason why Masaryk abandoned work on his Russian book appears to lie in his realistic appraisal of the revolutionary changes that had taken place in Russia in the meantime. Masaryk found it an impossible task to continue his analysis at the point where he had left off in 1913 with Volume Two of *Russland und Europa*.

The Revolution of 1905 had already made an indelible impression on Masaryk, as it is evident from the passages in his book that deal with the contemporary situation. The very circumstance that in the introduction to his book Masaryk refers to the 'Russian Question' is evidence of this. 'Questions' concerning certain nations only arise when their existence is threatened, or they even cease to continue as independent states, for example, the 'Polish Question' in the nineteenth century, or the 'German Question' after 1945. But the Russian Question? One can only talk of a Russian Question in this sense during the period of the October Revolution, when the Russian Empire appeared to fall to pieces, and all international contacts were broken off. At the Paris Peace Conference in 1919, the Russian Question in this sense came sharply into focus: there was no Russian state in sight from which representatives could have been invited to the conference table.

It is not an overinterpretation of the facts to maintain that in Masaryk's opinion, Russia had reached such an intense crisis after 1905 that he felt justified in referring to a 'Russian Question' in his preface to *Russland und Europa*. A further interpretation of this term must also be mentioned. Masaryk understood it in the wider sense in which he had treated the 'Czech Question' (*Česká otázka*) some years earlier: as an interpretation of the 'meaning of Czech history' based on the analysis of certain selected phases and phenomena of the whole of the nation's history.

Although Masaryk's life as an academic and politician had taken an abrupt turn since 1914, his journey to Russia, lasting from August 1917 until March 1918, meant for him further enlightenment on conditions there.[39] For the first time, Masaryk experienced conditions in a revolutionary civil war situation; his life was several times in danger, and as an unforeseen and extremely unmilitary commander-in-chief of an exile army[40] of a state which had not yet come into existence, his capacities were stretched to the utmost. On the basis of his previous theoretical and actual knowledge of Russian conditions, it was inevitable that Masaryk, in spite of almost constantly living among Czech legionaries during these weeks, should have gained genuine insights into events in revolutionary Russia, which convinced him of the depth of the changes taking place there.

It was not least on account of these impressions that Masaryk belonged to those few observers who were quick to come to a realistic evaluation of the emerging Soviet state, so far as Czech and Czechoslovak policies in the Russian Question were concerned.

4. MASARYK AND THE CZECH SUPPORTERS OF THE SLAVONIC IDEA

It is never easy for contemporaries to perceive far-reaching political changes in respect of their permanency. As is clear in his book *The New Europe*, Masaryk himself expected after 1918 that Russia would succeed in transforming the 'all too considerable negative effects of the revolution' into a 'revolution of heads and minds', which would ensure for it a 'great role' in the future 'Republic and Democracy' to be established on the basis of 'freedom and humanity'.[41] Masaryk's basic criticism of Bolshevism, which he had set forth in the period before World War I, and which he had consolidated in the revolutionary period, did not alter in the following decade. In contrast to other politicians and observers, Masaryk had a much more realistic assessment of the state of current affairs in Russia, much more so than those who came forward as the true protectors of Slavonic ideals (*slovanství*) in the new Czechoslovakia.[42]

The contrast becomes particularly evident when one looks at the relationship between Masaryk and the principal exponent of Neo-Slavism, Karel Kramář, and considers it during and after the World War. At the beginning of the 1890s, Kramář was just a junior partner of Masaryk's.[43] They had both entered parliament together, and at that time Kramář tended to adopt the style of life of Masaryk, who was his elder by ten years. Like Masaryk, Kramář worked to become a university academic, though in vain, and like him, he too undertook a long journey in Russia in 1890. In the course of his extensive public career, Kramář lost sight of the academic side of his work, which was almost completely subordinated to political considerations. Similarly, in his relations with Russia he allowed political, even emotional elements to gain the upper hand over rational analysis. What remained was – to a certain extent – mere outer imitation of Masaryk's attitudes. It is therefore very probable – even if impossible to prove – that Masaryk's book on Russia inspired Kramář to write one also. Already influenced by the Russian Revolution of February 1917, he began work on it during World War I and finished it around 1920. Its title was *The Russian Crisis*, and with nearly seven hundred pages it was about the same length as the two volumes of Masaryk's work. A further imitation of Masaryk is perhaps visible in the fact that the book, although financed by Kramář himself, appeared in a German translation published in 1925 by Duncker and Humblot in Munich and Leipzig.[44]

These similarities are entirely external. From the mid-1890s onwards, Masaryk had distanced himself from the mainstream of the Young Czech Party, and consequently from the Russophilia cultivated there largely under the influence of Kramář. Masaryk, who was already engaged in preparatory work on *Russia and Europe*, entertained a sceptical attitude towards the Neo-Slavism propagated by Kramář at the beginning of this century.[45] Later on, in 1919, the correspondence of the Czechoslovak President, Masaryk, and the Prime Minister, Kramář, reveals not only the misfortune of an irrevocably broken friendship, but also the fundamental differences in their comprehension of the role of Russia.[46]

This is not the place to discuss in detail that variation of Slavonic ideology which was one of the pillars of party doctrine adhered to by Kramář's National Democratic Party after World War I. Let us, however, list just some elements of it:

(1) The Czechoslovak Republic owed its existence to Russia (if Russia had not gone to war for the liberty of the Slavs, Czechoslovakia would not have come into existence, and so on.)
(2) Gratitude for this must be actively demonstrated. Czechoslovakia should either provide an interventionist army in the civil war, or, in the event of the defeat of the Russian Whites, it should support Russian émigrés.
(3) In matters of foreign policy, Czechoslovakia should place complete trust neither in the League of Nations nor in the Western powers because of their possible rapprochement with Germany. Her natural partner in an alliance could only be a 'strong, national, united, new and democratic' Russia which would emerge after the defeat of Bolshevism, in which the National Democratic Party under Kramář never lost hope.
(4) Czechoslovakia was to be a Czech-dominated national state, which on account of its Slavonic character must naturally tend towards Russia.
(5) In Czechoslovak politics, those forces most determined to fight against Bolshevism (that is, also domestic Communism) should receive support. This thesis was the basis for Kramář's temporary flirtation with Fascism.[47]

Against such a background, the attitude of the 'Castle' (*Hrad, Burg*)[48] faction toward Russia is thrown into sharp relief. It is certain that Masaryk with his undoubted authority was able to convey his views about Russia to this group of politicians which had gathered around him and Foreign Minister Edvard Beneš as a sort of informal extraparlamentarian leadership. Even though it may be necessary to examine critically Beneš's assertion that his and Masaryk's conceptions of the Slav Question were identical down to the last detail,[49] it is nonetheless possible to find that Masaryk's views on Russia were reflected in the official Czechoslovak foreign policy directed by Beneš.

After 1918, Masaryk was prudently reticent in his public statements on the Russian Question, since his obligations as state president required him to abstain from taking political sides. He expressed his opinions very clearly, though, in his correspondence with Karel Kramář which was partially published some twenty years ago. In it he expressed his undoubted scepticism about the possibility of actual intervention from outside in the Russian civil war, and he totally rejected the Czechoslovak intervention so vehemently demanded by Kramář.[50]

During the first months after the foundation of the Czechoslovak Republic, Masaryk and Beneš frequently issued statements on the Slavonic problem, referring thereby to the Russian Question. This was necessary in order to deflate popular Slavonic enthusiasm, the Czech *hejslovanství*, and lead it back into proper channels, so as to integrate the young state into the new European system orientated towards the Western allies with the least possible internal political friction. 'Slavonic dreams' such as were proposed in Kramář's National Democracy were an obstacle to this purpose, especially in view of the prevailing situation in Russia. The 'Castle' actually more or less succeeded in not throwing out the baby with the bath water, but in channelling existing Slavonic feeling. This was possible by directing it towards the neighbouring Slav states in the north and south. In view of the long drawn-out Czechoslovak conflict with Poland, that meant above all towards the Yugoslav partner within the Little Entente.

There was another reason why the Russian Question was an explosive issue as far as the stability of Czechoslovakia was concerned. Thousands of legionaries returning home from Russia had to be 'neutralised'. This applied not only to those who tended to extreme military and nationalistic views, but also to those who wanted to change the national revolution in Czechoslovakia into a socialist revolution. Masaryk had already discussed the problem of the different revolutionary groupings in Russia in his *Russland und*

Europa, and now he found himself obliged to continue the argument at home. Masaryk's various minor publications on Russia and the Slavs (mainly speeches and interviews),[51] which date from this period, were principally directed towards the Socialist Left on the home front.[52] In anonymous essays or in those published under a pseudonym (such as 'Český legionář') Masaryk propounded his views with utter frankness.[53]

The attitude of the 'Castle' towards the Slav problems of the inter-war years is graphically illustrated by the sponsorship it gave to the academic sphere. Research on Russia occupied only a secondary place in those institutions either established or sponsored by the Czechoslovak government at home and abroad; it was replaced by the cultivation of research on Slav affairs.[54] The focus of attention, including studies on Czechoslovakia itself, was directed towards the Western and South Slavs in those institutions abroad (London and Paris in particular) which were supported by the Czechoslovak state. All in all, it embraced Masaryk's conception of a 'New Europe'. However, neither the 'Castle' nor Masaryk lost a sense of proportion in this respect. Possibly, the enormous difficulties experienced by Masaryk in obtaining Russian literature while he was working on *Russland und Europa* was one of the reasons why after 1918 well-financed collections and research facilities (the Slavonic Library, the Russian Foreign Archive) were established in Prague. These made the capital a first-class research centre, especially for Russian affairs. Hand in hand with this went official and private support for émigré Russian scientists and scholars.

In contrast to this academic sponsorship, political support for the Russian émigrés receded into the background in Czechoslovak foreign policy, which was strongly influenced by the 'Castle'. Whether the accusation, made in the course of the strong official anti-Masaryk campaign of the fifties, that Masaryk had supported the Socialist Revolutionary, Boris Savinkov, with 200 000 inflation roubles in 1918 supposedly in order to murder Lenin[55] was of any relevance, can only be judged, if at all, when archives in Czechoslovakia and the Soviet Union are opened to researchers. In general, the 'Castle' was very reticent in its support of White Russian émigrés who received their backing from its opponents, in particular from the Kramářs, both husband and wife. But the foreign policy pursued by the Czechoslovak government kept the path open in a realistic and cautious manner for a rapprochement with the Soviet Union, albeit a late one.

The caesura that the years 1917–18 represented in the events of world history also influenced Masaryk's attitude towards the Russian Question. The reason for this was not only the fact that he had taken on the office of president, which was to last seventeen years and definitively alter his way of life, but also his perception of the transformed state of world affairs. The shift of official Czechoslovak interest within the Slav world from Russia to the Western and South Slavs, and the transfer of Masaryk's perspective from intellectual history to the problem of the revolution, also contributed to his failure to complete his book on Russia. In its assessment of *Russland und Europa*, the panegyric literature on Masaryk has concentrated above all on the reinterpretation of the interpretations offered by the work. The denigrating literature of the 1950s and later has placed greater emphasis on the background to the political conditions then prevailing, although it often fails to comprehend the heart of the matter. By taking a look at the German and Czech readership of his work, this paper has tried to illuminate from a slightly different angle the significance of Masaryk's book on Russia and his opinions on the Russian Question.

NOTES

1　　Anon., 'Masarykova bibliografie', *Masarykův sborník*, (Prague: Type-script, 1980) vol. VII, pp. 697–757. This is a supplement to (among others) Boris Jakovenko, *La bibliographie de T. G. Masaryk* (Prague: Bibliothèque Internationale de Philosophie, vol. 1, No. 9/10, 1935). Jakovenko's bibliography was severely criticised for being fragmentary in literature on Masaryk and Russia and in Masaryk's Russian articles; see Theodor Syllaba, *T. G. Masaryk a revoluce v Rusku* (Prague: Naše vojsko, 1959) p. 11, n. 7.

2　　Bidlo was professor of East European history at the Czech university in Prague. See Jaroslav Bidlo, 'Masarykovy studie Ruska', in *Sborník přednášek o T. G. Masarykovi*, ed. M. Weingart (Prague: Orbis, 1931) pp. 159–75: 'nejdůležitejší a nejdokonalejší vědecké dílo Masarykovo.' Similar is E. L. Radlov, cf. 'Ernest Leopol'dovič Radlov a T. G. Masaryk', *Masarykův sborník*, vol. III (1929) p. 367. Likewise: Pavel N. Miljukov, 'Masaryk jako historik ruské inteligence', *Masarykův sborník*, part VI *Vůdce generací*, vol. II, (1930/31) pp. 363–6; Andrej Pawlow, 'Die Grundzüge von T. G. Masaryks Werk "Russland und Europa"', *Jahrbücher für Kultur und Geschichte der Slawen*, vol. X (1934) pp. 516–23 and others.

3   Zdeněk Nejedlý, *T. G. Masaryk ve vývoji české společnosti a čs. státu* (Prague: Ministerstvo informací a osvěty, 1950) p. 34. For Masaryk's early relationship to Russia cf. also: Zdeněk Nejedlý, *T. G. Masaryk*, 4 vols (Prague: Melantrich, 1931–37), *passim*, and Julius Dolanský, *T. G. Masaryk a Rusko předrevoluční* (Prague: ČSAV, 1959).

4   František and Marie Laichter, *Bibliografie Masarykovských prací v předválečné Naší době* (Prague: Laichter, 1936).

5   Nevertheless, there was a second edition in 1893. T. G. Masaryk, *Slavjanofilství Ivana Vasiljeviča Kiřejevského* ('Slovanské studie, sv. I', (Prague: Bursík a Kohout, 1889); 2nd. ed. 1893).

6   Masaryk indeed intended to conduct a 'Slavonic Studies' programme to clarify the so-called Slav question'. Russian studies were to form the first part, Czech studies were to follow. Cf. Simon Rosengard Green, *Thomas Garrigue Masaryk: Educator of a Nation* (University of California, Berkeley, PhD dissertation, 1976; Ann Arbor: University Microfilms, 1976) p. 351.

7   T. G. Masaryk, *Rusko a Evropa*, 2 vols. (Prague: Laichter, 1919–21); 2nd. ed. Jan Slavík (Prague: Laichter 1930–33).

8   Some English reviews of *Russland und Europa* are reprinted in Jaroslav Černý, '"Rusko a Evropa" v Anglii', *Masarykův sborník*, vol. II (1927) pp. 256–61. Among reviews cited there are: *The Athenaeum* (1919) p. 541; J.W.N.S. 'Credo, ergo sum', ibid., p. 749.

9   T. G. Masaryk, *La Russia e l'Europa. Studi sulle correnti sprituali in Russia*, 2 transl. and ed. Ettore Lo Gatto (Rome: 'Pubblicazioni dell'Istituto per l'Europa Orientale a Roma. 2. serie', 2 vols.: Istituto romano editoriale, 1922; Naples: R. Ricciardi, 1922).

10   T. G. Masaryk, *Rusija i Evropa. Studije o duhovnim strujama u Rusiji*, trans. by Stjepan Musulin ('Izbrana djela T. G. Masaryka, knjiga druga, sv. I': *Sociologijske skizce za rusku filozofiju povijesti i vjere*) (Zagreb: Nakladni oddio jugoslovenskog novinskog D. D., 1923).

11   An earlier essay by Masaryk on Dostoyevsky from 1892 was re-edited in 1932: T. G. Masaryk, *Studie o F. M. Dostojevském* (s rukopisnými poznámkami), uspořádal Jiří Horák ('Prameny k dějinám vzájemných styků slovanských národů, sv. I', Prague: 'Slovanský ústav', 1932).

12   F. Kattenbach in his review in *Theologische Literaturzeitung*, 1915, no. 20–21, cols. 442–8, esp. 443.

13   This was criticised by N. (=Lev) Trotsky in the Austrian socialist journal *Der Kampf* in December, 1914; cf. also Alfred Thomas, 'Some Russian Responses to Masaryk's *Spirit of Russia*', paper for the T. G. Masaryk Conference, Dec. 1986, London (this paper is exclusively on Trotsky's review, although there were other Russian responses, even if Masaryk's book was immediately censored in Russia).

14   T. G. Masaryk, 'Výňatky z 3. části díla *Rusko a Evropa*', *Naše doba*, vol. XXXXV (1938), no. 4, pp. 203 ff.

15   George Gibian, 'Introduction', in T. G. Masaryk, *The Spirit of Russia* (London: Allen & Unwin, 1967) vol. III, pp. xiii–xxi; *idem*, 'Masaryk on Dostoyevsky', in Miloslav Rechcígl Jr. (ed.), *Czechoslovakia Past and Present* (The Hague; Paris: Mouton, 1968) vol. II pp. 951–61.

16   Cf. Sylvia E. Crane, 'The Crane-Masaryk Connection', Paper for the T. G. Masaryk Conference in Dec. 1986, London, pp. 1–2; on

Masaryk's lectures in Chicago cf. the literature cited by Eva Schmidt-Hartmann, *Thomas G. Masaryk's Realism. Origins of a Czech political concept* (Munich: Oldenbourg Verlag, 1984) p. 173 n. 41.

17   The existing studies concentrate mainly on the suffrage reform movement and on (mainly Czech) working-class party history. I take this opportunity to thank Stanley B. Winters for valuable advice on this matter and on others in this paper.

18   Eugen Diederichs, *Selbstzeugnisse und Briefe von Zeitgenossen* (Düsseldorf and Cologne: Eugen Diederichs Verlag, 1967) p. 341.

19   On a certain confusion in dating Masaryk's trips to Russia and also the dates of Masaryk's reading of Dostoyevsky cf. Green, *Thomas Garrigue Masaryk*, p. 363 n. 22, p. 341.

20   Most valuable for the following passage: Hans Hecker, *'Die Tat' und ihr Osteuropa-Bild 1906–1939* (Cologne: Wissenschaft und Politik, 1974); Eugen Diederichs, *Leben und Werk*, ed. L. Von Strauss und Thorney-Diederichs (Jena: Eugen Diederichs Verlag, 1936) pp. 205–7; Diederichs, *Selbstzeugnisse, passim.*

21   Jaroslav Papoušek, 'Masaryk a slovanstvo', *Masarykův sborník*, vol. VI *Vůdce generací*, vol. II, (1930/31) p. 284.

22   Günther Stökl, *Osteuropa – Geschichte und Politik* (Opladen: Westdeutscher Verlag, 1979).

23   Cf. the forthcoming book: Uwe Liszkowski, *Historische Osteuropaforschung und politische Bildung. Ein Beitrag zum historisch-politischen Denken und Wirken Otto Hoetzschs* (Habilitation dissertation, Universität Kiel, 1983).

24   Critical on the method Masaryk applied in *Russland und Europa*: James P. Scanlan, 'Masaryk as Interpreter of Russian Philosophy', (see vol. II of *T. G. Masaryk (1850–1937)* ed. R. B. Pynsent) and Paul I. Trensky, 'Masaryk and Dostoyevsky', (see vol. III of *T. G. Masaryk (1850–1937)* ed. H. Hanak); more positive: Hanus J. Hajek, *T. G. Masaryk Revisited. A Critical Assessment* (Boulder, CO.: East European Monographs, 1983) pp. 133–44.

25   Cf. Roman Szporluk, *The Political Thought of Thomas G. Masaryk* (Boulder, CO.: East European Monographs, 1981) pp. 55–79.

26   Jan Slavík, 'Methoda v knize Rusko a Evropa', *Masarykův sborník*, vol. V (1930/31) pp. 282–6.

27   For Diederichs's publishing programme before World War I, cf. Eugen Diederichs, *Aus meinem Leben*, 2nd ed. (Leipzig: Diederichs, 1938) pp. 38–64.

28   Thomas G. Masaryk, 'Russland und Europa', *Die Tat, Sozial-religiöse Monatsschrift für deutsche Kultur*, vol. V (1913/14) pp. 144–8. It may not be accidental that neither this article nor that one by Kuliš on Masaryk in the same journal (cf. note 31) was mentioned in Jakovenko's bibliography (cf. note 1) or in Jaromír Doležal, *T. G. Masaryk. Soupis tisků v cizích jazycích* (Prague: Orbis, 1938).

29   Cf. Hecher, *Die Tat.*

30   Hans Lemberg, 'Zur Entstehung des Osteuropabegriffs im 19. Jahrhundert. Vom "Norden" zum "Osten" Europas', *Jahrbücher für Geschichte Osteuropas*, New series, vol. XXXIII (1985) pp. 313–32.

31 For an appraisal of Masaryk in *Die Tat* see Fritz Kuliš, 'Masaryks Weltanschauung', *Die Tat. Monatsschrift für die Zukunft deutscher Kultur*, vol. XIII (1921) pp. 598–606. Masaryk's *Russland und Europa* was criticised by the Russian émigré Vl. Lazarevskii, *Rossija i chekhoslovatskoe vozrozhdenie* (Paris, K-vo 'Grad Kitezh', 1927) p. 79, for having been praised in the Pan-German journal *Das grössere Deutschland* in 1917 [*sic*] as the 'perhaps most ingenious and profound contribution to political literature of the last few years.' Lazarevskii even denounced Masaryk's two volumes as having been part of German psychological warfare against Russia in World War I (ibid., pp. 72–3).

32 In *Internationale Bibliographie der Zeitschriftenliteratur, Abteilung C: Bibliographie der Rezensionen und Referate*, Supplementsbände 19 (1914) – 37 (1921), ed. Dietrich, an incomplete and – for those times – far from exact listing of book reviews, twenty-two German reviews of *Russland und Europa* can to be traced, among them only four from Austria; some other listings being evidently incorrect (e.g. in medical journals, etc.).

33 E.g. Herman Kranold, 'Zur Kenntnis Russlands', *Die neue Rundschau*, vol. XXVIII (1917) pp. 1542–50; Georg von Lukács, *Archiv für Sozialwissenschaft und Sozialpolitik*, vol. XXXVIII (1914) pp. 871–75; Arthur Drews, in *Preussische Jahrbücher*, vol. CLXIX (1917) pp. 435–9.

34 E.g. L. Karl Goetz in: *Deutsche Literaturzeitung*, 5 Dec. 1914, col. 2620–2.

35 F. Kattenbusch in *Theologische Rundschau*, vol. XVIII (1915) pp. 367ff., referring to his positive review cited above, note 12. Cf. also Kranold, as above, note 33.

36 Robert W. Seton-Watson, 'The Origins of the School of Slavonic Studies', *The Slavonic and East European Review*, vol. XVII (1939) pp. 360–72, cited in Josef Kalvoda, *The Genesis of Czechoslovakia* (Boulder, CO.: East European Monographs, 1986) p. 54.

37 Hecker, *Die Tat*, p. 19.

38 Trensky, 'Masaryk'.

39 Cf. Karel Pichlík, *Zahraniční odboj 1914/1918 bez legend* (Prague: Svoboda, 1968).

40 Cf. some of the photographs in *Od Zborova do Bachmači. Památník o budování československého vojska na Rusi pod vedením T. G. Masaryka* (Prague: Vojáci svobody, Čin and Orbis, 1938) vol. II.

41 T. G. Masaryk, *Das neue Europa. Der slavische Standpunkt* (Berlin: Schwetschke, 1922) pp. 80–6.

42 *Slovanství v národním životě Čechů a Slováků* (Prague: Melantrich, 1968); Hans Lemberg, 'Tschechen und Russen. Die Slawische Idee in der Tschechoslowakei 1918–1938', in *Die demokratisch-parlamentarische Struktur der Ersten Tschechoslowakischen Republik*, K. Bosl (ed.), (Munich and Vienna: Oldenbourg, 1975) pp. 185–200; Josef Jirásek, *Češi, Slováci a Rusko* (Prague: Vesmír, 1933); Stanley B. Winters, 'Austroslavism, Panslavism, and Russophilism in Czech political thought 1870–1900', in S. B. Winters and J. Held (eds)

Intellectual and Social Developments in the Habsburg Empire (Boulder, CO: East European Monographs, 1975) pp. 175–202.

43   Cf. Stanley B. Winters, 'Masaryk and Kramář: Long years of friendship and rivalry', Chapter 7 of this volume.

44   Karel Kramář, *Die russische Krisis. Geschichte und Kritik des Bolschewismus* (Munich, Leipzig: Duncker and Humblot, 1925). Also, *idem*, *Russkii krizis* (Prague-Paris, 1925), a self-published translation into Russian. Compare Karel Herman and Zdeněk Sládek, *Slovanská politika Karla Kramáře* (Prague: Academia, 1971).

45   Paul Vyšný, *Neo-Slavism and the Czechs 1898–1914* (Cambridge University Press, 1977).

46   The correspondence between Masaryk and Kramář during the year 1919 was prepared for print in the late 1960s in Prague by Jarmila Menclová, but could not be published after 1968. Some of the letters are published in *Boj o směr vývoje československého státu*, 2 vols. (Prague: Academia, 1965–69).

47   Lemberg, 'Tschechen und Russen'.

48   *'Die Burg'. Einflussreiche politische Kräfte um Masaryk und Beneš*, K. Bosl (ed.), 2 vols. (Munich: Oldenbourg, 1973–74).

49   Oswald Kostrba-Skalicky, 'Pathologie einer Beziehung: Die Sowjetunion und die Tschechoslowakei 1918–1938', in K. Bosl (ed.), *Gleichgewicht, Revision, Restauration. Die Aussenpolitik der Ersten Tschechoslowakischen Republik im Europasystem der Pariser Vorortverträge* (Munich and Vienna: Oldenbourg, 1976) pp. 153–82. Edvard Beneš, *Úvahy o slovanství. Hlavní problémy slovanské politiky* (London: Lincoln-Prager, 1944) pp. 171 *passim*.

50   Cf. note 21. Also: Hans Lemberg, 'Karel Kramářs Russische Aktion 1919', *Jahrbücher für Geschichte Osteuropas*, N.F. vol. XIV (1966) pp. 400–28. *idem*, 'Karel Kramářs Reise zu Denikin 1919. Ein tschechischer Politiker im russischen Bürgerkrieg', in I. Auerbach et al. (eds), *Felder und Vorfelder russischer Geschichte. Studien zu Ehren von Peter Scheibert* (Freiburg: Rombach, 1985) pp. 220–40.

51   Many articles and interviews are reprinted in T. G. Masaryk, *Cesta demokracie*, 3 vols. (Prague: Čin, 1938–39).

52   T. G. Masaryk, *O bolševictví* (Prague: Knihovnička služby, 1921); *idem*, *Slovanské problémy*, compiled by Adolf Černý, (Prague: Státní nakladatelství, 1928). Compare also Věra Olivová, *Československo-sovětské vztahy v letech 1918–1922* (Prague: Naše vojsko, 1957) pp. 276–7 *passim*; Theodor Syllaba, 'K problematice vztahu T. G. Masaryka k Říjnové revoluce', *Slovanský přehled*, no. 5 (1968) pp. 386–91; other re-evaluations are Vladislav Šťastný, ibid., no. 2 (1969) pp. 134–9; Lubomír Nový, 'Fenomén Ruska v Masarykově filosofii', ibid., no. 3 (1969) pp. 201–8.

53   Český legionář, *Sovětské Rusko a my* (Prague: Knihovnička 'Času', 1920); Jaroslav Werstadt, *Skrytý Masaryk. O nepodepsané úvahy presidenta Osvoboditele* (Prague: Knihovna 'Soboty', 1938).

54   Hans Lemberg, 'Die Slavistik in der Tschechoslowakischen Republik – Wissenschaft im politischen Spannungsfeld', in K. Bosl and F. Seibt (eds), *Kultur und Gesellschaft in der Ersten Tschechoslowakischen*

Republik (Munich and Vienna: Oldenbourg, 1982) pp. 289–302; Milan Kudělka et al., *Československá slavistika 1918–1939* (Prague: Academia, 1977).

55 *Dokumenty o protilidové a protinárodní politice T. G. Masaryka* (Prague: Orbis, 1953) pp. 13–20; Syllaba, *T. G. Masaryk*, pp. 226–7, *passim*.

13 Masaryk and Czech Jewry: the Ambiguities of Friendship
Hillel J. Kieval

INTRODUCTION

The relationship of Thomas G. Masaryk to the Jews of Bohemia and Moravia revolved around two paradoxes. On the one hand, Masaryk enjoyed a reputation among both Jews and non-Jews as a staunch opponent of anti-Semitism, a relentless critic of the so-called 'blood libel', and a defender of Jewish political rights.[1] Yet, as this essay will attempt to demonstrate, the record of Masaryk's dealings with Jewish leaders, as well as his writings on Jews, leave little doubt that his attitudes were in fact highly ambiguous and, at times, overtly negative.

The second paradox concerns the nature of the political alliance that was forged between Masaryk's Realist party and the Czech-Jewish movement – the wing of the Jewish community that had committed itself both to the promotion of the Czech national cause and to the assimilation of Jews to Czech culture. Following the radicalisation of Czech politics at the end of the 1890s, it was largely Masaryk and the Realist Party who commanded the loyalties of Czech national Jews. Yet Masaryk and other leading intellectuals could not shed their fundamental, ideological discomfort at the idea of Jewish assimilation and, hence, at the prospect of Jewish participation in the Czech national movement. Masaryk, in fact, felt much closer in temperament to the European Zionists than to the leadership of the Czech-Jewish movement. His frequent endorsements of Jewish national positions and the tactical support which he and Edvard Beneš lent to the Czech Zionists after World War I produced genuine consternation in the Czech-Jewish camp. When the Czechoslovak state formally recognised Jewish national autonomy in the constitutional documents of 1920, it dealt a psychological defeat, at least, to some of its most fervent Jewish supporters. After decades of painstaking work promoting Czech national culture and Czech political loyalties among the Jews, the Czech-Jewish movement had to face the predicament of an independent Czechoslovakia that supported the principle of Jewish cultural autonomy.

This essay will explore the ambivalent relationship between Masaryk's Realists and the Czech-Jewish movement, and attempt to explain the uneasiness felt by Czech nationalists towards the Czech-Jewish partnership. In so doing, I shall consider the intellectual and emotional factors that determined the attitude of Masaryk and others towards the Jews, the role of residual anti-Semitism in the relationship, and the significance – both social and political – of the Realists' flirtation with Zionism. Lastly, the question of whether the ambivalence towards Jewish assimilation had any real effect on Jewish integration into inter-war Czech society will have to be examined. For there are good indications that the Zionists may have won the ideological and political battle only to lose the long-term war in the social arena.

THE CZECH-JEWISH AFFINITY FOR MASARYK

During the last quarter of the nineteenth century, the Jewish population of the Bohemian crownlands underwent a social, political, and cultural transformation of major proportions. In the process of this change, an organised movement emerged which promoted the political rapprochement of Czechs and Jews, a more thoroughgoing acculturation of Jews to Czech language and sensibilities, and Jewish support for Czech national aspirations. The lawyers, doctors, journalists, shopkeepers and clerks who made up the ranks of this 'Czech-Jewish' movement allied on the whole with the National Liberal, or Young Czech, Party, the most powerful political force at the time on the regional scene. They supported Young Czech candidates in local, provincial and imperial elections, promoted the party's cultural and educational programmes for Prague and rural Bohemia, and tolerated what many acknowledged to be the rhetorically excessive tones of such newspapers as *Národní listy*.[2]

One could say that the leaders of the Young Czech Party and the Czech-Jewish movement had arrived at an implicit *modus vivendi* concerning their mutual behaviour. Both sides, it was agreed, would place pressure on Bohemian Jewry to move into the Czech national camp and to cease supporting German national interests. Moreover, the National Liberals and their major institutions would remain faithful to the party's formal position, rejecting both anti-Semitism and clericalism, and would disassociate themselves from the more radical manifestations of Czech nationalism. This unwritten agreement worked until the second half of the 1890s. But it collapsed under pressure that came from a number of different directions: the radicalisation of student politics in Prague; the government's disastrous handling of the Badeni language ordinances of 1897; the Hilsner ritual-murder trial of 1899; and the irresistible appeal of popular anti-Semitism. It had already buckled during the outbursts of popular violence that erupted in Prague and elsewhere in 1897 and was probably dead before the Hilsner Affair provided the *coup de grâce* two years later.[3]

By the end of the following decade, the 'Czech national' Jews had searched for and found new political allies. They were the so-called 'Realists' of Masaryk's Czech People's Party and, to a lesser degree, the Radical Progressives, that is, Antonín Hajn, and the Czech Social Democrats. Together they constituted what could be called the progressive wing of the Czech national movement. Czech Jews on the whole demonstrated the greatest enthusiasm for Masaryk and his small party, seeing in him a staunch opponent of anti-Semitism, a defender of Jewish aspirations for social and political acceptance, and a promoter of the democratic, secular state.

Viktor Vohryzek (1864–1918), a Jewish physician and political figure in Pardubice, laid the foundations for an entirely new approach to Czech national politics in 1900 when he published in *Českožidovské listy* a series of articles entitled 'Letters to Czech Jews'.[4] Vohryzek's 'Letters' set a new tone for Czech-Jewish writing. It argued that the causes of Jewish suffering and persecution in all countries lay not in some misdirected historical evolution, in poorly-conceived governmental policies, or in the stubborn refusal of Jews to assimilate. The basic factors lay in human nature itself. Anti-Semitism was in the end a psychological and moral phenomenon, arising from humanity's atavistic instincts, and as such was primarily a European – and not a Jewish – problem.[5] On the local level, it stemmed from a moral defect in the character of the Czech people, one that was being exploited by nationalist politicians for selfish and short-sighted purposes. Finally, however, it was the Czech soul, not the Jewish, that suffered.

Vohryzek's advice to Czech Jewry was twofold. First, it should sit out the decline of the Liberal Party:

If the Czech nation were once again to return to Hussite liberalism,

I would not hesitate to proclaim that we would soon succeed in reaching that point at which all Czech Jews would be in the Czech camp as loyal sons; but it would have to be sincere liberalism, not the comic pre-elections kind in which Jews cannot and do not believe.[6]

Yet one could hardly expect to see a return to the ideals of the Czech past in the near future. Vohryzek advised Jews in the meantime to prepare an 'antidote' to the poison that had infected the Czech nation. 'Our antidote is the strengthening of all progressive influences ... the battle against hypernationalism and clericalism. The antidote is the struggle against the dark.'[7]

Vohryzek called upon Czech Jews to learn how to defend themselves – to stiffen their backs, as he put it – and not to 'fall down in the dust before every journalistic bandit'. They had to act with dignity and pride so that basic human consideration dictated the conduct of others towards them. This is not to say that there was not a great deal wrong with the nature of Jewish cultural and economic life in the Bohemian crownlands. Vohryzek felt that it was just as incumbent upon Jews to examine their faults as to defend their rights. Jews continued to pursue dangerous and unsavoury economic occupations such as money-lending and the production and distribution of liquor. Jewish life required a thorough, ongoing reform – a renewal, based on the spiritual purposefulness, on the social ethics and the progressive outlook of the Old Testament prophets. But the issue of internal reform and redirection, Vohryzek warned, was for Jews to face on their own. Society at large was in no position to pass judgement.[8]

Over the next four years, a formidable opposition to the mainstream of the Czech-Jewish movement developed around Vohryzek and two other individuals, Eduard Lederer (1859–1941) and Bohdan Klineberger (1859–1928). Based in the beginning in Vohryzek's home town of Pardubice, the Czech-Jewish 'progressives' organised a broad range of cultural and educational programmes. The group, which adopted the name 'Rozvoj' [development], sought to deepen the sense of Czech national identity among Jews, effect a social and economic reorientation and modernisation of Czech-Jewish life, and promote a new religious sensibility, to teach Jews the difference (as *Rozvoj* put it) between religion and piety.[9]

Between 1904 and 1907, Vohryzek financed, edited and did much of the writing for a new and independent Czech-Jewish newspaper. It, too, went by the name *Rozvoj*, and reflected his generally progressive, anti-establishment positions. By 1907 *Rozvoj* had succeeded in replacing *Českožidovské listy* as the paper of choice among Czech-national Jews. *Českožidovské listy* ceased publication that year; *Rozvoj* changed from a fortnightly to a weekly, expanded its format, and moved its editorial offices to Prague. From there it continued to publish the single most influential organ of Czech-Jewish opinion down to the German occupation of 1939.[10] Vohryzek completed *Rozvoj*'s 1907 *putsch* when he formed the Association of Progressive Czech Jews (*Svaz českých pokrokových židů*). Designed to serve as an alternative to the Czech-Jewish Political Union – which coordinated Jewish support for the Young Czech Party – Vohryzek's progressive association consisted primarily of Jewish supporters of Masaryk's Realist Party and encouraged Czech Jews to support socially 'progressive' political causes.[11]

What was it that the Czech-Jewish movement felt it had found in Masaryk? To begin with, the movement had discovered a political leader who appeared to eschew all manifestations of radicalism. The Realists publicly opposed the intransigence of the nationalist right, which based its argument for autonomy on the historic claims of the ancient Bohemian Kingdom rather than on the natural rights of the Czech people. They were equally opposed to revolutionary Marxism, arguing that only peaceful and democratic avenues could lead to social progress. Moreover, in his commitment to the scientific method and to Positivism in social analysis, as well as in his anti-clericalism, Masaryk may have been the most faithful heir on the Czech political scene to the legacy of the Enlightenment.[12]

Yet Masaryk's party undoubtedly made its greatest impact on Czech Jews as a result of its rejection of both economic and political anti-Semitism. *Naše doba* had been one of the few Czech periodicals at the turn of the century to be critical of 'Svůj k svému', the nationally-inspired boycott movement directed against Germans and Jews.[13] And at the height of the Hilsner murder trial, Masaryk rose – at some risk to his personal safety – to denounce the blood libel and to demand that Hilsner be given a new trial.[14]

In short, the reasons behind Masaryk's popularity among Czech Jews are not hard to find. In a highly contentious society, divided along national, class, and religious lines, and one in which much political capital could be gained by exploiting natural antagonisms and prejudices, Masaryk and his party offered the best hope for Jewish integration into a Czech milieu. Moreover, Czech-Jewish thinkers found in Masaryk, the philosopher and sociologist, a model and inspiration for their own creative work. Even Masaryk's idiosyncratic blend of anti-clericalism and concern for the religious foundations of modern culture had a direct influence on turn-of-the-century Czech-Jewish thought.[15]

The *Rozvoj* circle at the turn of the century consisted largely of secularised Czech-Jewish intellectuals – contributors to the newspaper *Rozvoj* (Development) and often leading members of the Association of Czech Academic Jews. Yet Viktor Vohryzek and others among this group issued what amounted to an 'anti-secularist' manifesto of their own in the years following 1900, in order to take the wind out of the sails of both the new anti-Semitism and the growing Zionist movement. A revitalisation of the religious element in national life, they reasoned, would rehabilitate the purely religious definition of Jewish distinctiveness – a definition denied by both racial anti-Semites and Jewish nationalists. It might also provide a much-needed boost to the involvement of Jews as Jews in the Czech national revival. Since the real value of a people was determined by its spirit, its religious character, a demonstration of the spiritual equality of Judaism to Christianity – indeed of Judaism's universality – might increase the desirability of Jewish cooperation in the eyes of the Czechs.[16]

The *Rozvoj* intellectuals also found in Masaryk's oft-repeated call for an infusion into national life of the spiritual values of the Czech Reformation, an opportunity to correct the abuses of Czech politics. Eduard Lederer was frankly echoing the words of his Czech mentor when he argued in his 1902 work, *Žid v dnešní společnosti* (*The Jew in Contemporary Society*), that the whole of society needed to operate along radically different lines, and that the idea of social justice as expressed in the Gospels had to temper that of nationality. The Czech Reformation – as reformulated by its turn-of-the-century interpreters – was said to rest on the foundations of religious and social democracy, the primacy of peaceful means and intentions, and the insistence on political and social justice.[17]

Finally, Masaryk and *Rozvoj* were in basic agreement over the proposition that a true national renewal could only emerge from moral regeneration. In a speech delivered in 1910, in which he made constant reference to the figure of Jan Hus, Masaryk insisted: 'The leaders of our reformation have but one message for us all, repeated and reechoed over our land: regenerate, reform the individual, regenerate, reform the whole people.'[18]

When *Rozvoj* opened its pages during its early years to a wide-ranging discussion of the moral transformation of Czech society, it did so not only out of devotion to the teachings of Masaryk, but also because it felt that Judaism had a special contribution to make in this regard. The Czech Jews were in a position to draw upon the resources of rabbinic and biblical Judaism – as well as nineteenth-century philosophy – to aid the creation of a new ethical consensus, a religious and philosophical synthesis that would 'unite us in a single cultural whole.'[19] Vohryzek in particular envisioned a morally-honed Judaism, which emphasised the hallowing of God's name through ethical behaviour as performing a specific national function. On the one hand, ethical Judaism would serve as a vehicle for the improved integration of the Jew into Czech society, but it also would affect the very foundations of that society. Czech Jews would help to direct the nation on a more moderate course, lead it away from the hyper-nationalism of the past towards a new humanism. In the end, Judaism's task amounted to nothing less than the modulation, even the sublimation, of the national impulse. It was perhaps paradoxical that this redefined and reshaped Jewish culture, once it was directed back towards Czech society, would result in the blunting of the very conflicts that had spawned it in the first place. Yet such was to be the ultimate task of Czech Jewry: to mediate the national struggle, eventually to overcome nationalism and arrive at a humanistic solution to social conflict.[20]

MASARYK'S AFFINITY FOR ZIONISM

For all the exuberance shown by the Czech-Jewish movement for its newly-found political and cultural allies, the relationship between the two parties was hardly smooth. To begin with, a veil of misunderstanding and wishful thinking clouded the judgement of the Czech national Jews. They may have recognised in Masaryk a man of religious tolerance and of the Enlightenment, but they consistently underestimated the importance to him of the National Revival and, in particular, the moral definition that he applied to this endeavour. 'It is the duty of every thinking person', he wrote in *Česká otázka* (*The Czech Question*), 1895, 'to participate actively in the rebirth of his nation.'[21] He elaborated on this theme in his 1905 publication, *Národnostní filosofie doby novější* (*National Philosophy of the Modern Era*), when he argued:

That which is most holy within the nation is its moral character . . . The Czech becomes German only out of impure motives; he is

without character, and what is remarkable is that the Germans are
willing to take him in.
. . . A person of solid character would under no circumstances be
untrue to his nation.[22]

In expressing disapproval of cultural assimilation, Masaryk probably had in mind the behaviour of the sizable Czech population in
Vienna. But in a 1909 interview with the Vienna correspondent of
Wschod, a Lwów weekly, he applied a similar judgement to the Jews.
Here he labelled national assimilation 'impossible and in fact laughable', adding that it had made no real progress over the past ten
years.[23]

Masaryk's remarks, which also appeared in the Prague Zionist
weekly, *Selbstwehr*, caused a stir among *Rozvoj*'s readership; its
editor, Viktor Teytz, asked the Czech leader to clarify his anti-
assimilationist stance. The reply appeared in *Rozvoj* on 9 April 1909.
Interestingly, it displayed only a minor retreat from Masaryk's
original position. Masaryk explained that he had been misquoted by
the Polish paper. He had not intended to promote any specific Jewish
Party, but rather had had in mind only the 'general idea' of Zionism.
What he found sympathetic in the movement was the awakening of
the self-awareness of the Jewish masses. The notion of colonising
Palestine he still held to be utopian.[24]

Masaryk cautioned that Zionism ought not to work at cross
purposes with Jewish emancipation. On the contrary, it was important for Jews to fight for their rights in those places where they
presently lived. Nor did he want to demean the value of the
Czech-Jewish movement. His views on assimilation, he explained,
had been meant to apply to racial assimilation and not to social or
cultural integration. But he equivocated on this point, unable to
accommodate the Czech-Jewish movement to the degree it would
have liked:

> The nation is not a single entity; it has a whole array of traits:
> language, origins, religion, traditions. And language is certainly
> the most important. Of course the Jews can become culturally
> Czech, but there still remains a difference: that of separate origins,
> of race – which of course cannot be exactly established – of
> religion, and of tradition.[25]

Moreover, Masaryk added, one ought not to underestimate the
importance that religion has had in preserving the cultural and social
isolation of the Jews in Europe. He concluded his explanation with a

remark that could not have pleased the Jewish assimilationists: 'It is certainly no misfortune if the Jews form a distinct element for a while within the nation.'[26]

In retrospect, Masaryk's position in the *Wschod* interview ought not to have surprised the editors of *Rozvoj*. He had expressed similar opinions on the question of Jewish nationalism as far back as 1883, when he reviewed Ernest Renan's *Le Judaisme comme race et comme religion* for the journal *Sborník historický*. Here Masaryk took issue with Renan's contention that Judaism was not a national religion and that the Jews were not a pure nationality, but rather a racial mixture.[27] The Jews, Masaryk contended, were in fact less racially mixed than their European neighbours. 'The antagonism between Jews and Europeans has always been so strong on both sides that one cannot conceive of the kind of mixing that occurred for example between Romans and Gauls, Romans and Germans, or Germans and Slavs.' We must consider the Jews, he argued, 'as a nation completely different from ourselves.'[28]

Masaryk went on to suggest that Jewish self-awareness provided the best means of insuring peaceful coexistence between Jews and non-Jews. One could not effectively fight anti-Semitism by arguing, as Renan had, that the Jews were not a pure race or nation. 'National hatred', Masaryk quipped, 'does not ask whether the blood of one's adversary is pure or not.' The issue at hand was not one of racial purity but of character. By this he meant to suggest that national antagonisms emerged from cultural defects, from character short-comings on both sides of a conflict:

> Under these circumstances, let us both – Semites and non-Semites – recognise what differentiates us, what character traits repel one another; let each recognise his own faults and shortcomings; and let us both work to find that cement which up to now has not been found.[29]

Although Masaryk harboured a deep-seated mistrust of assimilation-ist movements in general and argued in favour of a Jewish national-ity, it is not true that his attitudes towards Jews were uniformly positive. Masaryk justly gained notoriety in 1899 and 1900 as a defender of the Jews against the newly-revived, medieval blood libel. The conviction of Leopold Hilsner on murder charges in Kutná Hora had stemmed from a trial in which allegations of 'ritual murder' were aired long and loud. In two celebrated pamphlets, Masaryk railed against the ancient superstition and demanded a new trial for the luckless defendant.[30] Yet, as Masaryk later admitted on a number of occasions, he had not been drawn to defend either Hilsner or the Jews out of philo-Semitic motives.

Masaryk claimed to have become involved in the Hilsner trial to protect neither the Jews nor Hilsner, but 'to defend Christians from superstition.' It was only at the behest of a former student that he expressed any opinion at all about the Hilsner trial, this in the form of a letter that was subsequently published in Vienna's *Neue Freie Presse*. And only after the completion of the first trial was he moved first to investigate the matter carefully and then to intervene forcefully against the libel.[31]

In point of fact, Masaryk's pious Catholic mother had taught her children to fear Jews. She herself believed the blood libel and informed her children of the Jewish 'need' for Christian blood at Easter time. As a boy, Masaryk simply assumed that the libel was true, and used to go out of his way to avoid contact with the two or three Jewish families who lived in his village. Later he would find himself involuntarily inspecting the hands of Jews whom he met to see if they contained tell-tale traces of blood.[32]

Masaryk related on a number of occasions that his attitude towards Jews did not change until he became a grammar-school pupil in Hustopeče. There, for the first time, he had Jewish students in his classroom, one of whom, at least, caused him to appreciate the moral significance of an individual's commitment to Judaism.[33] Yet, as Masaryk admitted much later to Karel Čapek, he was never able emotionally to 'overcome ... the anti-Semitism of the common people.' Only in his 'reason', in his pursuit of rational justice, did he seek to combat it.[34] Reason and emotion, however, co-existed in an uneasy alliance in Masaryk's thought. And throughout his career he managed to combine support for the Jews of Bohemia with naive prejudices and expressions of resentment and mistrust. Thus, when he assessed the long-term political impact of his defence of Leopold Hilsner, he remarked:

> During the war I saw how useful the affair had been to me: the press of the world is largely managed or financed by Jews; they knew me from the Hilsner case, and repaid me for what I had done for them then by writing favourably about our cause – or at least not unfavourably.[35]

Later, during the early months of the World War, Masaryk would complain to the governor of Bohemia, Prince Thun, about the 'aggressive and excited' behaviour of the Germans of Prague, particularly the Jews. He urged the governor to 'hold back the Jews and render them less aggressive' lest a 'Jewish pogrom' ensue.[36] And, as he prepared to go into exile, Masaryk would offer the same advice to the Prague Jewish writer and Zionist leader Max Brod.[37]

When Masaryk again picked up his pen to write on the Jewish question in 1898, he did so in the context of a long essay on the philosophical and sociological foundations of Marxism.[38] In it he criticised Marx for underestimating both the religious and the national sides of the Jewish question, and for drawing his generalisations concerning Jews and the nature of Judaism, not from empirical observation, but from Feuerbach's critical imagination.

> Marx refuses to see in the Jewish question a national and racial dimension, which nevertheless is there. The Jews are a distinct nation even though they have long given up their spoken language. But language is not the only, nor the most important, attribute of nationality.

> . . . Marx does not sufficiently analyse the particular character of the Jews, and therefore does not differentiate between the good and bad sides of their character. Nor does he investigate the good and bad characteristics of Christians in different nations. Thus his judgement of the Jews does not differ much from that of [Max] Stirner. And yet the Jewish nation is characterised not only by barterers, but also by Jeremiah, Spinoza, and also Christ.[39]

While accepting Marx's call for a universal, human emancipation, Masaryk was quick to point out that such efforts were being made precisely within the Jewish national movement. 'I see a bit of this work at revitalisation in Zionism', he wrote. 'By this I do not mean the emigration of Jews to Palestine. They can calmly stay where they are. But they must understand that their moral condition and their entire outlook on the world is in need of reform.'[40]

> Today's Jews lack the self-criticism of the prophets. . . . Out of fear of the majority, the Jews do not dare look into their own consciences. It is true that Christians are partly to blame for this, but only partly. The Jews – that is their current shortcoming – are all too self-satisfied. The same holds true by the way for the Christian anti-Semites.'[41]

Three main themes emerge from Masaryk's discussion of Marx and the Jewish Question. First, the Jews – whatever the arguments to the contrary and despite the fact that they appeared to have lost their common spoken language – are seen as forming a separate nationality among the European family of nations. Other Czech Realists, such as the journalist Jan Herben and the philosopher František Krejčí, would later echo this point of view. Krejčí would build his case for a distinct Jewish nationality on the argument that the unique religion of the Jews functioned in much the same way that linguistic culture did for other groups.[42] Herben would admit to a more basic, emotional response to the question. He considered the Jews to be a nation for the simple reason that 'one could see that they were' [his words were 'protože je to na nich vidět']; and he was bemused by the fact that statements of this nature caused his Czech-Jewish acquaintances such pain.[43]

In Masaryk's writings, both reasons for regarding the Jews as a separate nation exist side by side. Since he bestowed on religion a major role in the formation of national culture in general, he was prone to do the same with regard to the specific case of Judaism and the Jewish people. Yet it was also completely natural for him, as well as for most other children of rural and small-town Moravia, to view the Jews as a distinct cultural element, alien from Czech or Slovak Catholic society, because, to paraphrase Herben, that was simply how they were.[44]

The second point is that Jewish society on the whole, like post-Enlightenment society in general, was in need of ethical reform. Here Masaryk offered little in the way of elaboration, feeling, perhaps, that the criticism was obvious. He made oblique references to the 'materialism' and the 'moral complacency' of the Jews, but had few specific complaints to lodge. One suspects that here, too, the combination of inbred cultural attitudes and more formal cultural criticism came into play. Lastly, Masaryk credited the Zionist movement with pointing the way to the moral regeneration of modern Jewry, a regeneration which all the nations of Europe could use, and which Masaryk himself was urging upon the Czech people.

Over the years Masaryk did not move very far from these three basic positions. Contributing to a 1900 publication entitled *Zionisten und Christen*, which incidentally was dedicated to him, Masaryk wrote: 'I understand Zionism . . . from a primarily moral perspective. The thinking, progressive Jew becomes conscious of the defects in his character and *Weltanschauung*. I see in Zionism, to borrow a well-known phrase, "a drop of the oil of the prophets".'[45]

The 'thinking Jew', Masaryk explained, acknowledges his own

responsibility for the deficiencies of cultural work (*Kulturarbeit*) in the past. He wants to be 'born again', and therefore must proceed forward, far beyond the 'general shortcomings' of our civilisation. 'For this, changing the local milieu alone will not help; for this, what is needed is a regeneration from within, one to which, to be sure, Christians must also contribute, as [they are] equally guilty.'[46]

Masaryk's fascination with 'regeneration from within' led him, with the help of young Zionist intellectuals in Prague, to discover and appreciate the work of the Russian Jewish writer Aḥad Ha'am (Asher Ginsberg, 1856–1927). Reviewing religious and ecclesiastical developments for *Naše doba* in 1905, Masaryk wrote: 'I am indebted to several Jews who understood my interest in their religious question, and who brought to my attention a thinker from whom one can draw very positive instruction.'[47] The fact that Aḥad Ha'am was a master of Hebrew prose style and a major figure in the Hebrew literary renaissance did cause Masaryk to step back admiringly. But what impressed him the most was Aḥad Ha'am's critical stance towards Western liberalism, his cultural modernism, which nevertheless was infused with spiritual concerns:

> Aḥad Ha'am is in the first instance an opponent of liberalism and hence an opponent of Western Judaism [literally, 'Jewish Westernness']. He is not impressed with the freedom of Western Jewry, its liberal blend of chauvinism and cosmopolitanism. 'Should I envy these our brothers their rights? No, and again, no! I, it is true, have none, but neither have I had to give up my soul for them . . .' Aḥad Ha'am is a Jew, simply a Jew; he does not understand at all the question of why he remains a Jew.[48]

Aḥad Ha'am's views appeared to Masaryk to highlight his own. Neither advocated that their people forsake the Enlightenment or remove themselves from European culture; but neither wished for their people to lose their 'national nature' in the process of becoming 'modern'. Masaryk, who felt that one could be anti-clerical without becoming anti-religious, modern without abandoning traditional culture, showed a particular interest in what to some must have appeared to be an arcane dispute within the Jewish national movement. It involved Aḥad Ha'am and writers such as M. J. Berdyczewski, who were strongly influenced by Nietzsche and his concept of the 'transvaluation of all values.' To this group, all elements of traditional Judaism had to be left behind if a true cultural renaisance were to be achieved. To Masaryk's obvious satisfaction, Aḥad Ha'am denounced this anarchistic approach to culture, arguing instead for a renaissance of Hebrew language and literature which used the religious-literary tradition as a necessary base on which to build.[49]

Most important for Masaryk, Aḥad Ha'am called upon the Jews to effect a 'reawakening of the heart', an internal rebirth. In this Masaryk clearly recognised a kindred spirit. But he also found in Aḥad Ha'am a nobility of character which he felt was lacking in the Czech Jewish assimilationists, even those who had determined to stand up to anti-Semitism within the Czech national movement. 'Thus he approaches anti-Semitism in an entirely different way from most Jews: anti-Semitism must not be the reason and motive for the efforts at national revival; these efforts must emerge from one's own deepest consciousness.'[50]

'In a word', Masaryk concluded, 'Aḥad Ha'am points to the improvement of Jewry through a spiritual and religious awakening.'[51] This, Zionism's emphasis on self-improvement, provided the movement with unassailable moral strength.

POLITICAL NEGOTIATIONS UNDER THE NEW ORDER

Whatever differences had separated Czech-nationalist progressives from the Czech-Jewish movement in the past, by the close of 1918 they stood united as promoters and defenders of a new political order. With the establishment of an independent Czechoslovakia, a major part of the political, if not the cultural, programme of the Czech-Jewish movement had by then been realised. Czech-speaking Jews no longer needed to defend the legitimate aspirations of a national minority in a provincial capital. Their political purpose appeared now to be reduced to ensuring Jewish support for the new state, their cultural programme to achieving a more effective integration with the Czech national majority.

Yet the very tensions that had led to cleavage during the last decades of the Austrian Empire continued to frustrate relations between Czech-national Jews and the Realists in the new state. One source of discomfort was popular anti-Semitism, which erupted intermittently between 1918 and 1920, and which fused demonstrations against the German minority with physical attacks on Jewish property and institutions.[52] Ultimately more troubling for Czech-national Jews, however, was the growing number of political successes registered by the Zionists. Zionist efforts to organise Czechoslovak Jewry along national lines and to promote Jewish national interests in the new state threatened the integrationist programme of the Czech-Jewish movement. Not surprisingly, the Zionists received a sympathetic hearing from the heads of the Czech government; this fact alone was enough to throw the Czech-Jewish camp into alarm.

The Zionists emerged from the war on the whole better organised and more adroit politically than the assimilationists. Yet all of their energy and readiness would have mattered little had it not also been for the fact that during the war Masaryk and Edvard Beneš had acquired for themselves the status of symbolic representatives of a future state in the eyes of the Western powers. This recognition from the outside world placed Masaryk's Realists in a position of authority far above their true electoral strength. The World Zionist Organisation, in turn, exploited the situation skilfully, offering support for Czech national aspirations during the war while capitalising on the friendly relations that already existed between Masaryk and the Czech Zionists.

In September 1918, following verbal assurances from President Wilson that the 'Czechoslovak nation' would enjoy independence in the new European order, the Zionist Organisation of America sent a telegram of congratulations to the Czech leader. Masaryk replied with a promise that the same rights that were to be granted the German national minority in Czechoslovakia would also apply to the Jews. 'As regards Zionism', he added, 'I can only express sympathy with it and with the national movement of the Jewish people in general, since it is of great moral significance.'[53] Masaryk also sent an unsolicited telegram to Max Brod, recalling a meeting that they had had at the start of the war, and guaranteeing that Jewish rights would be respected fully in the future state.[54]

On the eve of the proclamation of the new Republic, the Jewish nationalists, including a number of non-Zionists, organised themselves into a Jewish National Council (*Národní rada židovská/ Jüdischer Nationalrat*). Six days later, on October 28, the council approached the Czech National Committee (*Národní výbor*) and presented it with the demands of the Jewish community.[55] The memorandum of the Jewish National Council called for official recognition of the Jewish nationality and for the right of Jews to declare it in censuses and elections. No individual was to be compelled to list his nationality as Jewish, 'but by the same token no one desiring to profess it [was to] be prohibited from doing so officially or unofficially.'[56] The memorandum went on to call for the full civil and legal equality of the Jews. Jewish minority rights, in other words, were not 'to be construed as affecting those rights which are their due as Czech citizens.' Rather, Jews would enjoy what had been denied them previously under the terms of the emancipation of 1867: full civil equality combined with full national rights.[57]

The Jewish nationalists demanded cultural autonomy in the areas of education, the cultivation of the Hebrew language, relations with Palestine, and social welfare. They asked for the right to establish Jewish elementary and high schools – 'along modern (not sectarian) lines' – where circumstances permitted. The Jewish religious communities, recognised as a corporation in public law, were to be recast along democratic lines and were to choose a 'joint representative body' with headquarters in Prague. Finally, to the extent that cultural projects were to be recipients of state funds in the future, Jewish institutions would be entitled to proportionate assistance.[58]

During the first fifteen months of the new Republic, the Czech Zionists worked the political fields of Prague and of Paris – where the peace treaties ending the war were being negotiated – with unusual sophistication and self-assurance. They had prepared themselves for this role during the last years of the war and certainly gave the appearance of being seasoned political professionals. Yet the secret of their success lay not so much in knowing how and when to apply pressure, as in their sympathetic appreciation of the underlying assumptions of liberal Czech nationalism. Masaryk and his associates, the Zionists understood, would not readily deny the Jews the cultural self-determination that the Czechs themselves had treasured. In addition, the Czech Zionists relied on the self-interest of the Czechoslovak government to achieve recognition of the Jewish nationality. If the Jews of Bohemia and Moravia were given the opportunity to register their nationality as Jewish, the result might be a significant reduction in the size of the German national camp. Similarly, the Jews of Slovakia might thereby be induced to abandon the Hungarian cause. Hence, to some within the government, accommodating the Zionists made good political sense, if only to weaken the national rivals of the Czechs and Slovaks.[59]

As it turned out, the road to recognition of the Jewish nationality in Czechoslovakia was not to be free of obstacles. The Foreign Minister, Beneš, resisted efforts to include specific references to Jewish minority rights in the Treaty of St Germain because, as he explained in a letter to Ludvík Singer, the new state regarded human rights as a matter of course. 'We have fulfilled our obligations thus far and will continue to do so.' Beneš acknowledged, moreover, the difficult position that the government was being asked to assume: to render judgement on the relative merits of Jewish nationalism versus assimilationism. 'The Czechoslovak delegation is not competent to broach this question', he concluded, 'and therefore cannot broach it.'[60] Not competent in a formal sense, perhaps, but both Beneš and Masaryk undoubtedly had strong personal sentiments on this matter. A few days later Beneš tried to reassure Nahum Sokolow, chairman of the *Comité des délégations juives* at the Paris Peace Conference, of his sympathy for Jewish nationalism. He insisted, however, that to sign the so-called 'Jewish articles' of the Polish Treaty, for example, would represent a 'yellow badge' for Czechoslovakia, a stigma of which only Poland and Romania were deserving because of their long history of anti-Semitism.[61]

In the end neither Masaryk nor Beneš would agree to the inclusion of so-called 'Jewish clauses' in the Treaty of St Germain. It was not until the promulgation of the Czechoslovak Constitution in February 1920 that the government formally announced its recognition of the Jewish nationality.[62] Now the Jewish National Council received essentially what it had been asking for all along. Jews who regarded themselves as members of a separate nationality had the right to express this choice in censuses and elections, yet they could not be required by the state to do so. The Jews, moreover, were the only national minority not to be defined by a linguistic criterion, nor did they necessarily have to identify with the Jewish religion.[63]

CONCLUSION

Czechoslovakia's concessions to Jewish nationalism were, in fact, unprecedented. For the first time in European history, an industrialised parliamentary democracy with a long prehistory of Jewish emancipation recognised the claim to Jewish national distinctiveness. The state, moreover, made room for Jewish cultural and national self-expression without diminishing the value of emancipation, and free of any underlying motive to reduce Jewish social and political integration. Masaryk's government had, as it were, fulfilled the demands once voiced by the historian Simon Dubnov, to realise emancipation for Jews not as individuals – which had been the model of the French Revolution – but as a nation, according to the new model of Eastern Europe.[64]

In legitimising Jewish national politics in the new state, Masaryk and the Realists remained faithful to long-held, if conflicting, convictions. On the one hand, childhood impressions had combined with popular attitudes to produce in the Czech leaders a general stance of distance and suspicion towards the Jews. Moreover, the lessons of inter-communal conflict and coexistence in the Czech-dominated countryside had taught even the most liberal of Czech nationalists that the Jews formed a separate ethnic group. Often Czech leaders simply lumped the Jews together with the more sizable German minority; on occasion they viewed the Jews as a third player in the national struggle. Rarely, however, did they entertain the conviction that the Jews were, or could become, fully Czech.

And yet the emotional distance that separated Czech and Jewish society did not prevent Realist intellectuals from sympathising with the goals of European Jewish nationalism. This is not an entirely surprising fact, since some of Zionism's more vocal supporters in the past – the National Democrats in inter-war Poland, for example – were by no stretch of the imagination friends of the Jews. Two things, I feel, distinguished the Realists' approach to both Jewish emancipation and Jewish nationalism from that of other East European political parties. The first was the ability to separate their emotional predisposition towards the Jews from their philosophical commitment to democracy and social equality. The second, more telling, factor was the Czech propensity to see in Jewish nationalism on the European continent a version of their own national renascence, an echoing of their own efforts to secure a Czech future through cultural and political autonomy.

On both points credit must be given to Masaryk for having broken the chains of habit. He consciously strove to overcome popular prejudice through a commitment to European rationalism and empirical science (though in his own case the mythical foundation for his cultural attitudes was particularly strong). He then translated this personal stance into a courageous, and personally costly, public crusade. Secondly, his peculiarly moralistic interpretation of Czech nationalism encouraged a sympathetic encounter with the cultural nationalism of Aḥad Ha'am and the Prague Zionists. Masaryk could not help but approve of what he saw going on in the small camp of Jewish nationalists, but he also lent the weight of his own personal prestige to the Zionist endeavour. Unlike Polish nationalism, then, which was happy to endorse Zionism if that meant removing from the scene a large and problematic national minority, Czech nationalism –

largely through Masaryk's tutelage – could straddle two apparently contradictory rails. In the eyes of East European Zionism, of course, there was no contradiction. National identity and cultural autonomy were seen as vehicles for a truer, deeper, more successful integration in a multi-national environment. Masaryk and the Czech Realists agreed.

Leaders of the Czech-Jewish movement, meanwhile, reacted to the Realist-Zionist relationship with disappointment bordering on anger. A front-page editorial that appeared in *Rozvoj* in June 1919 complained bitterly of Zionist policies in the new state. The unsigned article contended that Zionist support for the state and its overt neutrality on the Czech-German issue was a masquerade designed to conceal its basically German make-up. Sardonically it recalled how the Czech Zionists had demonstrated in favour of Masaryk and an independent Czechoslovakia after the national revolution had already taken place, how everyone was careful to speak only Czech at the meetings of the Prague Zionists though their Czech was really quite hopeless.[65]

Max Lederer (1875–1937), an activist in the Czech-Jewish movement since the early 1900s, reviewed Karel Čapek's *Hovory s TGM* (*Conversations with Masaryk*) in April 1929, and used the occasion to highlight Masaryk's fundamentally ambiguous relationship to the Jews. The title of the piece itself, 'Staronový Masaryk' (The Old-New Masaryk), contained a *double entendre*. On the one hand it alluded to the venerable history of the Prague Jewish community and to its symbolic representation, the thirteenth-century *Alt-neu* [*Staronový*] *synagogue*. The title's second meaning referred to Masaryk himself. He was a creative genius, continually surprising his public with seemingly new and unexpected pronouncements. In reality, however, his views demonstrated remarkable stability over time; and his seemingly startling statements about Jews in Čapek's *Conversations* in fact reflected basic attitudes.

'In the end', Lederer writes, 'all of us who have had close relations with Masaryk recognise that he was never a philo-Semite.'[66] He was never able completely to overcome childhood fears and prejudices. In the end, Lederer concluded, there were two Masaryks: one passionately committed to rationality and justice, and one who had a 'fundamentally emotional misunderstanding' of the Jewish question.[67]

Lederer's assessment, though ultimately incorrect, does suggest a useful psychological model in understanding the ambiguity of

Masaryk's relationship to Czech Jewry. Masaryk's attitudes turned on the dichotomy between his affective, or emotional, disposition and his rational/ideological convictions. Emotionally, Masaryk never completely overcame the mistrust and suspicion of Jews that he had learned as a child. Similarly, his intuition that the Jews constituted a distinct national element in the larger social body stemmed from a naive reading of his early social-cultural environment. However, the village boy in Masaryk and the university professor, the Moravian Catholic and the Enlightenment rationalist, were constantly at odds. It was this struggle that produced the creative tension in Masaryk's life and work. Thus, it was the reasoning ideologist of political democracy and the enemy of cultural backwardness who defended the right of Jews to enter Czech society as equal members. And it was the critic both of Marxism and of Western liberalism, the ideologist of national renewal, who discovered in Aḥad Ha'am and the Zionist movement the spirit of Hus and the 'oil of the prophets'.

In the end, both the Zionist victory and the Czech-Jewish defeat proved to be more ephemeral than real. The government's recognition of the Jewish nationality did not alter long-term social and cultural developments within Czech Jewry. The Zionists did not achieve a revolution in Jewish consciousness, nor did the pace of Jewish integration slow down. In fact the reverse was true. Most indicators showed a dramatic increase in Jewish integration into Czech society at all levels between 1918 and 1939.[68] Masaryk's religious and cultural inclinations may have favoured the Zionists over the assimilationists, but the liberal foundations of the new political order, together with the force of Czech nationalism in general, had the overall effect of encouraging Czech-Jewish self-definition and the progressively stronger movement of Jews into the Czech mainstream. The real loser in the Realist-Czech Jewish-Zionist confrontation was the older German orientation of the Jewish community. Historical forces that were well in place since the late nineteenth century had long been eroding the German-Jewish synthesis of the emancipation era. The Czech national Jews, the Zionists, and the Realists combined to deliver it the final blow.

NOTES

1 On Masaryk's role in combatting anti-Semitism, see Ernst Rychnovsky, 'Im Kampf gegen den Ritualmordaberglauben', in *Masaryk und das Judentum*, Ernst Rychnovsky (ed.) (Prague: Marsverlagsgesellschaft, 1931) pp. 166–273; Jaroslav Rokycana, 'Freunde in der Not', in *Masaryk und das Judentum*, pp. 300–15; and Jan Herben, 'T. G. Masaryk über Juden und Antisemitismus', in *Masaryk und das Judentum*, pp. 274–99. Radical anti-Semites were just as prone as Masaryk's Jewish admirers to equate him with pro-Jewish policies. See Jan Rys, *Hilsneriáda a TGM: K čtyřicátému výročí vražd polenských* (Prague: Wiesner, 1939).

2 See Hillel J. Kieval, *The Making of Czech Jewry: National Conflict and Jewish Society in Bohemia, 1870–1918* (New York: Oxford University Press, 1988) Chs. 1–2.

3 Leopold Hilsner, a Jewish vagabond, was accused of murdering a nineteen-year-old dressmaker, Anežka Hrůzová, in the town of Polná. The former Young Czech politician, Karel Baxa, participated in the trial as counsel for the victim's family and did much to promote 'ritual murder' as the motive behind the killing. See František Červinka, 'The Hilsner Affair', *Leo Baeck Institute Yearbook*, vol. XIII (1968) pp. 142–57; and Arthur Nussbaum, 'The "Ritual Murder" Trial of Polná', *Historia Judaica*, vol. IX (1947) pp. 57–74.

On Czech nationalist politics in the 1890s, see Kieval, *The Making of Czech Jewry*, Ch. 3; Bruce M. Garver, *The Young Czech Party, 1874–1901, and the Emergence of a Multi-Party System* (New Haven: Yale University Press, 1978), pp. 121ff.; Stanley B. Winters, 'Kramář, Kaizl, and the Hegemony of the Young Czech Party, 1891–1901', in P. Brock and H. G. Skilling *The Czech Renascence of the Nineteenth Century* (University of Toronto Press, 1970) pp. 282–314; and Tomáš Vojtěch, *Mladočeši a boj o politickou moc v Čechách* (Prague: Academia, 1980). For Czech-Jewish reactions, see Hillel J. Kieval, 'Nationalism and Antisemitism: The Czech-Jewish Response', in Jehuda Reinharz (ed.), *Living with Antisemitism: The Jewish Response in the Modern World* (Hanover, N.H.: University Press of New England, 1987).

4 Viktor Vohryzek, 'Epištoly k českým židům', *Českožidovské listy*, 1900; repr. in Vohryzek, *K židovské otázce* (Prague: Akademický spolek 'Kapper', 1923) pp. 15–40.

5 Vohryzek, 'Epištoly', pp. 15–16.

6 Ibid., pp. 33–4.

7 Ibid., p. 34.

8 Ibid.

9 'Zpráva o činnosti spolku "Rozvoj"', *Kalendář českožidovský*, vol. XXV (1905–06) pp. 178–9. See also Kieval, *The Making of Czech Jewry*, Ch. 3.

10 Oskar Donath, *Židé a židovství v české literatuře 19. a 20. století*, 2 vols. (Brno: O. Donath, 1930) II pp. 186–94.

11 *Dějiny českožidovského hnutí* (Prague: Svaz Čechů-židů v Československé republice, 1932) pp. 10–11.

12   On Masaryk's national and religious thought, see: Roman Szporluk, *The Political Thought of Thomas G. Masaryk* (Boulder, CO: East European Monographs, 1981) pp. 55–125; Hanuš J. Hajek, *T. G. Masaryk Revisited: A Critical Assessment* (Boulder, CO: East European Monographs, 1983) and Masaryk's own works: *Česká otázka: snahy a tužby národního obrození* (Prague: 1895); *Naše nynější krise. Pád strany staročeské a počátkové směrů nových* (Prague: 1895); and *Otázka sociální: základy marxismu filosofické a sociologické* (Prague, 1898).
       On Czech-Jewish receptivity, see Evžen Stern, *Názory T. G. Masaryka* (Prague: Grossman a Svoboda, 1910); Rychnovsky, '*Im Kampf gegen den Ritualmordaberglauben*', pp. 166–273 and Rokycana, 'Freunde in der Not', pp. 300–15.

13   See, for example, the piece by J. Svozil, 'Několik slov o hesle 'Svůj k svému''', *Naše doba*, vol. VIII (1900–01) pp. 641–46. Though the author argues in favour of limiting the influx of 'foreign capital' and of building up the 'productive forces' of the Czech nation, he sets limits on the legitimate use of economic boycott as a weapon in the national struggle.

14   T. G. Masaryk, *Nutnost revidovat proces polenský* (Prague: Čas, 1899) and *Die Bedeutung des Polnaer Verbrechens für den Ritualaberglauben* (Berlin: Hermann, 1900). On Masaryk's role in the defence of Hilsner, see Ernst Rychnovsky, 'Im Kampf gegen den Ritualmordaberglauben', and Červinka, 'The Hilsner Affair'.

15   On this theme, see Hillel J. Kieval, 'In the Image of Hus: Refashioning Czech Judaism in Post-Emancipatory Prague', *Modern Judaism*, vol. V (1985) pp. 141–57.

16   Viktor Vohryzek, 'Několik slov úvodem', *Rozvoj*, 1904; reprinted in his *K židovské otázce*, pp. 41–7. Also Vohryzek, 'K myšlenkové kristi našich dnů', *Rozvoj*, 1904; in *K židovské otázce*, pp. 103–18.
       In an apologetic tone, Eduard Lederer argued that modern Jews, on the strength of Judaism's ethical teachings, could grow to the same moral and humanistic heights as their Christian neighbours. Moreover, the values of Judaism, as manifested in the ideals of the prophets, were worthy of serving as ethical models for all people the world over (Lederer, *Žid v dnešní společnosti* (Prague: E. Lederer, 1902) pp. 73–4.

17   Lederer, *Žid v dnešní společnosti*, p. 152. The most succinct statement of Masaryk's views on Hus, the Czech Reformation, and contemporary Czech nationalism can be found in a speech which he delivered in 1910 entitled 'M. J. Hus a česká reformace.' It has been translated and reprinted as 'Jan Hus and the Czech Reformation' in T. G. Masaryk, *The Meaning of Czech History* (Chapel Hill, NC: University of North Carolina Press, 1974) pp. 3–14.

18   Masaryk, 'Jan Hus and the Czech Reformation', p. 14.

19   Vohryzek, 'Národohospodářské úvahy', *Rozvoj*, 1904; repr. in *K židovské otázce*, p. 127.

20   See Kieval, 'In the Image of Hus', pp. 148–53.

21   Quoted in Felix Weltsch, 'Masaryk und der Zionismus', in *Masaryk und das Judentum*, p. 104.

22 Masaryk, *Národnostní filosofie doby novější* (Jičín: Holvek, 1904)
    p. 14; quoted in F. Weltsch, 'Masaryk und der Zionismus', p. 102.
23 The *Wschod* interview quoted Masaryk as saying: 'I confess that
    assimilation as a popular movement is downright impossible and
    laughable. The last decade, after all, has demonstrated this: despite all
    its efforts assimilation has not achieved real results.' (Quoted in
    'Rozmluva s Prof. Masarykem', *Rozvoj*, 9 April 1909. See also
    Weltsch, 'Masaryk und der Zionismus', pp. 72–4.)
24 'Rozmluva s Prof. Masarykem', *Rozvoj*, 9 April 1909.
25 Ibid.
26 Ibid.
27 T. G. Masaryk, 'Ernest Renan o židovství jako plemenu a náboženství
    (*Le Judaisme comme race et comme religion*, 1883)', *Sborník histor-
    ický*, 1 (1883); repr. in V. K. Škrach (ed.), *Masarykův sborník*, 6 vols.
    (Prague: Čin, 1924–30) I, pp. 61–8.
28 Masaryk, 'Renan o židovství', pp. 67–8.
29 Ibid.
30 See note 14 above.
31 From Masaryk's comments to the Austrian Reichsrat of 5 December
    1907, quoted in Ernst Rychnovsky, *Masaryk* (Prague: Staatliche
    Verlagsanstalt, 1930) pp. 92–5. He later repeats much the same story
    to Karel Čapek, who records it in his *Hovory s TGM* (Prague,
    1928–1935. See Čapek, *Hovory s T. G. Masarykem* (Prague: Česko-
    slovenský spisovatel, 1969) pp. 101–2.
32 Rychnovsky, *Masaryk*, pp. 93–4; Čapek, *Hovory s TGM*, p. 17.
33 This lesson was learnt by him one day during a class outing. After
    lunch, while his classmates ran about and amused themselves, a Jewish
    student slipped away. Masaryk followed him out of curiosity and
    discovered that he had gone behind a gate in order to say his prayers.
    The action of the Jewish student elicited in Masaryk a naive, emotional
    response:

> I was ashamed somehow that a Jew should be praying while we were
> playing about. I could not get it out of my head that he had been
> praying as devoutly as we did, and that he had not forgotten his
> prayers, even for games . . . (*Hovory s TGM*, p. 17; English trans. in
> *President Masaryk Tells his Story* (New York: Arno Press and *The
> New York Times*, 1971) p. 29).

34 *Hovory s TGM*, p. 17; *President Masaryk*, p. 29.
35 *Hovory s TGM*, p. 102; *President Masaryk*, p. 189. Masaryk makes a
    less extreme claim in his memoirs of the war years, *Světová revoluce, za
    války a ve válce, 1914–1918* (Prague: Čin and Orbis, 1925). English
    trans., *The Making of a State: Memoirs and Observations, 1914–1918*
    (New York: Stokes, 1927):

> I had many personal meetings with representatives of Orthodox
> Jewry as well as with Zionists. Among the latter I must mention Mr.
> Brandeis, a Judge of the Supreme Court, who came originally from
> Bohemia and enjoyed President Wilson's confidence. In New York
> Mr. Mack was a leading Zionist and I met Nahum Sokoloff, the

influential Zionist leader. In America, as in Europe, Jewish influence is strong in the press, and it was good that it was not against us. Even those who did not agree with my policy were reserved and impartial.

(*The Making of a State*, pp. 236–7.)

36   'Memorandum on Conversations with Masaryk (October 1914)' in R. W. Seton-Watson, *Masaryk in England* (Cambridge University Press, 1943) pp. 40–1.

37   Max Brod, *Streitbares Leben* (Munich: Herbig, 1969), pp. 95–8.

38   T. G. Masaryk, *Otázka sociální: Základy marxismu filosofické a sociologické* (Prague: Laichter, 1898). A German version appeared the following year: *Die philosophischen und sociologischen Grundlagen des Marxismus* (Vienna: Carl Konegen, 1899).

39   Masaryk, *Otázka sociální*, 1946 edition, 2 vols. (Prague: Čin) II, pp. 180–1. See also Jaroslav Dresler (ed.), *Masarykova abeceda: Výbor z myšlenek Tomáše Garrigua Masaryka* (Zurich: Konfrontace, 1976) p. 110.

40   Masaryk, *Otázka sociální*, II, p. 182; cited in F. Weltsch, 'Masaryk und der Zionismus', p. 70.

41   Masaryk, *Otázka sociální*, cited in F. Weltsch, 'Masaryk und der Zionismus', p. 70.

42   Krejčí's remarks were published in *Selbstwehr* (Prague), 11 June 1909, under the title 'Assimilation und Zionismus vom ethischen Standpunkt'.

43   Jan Herben recalls the incident in 'Julius Taussig', *Kalendář českožidovský*, vol. XXXII (1912–13), pp. 15–16. See also Vohryzek's remarks in 'Náboženská společnost, či národnost?' *Rozvoj*, 1906; repr. in *K židovské otázce*, pp. 218–28.

44   See the chapter in *Hovory s TGM* entitled 'Dítě a jeho svět', and also the autobiographical fragment, 'Náš pan Fixl', published originally in *Besedy Času*, 24 February 1911, and repr. in Jaromír Doležal, *Masarykova cesta životem*, 2 vols. (Brno: Polygrafia, 1920–21) II, pp. 37–9.

45   Kronberger, *Zionisten und Christen* (Leipzig, 1900); quoted in Weltsch, 'Masaryk und der Zionismus', p. 71.

46   Ibid.

47   T. G. Masaryk 'Život církevní a náboženský roku 1904', *Naše doba*, vol. XII (1905) p. 522. In this article, Masaryk reviewed the first German translation of Aḥad Ha'am's collected essays 'Al parashat derakhim (Am Scheidewege: Ausgewählte Essays*, authorised trans. by Israel Friedländer (Berlin: Jüdischer Verlag, 1904).

48   Masaryk, 'Život církevní', pp. 522–3.

49   'Aḥad Ha'am fights against Nietzschean individualism; he demonstrates that the Old Testament in the end is social, demanding loyalty to the collective' (Ibid., p. 523).

50   Ibid.

51   Ibid.

52   In early December 1918, recently demobilised troops and other civilians together marauded through the streets of Prague physically attacking Jews and Jewish property. Demonstrations in May 1919,

against profiteering and high prices, led to the looting of shops and businesses in Prague and the suburbs. Many, but not all, of the establishments affected were owned by Jews. The most disturbing acts of violence occurred in November 1920, when mobs broke into the ancient Jewish Town Hall, tore to pieces paintings and furnishings, rifled desk drawers, and destroyed priceless documents relating to the history of the Jews in the city. See Antony Polonsky and Michael Riff, 'Poles, Czechoslovaks, and the "Jewish Question", 1914–1921', in Volker Berghahn and Martin Kitchen (eds) *Germany in the Age of Total War* (London: Croom Helm, 1981) pp. 88–93, 99; and Christoph Stölzl, 'Die "Burg" und die Juden: T. G. Masaryk und sein Kreis im Spannungsfeld der jüdischen Frage', in Karl Bosl, *Die 'Burg': Einflussreiche politische Kräfte um Masaryk und Beneš*, 2 vols. (Munich; Vienna: Oldenbourg, 1973–1974) especially II, pp. 94–8.

53 Quoted in Aharon Moshe Rabinowitz, 'The Jewish Minority', in *The Jews of Czechoslovakia*, 3 vols. (Philadelphia: Jewish Publication Society, 1968–84) I, p. 165.

54 Brod, *Streitbares Leben*, p. 104.

55 'Der jüdische Nationalrat beim Národní výbor', *Selbstwehr*, 1 November 1918. See also: Max Brod, 'Prag – Wien – Erinnerungen', in Josef Fränkel (ed.) *The Jews of Austria* (London: Valentine, Mitchell, 1967) pp. 241–2; Oskar K. Rabinowicz, 'Czechoslovak Zionism: Analecta to a History', in *The Jews of Czechoslovakia*, II, p. 31, and Weltsch, 'Masaryk und der Zionismus', pp. 79–86.

56 *Selbstwehr*, 8 November 1918, p. 2; Weltsch, 'Masaryk und der Zionismus', pp. 79–86; A. M. Rabinowicz, 'The Jewish Minority', pp. 159–61. Rabinowicz produced an English translation of the memorandum, ibid., pp. 218–21.

57 *Selbstwehr*, 8 November 1918, p. 2; A. M. Rabinowicz, 'The Jewish Minority', pp. 218–19.

58 *Selbstwehr*, ibid., p. 2; Rabinowicz, ibid., pp. 219–20.

59 See the discussion in Ezra Mendelsohn, *The Jews of East Central Europe Between the World Wars* (Bloomington: Indiana University Press, 1983) pp. 148–9.

60 Edvard Beneš to Ludvík Singer, 25 August 1919 (Central Zionist Archives, Jerusalem, Z4/583). Full text of the letter quoted (in English translation) in Rabinowicz, 'The Jewish Minority', pp. 172–3.

61 Report of N. Sokolow (Central Zionist Archives, Z4/583); reproduced in Rabinowicz, 'The Jewish Minority', pp. 174–7.

62 The Constitution itself did not indicate expressly who the legally recognised, national minorities were. Instead, this was spelled out in documents which accompanied and clarified the Constitution.

63 Weltsch, 'Masaryk und der Zionismus', pp. 88–9; Rabinowicz, 'The Jewish Minority', pp. 186–7, 199.

64 See Simon Dubnov, *Nationalism and History: Essays on Old and New Judaism* (New York: Atheneum, 1970), esp. pp. 100–15.

65 'Falešná hra sionistů', *Rozvoj*, 28 June 1919.

66 Max Lederer, 'Staro-nový Masaryk', *Rozvoj*, 26 April 1929.

67 Ibid.

68 Jan Heřmann, 'The Development of Bohemian and Moravian Jewry,

1918–1938', in U. O. Schmelz, P. Glikson, and S. Della Pergola (eds), *Papers in Jewish Demography 1969* (Jerusalem: Institute of Contemporary Jewry, 1973) pp. 191–206; Idem, 'The Evolution of the Jewish Population of Prague 1869–1939', in *Papers in Jewish Demography 1977* (1980) pp. 53–67; and František Friedmann, 'Židé v Čechách', in Hugo Gold (ed.), *Židé a židovské obce v Čechách v minulosti a v přítomnosti* (Brno-Prague: Židovské nakladatelství, 1934) pp. 733–4.

One extreme of Jewish integration, that of mixed marriages, indicates a dramatic shift after 1918. For the city of Prague, the percentage of mixed couples out of all marriages involving at least one Jewish spouse was 9.8 between 1911 and 1914, 16.4 in 1921–1922, 40.1 in 1925, and 43.6 from 1926 to 1930. See Heřman, 'Jewish Population of Prague', pp. 60–1.

Index

A page number followed by 'n' refers to an end note. Names in parentheses are places of publication of newspapers and periodicals. The name of T. G. Masaryk is cited in cross reference only, not in a main entry.